LIBYTHEIDAE

RIODINIDAE

Libythea celtis [32]

Hamearis lucina [24, 31]

LYCAENIDAE

Quercusia quercus [14]

Nordmannia ilicis [14]

Heodes virgaureae [15]

Lycaena phlaeas [15]

Cigaritis zohra [16]

Aricia agestis cramera [19]

Plebicula dorylas [20]

Lysandra albicans [21]

Lysandra coridon [21]

HESPERIIDAE

Syrichtus proto [62]

Carterocephalus palaemon [63]

Gegenes pumilio [63]

CANTERBURY COLLEGE OF TECHNOLOGY

LIBRARY
Tel: Canterbury 66081

Conditions for the loan of books

1. Books may be kept on loan for three weeks, at the end of which time they must be returned or the loan renewed by arrangement with the librarian.

2. No user of the library may have more than three non-fiction books on loan at any time.

3. When a book is borrowed, the borrower must write his name, and details of the book, on an issue slip. In the case of this book, the details to be recorded are:

   Author: *L. G. HIGGINS ∂ N. D. RILEY*

   Title: *Butterflies - Britain & Europe*

   Book No.: **35062**

   It is important that these details be copied exactly.

4. No book marked "For Reference Only" may be removed from the library, except by arrangement with the librarian.

A FIELD GUIDE TO THE
Butterflies of Britain and EUROPE

COLLINS GUIDES

THE BIRDS OF BRITAIN AND EUROPE, NORTH AFRICA AND
THE MIDDLE EAST
Hermann Heinzel, Richard Fitter and John Parslow

THE WILD FLOWERS OF BRITAIN AND NORTHERN EUROPE
Marjorie Blamey, Richard Fitter and Alastair Fitter

THE ALPINE FLOWERS OF BRITAIN AND EUROPE
Christopher Grey-Wilson and Marjorie Blamey

A FIELD GUIDE TO THE TREES OF BRITAIN AND NORTHERN EUROPE
Alan Mitchell

A FIELD GUIDE TO THE INSECTS OF BRITAIN AND NORTHERN EUROPE
Michael Chinery

A FIELD GUIDE TO THE REPTILES AND AMPHIBIANS OF BRITAIN AND
EUROPE
E. N. Arnold, J. A. Burton and D. W. Ovenden

A FIELD GUIDE TO THE NESTS, EGGS AND NESTLINGS OF BRITISH AND
EUROPEAN BIRDS
C. J. O. Harrison

A FIELD GUIDE TO THE LAND SNAILS OF BRITAIN AND NORTH-WEST EUROPE
M. P. Kerney, R. A. D. Cameron and Gordon Riley

A FIELD GUIDE TO THE SEABIRDS OF BRITAIN AND THE WORLD
Gerald Tuck and Hermann Heinzel

A FIELD GUIDE TO THE BIRDS OF BRITAIN AND EUROPE
Roger Peterson, Guy Mountfort and P. A. D. Hollom

COLLINS GUIDE TO ANIMAL TRACKS AND SIGNS
Preben Bang and Preben Dahlstrom

COLLINS GUIDE TO THE FERNS, MOSSES AND LICHENS
OF BRITAIN AND NORTHERN AND CENTRAL EUROPE
Hans Martin Jahus

COLLINS GUIDE TO MUSHROOMS AND TOADSTOOLS
Morten Lange and F. Bayard Hora

COLLINS POCKET GUIDE TO THE SEA SHORE
John Barrett and C. M. Yonge

A FIELD GUIDE TO THE STARS AND PLANETS
Donald Menzel

A FIELD GUIDE TO THE
Butterflies of Britain
and Europe

Lionel G. Higgins

and

Norman D. Riley

Over 800 illustrations in colour by
Brian Hargreaves

COLLINS
Grafton Street, London

First edition 1970
Second edition 1973
Third edition 1975
Fourth edition, revised and reset 1980
Fifth edition, revised 1983

© Lionel G. Higgins and Norman D. Riley 1970

ISBN 0 00 219241 1

Filmset by Jolly & Barber Ltd, Rugby
Made and printed in Hong Kong by
South China Printing Co

Preface to the Fifth Edition

Since the first appearance of this Field Guide in 1970 there has been great activity among European lepidopterists and many new species and subspecies have been identified making substantial changes and revisions necessary in successive editions. Three completely new plates of illustrations were added for the last edition and this new edition has accounts of ten species and eight subspecies, all recently described, which were not previously included. No fewer than five of these newly described forms are small brown butterflies of the difficult genus *Agrodiaetus* Hübner. The others include two forms of *Pseudochazara* de Lesse, also a difficult group, but I have not been able to examine any specimens. These recently described forms are all included in the Check List, sometimes with a query to emphasise the uncertainty of their status. Other matters of some interest include the adoption of a new genus: *Neolysandra* Eckweiler & Schurian for *coelestina* Eversmann, not well placed in *Lysandra*, and the omission of the small lycaenid *Cupido carswelli* Stempffer as a distinct species, since the specific characteristics are so ambiguous.

Discoveries in the south-eastern countries of our region have shown the unexpected richness of their butterfly fauna, with several species clearly related to western Asia, pointing to the importance of Macedonia as a pontic refugium. It is not surprising that several of these newly described species are known from single localities, so a 'distribution' in the ordinary sense cannot be described or mapped. Several of these species are known only to their captors and specimens were not available for illustration, our readers must forgive their absence.

My colleague and co-author, Norman Riley, died in May 1979. He was able to participate fully in the revision of the last edition but his participation was sadly missed in preparing this one. Both of us have been indebted in the past to the numerous friends who have given their help and I would like to thank them and express the hope that they will continue to assist in keeping this book fully up-to-date in future.

LIONEL G. HIGGINS
Focklesbrook Farm
Chobham
Woking

Abbreviations

Contents

How to use this book

The *endpapers*, inside the front and back covers, illustrate butterflies characteristic of 8 of the 9 families occurring in Europe. For the 9th family see the unmistakable species of Danaidae on Plate 24. Note the butterfly most like the specimen you want to identify and turn to the plates indicated by the numbers alongside the names. This should lead you to the correct group of illustrations.

On the *plates* are illustrated all the butterflies known to occur in Europe, including both sexes and all major subspecies. The left half of each illustration shows the upper sides of the wings, the right half the under sides. All are life size. When comparing specimens with the illustrations bear in mind that both pattern and colour are liable to variation and that colours are brightest in fresh specimens.

On the *caption pages*, facing the plates, will be found the names of the butterflies, their key characters, and page references to the full text descriptions. Sometimes it has not been possible to group together on a single plate all the varieties of a species that needed illustration. In all such cases cross references to other plates are given on the caption pages.

The *text descriptions* are restricted to characters important for identification. Pay particular attention to notes on 'Similar species' whenever these are given. Anatomical features are explained in the Introduction (p. 11) and Glossary (p. 369). *Flight periods* given are those normal to the species but are liable to considerable variation according to altitude and latitude. *Habitats* also vary and it has only been possible to give general indications of the kind of terrain in which the butterfly is normally found. Food plants of the caterpillars are also given here.

The text information on *Distributions*, necessarily condensed, is summarised on the *Maps* pp. 341–65. It should not be assumed that every species occurs everywhere throughout the area indicated on its map: it may be localised in widely separated colonies; it may regularly migrate beyond it, as indicated by the striped black and white areas. The map shows the whole range. The Atlantic islands are indicated by initials: A (Azores), C (Canary Islands) or M (Madeira).

Taken together, the descriptions and the information under flight, habitat and distribution, including the maps, should enable you to identify your specimens, to find a particular species you want, and also to know what to expect in any given area.

A *Checklist* of all the species described will be found on p. 366, and a selective *Bibliography* on p. 372. For *Abbreviations* see p. 6.

Additions to the Fifth Edition

Since the publication of the fourth edition in 1980 new discoveries and changes in scientific opinion have required a number of amendments and additions to the text. In many cases it has not been possible to examine specimens of newly described forms but short descriptions have been included to record the publication. Most have been incorporated in the body of the book but space has prevented the placing of some new forms in their correct sequence in the text. They are given below with indications of their place in the systematic order. They are not illustrated or mapped but bring the book as up-to-date as possible at the time of going to press.

After *Pseudophilotes panoptes*, page 67

PSEUDOPHILOTES BARBAGIAE   *Sardinian Blue*
Range. Confined to Sardinia.

P. barbagiae   De Prins & v.d. Poorten   1982   TL: Sardinia (Nuoro) No map
Description. ♂ like *P. panoptes* in size, ups grey-brown upf blue suffusion at wing-base not conspicuous, absent in postdiscal area. Uns grey-brown with usual macular markings. ♀ ups dark brown, uns resembles ♂. Fringes chequered dark and paler on both sexes. Male genitalia are most distinctive.

After *Agrodiaetus ripartii*, page 87

AGRODIAETUS VIOLETAE   *Andalusian Anomalous Blue*

A. violetae   Gomez Bustillo & Borrego 1979   TL: Andalusia, Sierra de Almijarra.
Description. Like *A. ripartii*, ups chestnut brown, uns ground colour quite pale, unh white stripe usually present, sometimes reduced or absent.
Flight and **Habitat.** Flies in late July at 1600m or over, appears to be local and uncommon.

AGRODIAETUS NEPHOHIPTAMENOS   *Higgins' Anomalous Blue*

A. nephohiptamenos   Brown & Coutsis 1978   TL: NE. Greece
Description. A small form, fw 15–16mm. Ups the pale wing-fringes are noticeable with the ground colour also in rather a pale tone of brown; unh the pale stripe is prominent.
Flight and **Habitat.** Flies in August over grass slopes at 600m and appears to be local and uncommon.
A. n. galloi   Bolleto & Toso 1979   *Gallo's Anomalous Blue*   TL: Monte Pollino, Reggio Calabria, S. Ital.
Description. A small form with some of the characters of *A. nephohiptamenos*, especially on ups the pale wing-fringes are prominent; unh a pale stripe is well developed. The butterfly is named with full specific rank.
Flight and **Habitat.** Flies in August over grass slopes at 1500m. Not uncommon.

After *L. coridon*, page 90

LYSANDRA PHILIPPI   *Macedonian Chalk-hill Blue*

L. philippi   Brown 1978   TL: NE. Greece
Description. ♂ ups very pale blue, resembling some of the Spanish races, e.g. *L. c.*

asturiensis Sag., with characteristic generic markings; uns pale, the usual black spots often small. ♀ brown.
Flight and **Habitat.** Occurs in hilly country flying in late July at altitudes of 700m and upwards. It appears to be uncommon. Also recorded from Drama.

After *Hipparchia semele cadmus*, page 263

H. semele lieghebi   Kudrna 1976   TL: Stromboli, Eolian Ils.
Description. Like *H. aristaeus blachieri*, ♂ fw 29–30mm, upf pd area broadly yellow buff, shaded, cell and sex brand dark, prominent, uph yellow-buff, basal area slightly shaded. ♀ larger, fw 30–32mm, ups markings as for *H. a. blachieri*. Identified by ♂ genitalia, uncus long, brachia long, regularly curved. Described and named as subspecies of *H. semele*.
Flight and **Habitat.** Flies in June/July at all levels to 500m. Recorded from Stomboli and Panarea.

After *Pseudochazara graeca*, page 269

PSEUDOCHAZARA ORESTES

P. orestes   De Vries & v.d.Poorten 1981   TL: Drama, N. Greece
Description. ♂ like *P. cingovskii*, large, ♂ fw 28–30mm, wing-base and sical area dark, pd band entire, pale buff, colour more intense distally, white pd spots present in s3 and s4; uph pd band wide, complete from v2 to v7, white, shading distally to buff, darker basal and discal areas well defined, uns as above but all markings paler. ♀ similar but slightly larger, fw 32–34mm, upf distal border of dark basal area sharply angled at v5.
Flight. July, in mountains at 1700m.
Distribution. Recorded only from N. Greece.

After *Pseudochazara geyeri*, page 270

PSEUDOCHAZARA TISIPHONE   *Dark Grayling*

P. tisiphone   Brown 1980   TL: NW. Greece.
Description. ♂ ups like *P. cingovskii*, usual markings present but somewhat obscured by general dark suffusion; ♂ fw 25–29mm, upf pd band yellowish or fulvous, broken along v4 by dark ground-colour, white spots in s3 and s4 prominent; uph band crossed by darkened veins, often with white-pupilled ocelli in s2 and s3. ♀ similar but larger, fw 28–29mm; in both sexes unh with confused dark markings pd area not well defined.
Flight and **Habitat.** Recorded in July flying over rough, stony places at about 1200m on Mt. Smolikas in NW. Greece.

After *Carcharodus alceae*, page 333

CARCHARODUS TRIPOLINUS   *False Mallow Skipper*

C. tripolinus   Verity 1925
Description. ♂ like *C. alceae* but usually smaller (*C. alceae* exp. circ. 27mm, *C. tripolinus* exp. circ. 23mm), ups often yellowish, identification by inspection probably impossible but distinctive characters are present in the ♂ genitalia.
Distribution. Flies, often with *C. alceae*, on coastal areas of Portugal (Estoril etc.), S. Spain (Malaga, Huelva etc.) and N. Africa, especially Tunisia. *C. alceae* is present in the Middle Atlas (Ifrane etc.).

Introduction

Butterflies (*Rhopalocera*) and Moths (*Heterocera*) form together the very large Insect Order *Lepidoptera*, so-called because their wings are covered with scales. The coiled proboscis, through which nourishment is sucked up, is peculiar to Lepidoptera. In western Europe butterflies can be distinguished from moths by having clubbed antennae; by having the two wings on either side held together by the shape of the wings instead of the 'bristle and catch' frenulum of moths; by flying by day; and by sleeping with their wings closed together over the back. Brightly coloured day-flying moths and other similar insects that occur in Europe can be distinguished from butterflies by one or more of these characters.

European Butterflies. For the region covered in this book see the map on p. 16 and its explanatory note.

This region forms a subcontinent of great zoological interest. Of about 380 species of butterflies that are known to occur in it, at least 112 (just under 30%) are endemic, not found elsewhere.

Comparison of the distribution maps p. 341–65, will show a number of interesting recurrent patterns: groups of species confined to the central Alps, others dotted on isolated mountain ranges over a wide area, some almost confined within the Arctic Circle, many restricted to the Mediterranean sub-region or to one end of it, a few that hardly extend beyond the lowlands of central Europe, from France to Russia, and a wide-ranging group failing only to reach the Arctic and high alpine zones, and so on. These distribution patterns all mean something. They can be explained by, and help to explain, the great land movements and climatic changes to which Europe was subjected before and during the Great Ice Ages.

Most European butterflies can be recognised fairly easily as belonging to one or other of the *species* described in this guide. There are others, however, like the Brown Argus butterflies (p. 75) of which it is difficult to say whether they are a single species or a group of species so closely allied as to be virtually indistinguishable. Such a complex may be looked upon as a group still in the process of evolution, in which the various components are not yet separated and stabilised. On this view they are approaching the status of *subspecies*, i.e. geographical races which we define as differing populations of a single species that occur in different parts of the range of that species. By definition no two subspecies of any species ever fly together; but if and when their ranges meet they can, and usually do, interbreed and produce intermediate forms. This does not happen between species.

The large number of described and named subspecies has proved embarrassing, since only very few could find a place in this book. In the main only those that may be termed major subspecies have been described, i.e. those with clearly recognisable constant characters and well defined geographical distributions. Others, with less distinctive characters are referred to as 'forms', a term we use in a non-committal sense for any kind of recognisable variety of a species, whether expressly defined or not, such as a local race, a recurrent variety, an incipient subspecies, a seasonal, female or other special form.

11

In Europe there are many examples of a continuous type of variation that extends in a series of gradations throughout a butterfly's range. This kind of variation is known as a *cline*. No doubt clines are evolutionary stages that could give rise eventually to subspecies if the range of the species became interrupted by barriers to free movement. A good example is the Meadow Brown (*Maniola jurtina*, p. 302) which is large and brightly marked in southern Europe, small and dull in the north, the extremes linked by intermediates. There seems good reason to suppose that variation of this kind reflects the influence of climatic conditions.

Seasonal variation occurs only in butterflies that have two or more annual broods. Individual butterflies do not vary with the season. Most European butterflies are single-brooded, and this is particularly true of those that live at high altitudes and latitudes, where the season favourable to development is short. Double-brooded species are not numerous, and are mostly insects of the lower levels. Some species that are double-brooded in southern Europe are single-brooded in the north. Several of these differ greatly from one brood to the next. Good examples are the Green-veined White (p. 25) and the Map Butterfly (p. 104). A few species have more than two annual broods. Most of these will go on breeding so long as conditions are favourable. Good examples are the Bath White (p. 27) and the Longtailed Blue (p. 56). In many species that have more than one annual brood a small proportion of each brood may hibernate as pupae or larvae till the following spring.

In most European butterflies the males and females are noticeably different, and in a few species the females themselves are dimorphic, as in the Clouded Yellows of the genus *Colias* (p. 34), many of which have both 'yellow' and 'white' forms.

Individual variations occur in all species, but are more common in some than others. In the Ringlets and Heaths (Satyridae) the characteristic eye-spots tend to increase or decrease in size and number; in the Fritillaries the black spots of the upperside tend to form streaks, or to overrun the whole wing, and the silver spots of the underside may do the same; in the Blues the spots on the underside similarly may lengthen to form streaks between the veins, may be greatly reduced in number or even absent, and so on. Individuals with an excess of black pigment are melanics. Lack of pigment produces albinos. Curious specimens occur sometimes in which one side is male, the other female. These are gynandromorphs or intersexes, and are very rare. A male with scattered patches of female characters, or vice versa, is known as a mosaic. Pathological conditions, due to disease, which are common in some species, usually result in bleaching effects or the distortion of wings and veins.

All these freaks and 'aberrations' are worth keeping. Most of them have been given names, but they are far too numerous to be dealt with in this Guide.

Names (nomenclature). Less than a hundred of the European butterflies have English names. Our experience is that English names are especially welcome to beginners, so we have invented English names for all those that needed them. For this we offer no apology. As knowledge grows these vernacular names will lead on inevitably to the use of the 'Latin' names that are the international currency of butterfly nomenclature.

One of the troubles with scientific names is their multiplicity. Which of the many names (synonyms, homonyms etc., see Glossary p. 369) given to any species is the *correct* name for that species is now fortunately determinable by the rules laid down in the International Code of Zoological Nomenclature. We have been at great pains to follow these rules, as their purpose is to establish the stable nomenclature that we all need so badly. As a result we have had to make a few changes which we hope are final.

Of synonyms we have thought it most useful to include only those in current use.

THE BUTTERFLY

During its life a butterfly passes through four stages, from egg (ovum) to caterpillar (larva), chrysalis (pupa) and butterfly (imago), each stage undergoing a complete metamorphosis. This book is concerned only with the fourth stage—the adult butterfly.

To understand the characters used in the descriptions in this guide you will need to know something about the structure of a butterfly. Take a common butterfly, like a Small Tortoiseshell, and run through the following paragraphs looking for the various structures as they are mentioned. Most of these can be seen with the naked eye, but a hand lens with a magnification of about × 10 will be a great help.

A butterfly has all its hard parts on the outside. This external covering (exoskeleton) is mainly composed of chitin, and to its inner surface the muscles are attached. The *head* is a small brittle capsule and its appendages are sensory. The proboscis, which takes the place of a mouth, is formed of two tubes joined together so as to form a third through which the insect drinks. There are no jaws. On either side of the proboscis is a sensory 3-jointed *palp*. Close behind the palpi are the two conspicuous *compound eyes*. The face between the eyes and below the antennae is called the *frons*. The *antennae* are wide apart in the Skippers, close together in all other butterflies; they are both sense organs and balancers.

The *thorax* bears the wings and legs and is made up of three segments. Each segment bears a pair of legs but only the second and third bear wings.

The three pairs of legs are all of the same pattern. They are made up of a basal hip-joint (coxa), which is immobile, and three mobile segments, the femur, tibia and tarsus, the last, corresponding to the foot, five-jointed and usually clawed. In the Nymphalidae and Satyridae the front legs are clawless and so small that butterflies of these two families seem to have only four legs.

Side view of a Pierid butterfly

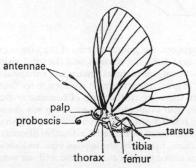

antennae

palp
proboscis

tarsus

tibia
femur

thorax

In the identification of butterflies the *wings* are of course of prime importance. The scales that cover them are minute flattened plates fixed to the wings by tiny stalks and overlapping like the tiles on a roof. These scales contain the pigments that give colour to the wings, and their arrangement forms the pattern of markings. The microscopic structure of some scales breaks up the light that falls on them, as does a thin film of oil, to produce the 'metallic' colours of the Blues and Coppers. These are interference colours and they disappear if the scales are wetted. Pigments are not affected in this way. Scattered amongst the ordinary scales are other scales peculiar to males and called androconia. At the base of such scales there are gland cells. These produce scents, believed to be attractive to females, which are diffused through the tufts of fine fibres at the tips of the scales. Very often these androconia are grouped together in patches to form sex-brands.

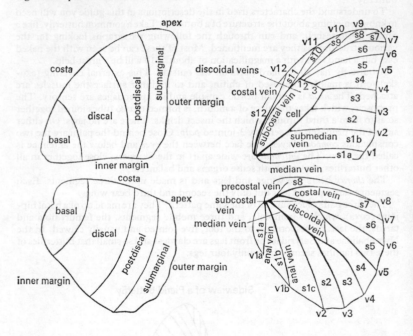

For descriptive purposes, the principal areas of the wing are the *costa* (front edge), *inner margin* (back edge), the outer margin, and the subdivisions of its surface, i.e., the basal, discal, postdiscal, submarginal, marginal, subapical and apical areas. The veins (fig. above) are of great importance. It is easiest to see them on the underside. If it is difficult, moisten the wing with a drop of benzene or alcohol. This will show them up momentarily and evaporate without doing any damage. Look first at the basal half of the wing towards the costa. You will see a largish clear area surrounded by veins. This is the *cell*, sometimes called the discal or discoidal cell. It is bounded in front by the *subcostal vein*, behind by the *median* vein, and outwardly by one to three short transverse veins called the discoidal or discocellular veins, one or even two of which may be absent. The veins of the fore-wing are numbered 1 to 12. Vein 1 arises from the base of the wing and runs roughly parallel to the inner margin. As it is largely hidden (when seen from beneath) behind the costa of the hind-wing it is best to start counting the veins from vein 2, which originates from the median vein about halfway along the lower edge of the cell. Count forwards from this vein and you will find that the last vein, which also arises from the base of the wing, is number 12. On the hind-wing start counting in the same way from vein 2; you will find that the last long vein is number 8, which usually has a short forward branch (precostal vein) arising near its base. This simple system contains one or two minor snags. Sometimes, particularly in the Lycaenidae, the fore-wing will be found to have only 10 or 11 veins. In such cases it is vein 7, 8 or 9 that is missing, or two of them. The veins we call 10, 11 and 12 are always present. Again, except in the Papilionidae there are two anal veins on the hindwing, between the inner margin and vein 2; to avoid altering the numbers of the other veins these are called vein 1a and vein 1b.

The wing surfaces between the veins we call the *spaces*. Having learnt the veins, you should have no difficulty in identifying them. The system follows that of the veins. Space 2 (s2) lies above v2 and between it and v3, and so on to space 12 (s12). When only one anal vein is present on the hind-wing, the spaces starting from the inner margin, are numbered 1a and 1b; if two anal veins are present the third space so created is called s1c. A statement such as 'ocelli in s2, 3 and (4)' implies that ocelli are always present in s2 and s3 but may or may not be present in s4.

The *abdomen* is much less heavily chitinised than the head and thorax. It is composed of 10 segments, only seven of which are externally recognisable, namely segments 2 to 8. Besides the organs of digestion and reproduction it contains the vascular heart (dorsally) and the nerve cord (ventrally) which both extend into the head. The chitinous parts of the genitalia, at the tip of the abdomen, are of very great importance in classification. They also provide a means of *sexing* specimens in difficult cases. Look at the tip of the body from beneath—it may be necessary to brush away the hairs and scales first. If it is a male the valves (claspers), one on each side, will be visible, and perhaps also the tip of the penis. The female abdomen is blunt-ended with at the most the end of the ovipositor showing.

MAPPING SCHEME

An international scheme has recently been set up which will provide far more detailed information on the present distribution of European butterflies than is possible in this Guide. Maps are being produced on a 50 km basis, but it is hoped that the records from each European country will be collected on a 10 km basis. A special species-list card based on the check list used in this book is available with detailed instructions for those wishing to take part in the scheme. Further details are obtainable from The European Invertebrate Survey, c/o Biological Records Centre, Monks Wood Experimental Station, Abbots Ripton, Huntingdon, England.

The area covered extends from the North Cape within the Arctic Circle to the southern slopes of the Atlas Mountains north of the Saharan Desert, and from the Azores, Canary Islands and Madeira to Tripoli, the Bosphorus and the western frontier of Russia but not to the Aegean islands or Cyprus. In Iceland there are no indigenous butterflies.

PAPILIONIDAE

Latreille 1809

A large family including species that vary greatly in appearance and in structural details. All are alike in two important characters: the butterflies (imagines) have six functional legs of nearly equal size and each tarsus has a single pair of claws. In the hind-wing there is a single anal vein and the inner margin is slightly concave.

PAPILIO MACHAON Swallowtail
Range. From N. Africa across Europe and temperate Asia to the Himalaya Mts. and Japan. Represented in N. America by closely related species or subspecies.   Map 1

P. machaon Linnaeus 1758   TL: Sweden (Verity 1947)   **Pl. 1**
   syn: *sphyrus* Hübner 1823
Description. ♂fw 32/38mm; *first brood* ups yellow with dense black markings; upf basal area black; uph inner margin and s1 black, blue spots in black pd band obscure; abdomen black. *Second brood* (f. *aestivus* Zeller 1847) ups markings dusted with pale scales; uph inner margin narrowly dark, s1 pale, black pd band less wide, blue markings better defined; abdomen yellow with black dorsal stripe. In S. Europe seasonal difference may be striking. ♀ similar.
Flight. April/May and July/August in two or three broods in S. Europe and N. Africa. In northern districts usually single-brooded.
Habitat. Meadows and flowery banks from lowlands to 1800m. Larval food plants, wild carrots, fennel and other Umbelliferae and Rutaceae.
Distribution. Throughout the region from N. Africa to North Cape; in England now confined to Norfolk, very local in fens, formerly more widely distributed. The species is a vagrant: continental specimens, usually of the second brood, occasionally reach England.
Variation. Apart from the seasonal changes the wing-markings are stable, showing little evidence of geographical variation in Europe. Rare abnormal forms include f. *nigra* Reutti, ups wings black except the uph blue spots in pd band; f. *nigrofasciata* Rothke, uph black pd band extends to blend with marginal border; f. *aurantiaca* Speyer ups wings deep yellow or orange-yellow.
Similar species. *P. hospiton* below, unf marginal band narrow, composed of dark-bordered grey-blue lunules; occurs only in Corsica and Sardinia.

PAPILIO HOSPITON Corsican Swallowtail
Range. Restricted to Corsica and Sardinia.   Map 2

P. hospiton Géné 1839   TL: Tortoli, Sardinia   **Pl. 1 and front end paper**
Description. ♂fw 36/38mm, resembles *P. machaon* closely, but differs as follows: tail at v4 on hw shorter; uph blue spots in dark marginal border small and well defined; unf pd band composed of a series of grey lunules bordered black. On both surfaces the red anal spot is small, sometimes nearly absent. ♀ similar.
Flight. May/July in a single brood with prolonged emergence.
Habitat. Mountains to 600–1200m. Larval food plants Umbelliferae, esp. fennel.
Distribution. Corsica and Sardinia only.
Similar species. *P. machaon* above.

17

PAPILIO ALEXANOR *Southern Swallowtail*
Range. From Provence, S. Italy and S. Balkans across W. Asia to Iran, W. Pakistan and Turkestan. Map 3

P. alexanor Esper 1799 TL: Nice, France **Pl. 1**
Description. ♂fw 31/33mm, antennal club straight; ups bright yellow, outer margins narrowly bordered black; upf with four broad black transverse stripes, the black pd band with narrow blue central stripe; uph black pd band filled with blue and greatly enlarged in s2. ♀ often larger.
Flight. April to July in a single prolonged emergence.
Habitat. Mountainous districts to 1200m or more, attracted by thistles. Larval food plants Umbelliferae, esp. *Trinia vulgaris, Seseli montanum* and *Ptychotis heterophylla*.
Distribution. Alpine foothills in Provence to Ardèche, Drôme and Isère, esp. in Var and Basses Alpes, e.g. Draguignan, Beauvezer, St Martin Vésubie, valley of the Tinée, etc. Italy, local and rare on eastern slopes of Maritime Alps, esp. San Martino Lantosca, also Aspromonte and E. Sicily. Yugoslavia in Istria and Dalmatia. Greece on Mt. Parnassus, Taygetos, Corfu, but generally very local and scarce in all eastern localities.

IPHICLIDES PODALIRIUS *Scarce Swallowtail*
Range. From N. Africa across Europe and temperate Asia to China. Map 4

I. podalirius podalirius Linnaeus 1758 TL: Livorno, Tuscany (Verity 1947) **Pl. 1**
syn. *sinon* Poda 1761
Description. ♂fw 32/40mm, female larger; *first brood* ups very pale yellow, black markings heavy; upf six transverse stripes; uph wing-border along inner margin black but s1 narrowly pale, variable, sometimes obscured, anal ocellus with orange crescent above; unh double discal band filled orange; abdomen black. In *second brood* (f. *zancleus* Zeller) ups cream-white; uph dark wing-border along inner margin clearly divided, s1 pale and black stripes not heavy; unh double discal band not filled orange; apex of abdomen pale grey.
Flight. March/September in one or two broods, usually May/June and August/September.
Habitat. Lowlands to 1800m or more, often around fruit orchards. Larval food plants sloe and cultivated fruit trees.
Distribution. Pyrenees, excluding E. Pyrenees, thence eastwards through Europe to 54°N, including the Mediterranean islands. Occasional vagrants have occurred in Britain.

I. podalirius feisthamelii Duponchel 1832 TL: Barcelona and Algeria **Pl. 1**
Description. ♂fw 35/42mm; *first brood* ups grey-white, wings thickly scaled, black markings heavier; uph inner border broadly black; abdomen black. ♀ larger, ups gc pale yellow. In *second brood* (f. *latteri* Austaut) wings less thickly scaled; ups black markings less dense; uph wing-border along inner margin clearly divided, s1 pale and black stripes obsolescent; abdomen grey with black dorsal stripe. ♀ generally slightly flushed yellow, sometimes very large.
Flight and **Habitat** as for *I. p. podalirius*.
Distribution. Morocco, Algeria, Tunisia. Portugal and Spain northwards to southern slopes of Pyrenees. France, E. Pyrenees.

ZERYNTHIA POLYXENA *Southern Festoon*
Range. Local in S. Europe and W. Asia Minor. Map 5

Z. polyxena polyxena Denis and Schiffermüller 1775 TL: Vienna
syn: *hypsipyle* Schulze 1776; *hypermnestra* Scopoli 1763 (invalid homonym) **Pl. 2**
Description. ♂fw 23/26mm, ups gc yellow; upf black transverse markings with *small red costal spot in* s9, outer margin with border of deep lunules; uph a series of red pd spots and deep marginal lunules as on fw, the row of blue submarginal spots lying between, sometimes vestigial or absent. ♀ similar.
Flight. End April/May in a single brood.
Habitat. Rough stony places, lowlands to 900m. Larval food plants *Aristolochia pistolochia, A. rotunda* and *A. clematitis.*
Distribution. Widely distributed but local in SE. Europe to 50°N in S. Slovakia. Austria, Hungary, Romania, Balkans to Greece. Sicily.

Z. polyxena cassandra Geyer 1828 TL: not stated **Pl. 2**
syn: *creusa* Meigen 1829
Description. Resembles *Z. p. polyxena* but ups *black markings slightly more extensive*; upf *red costal spot in s9 absent*; uph marginal lunules slightly wider and less deep; unh reddish suffusion more noticeable.
Flight and **Habitat** as for *Z. p. polyxena.*
Distribution. France in Var, Maritime Alps and Bouches du Rhône, very local in Basses and Hautes Alpes. Italy, common near Florence, Milan, Turin, etc., more rare in peninsular Italy and Sicily, upf sometimes with red costal spot.
Variation. Ups gc sometimes deep yellow, *f. ochracea* Staudinger.
Similar species. *Z. rumina* below, upf has red spots in cell; may be confusing in SE. France.

ZERYNTHIA RUMINA *Spanish Festoon*
Range. Confined to SW. Europe and N. Africa. Map 6

Z. rumina rumina Linnaeus 1758 TL: S. Europe **Pl. 2**
Description. ♂fw 22/23mm, ups gc pale yellow. Differs from *Z. polyxena* as follows: Upf *red spots are present at base of cell, in discal area in* s1b (usually), at cell-end and in pd area in s4, 5, 6, 9, with *vitreous cells beyond*, lunular marginal border less deep; uph with red spots on costa in s7 and pd red spots in s1–5. ♀ similar.
Flight. February/May depending upon altitude, etc., in a single brood.
Habitat. Rough places and rocky slopes on hills and mountains. Larval food plant *Aristolochia pistolochia* on dry hillsides.
Distribution. SE. France, in Provence, Languedoc, Rousillon and E. Pyrenees. Spain and Portugal, widely distributed from sea-level to 1500m, especially common on rocky coastal hills.
Variation. A red spot is sometimes present at the base of the cell on the hind-wing, almost constant in specimens from S. France, *f. medesicaste* Hoffmannsegg Pl. 2. Very rarely the red markings may be greatly enlarged, *f. honoratii* Boisduval Pl. 2; a recurrent variant with gc deep orange-yellow is more frequent, *f. canteneri* Staudinger, almost confined to females.

Z. rumina africana Stichel 1907 TL: Morocco **Pl. 2**
syn: *ornatior* Blachier 1908; *mauretanica* Schulze 1908

Description. ♂fw 25/26mm, larger, with brilliant markings, uph red pd spots larger and enclosed in the solid black marginal border; upf red spot in s1b absent. ♀ similar, f. *canteneri* common Pl. 2.
Flight. February or later.
Habitat as for *Z. r. rumina*.
Distribution. Morocco, Algeria, Tunisia, restricted to northern slopes of Atlas Mts., flying from sea-level to 1500m.
Similar species. *Z. polyxena* p. 19.

ZERYNTHIA CERISYI   *Eastern Festoon*
Range. SE. Europe through Asia Minor (TL of *Thais cerisyi* Godart 1822), Cyprus, Lebanon, Iraq, Iran.   Map 7

Z. cerisyi ferdinandi   Stichel 1907   TL: Bulgaria   **Pl. 2**
Description. ♂fw 26/31mm, generally large; ups pale yellow; upf with scanty black costal and pd markings; uph with small red pd marks in s1–5 and on costa in s7. ♀ similar, ups black markings more extensive.
Flight. April/June in a single brood.
Habitat. Rough ground on hills or mountains to 1200m. Larval food plants *Aristolochia* species.
Distribution. N. Greece, Albania, SE. Yugoslavia, Romania, Bulgaria.
Variation. Size varies in different localities; the Bulgarian race is the largest known.

Z. cerisyi cretica   Rebel 1904   TL: Crete   **Pls. 2, 23**
Description. ♂fw 21–26mm, like *A.c. ferdinandi* but smaller and hw outer margin rounded. Ups markings scanty, uph red submarginal spots vestigial or absent. ♀ ups markings well developed, uph blue submarginal lunules present but small.
Flight. April/May.
Habitat. Rough ground from sea level to 1100m (Mt. Omalos).
Distribution. In Europe confined to Crete.

ARCHON APOLLINUS   *False Apollo*
Range. Bulgaria and the Near East.   Map 8

A. apollinus   Herbst 1798   TL: Ourlac (Bay of Izmir)   **Pl. 2**
Description. ♂fw 27/30mm, largely hyaline, sometimes brownish; upf with fine transverse striae, large black spots in cell, at cell-end and on costa; uph yellowish, the dark marginal border enclosing six submarginal ocelli pupilled blue, bordered internally with red. ♀ darker, markings more complete.
Flight. March/April in a single brood, one of the first species to emerge in spring.
Habitat. Rough ground, usually in mountainous districts, to 1500m. Food plant *Aristolochia hastata*.
Distribution. Recorded occasionally from Romania, Greece and European Turkey.

PARNASSIUS APOLLO   *Apollo*
Range. On all major mountains from Spain through Europe, including Fennoscandia, to C. Asia.   Map 9

P. apollo   Linnaeus 1758   TL: Sweden   **Pl. 3**
Description. ♂fw 35/42mm, ups white with markings of characteristic pattern; *upf round black pd spot in s1b*; uph spots red or more rarely yellow, usually large,

ocellated. ♀ similar, ups usually with considerable grey suffusion, uph red spots often larger, sometimes with additional red spots in pd area of fw and at anal angle of hw. In both sexes *antennal shaft pale grey, ringed slightly darker grey.*
Flight. July/August.
Habitat. Among mountains at subalpine levels from 700–1800m in S. and C. Europe, at lower levels in N. Europe. Larval food plants stonecrop (*Sedum*, esp. *S. album, S. telephium, S. purpurascens* and *Sempervivum*).
Distribution. Widely distributed in mountains of W. Europe and S. Fennoscandia but extinct in some districts, e.g. C. Germany, Czechoslovakia and Denmark. In Poland found only on the Tatra Mts. Absent from Britain.
Variation. A very large number of local races and subspecies have been described and named. Description of these is beyond the scope of this Guide. Those illustrated are *P. apollo hispanicus* Oberthur ♀, a large race, usually only slightly suffused grey, with ocelli orange (usually red) on hw (Pl. 3); and *P. apollo rhodopensis* Marković ♂, very large, uph ocelli brilliant red with white pupils Pl. 3. Among other named subspecies the following should be mentioned. *P. a. apollo* Linnaeus, TL: Sweden; large ♂ gc pure white. *P. a. geminus* Stichel, TL: Switzerland; ♂ gc faintly yellowish, red spots smaller. *P. a. bartholomaeus* Stichel, TL: Bavaria; small ♂ ups heavily marked (illustrated on front endpaper). *P. a. pumilus* Stichel, TL Calabria, very small. *P. a. nevadensis* Oberthur, TL: S. Spain; ♂ ups ocelli yellow. *P. a. siciliae* Oberthur, TL: Sicily; ups lightly marked, red markings reduced.

PARNASSIUS PHOEBUS *Small Apollo*
Range. Alps, Urals and through Siberia (TL of *P. phoebus* Fabricius 1793) to Kamschatka. N. America in British Columbia and Rocky Mts. Map 10

P. phoebus sacerdos Stichel 1906 TL: Pontresina, Engadin **Pl. 3**
  syn: *delius* Esper 1800 (invalid homonym)
Description. ♂fw 30/33mm, resembles *P. apollo*; *ups faintly yellowish-white*; upf pd costal spot in s8 usually red-centred, spot in s1b usually absent; uph pd area clear white, red spots often small. ♀ similar, more or less suffused grey, more heavily marked and uph red spots larger, upf black spot in s1b generally present, often red-centred. In both sexes *antennal shaft white clearly ringed black.*
Flight. July/August.
Habitat. Grass slopes at 1800m or above. Larval food plants *Saxifraga aizioides, Sempervivum montanum.*
Distribution. Maritime Alps and eastwards to Styria and Grossglockner, rare in north, occasional in Allgäuer Alps, absent from Limestone Alps of N. Tirol. Absent from Jura, Pyrenees, Julian Alps, Balkans and Carpathians.
Variation. On uph red ocelli united by black bar, f. *cardinalis* Oberthur, not rare in eastern Alps. The female illustrated is typical of the Styrian race, f. *styriacus* Fruhstorfer.

P. phoebus gazeli Praviel 1936 TL: Vallée du Boréon, Alpes Maritimes
Description. ♂ resembles *P. p. sacerdos*, but ups gc is chalk-white; upf grey marginal border wide and extending nearly to the submarginal band, which is less dense than usual, pd costal spot in s8 not red-centred; uph red spots small, without white pupils.
Flight and **Habitat** as for *P. p. sacerdos.*
Distribution. Known only from a few high valleys in the Maritime Alps, where it appears to replace the usual form.

Similar species. *Parnassius apollo* p. 20, shaft of antenna white indistinctly ringed pale grey; upf black pd spot in s1b always present, usually large; flies at subalpine levels.

PARNASSIUS MNEMOSYNE   *Clouded Apollo*
Range. From Pyrenees and C. France across C. and N. Europe to 64°N and eastwards to Iran, Caucasus and C. Asia.   Map 11

P. mnemosyne mnemosyne   Linnaeus 1758   TL: Finland   **Pl. 3**
Description. ♂fw 26/31mm, ups gc white without red spots; upf black markings reduced to two spots, upf wide marginal border grey; uph without marginal markings except on inner margin; uns glabrous. ♀ similar, often suffused dark grey, uph markings sometimes more extensive; dorsum of abdomen black and glabrous; sphragis large, extending from third abdominal segment to anal extremity.
Flight. May to July in a single brood.
Habitat. Hilly or mountainous districts to 1500m in C. Europe, a lowland species in the north, frequents damp meadows. Larval food plant *Corydalis*.
Distribution. Widely distributed in W. Europe to 64°N, including Pyrenees, Central Massif of France, Alps and Carpathians; Apennines, N. Sicily and Balkans. Very local and rare in Norway. Absent from Britain, Spain, Portugal, NW. Switzerland, Denmark (except Baltic islands).
Variation. Females with extensive fuscous suffusion are common in the Pyrenees and in other mountainous areas, f. *melaina* Honrath, Pl. 3.

P. mnemosyne athene   Stichel 1908   TL: Mt. Chelmos and Olenos, Greece   **Pl. 3**
Description. Resembles *P. m. mnemosyne*, but ups black markings less intense, usually smaller, the grey marginal border on upf divided by a chain of five or six faint white spots. ♀ sphragis noticeably longer.
Flight and **Habitat** as for *P. m. mnemosyne*.
Distribution. Southern Greece as a constant race; similar forms are not rare in the Apennines, Sicily, Alps of Provence and E. Pyrenees. This subspecies is clearly an outlier of the near-eastern races of the species.
Similar species. *Aporia crataegi* p. 23, easily distinguished by the absence of black markings.

PIERIDAE

Duponchel 1832

This is a very large family, but the species are generally easy to recognise, with white or yellow wings, the upper surface with scanty black markings. In nearly all species the sexes differ considerably, and many have two or more annual broods which may show marked seasonal variation. The butterflies have six functional legs of nearly equal size, each tarsus with a pair of double claws. In the hind-wing there are two anal veins, the inner margin slightly convex.

APORIA CRATAEGI *Black-veined White*

Range. From N. Africa and W. Europe across temperate Asia to Korea and Japan. Map 12

A. crataegi Linnaeus 1758 TL: Sweden (Verity 1947) **Pl. 13**

Description. ♂fw 28/34mm, ups gc white, veins pigmented dark brown or black, a narrow dark discoidal mark; uns similar, often with thin scattering of black scales, esp. on unh. ♀ larger, fw glabrous showing light brown membrane, veins brown, dark discoidal mark absent; hw thinly scaled.

Flight. May to July in a single brood.

Habitat. Open country, sea-level to 1800m. Food plants hawthorn, *Spiraea, Prunus*. Sometimes an orchard pest.

Distribution. C. and S. Europe to 62°N, rarely farther north; extinct in Britain. Common locally in Morocco and Algeria. Absent from Corsica, Sardinia and Atlantic islands.

Variation. The dark scales along veins expand at outer margin of fw into dark triangles which may be exaggerated.

Similar species. *P. mnemosyne* p. 22.

PIERIS BRASSICAE *Large White*

Range. From N. Africa across Europe and Asia to Himalaya Mts. Map 13

P. brassicae brassicae Linnaeus 1758 TL: Sweden (Verity 1947) **Pl. 4**

Description. ♂fw 28/33mm; *first brood*, costa and apical border black powdered white, *the latter extending down outer margin to v3 or beyond*; uph with costal mark in s7; unf black spots present in s1b and s3; unh densely powdered with dark scales with greenish effect. ♀upf with black streak in s1a and round spots in s1b and s3; hw yellowish (f. *chariclea* Stephens 1827). In *second brood* upf apical border intensely black; unh dark dusting slight if present. ♀hw usually white.

Flight. April/May and July/August in two or three broods.

Habitat. Gardens and flowery places, lowlands to 1800m. Food plants various *Cruciferae*, esp. *Brassica*, and *Tropaeolum*.

Distribution. Throughout N. Africa and W. Europe, including all Mediterranean islands, Azores, scarce or occasional north of 62°N. A well-known migrant, its abundance in Britain in late summer depends upon successful immigration in early months.

23

P. brassicae cheiranthi   Hübner 1808   TL: Canary Islands   **Pl. 4**
Description. ♂fw 33mm, uph costal mark enlarged; unf apex brilliant yellow, black spots in s1b and s3 enlarged and fused to form a large discal mark; unh bright yellow. ♀ all markings greatly enlarged; upf discal spots fused into a large black mark.
Flight. April and later, perhaps with several broods.
Habitat. Flies over the *maquis* of bushes and brushwood from sea-level to 1200m or more.
Distribution. Restricted to W. Canary Islands; La Palma, Tenerife and Gomera. A less exteme form occurs on Madeira (*P. b. wollastoni* Butler 1886).
Similar species. *A. rapae*, below, upf apical dark border extends down outer margin to v6 only, but more widely along costa.

ARTOGEIA RAPAE   *Small White*
Range. From N. Africa across Europe and Asia to Japan; introduced into N. America and Australia.   Map 14

A. rapae   Linnaeus 1758   TL: Sweden (Verity 1947)   **Pl. 5**
Description. ♂fw 23/27mm; *first brood* (f. *metra* Stephens 1827) upf markings grey, generally with spot in s3, apical border extends along costa but only to v7 or v6 down outer margin; unf spots present in s1b and s3, apex yellow; unh yellow with grey dusting along lower margin of cell. ♀ups yellowish with grey suffusion at wing-bases; upf additional oblique mark in s1b. In *later broods* ups markings dark grey or black; unh grey dusting greatly reduced.
Flight. March or later in two or more broods.
Habitat. Meadows, gardens, etc., from sea-level to 1800m. Larval food plants *Brassica* and other Cruciferae and Resedaceae.
Distribution. From Canary Islands, Azores and N. Africa throughout Europe; generally common to 62°N, rarely to 70°N. Known from Madeira since 1974.
Variation. In N. Africa generally small, unh in late broods plain white.
Similar species. *A. mannii*, below, only in S. Europe, upf apical border black and continued by a few dark scales down outer margin to v4 or v3. *A. napi* p. 25, esp. extreme summer form, upf apical border extends down outer margin as spots or triangles at vein ends, traces of pre-apical spot often present in s6. *A. ergane* below, unf unmarked. *P. brassicae* p. 23.

Note. This and the next four species are morphologically separable from *Pieris brassicae*, which is the type species of the genus *Pieris*. For this reason the generic name *Artogeia* is now used for them in place of *Pieris* of earlier editions.

ARTOGEIA MANNII   *Southern Small White*
Range. From Morocco across S. Europe to Asia Minor and Syria.   Map 15

A. mannii   Mayer 1851   TL: Split (Spalato), Dalmatia   **Pl. 5**
Description. ♂fw 20/23mm; *first brood* (f. *farpa* Fruhstorfer 1909) resembles *A. rapae*; upf apical *black border*, extending down outer margin to v4 or v3, outer margin of spot in s3 flat or concave, sometimes connected to dark outer margin by a few black scales along v4; uph costal mark in s6 moon-shaped, concave outwards; unh rather densely dusted with dark scales. ♀upf apical border wider, spot in s3 generally clearly connected with outer margin. *Later broods* generally larger, ♂fw 26mm, black markings enlarged esp. in ♀; unh dark dusting slight or absent.
Flight. March or later in three or four broods during summer.

Habitat. Rough rocky places from sea-level to 1500m. Larval food plants *Iberis sempervirens, Sinapis, Cardamine* etc. (Cruciferae).
Distribution. France, widely distributed S. of R. Loire. E. Spain to Murcia, local and scarce in Catalonia. Switzerland, local in Tessin and Valais. Italy, widely distributed, including Sicily. Austria. Slovakia. Hungary. Balkans, including Greece. Romania in Retezat Mts. Morocco, very local in Atlas Mts. Absent from Corsica, Sardinia and small Mediterranean islands except Sicily.
Similar species. *A. rapae* p. 24.

ARTOGEIA ERGANE *Mountain Small White*
Range. SE. France and eastwards to Asia Minor, Syria, Iraq and Iran.   Map 16

A. ergane   Geyer 1828   TL: Ragusa (Hemming 1937)   **Pl. 5**
Description. ♂fw 19/24mm, resembles *A. rapae*; upf markings grey, apical mark square, extending to v5, pd spot in s3 sometimes absent; uph a small grey mark on costa in s6, often absent; *unf apex yellow otherwise unmarked*, but pattern from ups may show through; unh yellow, lightly dusted with grey. ♀ups faintly yellowish esp. uph, usually with extensive grey suffusion; upf additional often ill-defined grey spot in s1b, spot in s3 larger; uph costal spot constant.
Flight. March or later in two or more broods.
Habitat. Rocky slopes with grass from lowlands to 1800m. Food plant *Aethionema saxatile.*
Distribution. Scarce and local in NE. Spain and in France in E. Pyrenees, Aude and northwards occasionally to Briancon. Local in some warm valleys in S. Tirol. More common, sometimes abundant in Apennines (Abruzzi and Lucania) and Romania and Balkans including Greece.
Similar species. *A. rapae* p. 24.

ARTOGEIA NAPI *Green-veined White*
Range. N. Africa, Europe and east to N. America.   Map 17

A. napi napi   Linnaeus 1758   TL: Sweden (Verity 1947)   **Pl. 6**
Description. Both sexes unh gc yellow, veins lined grey. First brood ♂ upf with or without pd spot in s3; ♀ ups veins lined grey, upf with additional spot in s5. Second brood often larger, unh grey stripes reduced or vestigial; ♀ ups veins not lined grey.
Flight and **Habitat.** March or later in 2 or 3 broods, often in light woodland. Food plants various crucifers.
Distribution. Europe, except southern and boreal regions.

A. napi meridionalis   Heyne 1895   TL: C. Italy
   syn: *dubiosa* Röber 1907 (part)
Description. First brood like *A. n. napi*, later broods often larger with extreme summer-brood characters. Distinction from *A. n. napi* is not entirely due to ecological conditions; larvae from Germany (*napi*) and from S. Italy (*meridionalis*) were bred alongside, but distinctive *meridionalis* characters remained very evident in Italian specimens (Bowden).
Distribution. Spain, S. France, Corsica etc.

A. napi adalwinda   Fruhstorfer 1909   TL: Finmark   **Pl. 6**
   syn: *arctica* Verity 1911
Description. Like *A. n. bryoniae* but smaller. Cross-breeding with *A. n. napi* easy and successful, with *A. n. bryoniae* rarely satisfactory (Bowden).

Flight and **Habitat** as for *A. n. bryoniae*. Food plants *Draba*, *Arabis* etc.
Distribution. Fennoscandia north of 65°N latitude.

A. napi bryoniae   Hübner 1806   TL: Germany   **Pl. 6** ♂; **Pl. 13** ♀
Description. Like *A. n. napi*; ♂ ups veins firmly lined black. ♀ variable, ups more or
less suffused grey along veins etc., upf a short marginal streak between v1 and v2
(bryo-streak) will confirm *bryoniae* in pale specimens.
Flight and **Habitat.** Occurs in a single brood at altitudes of 1200m and over.
Foodplant *Biscutella*, rarely *Thlaspi*.
Distribution. In mountains, W. Alps, Jura, Tatra and Carpathians to Caucasus.
Absent from Pyrenees and Balkans including Greece.
Similar subspecies. *A. n. flavescens*, distinction very difficult.

A. napi flavescens   Wagner 1903   TL: Mödling, Vienna   **Pl. 6**

Description. ♂ like *A. n. napi*, ♀ extremely variable with all possible combinations
of characters between *napi* and *bryoniae*.
Flight and **Habitat** as for *A. n. napi*, flying at low to moderate altitudes. Food plant
Biscutella.
Distribution and **Variation.** Eastern Europe, extremely variable, f. *subtalba*
Schima (Pl. 6g) common, unh gc white; genetically dominant. Different ♀-forms,
varying from *napi* to *bryoniae*, may appear in offspring of a single ♀. Large races
flying in the Karawanken Mts. are often referred to f. *neobryoniae* Sheljuzhko,
described from Maritime Alps.
Note. In its western range *A. n. bryoniae* is isolated ecologically; it can be crossed
with *A. n. napi* but the broods have poor viability and f. *subtalba* is extremely rare; in
its eastern range as *flavescens*, crossed with *napi*, the resulting broods have good
viability, there is no evidence of ecological isolation, variation is extreme and the f.
subtalba is common, often preponderating.
The following taxa of unknown genetic relationships are described here as subspecies of *A. napi*.

A. napi maura   Verity 1911   TL: Glacières de Blida, Algeria   **Pl. 13**
    syn: *blidana* Holl 1912; *atlantica* Rothschild 1917

Description. ♂ like *A. n. napi*, summer brood; unh veins weakly lined grey in first
brood only. Flies at 1000m, at Glacières de Blida, in 3 annual broods from April.

A. napi atlantis   Oberthur 1923   TL: Azrou, Morocco   **Pl. 13**
♂fw 24–26mm, ups black markings reduced but upf spot in s3 large, ♀upf discal
spot conspicuous as in ♂. In both sexes unh slightly or not at all lined grey.
Flight and **Habitat.** Occurs in May, only first brood known, flying at about 1500m
near Azrou.

A. napi segonzaci   le Cerf 1923   TL: High Atlas   **Pl. 6**
Description. ♂fw 25–26mm, upf spots in s3, s5 and s6 constantly present, unh veins
broadly striped. ♀ ups all veins lined grey.
Flight and **Habitat.** Flies from end June at 2500m, Toubkal Massif only.

A. n. canidiaformis   Drenowsky 1925   TL: Bosnia and Macedonia
    syn: *balcana* Lorković.
Description. Like *A. napi napi* but unh suffused grey, veins not well defined. Cross
breeding with *A. n. napi* proved sterile. (Lorković).
Similar species. *A. rapae* p. 24; *A. callidice* p. 28.

ARTOGEIA KRUEPERI *Krueper's Small White*
Range. S. Balkans and eastwards to Iran and Baluchistan.   Map 18

A. krueperi   Staudinger 1860   TL: Arcana, Greece   **Pl. 5**
Description. ♂fw 21/25mm; *first brood* upf *large round spot in s3*, preapical costal mark and border of marginal triangles on each vein from apex to v3 all black; uph costal mark in s6 black; unh basal and discal areas grey-green, pd area white, with small grey marginal marks at vein endings. ♀ similar. In *second brood* ups black markings often smaller; unh usually yellow, dark basal shade paler, yellow-green or absent, but dark costal mark in s5, 6, 7 always present.
Flight. March/April or later in two or more broods.
Habitat. Rocky or precipitous places from lowlands to 1800m or more. Larval food plant *Alyssum saxatile*.
Distribution. SE. Europe, Bulgaria in Rumelia. Albania and SE. Yugoslavia. Greece, widespread.

PONTIA DAPLIDICE *Bath White*
Range. From Africa and S. Europe to Japan (not resident).   Map 19

P. daplidice   Linnaeus 1758   TL: Africa and S. Europe   **Pl. 7**
Description. ♂fw 21/24mm; *first brood* (f. *bellidice* Ochsenheimer) upf with usual markings; uph dark pattern shows through from uns, sometimes with black mark in s7; *unf discoidal spot large, extending to costa, apical markings green*; unh basal, discal and marginal spots in series all dark green. ♀upf black markings larger; uph large post-discal and small marginal black spots in series; unh green markings generally confluent from base to discal series. *Second and later broods* uns green markings often less extensive; unh usually paler and suffused yellow but variable. Seasonal distinction often poorly defined.
Flight. February/March and later in two or more broods.
Habitat. Rough ground and flowery meadows from lowlands to 1800m. Larval food plants *Arabis, Reseda, Sinapis*, etc., various Cruciferae.
Distribution. N. Africa and Europe to 66°N. The species is strongly migratory, and sometimes reaches Britain.
Similar species. *P. chloridice* below, in Europe only in S. Balkans, smaller, unf discoidal spot does not reach costa; unh marginal markings linear.

PONTIA CHLORIDICE *Small Bath White*
Range. Bulgaria (Sliven), NE. Greece, Albania and European Turkey, reported from SE. Yugoslavia, extending across W. Asia and Siberia to W. North America (*P. c. beckeri* Edw.).   Map 20

P. chloridice   Hübner 1808   TL: not stated   **Pl. 7**
Description. ♂fw 20/22mm, *first brood* resembles *P. daplidice* but small, lightly marked; uph unmarked; unf discoidal spot narrow, not reaching costa; unh regular short green marginal stripes connected basally by green pd band. ♀upf apical markings better developed; uph with vestigial pd and marginal markings. In *second brood* slightly larger, ♀ups all markings larger, upf spot in s1b constant and pd and marginal spots well developed on both wings.
Flight. April/May and June in two broods.
Habitat. Rocky places from lowlands to 1500m. Larval food plant not known.
Distribution. Bulgaria. Macedonia. Albania. NE. Greece. European Turkey.
Similar species. *P. daplidice* above.

PONTIA CALLIDICE   *Peak White*
Range. From Pyrenees and Alps through Asia Minor and Lebanon to Himalaya Mts., Tibet and Mongolia. N. America, on high western mountains of Alaska, Colorado and California (*occidentalis* Reakirt), where it is associated with a lowland form (*protodice* Boisduval and Leconte).   Map 21

P. callidice   Hübner 1805   TL: Swiss Alps   **Pl. 7**
Description. ♂fw 21/26mm, ups markings scanty; upf discoidal spot narrow; uph unmarked; unf markings as on ups; unh generally yellow with veins heavily lined greenish-grey, united in pd area by a series of V-shaped marks. ♀ups more heavily marked with well-developed pd and marginal markings; uns as in ♂.
Flight. End June/July/August.
Habitat. Grass slopes from 2000m upwards, restricted to higher alpine zone. Larval food plants *Erysimum pumilum, Reseda glauca.*
Distribution. Pyrenees, Hautes Alpes, Graian Alps and eastwards on higher summits to Dolomites, Austrian and Bavarian Alps. Absent from Tatra Mts, Balkans, Apennines and Cantabrian Mts.
Similar species. *A. napi* p. 25, which lacks a black discoidal spot.

EUCHLOE AUSONIA   *Mountain Dappled White*
Range. From N. Spain (Cantabrian Mts.), Pyrenees and Alps, as a mountain butterfly across Asia to Amurland; also in N. America from Alaska to Colorado (*ausonides* Lucas).   Map 22

E. ausonia ausonia   Hübner 1806   TL: N. Italy   **Pl. 7**
   syn: *simplonia* Boisduval 1828, nom. nud.; 1832 invalid homonym; *marchandae* Geyer 1832 invalid synonym
Description. ♂fw 20/24mm, ups white; upf *black discoidal spot narrow, often externally concave and fusing with dark shade along costa; hw with obtuse marginal angle at v8*; uph unmarked; unf discoidal spot angled and white centred, apex green with white markings; unh with extensive irregular green markings. ♀ similar, upf discoidal spot larger; uph yellowish.
Flight. June/July in a single brood.
Habitat. Subalpine meadows at 1500–1800m. Larval food plants *Iberis, Sisymbrium, Barbarea*, etc. (Cruciferae).
Distribution. Cantabrian Mts., esp. Picos de Europa; Pyrenees and through S. Alps to San Bernardino Pass and Splugen Pass. Absent from Jura, E. Alps, Carpathians, Apennines and Balkans.

EUCHLOE SIMPLONIA   *Dappled White*
Range. From N. Africa across S. Europe to Asia Minor, Lebanon and the Himalaya Mts. USA in California etc. (*E. hyantis* Edw.)   Map 23

E. simplonia simplonia   Freyer 1829   TL: Croatia   **Pl.7**
   syn: *belia* Stoll 1782, invalid homonym; *esperi* Kirby 1871; *crameri* Butler 1869; *orientalis* auct.
Description. Like *E. ausonia; first brood* (f. *kirbyi* Rothschild) upf discoidal spot usually larger, extending to v12 but *not reaching costa*; unf discoidal spot often round or square; unh green markings dense with little yellow mixture, white spots sometimes shining (nacreous). ♀unf discoidal spot generally very large. In *second brood* unh green markings paler, green mixed with yellow, white spots not shining (matt). These forms are not always well defined and may fly together.
Flight. March/April and May/June in two broods.

Habitat. Open meadows and hillsides from sea-level to 1400m.
Distribution. Switzerland, known only from Rhône valley; local in Portugal; Spain, south of the Cantabrian Mts.; Morocco up to 2400m in Atlas Mts.; Algeria; Tunisia; widespread in Italy with Sicily and southern Balkan countries; Montenegro; Albania; Greece and Bulgaria. Not recorded today from Croatia (Lorković). Absent from Corsica and Sardinia. *Pontia simplonia* Freyer 1829 appears to be the first valid name for the lowland butterfly, described from the Balkans where the mountain species *ausonia* Hb. does not occur. It is not entirely certain what Freyer was describing. It seems that the species is complex with marked differences in markings between larvae from western and from eastern Europe (H. E. Back 1979).

EUCHLOE INSULARIS   *Corsican Dappled White*
Range. Confined to Corsica and Sardinia. No map.

E. insularis   Staudinger 1861   TL: Corsica   **Pl. 7**
Description. ♂fw 18/22mm, like *E. t. bellezina*, upf discoidal spot narrow with extension along v12; white spots in s4 and s5 enclosed in black apical mark extend to wing-margin; unf discoidal spot very small; unh white spots reduced in size by extension of green markings. ♀ similar.
Flight and **Habitat.** May/June, local in mountains at about 900m.
Distribution. Occurs in Corsica and Sardinia.
Similar species. *E. tagis* below, in which hw costa has a smooth even curve. *A. cardamines* p. 31, ♀ has superficial resemblance on ups; unf apex greenish-grey, unmarked; in *ausonia* unf apex clearly marked with green striae.

EUCHLOE TAGIS   *Portuguese Dappled White*
Range. Confined to SW. Europe and N. Africa.   Map 24

E. tagis tagis   Hübner 1804   TL: Peidade, Portugal   **Pl. 8**
   syn: *lusitanica* Oberthur 1909
Description. ♂fw 15/22mm, resembles *E. ausonia*; upf grey apical mark completely enclosing white spots in s4, 5; hw *costa in gentle curve without angle at v8*; unh gc greygreen, white spots small, nearly obsolete in some specimens. ♀ similar, fw apex less pointed.
Flight. February to April according to locality, probably a single prolonged generation.
Habitat. Flies from lowlands to 900m or more in rough stony places. Food plant *Iberis pinnata*.
Distribution. Portugal, local on south bank of Tagus; Spain, widely distributed in south, but local. Algeria, Morocco.

E. tagis bellezina   Boisduval 1828   TL: Provence   **Pls. 1, 8**
Description. ♂fw 18/19mm, unf white markings in green apical area more extensive; unh gc green, white spots more numerous and larger. ♀ similar.
Flight. April/early May.
Habitat. Rough open places in mountain foothills.
Distribution. France, in Provence, esp. Basses Alpes, Bouches du Rhône, Ain. etc. Aix and Digne are well-known localities.
Variation. A small form, ♂fw 14/15mm, ♀larger, unh white markings slightly reduced, transitional to *E. t. tagis*, flies in a few localities in C. Spain, e.g. Aranjuez, f. *castellena* Verity Pl. 1.
Similar species. *E. ausonia* p. 28.

EUCHLOE PECHI *Pech's White*
Range. Confined to Algeria. Map 25

E. pechi Staudinger 1885 TL: Lambessa, Algeria **Pl. 8**
Description. ♂fw 17mm, upf apex grey without white spots, grey discoidal mark extending along v12; unf apex smooth green, umarked; unh *smooth green with small white discoidal mark.* ♀ not seen.
Flight. March/April.
Habitat. Recorded from Djebel Aures, flying at 1800m.
Distribution. Algeria, recorded from Lambessa, El Kantara, Guelt-es-stel, El-Outaya, and Djebel Aures. A rare and very local species.

EUCHLOE FALLOUI *Scarce Green-striped White*
Range. N. Africa, including Tibesti, Fezzan, Tripoli, Egypt and Sinai. Map 26

E. falloui Allard 1867 TL: Biskra, Algeria **Pl. 8**
Description. ♂fw 18/19mm, resembles *E. belemia*; upf costa not striated, black discoidal spot does not extend to costal margin; unf *discoidal spot small, dense black, without white central mark*; unh green markings forming well-defined stripes. ♀ similar, upf discoidal spot larger; unh green markings sometimes flushed yellow.
Flight. January/June, with a partial autumn brood in some localities.
Habitat. Atlantic coastal areas and southern slopes of Atlas Mts., recorded by Oberthur at 1800m. Food plant *Reseda muricata*.
Distribution. Morocco, Algeria, Tunis, esp. Biskra and Bou Saada. Range extends far into desert oases.
Similar species. *E. belemia* below.

EUCHLOE BELEMIA *Green-striped White*
Range. N. Africa, SW. Europe, Tibesti to Iran and Baluchistan. Map 27

E. belemia belemia Esper 1799 TL: Belem, Portugal **Pl. 8**
Description. ♂fw 19/22mm; *first brood*, apex of fw and anal angle of hw pointed; ups markings like *E. ausonia*; uns apex of fw and all hw green, marked with white transverse stripes, well defined, brilliant, often nacreous; unf discoidal spot large, enclosing narrow white curved crescent. ♀fw outer margin more rounded, apex less pointed. *Second brood* often larger, fw less pointed; unh green mixed with yellow, stripes less well defined. Both forms may fly together.
Flight. February/March and April/May in two broods.
Habitat. Rough places with flowers from sea-level to 900m. Larval food plants not known.
Distribution. N. Africa, on coastal plain and foothills of Atlas Mts., where it may fly in December. Portugal; local near Lagos, Lisbon, etc. Spain, from Mediterranean coast to Burgos but principally in south, Cadiz, Seville, Granada, Malaga, Cordoba, etc.
Similar species. *E. falloui* above, only in N. Africa; unf discoidal spot small, oval, dense black without central white crescent.

E. belemia hesperidum Rothschild 1913 TL: Canary Islands **Pl. 1**
Description. ♂fw 16/17mm, wings less pointed; upf discoidal spot narrow; unh green stripes sometimes indefinite. ♀ similar.
Flight. End March/June in two broods.
Habitat. Mountains at 700–2500m. Larval food plant *Sisymbrium bourgeanum*.

Distribution. Canary Islands, recorded from Gran Canary, Fuerteventura and Tenerife. There may be slight differences between the forms flying on different islands.

ELPHINSTONIA CHARLONIA *Greenish Black-tip*
Range. Canary Islands, Morocco, Algeria, Tunisia, Tibesti, Macedonia, Egypt, Sudan, W. Asia to Iran, Baluchistan and Punjab. Map 28

E. charlonia charlonia Donzel 1842 TL: Emsilah, Algeria **Pl. 8**
Description. ♂fw 14/16mm, ups *gc sulphur-yellow*; upf with *large dark brown apical patch* with obscure paler markings and a large dark discoidal spot; unf red marginal lines along costa and outer margin, apex uniform grey-green, discoidal spot black; unh grey-green with a few obscure paler markings, most distinct along costa. ♀ similar.
Flight. February or later, often March/April with a series of two or more broods.
Habitat. Around cliffs or on rocky slopes, usually at considerable altitudes. Food plant not known.
Distribution. Morocco, Algeria, Tunisia, esp. in southern districts near desert, common in spring. Canary Islands, very local, flying at about 600m, recorded from Tenerife, Fuerteventura, Lanzarote.

E. charlonia penia Freyer 1852 TL: not stated **Pl. 8**
Description. ♂fw 18mm, fw less pointed; upf pale markings in dark apex inconspicuous; unf red marginal lines absent. Larval marking distinct, pupa with marked cephalic prominence (Back).
Flight. April and June in two broods.
Habitat. Flies at low levels in rocky or precipitous places. Larval food plant *Mathiola tessala*.
Distribution. SE. Yugoslavia, very local, Bitola, Skopje. Bulgaria. N. Greece.

ANTHOCHARIS CARDAMINES *Orange Tip*
Range. From W. Europe eastwards through temperate Asia to Japan. Map 29

A. cardamines Linnaeus 1758 TL: Sweden (Verity 1947) **Pl. 8**
Description. ♂fw 19/24mm, *ups gc white*; upf small black discoidal spot just enclosed in wide orange apical area, apex and marginal border grey; uns with confused yellow-green markings at apex of fw and over hw. ♀upf no orange apical patch; uph often flushed pale yellow; unf apex white or yellowish, *almost umarked*.
Flight. April or later in a single brood.
Habitat. Flowery meadows from sea-level to 1500m. Food plants Cruciferae, including cuckoo flower, hedge mustard, etc. (*Cardamine, Sisymbrium*, etc.).
Distribution. Throughout W. Europe to Arctic Circle. Absent from Crete, Elba, N. Africa, Balearic Islands and Malta.
Similar species. *E. ausonia* p. 28, ♀ only.

ANTHOCHARIS BELIA *Morocco Orange Tip*
Range. N. Africa and SW. Europe. Map 30

A. belia belia Linnaeus 1767 TL: 'Barbaria' (Morocco) **Pl. 8**
syn: *eupheno* Linnaeus 1767
Description. ♂fw 18/20mm, ups yellow; upf wide orange apical patch with dusky proximal border enclosing a small black discoidal mark, extreme apex dusky; uph yellow, unmarked; unh yellow with slightly variable grey *markings indistinct except*

on costa, in Anti Atlas often almost obliterated, sometimes slightly suffused fuscous. ♀ups white, dark apical markings more extensive, with orange scales between veins; uph flushed yellow; unh grey or reddish markings as in male, sometimes better defined.

Flight. April/May in a single brood.

Habitat. Rough ground or light woodland, sea-level to 1700m. Larval food plant *Biscutella lyrata*.

Distribution. Morocco, Algeria, Tunisia, esp. from Atlas Mts. to Mediterranean coast.

A. belia euphenoides   Staudinger 1869   TL: Gibraltar   **Pl. 8**
Description. ♂ups like *A. b. belia*; unh markings grey, more extensive and well defined, transverse narrow sub-basal and discal bands joined by band along anal vein, a series of white pd patches in s2–s7. ♀ups resembles *A. b. belia*; unh markings as in ♂.

Flight. May/June/July.

Habitat. Usually in mountainous country from low levels to 1500m. Larval food plant *Biscutella laevigata*.

Distribution. Spain and Portugal, widely distributed, often common in mountainous districts. France, from Pyrenees and Provence to Isère. Reported from Corsica. Italy, local in Maritime and Cottian Alps to Susa; Apennines, very local on a few high mountains. Monte Majella, Gran Sasso, Monte Terminillo, etc.; reported occasionally from warm valleys in S. Alps, Gondo, Lugano, Locarno, etc. in Switzerland. Ranked specifically distinct by some authors.

Similar species. *A. damone* below and *A. gruneri* below, unh mottled green in complicated pattern resembling *A. cardamines*.

ANTHOCHARIS DAMONE   *Eastern Orange Tip*
Range. Sicily and S. Italy, Greece, Syria to Iran.   Map 31

A. damone   Boisduval 1836   TL: Sicily   **Pl. 8**
Description. ♂fw 19/20mm, ups resembles *A. belia, gc bright yellow*; unh gc yellow with *confused greenish-grey markings* resembling those of *A. cardamines*. ♀upf gc white, apex grey, orange apical patch absent; *uph gc yellowish*; uns apex of fw and all hw gc yellow with markings as in ♂.

Flight. April/May.

Habitat. Rocky mountain slopes to 900m or more. Larval food plant *Isatis tinctoria*.

Distribution. Sicily, local in neighbourhood of Mt. Etna absent from W. Sicily; Italy, recorded from Aspromonte and Calabria. Greece, very local on Mt. Parnassus and Mt. Ghiona at 600–800m. SE. Yugoslavia, Skopje.

Similar species. *A. gruneri* below, ♂ smaller, unh gc white; ♀upf with very large grey discoidal mark; *A. belia* p. 31.

ANTHOCHARIS GRUNERI   *Grüner's Orange Tip*
Range. Greece, Asia Minor and Syria to Iraq (Kurdistan). Iran.   Map 32

A. gruneri   Herrich-Schäffer 1851   TL: 'Crete' (Greece?)   **Pl. 8**
Description. ♂fw 15/18mm, ups *gc light yellow*; upf orange-yellow apical patch enclosing small black discoidal spot, apical border grey, base of costa grey and fringe grey-chequered; unf apex yellow with grey mottling along veins; *unh gc white*, marbled with green markings resembling those of *A. cardamines*. ♀ white, upf a *large*

grey discoidal spot, apical border wider than in ♂; uph yellow flush along costa; uns as in ♂ but unf orange area absent.
Flight. March/May.
Habitat. Lowlands to 900m, flying on open stony ground. Larval food plant *Aethionema saxatile*.
Distribution. Greece, esp. near Mt. Parnassus, Mt. Chelmos, etc. Albania. SE. Yugoslavia, Vardar valley. Turkey in Europe.
Similar species. *A. damone* p. 32.

ZEGRIS EUPHEME   *Sooty Orange Tip*
Range. Morocco, Spain, S. Russia (TL of *Papilio eupheme* Esper 1782), Asia Minor and eastwards to Iran.   Map 33

Z. eupheme meridionalis   Lederer 1852   TL: S. Spain   **Pl. 9**
Description. ♂fw 23/25mm, ups gc white; upf C-shaped discoidal mark black, *apex broadly dark grey clouded white, enclosing an oval orange patch*; unf apex yellow; unh gc yellow with irregular green-grey markings recalling *A. belia euphenoides*.
♀ often slightly larger, orange apical patch reduced or absent.
Flight. April/May in a single brood.
Habitat. Rough slopes with flowers, cornfields, etc., lowlands to 1000m. Food plant *Sinapis incana*.
Distribution. Morocco, Middle Atlas at Ifrane, Anosseur, Foum-Kharig, 1700m; High Atlas, at Oikemaden, 2500m. Spain, from Mediterranean northwards to Lerida, Soria, Burgos, but absent in west.

COLOTIS EVAGORE   *Desert Orange Tip*
Range. Widely distributed in Africa and in S. Arabia (TL of *C. evagore* Klug) in a bewildering range of local and seasonal forms.   Map 34

C. evagore nouna   Lucas 1849   TL: Djebel Aures, Algeria   **Pl. 7**
Description. ♂fw 15/18mm, ups white with variable black markings and vermilion apical patch; *first brood* upf with black streak along inner margin; uph with black shade at base and along costa. ♀ apex of fw rounded, red apical patch narrow with black proximal border. *Late broods* generally small, all black markings reduced, sometimes absent, thorax and abdomen pale.
Flight and **Habitat.** February/March or later in a succession of broods, flying in hot rocky gorges at 900–1500m. Larval food plant caper bush (*Capparis*).
Distribution. Morocco, Algeria and Tunisia, S. Spain.

CATOPSILIA FLORELLA   *African Migrant*
Range. All Africa south of the Sahara, Canary Islands and through Egypt to India and China.

C. florella   Fabricius 1775   TL: Sierra Leone   **Pl. 13**
Description. ♂fw 31mm, *ups pale greenish-white*, scaling appears mealy except over basal area of hw where surface is smooth; upf discoidal spot minute and margin of costa grey-brown; uph unmarked; uns apical and costal areas of fw and all hw pale yellow, *lightly irrorated pale grey-brown*; unf with hair-pencil arising from inner margin and associated with sexbrand on uph in s7 along upper margin of cell. ♀ dimorphic, closely resembling ♂ or with gc yellow-buff; upf discoidal spot brown,

dark costal margin slightly more prominent and continued down outer margin as small dark marks on veins.
Flight and **Habitat.** In flowery places from sea-level to moderate altitudes, flying perhaps throughout the year. Larval food plants include *Cassia*.
Distribution. Within the region recorded only from Gran Canary and Tenerife, for the first time in 1964 and Gomera 1974. There are casual records from Malta (1963) and Germany (1964) and from other unlikely places.

COLIAS PHICOMONE   *Mountain Clouded Yellow*
Range. Restricted to Europe.   Map 35

C. phicomone   Esper 1780   TL: Styria   **Pl. 9**
Description. ♂fw 20/25mm, ups pale yellow-green *heavily suffused dark grey*; upf darker submarginal area enclosing yellow submarginal spots; uph grey-green from base to band of yellow submarginal spots, discoidal spot yellow. ♀ greenish-white, markings as in ♂ but upf grey suffusion reduced.
Flight. End June/July/August in a single brood, occasionally in September.
Habitat. Grass slopes from 1800m upwards. Larval food plants vetches, esp. *Vicia* and *Hippocrepis* (Leguminosae).
Distribution. Cantabrian Mts., Picos de Europa. Pyrenees and main alpine chain eastwards to Hohe Tauern and N. Carpathians, Bavarian and Salzburg Alps. Absent from Jura, Apennines, S. Carpathians and Balkans.
Similar species. *C. nastes* below, a purely arctic species.

COLIAS NASTES   *Pale Arctic Clouded Yellow*
Range. Arctic Europe, Greenland, Labrador (TL of *C. nastes* Boisduval 1832), probably circumpolar.   Map 36

C. nastes werdandi   Zetterstedt 1840   TL: Torne-Lapland   **Pl. 9**
Description. ♂fw 22/24mm, ups pale yellow-green *without general grey suffusion*, veins lined fuscous; upf grey border enclosing pale submarginal spots; uph *yellow discoidal spot minute.* ♀ similar, ups gc less yellow, more variable, uph often suffused grey. In both sexes antennae, collar and fringes usually red but variable.
Flight. June.
Habitat. Rough ground, usually in hilly country at 300m or more. Larval food plant *Astragalus alpinus*.
Distribution. NW. Scandinavia, from 66° to 70°N.
Similar species. *C. phicomone* above, ups ♂ suffused dark grey; uph yellow, discoidal spot large; only flies in Pyrenees and Alps.

COLIAS PALAENO   *Moorland Clouded Yellow*
Range. From C. and N. Europe through Siberia to Amur and Japan. Also in N. America.   Map 37

C. palaeno palaeno   Linnaeus 1761   TL: Sweden and Finland   **Pl. 9**
Description. ♂fw 25/27mm, ups gc pale sulphur yellow tending to white, fringes red; upf discoidal mark small, oval, black marginal band dense; uph black marginal border narrower; unf gc pale yellow; unh densely irrorated grey-green except the marginal band, discoidal spot small, white. ♀ups white, dark marginal markings as in ♂ but less well defined.
Flight. Late June/July in a single brood.

Habitat. Bogs and moorland with *Vaccinium* bushes, usually at low levels. Food plant bog whortleberry (*Vaccinium uliginosum*).
Distribution. Fennoscandia, widely distributed, ups often very pale in far north.

C. palaeno europome Esper 1779 TL: Saxony **Pl. 9**
Description. ♂fw 24/27mm, resembles *C. p. palaeno* but ups gc sulphur yellow; upf dark marginal band usually wide, discoidal spot black or, more rarely, white; uns yellow, darker in tone at fw apex and over hw, which is finely irrorated with dark scales. ♀gc generally white, occasionally yellow, f. *illgneri* Rühl.
Flight. Late June/July.
Habitat. Flies over bogs, etc., with *Vaccinium*, typically in lowland localities but in places to 700m.
Distribution. Local in NE. France in Vosges and Jura. Germany, esp. Bavarian moors. Rare in N. Czechoslovakia, Carpathians and Romania. Absent from Central Massif of France, Pyrenees, Apennines and Balkans. Extinct in Belgium.
Variation. At high altitudes in main Alpine chain, smaller, unh more heavily irrorated with dark scales, f. *europomene* Ochsenheimer.

COLIAS CHRYSOTHEME *Lesser Clouded Yellow*
Range. E. Europe and S. Russia to Altai Mts. Map 38

C. chrysotheme Esper 1781 TL: Cremnitz, Hungary, **Pl. 10**
Description. ♂fw 20/24mm, apex of fw pointed; ups gc yellow with wide black marginal borders regularly crossed by yellow veins; upf discoidal spot small, often reddish; uph without sex-brand; *uns black pd spots in regular series across both wings*; fringes red. ♀ resembles *C. crocea* and *C. myrmidone* but fw more pointed; upf costal margin broadly and *conspicuously green-grey*.
Flight. May and July/August in two broods.
Habitat. Flies on grass slopes from lowlands to 900m. Food plant *Vicia hirsuta*.
Distribution. Austria (Burgenland), Hungary, Czechoslovakia and Romania, in localised colonies. The species is a member of the Russian steppe fauna, reaching its most westerly point near Vienna.
Variation. White or pale yellow female forms occur but are rare.
Similar species. *C. crocea* and *C. myrmidone* p. 36: ♂ups veins crossing dark marginal bands only slightly or not at all lined yellow, uph sex-brand present, ♀upf lacks broad grey-green band along costal margin.

COLIAS LIBANOTICA *Greek Clouded Yellow*
Range. From mountains of Greece to Asia Minor and Lebanon (TL of *Colias libanotica* Lederer 1858). Map 39

C. libanotica heldreichii Staudinger 1862 TL: Mt. Veluchi, Greece **Pl. 10**
Description. ♂fw 27/28mm, fw pointed, *ups gc dull orange with purple reflections in oblique lights*; upf wide black marginal border crossed by yellow-lined veins; uph prominent sex-brand above median vein, *veins yellow-lined as they cross the black marginal border*; unh gc yellow-green, pd spots if present reddish. ♀ resembles *C. myrmidone* but larger; ups wide black marginal border broken by rather large greenish-yellow spots; uns *gc grey-green, almost unmarked, a small white discoidal spot* and pale submarginal spots.
Flight. June/early July.
Habitat. Rough open places at 1500–2400m. Larval food plant *Astragalus cyleneus*.

Distribution. Greece, on Mt. Veluchi, Mt. Chelmos, Mt. Parnassus.
Variation. A white ♀ form occurs rarely.

COLIAS MYRMIDONE *Danube Clouded Yellow*
Range. From E. Europe through Russia to W. Asia (Steppe fauna). Map 40

C. myrmidone Esper 1781 TL: Turnau, Hungary **Pl. 10**
Description. ♂fw 22/25mm, resembles *C. crocea*, ups gc *deeper, more reddish orange-yellow*; upf discoidal spot smaller, dark border usually dense, rarely v5–8 lined yellow; uph narrow dark marginal border with rather obscure pale orange submarginal lunules, conspicuous sex-brand at base of s7, discoidal spot red; uns resembles *C. crocea* but unf *black pd spots in s1b, 2, 3 small or absent.* ♀ups gc orange-yellow or greenish-white, ♀f. *alba* Staudinger, rarely with intermediate colour; uph yellow submarginal spots often prominent and tending to form a band. Specimens of *second brood* perhaps slightly larger.
Flight. May and July/August in two broods.
Habitat. A lowland species flying over heaths and open spaces. Foodplant *Cytisus capitatus*.
Distribution. Eastern Europe, mostly in Danube basin, Romania, Hungary, Austria and S. Germany to Munich. A very local species but often abundant in an established colony. Recorded from Bulgaria.
Similar species. *C. crocea*, ♂upf black marginal border near apex crossed by a few yellow veins, unf black pd spots in s1b, 2, 3 conspicuous in both sexes; ♂uph pale submarginal spots often irregular and series incomplete. *C. chrysotheme* p. 35; *C. balcanica* p. 37.

COLIAS CROCEA *Clouded Yellow*
Range. N. Africa, including Fezzan and Cyrenaica, S. and C. Europe and eastwards across W. Asia to Iran. Map 41

C. crocea Geoffroy in Fourcroy 1785 TL: Paris **Pl. 10**
  syn: *edusa* Fabricius 1787
Description. ♂fw 23/27mm, ups gc bright orange-yellow with wide black marginal borders; upf veins near apex lined yellow across border; uph body-groove pale yellow-green, black border rarely crossed by yellow veins, conspicuous sex-brand near base in s7. ♀upf with grey basal suffusion, wing-border enclosing yellow spots in s2 and near apex; uph gc dusky yellow-grey with large orange discoidal spot, irregular yellow spots in dark marginal band rarely in complete series. Unf pd spots black in both sexes, well-marked in s1b, 2, 3, fw outer margin and all hw yellow tinted green; unh twin white red-ringed discoidal spots, pd spots small, reddish.
Flight. April/May and later with succession of broods until autumn.
Habitat. Heaths and open places from lowlands to 1800m. Food plants various Leguminosae, esp. vetches.
Distribution. Throughout N. Africa and Europe to 60°N, including Mediterranean islands, Canary Islands, Madeira and Azores.
Variation. A white ♀ f. *helice* Hübner pl. 10, is genetically controlled and behaves as a dominant to the common yellow form, in a balanced polymorphism with a ratio of about 10% in most populations. Rarely females with an intermediate yellowish-white gc occur, ♀ f. *helicina* Oberthur.
Similar species. *C. myrmidone* above.

COLIAS BALCANICA *Balkan Clouded Yellow*
Range. Restricted to Balkan Mts.   Map 42

C. balcanica   Rebel 1903   TL: Bulgaria   **Pl. 11**
Description. ♂fw 25/27mm, *slightly larger* than *C. myrmidone; ups gc deep reddish-orange with dense dark borders* lightly powdered yellow on fw; uph slightly dusky, oval sex-brand gleaming yellow above median v near wing-base, pale orange submarginal lunules generally present bordering black border; uns resembles *C. myrmidone.* ♀upf dark border fully encloses small yellow spots; uph gc slightly dusky, prominent pale yellow submarginal spots between veins; the 'white' form of the female is not common, f. *rebeli* Schawerda.
Flight. July in a single brood.
Habitat. Open spaces in light woodland at 1300–1700m. Food plant not known.
Distribution. Higher Balkan Mts. from Trebević southwards to Durmitor, Mt. Perister in S. Yugoslavia; also Rila, Rhodope Mts. and Pirin Mts. in Bulgaria. NW. Greece.
Similar species. *C. myrmidone* p. 36, smaller, ♂ups gc paler orange-yellow, a lowland species occurring in the countries of the Danube basin.

COLIAS HECLA *Northern Clouded Yellow*
Range. Arctic Europe and N. America, Greenland (TL of *C. hecla* Lefèbvre 1836), probably circumpolar.   Map 43

C. hecla sulitelma   Aurivillius 1890   TL: Mt. Sulitelma, Sweden   **Pl. 11**
Description. ♂fw 20/23mm, ups *gc orange-yellow with rosy reflection* in oblique light; upf discoidal spot small, black marginal border usually with yellow cross-veins and powdered with yellow scales; uph red discoidal spot indistinct, black marginal border only very rarely with crossing veins; unf discal area paler yellow, *apex and margin and all unh grey-green*; unh small white red-ringed discoidal spot; uns marginal pale grey-green borders paler in both sexes. ♀upf veins dark, marginal band enclosing yellow-green elongate spots between veins; uph suffused grey, yellow submarginal spots prominent and regular, orange discoidal spot indistinct.
Flight. Late June/July.
Habitat. Usually flies over rough grassy places from sea-level to 900m. Larval foodplant *Astragalus alpinus.*
Distribution. Fennoscandia, from 68°N to North Cape. On Mt. Nuolja flies at 900m, but on Porsanger Fjord at sea-level; often common in established colonies.

COLIAS HYALE *Pale Clouded Yellow*
Range. From C. Europe, including Denmark and S. Sweden through S. Russia to Altai Mts. Range uncertain owing to confusion with *C. australis.*   Map 44

C. hyale   Linnaeus 1758   TL: S. England (Verity 1947)   **Pl. 11**
Description. ♂fw 21/25mm, ups gc pale yellow with dark grey or black marginal markings and red fringes. ♀ white with slightly yellow-green tint; uph discoidal spot pale orange; dark markings as in ♂. Females with yellow gc do occur but they are very rare.
Flight. May/June and August/September in two broods.
Habitat. Flowery meadows, clover fields, etc, lowlands to 1800m or over. The late brood is the more abundant. Larval food plants lucerne, *Coronilla, Vicia* and other Papilionaceous plants.

Distribution. Europe to 60°N, commoner in N. and E.; migrant to 65°, probably absent from Spain and S. Italy.
Similar species. *C. australis* below, identification may be very difficult but early stages are distinct. *C. erate* below.
Note. The species is strongly migratory, dispersing northwards and occurring occasionally in southern England.

COLIAS AUSTRALIS   *Berger's Clouded Yellow*
Range. From S. and C. Europe through S. Russia to Asia Minor.   Map 45

C. australis   Verity 1911   TL: Spain, Andalusia   **Pl. 11**
   syn: *alfacarensis* Berger 1948
Description. ♂fw 21/27mm, resembles *C. hyale*; ups *gc brighter yellow; upf dark apical markings less extensive*, dark basal shade *usually restricted to s1a* without spreading across base of cell; uph discoidal spot *bright orange.* ♀ white like that of *C. hyale*, very rarely yellowish.
Flight. May/June and August/September in two broods, often three broods in S. Europe.
Habitat. Rough ground, rocky slopes at moderate levels. Larval food plants *Hippocrepis comosa* (Tufted Horseshoe Vetch), *Coronilla varia*.
Distribution. S. and C. Europe to 54°N, including Greece, most commonly in SW., occasionally recorded from England and from Algeria; often flies with *C. hyale*.
Similar species. *C. hyale* above. The wing-markings of *C. hyale* and of *C. australis* differ only slightly and identification may be difficult. The most useful distinctive characters are on the upper surface and are compared as follows:
Ground-colour: in *hyale* ♂ pale greenish-yellow; in *australis* ♂ brighter lemon-yellow. This character is not entirely constant.
Fore-wing shape: in *hyale* apex more pointed; in *australis* apex more rounded; distinction is not present in all specimens.
Fore-wing markings: in *hyale* dark apical markings more extensive, black basal shade fan-shaped extending into s1b; in *australis* apical markings less extensive, dark basal shade spreads below submedian vein in s1a along lower margin of wing.
Hind-wing markings: in *hyale* submarginal markings not infrequent and black marginal markings constant, orange discoidal spot pale, not prominent; in *australis* submarginal markings absent, black marginal markings small if present, orange discoidal spot more brilliant orange.
Both species are variable and there is no reliable single external character for identification. The shape of the dark shading at base of fore-wing and the hind-wing markings are the most constant, most easily recognised and helpful characters. Identification of females may be very difficult. The two species may fly together.

COLIAS ERATE   *Eastern Pale Clouded Yellow*
Range. E. Europe and across temperate Asia to Japan, Formosa and Kashmir. Recorded also from Abyssinia and Somalia.   Map 46

C. erate   Esper 1804   TL: Sarepta, S. Russia   **Pl. 11**
Description. ♂fw 23/26mm, *ups bright lemon-yellow*; upf marginal black border dense, usually without yellow cross-veins; uph black marginal border narrower, orange discoidal spot often prominent. ♀upf dark margin broken by included yellow spots in s2 and near apex; uph marginal black border broken between veins and with clear yellow submarginal spots forming a somewhat indefinite band.

Flight. May/June and August/September in two broods.
Habitat. Open spaces and grass slopes at lowland levels. Larval food plants not recorded. All European specimens seen have been of the second generation.
Distribution. Romania, locally common especially the late brood. Occasional in Hungary, Bulgaria, N. Greece, Thrace and Turkey in Europe.
Similar species. *C. australis* and *C. hyale*, upf dark apical areas are broken by spots of ground colons.

GONEPTERYX RHAMNI *Brimstone*
Range. From N. Africa and W. Europe through Russia, to Siberia? and Japan. Map 47

G. rhamni Linnaeus 1758 TL: Sweden (Verity 1947) **Pl. 12**
Description. ♂fw 26/30mm, head and antennae red; ups *gc lemon-yellow* uniform on both wings, a small orange discoidal spot on each wing, veins marked at wing-margins by minute brown points, except at v1, 2, 3 on fw; uns markings similar; unh small brown pd points occasional between veins. ♀ greenish-white with similar wing-markings.
Flight. June or later in a single brood in Europe, hibernated specimens reappearing in early spring; a partial second brood in Africa flying in August/September.
Habitat. Light woodland and open places from sea-level to 1800m. Food plant Buckthorn (*Rhamnus*).
Distribution. Widely distributed in N. Africa and in Europe to 67°N or beyond. Absent from Balearic Islands, Crete and Atlantic islands.
Variation. Large specimens with fw 33mm occur in S. Europe and in N. Africa, f. *meridionalis* Roeber 1907.
Similar species. *G. cleopatra* below, ♀ only; *G. farinosa* p. 41.

GONEPTERYX CLEOPATRA *Cleopatra*
Range. From Madeira and Canary Islands through N. Africa and S. Europe to Syria. Map 48

G. cleopatra cleopatra Linnaeus 1767 TL: Algeria **Pl. 12**
Description. ♂fw 25/30mm, resembles *G. rhamni*, but upf *vivid orange-red*, yellow marginal border 5–6mm wide; uns costa of fw and all hw pale green or yellow (f. *italica* Gerhard syn. *massiliensis* Foulquier), both forms common in N. Africa. ♀ resembles *G. rhamni*, but unf with faint orange streak above median vein through cell.
Flight. May/June and later, depending upon locality. Perhaps two annual broods in S. Spain and N. Africa.
Habitat. Frequent near light woodland and in open places, from sea-level to 1800m. Larval food plant *Rhamnus*.
Distribution. Morocco, Algeria, Tunisia, Sicily. Greece and all Mediterranean islands including Balearics and Crete.
Note. The angle at margin of hw at v3 is often feebly developed, sometimes scarcely noticeable.

G. cleopatra europaea Verity 1913 TL: Florence
Description. ♂upf orange discal field is slightly larger and deeper orange, yellow marginal border only 3–4mm wide; angle at v3 on hw well defined, but distinctive

characters slightly variable and not always well marked. Form *italica* is recorded as a rarity from coastal districts of Mediterranean.

Flight. May/June, a partial emergence in August/September has been reported; hibernated specimens from March onwards.

Habitat. Usually in mountain foothills at 600–900m.

Distribution. Spain. Portugal. C. and S. France, northwards to Grenoble, Dordogne, etc. Italy, generally distributed; occasional in southern Alpine valleys.

Similar species. *C. rhamni* p. 39 and *C. farinosa* p. 41, ♀ only, unf lacks orange longitudinal flush from base through cell.

Variation. Dimorphism in males varies locally. Form *italica* is rare in France, Spain and in N. Italy, common in S. Italy and Sicily, probably preponderates in the Canary Islands and in N. Africa, probably constant in the Balearic Islands, Corsica, Sardinia, Crete and in the E. Mediterranean where females are often yellowish or yellow.

Note. In early autumn at hibernation, females are already fecund, but eggs are not laid until the following spring.

G. cleopatra maderensis   Felder 1862   TL: Madeira   **Pl. 23**
Description. ♂fw 28–30mm, hw angle at v3 usually developed; upf deep orange, marginal yellow border narrow. ♀ ups greenish with very slight yellowish flush.
Flight and **Habitat.** Most common April to October, but probably flies throughout the year. Widely distributed but local in mountains flying over the *maquis* of rough bushy undergrowth rarely below 700m, and up to 1400m or more.
Distribution. Confined to Madeira. Larval food plant *Rhamnus glandulosa*.

G. cleopatra palmae   Stamm 1963   TL: Canary Islands, La Palma   **Pl. 12**
Description. ♂fw 30/33mm, outer margin nearly straight, apex slightly falcate; upf lemon-yellow with pale orange flush which fades to yellow near outer margin, red-brown marginal line and spots marking veins often conspicuous; hw margin bluntly angled at v3; uph lemon yellow; uns pale yellow-green, unf disc paler. ♀ upf white, flushed yellowish at apex; uph palest orange; uns palest green, disc of fw white.
Flight. March/June, perhaps also later.
Habitat. Rough bushy ground at 600m.
Distribution. Canary Islands, confined to La Palma.

G. cleopatra cleobule   Hübner 1825   'Canary Island Brimstone'   **Pl. 12**
TL: Tenerife
Description. ♂fw 32/34mm, resembles *G. c. palmae*, fw outer margin more sinuous and apex more falcate; upf orange area extending nearly to outer margin; hw angle at v3 faint or absent, veins marked by conspicuous red-brown spots; uph lemon-yellow slightly flushed orange. ♀ups lemon-yellow broadly flushed orange on fw and over pd area of hw.
Flight. February/March and later until mid-August.
Habitat. Rough ground at 600–1800m. Larval food plants *Rhamnus crenulata* and *R. glandulosa*.
Distribution. Confined to Tenerife, Gomera. Females from Gomera are paler yellowish-white with minimal pale orange flush, probably a minor local race. In the Canary Islands the life-history of this species is not well understood. It is known to fly in January, February, March, May, June, July, August and perhaps later. It seems possible that the butterfly flies throughout the year; the usual period of hibernation has not been reported.

GONEPTERYX FARINOSA *Powdered Brimstone*
Range. From SE. Europe through Asia Minor and Syria to Iran.   Map 49

G. farinosa Zeller 1847   TL: Macri (Fethiye), SW. Turkey   **Pl. 12**
Description. ♂fw 28/32mm, resembles *G. rhamni*; upf scales uneven (mealy) with apices upturned, producing a slightly roughened appearance best seen with a hand lens; hw outer margin often rather deeply dentate between v1 and v3; upf gc lemon-yellow at base, becoming paler near outer margin, red discoidal spot minute or absent; *uph yellow gc distinctly paler than upf.* ♀ resembles *G. rhamni*.
Flight. May/June in a single brood.
Habitat. Usually in hilly or mountainous country from 300–1500m. Larval food plant buckthorn (*Rhamnus*).
Distribution. Only in extreme SE. Europe, Turkey, Greece, SE. Yugoslavia, Albania.
Similar species. *G. rhamni* p. 39, ♂ups yellow gc uniform in tone over both wings; in both sexes specimens from W. Europe usually have hw margin between v1b and v3 less deeply dentate; flies with *G. farinosa* but usually at higher altitudes.

LEPTIDEA SINAPIS *Wood White*
Range. From N. Africa (Er Rif) and W. Europe through Russia to Syria and Caucasus Mts. and eastwards to Siberia.   Map 50

L. sinapis Linnaeus 1758   TL: Sweden (Verity 1947)   **Pl. 13**
Description. ♂fw 19/24mm, antennal club black, extreme tip chestnut-brown with white patch beneath; ups paper white. *First brood* upf apical mark large, grey; unf costa grey, apex yellowish; unh yellowish with obscure dusky markings across most of wing excepting cell and area beyond. ♀upf apical mark reduced to grey streaks along veins. *Second brood* (f. *diniensis* Boisduval) ♂upf apical mark black, smaller, round; unh markings reduced to obscure yellow-grey marblings but usually with grey band above anal region. ♀upf apical mark vestigial or absent.
Flight. April/May and later in two or more broods.
Habitat. Light woodland from lowlands to 1500m. Larval food plants various Leguminosae, including tuberous pea, birds-foot trefoil, etc.
Distribution. Widely distributed through W. Europe to 66°N, rarely to 70°N, including the Mediterranean islands. Morocco (Er Rif.). Absent from Scotland and Malta.
Similar species. *L. duponcheli* below; *L. morsei* p. 42 larger, fw in first brood slightly falcate but more rounded in second brood; unh paper-white, unf veins lined grey near outer margin; unh grey pd markings better defined.

LEPTIDEA DUPONCHELI *Eastern Wood White*
Range. SE. France and Balkans to Asia Minor and Iran.   Map 51

L. duponcheli Staudinger 1871   TL: S. France   **Pl. 13**
   syn: *lathyri* Duponchel (invalid homonym)
Description. ♂fw 17/21mm, resembles *L. sinapis*, apex more pointed; antennal club without white spot beneath. *First brood* ups generally faintly flushed yellow; upf apical mark grey; uph extensive grey markings show through from uns; unh uniformly suffused grey-green except white mark at base of s5 and white area on outer margin. ♀ similar, upf apical mark pale grey. *Second brood*, f. *aestiva* Staudinger, ♂upf apical mark smaller, black; unh yellow flush generally well marked but dark markings absent. ♀upf apical mark often absent; unh as in ♂.

Flight. April or later in two broods.

Habitat. Open places generally at moderate altitudes, in mountainous districts. Larval food plants sainfoin and various Leguminosae.

Distribution. France in Var, Basses and Hautes Alpes, Alpes Maritime and Cantal to Briançon. Lower Austria, Czechoslovakia, Romania, Yugoslavia and Central and N. Greece. Appears to be absent from Peloponnesos.

Similar species. *L. sinapis* p. 41; *L. morsei* below. Both species have a white mark beneath antennal club.

LEPTIDEA MORSEI *Fenton's Wood White*

Range. From Europe across Siberia to Japan (TL of *L. morsei* Fenton 1881). Map 52

L. morsei major Grund 1905 TL: Zagreb, Yugoslavia **Pl. 13**

Description. *First brood*, f. *croatica* Grund, resembles *L. sinapis*; ♂fw 21/23mm, slightly falcate at v6; upf apical mark grey, streaky, v3 and v4 darkened near margin; unf apex and all unh yellow-grey with darker markings as in *L. sinapis*; all veins grey except in basal half of fw. ♀fw falcate tip well marked. *Second brood*, f. *major*, ♂fw 23/25mm, apex rounded with slight angle on outer margin at v6, not definite in all specimens; apical mark round, dark grey; unh paper-white with usual markings in palest grey. ♀upf apical mark of grey streaks along veins. Antennal club with small brown tip, uns white.

Flight. April and June/July in two broods.

Habitat. Light woodland at lowland levels. Food plant *Lathyrus yerna*.

Distribution. Lower Austria. Czechoslovakia. Romania, Mehadia. NW. Yugoslavia to Rijeka (Fiume) (farthest west) Olympus, Parnassos, Chelmos.

Similar species. *L. sinapis* p. 41; *L. duponcheli* above.

Acceptable specific characters are hard to find in this group.

LYCAENIDAE

Leach 1815

The Blues, Coppers and Hairstreaks that comprise this very extensive family are small or very small butterflies, the males characteristically blue, coppery or brown, females normally less brilliant. Some 100 species occur in the region. Structural characters are remarkably uniform throughout the family. Specific identification may be difficult. The best characters are found on the undersides, especially of the hind-wings, in the precise arrangement of the small markings, spots and striae, which are usually identical in both sexes.

CIGARITIS ZOHRA *Donzel's Silver-line*
Range. Restricted to N. Africa.   Map 53

C. zohra   Donzel 1847   TL: Algeria   **Pl. 16**
Description. ♂fw 12/13mm, upf small black spot in cell, pd row irregular, spot in s4 displaced distad; uph discoidal spot large; uns *gc of hw and costa of fw white*; unh with many brown silver-centred spots, the *crowded pd series sharply angled at v4*, base sometimes entirely black. ♀ similar.
Flight. March/June depending upon locality and season.
Habitat. Mountains up to 1700m, exact information not available. Larval food plant unknown.
Distribution. Morocco; Anosseur, Ifranc. Algeria; Sebdou, Saida, Kralfalih, Tunisia.
Variation. Ups markings variable; upf spots may be reduced to discoidal spot, costal and marginal spots; uns gc may be grey-brown, f. *jugurtha* Oberthur. Minor local variation is considerable.
Similar species. *C. allardi* p. 44, unh macular markings in straight rows. *C. siphax* below, unh spots smaller, gc usually darker, often reddish.

CIGARITIS SIPHAX *Common Silver-line*
Range. Confined to Algeria and Tunisia.   Map 54

C. siphax   Lucas 1847   TL: Algeria   **Pl. 16**
Description. ♂fw 11/12mm, ups marginal markings not well defined; upf pd spots irregular, spot in s4 displaced distad; uns *gc of apex of fw and all hw some shade of brown*, often with reddish tint, with *obscure small round silver-centred spots* arranged as in *C. zohra*. ♀ similar.
Flight. March or later, sometimes in two broods April/May and September.
Habitat. Dry hillsides at moderate altitudes.
Distribution. Algeria; Bône, Aflou, Collo, Khenchela. Tunisia; Ain Draham. Not reported from Morocco.
Variation. On ups all markings are variable, esp. black marginal spots which are sometimes obsolete; uns gc of hw varies from brown to near purple.
Similar species. *C. zohra* above.

43

CIGARITIS ALLARDI *Allard's Silver-line*
Range. Confined to N. Africa. Map 55

C. allardi Oberthur 1909 TL: Sebdou, Algeria **Pl. 16**
Description. ♂fw 12mm, upf black spots in oblique discoidal row with twin spots in s4, 5 isolated; submarginal spots large and regular on both wings; unh gc white, with large silver-centred *spots in straight basal, discal and pd rows.* ♀ similar.
Flight. May.
Habitat. No information; food plant unknown.
Distribution. Algeria; Sebdou, Masser Mines, Djebel Maktar at 1500–1800m, Abu Safra. Morocco.
Variation. In Morocco larger, more brightly coloured, ups black markings larger.
Similar species. *C. zohra* p. 43.

THECLA BETULAE *Brown Hairstreak*
Range. C. and S. Europe and across Asia to Amurland and Korea. Map 56

T. betulae Linnaeus 1758 TL: Sweden (Verity 1943) **Pl. 14**
Description. ♂fw 17/18mm, ups gc brown; upf with vertical mark at cell-end followed by orange patch, sometimes poorly developed; uph with small orange marks on margin at v1 and v2; uns orange-yellow, darkened towards outer margins; unf a narrow mark at cell-end, pd transverse line white; *unh with short discal and complete pd white transverse lines* with darker orange between, and narrow dark marginal line before white fringe. ♀ larger, upf with wide orange-red pd transverse band; uns gc more intense orange-red, markings more brilliant.
Flight. July/August.
Habitat. In light woodland at low to moderate altitudes. Larval food plants sloe, plum, birch, etc.
Distribution. From N. Portugal and N. Spain across C. Europe to 62°N, including S. Ireland, England and S. Fennoscandia, eastwards to the Baltic countries, Poland, Romania, Bulgaria and N. Greece. Absent from Mediterranean area.

QUERCUSIA QUERCUS *Purple Hairstreak*
Range. Europe and N. Africa and across Russia and Asia Minor to Armenia. Map 57

Q. quercus quercus Linnaeus 1758 TL: England (Verity 1943) **Pl. 14**
Description. ♂fw 12/14mm, ups *both wings gleaming purple-blue* with black marginal borders; uns gc dove grey with white transverse pd line on each wing and obscure sub-marginal markings; unf yellow marks at anal angle in s1 and s2 (3), best marked in N. Europe; unh anal lobe and circle round black spot in s2 both yellow. ♀ gleaming royal blue in s1b and in cell; unh submarginal markings more distinct.
Flight. July/August.
Habitat. In woodlands from lowlands to 1500m. Larval food plant oak, rarely ash.
Distribution. Throughout Europe to 60°N, including Britain, Mediterranean islands and Crete. Absent from Balearic Islands. Replaced in SW. by following subspecies.

Q. quercus ibericus Staudinger 1901 TL: S. Spain and Morocco. **Pl. 14**
Description. Ups like *Q. q. quercus*; uns gc very pale-grey, markings reduced, often vestigial; unh black spot in s2 often absent.
Flight. June/July.

Habitat. Flies around ash and oak trees from 900–2100m.
Distribution. Portugal. Spain, widely distributed in C. and S. districts. Morocco and Algeria, common.

LAEOSOPIS ROBORIS   *Spanish Purple Hairstreak*
Range. Restricted to Portugal, Spain and SE. France.   Map 58

L. roboris   Esper 1793   TL: 'Frankfurt am Main' (error)   **Pl. 14**
Description. ♂fw 12/15mm, upf dark purple-blue with wide black marginal borders; uph black with basal purple patch, sometimes small; uns yellow-grey with yellow marginal borders and small black marginal dots between veins. ♀ larger, fw more rounded; upf a shining blue patch in s1b extending into cell; uph black; uns marginal markings better defined with broken silver antemarginal line on hw and black marginal spots capped with blue-white chevrons, sometimes partly developed also in ♂.
Flight. End May/June/early July.
Habitat. From sea-level to nearly 1500m, on mountains, flying round ash trees, esp. small isolated trees. Larval food plant ash (*Fraxinus excelsior*).
Distribution. France, widely distributed in Provence, Cevennes and E. Pyrenees. Spain, esp. in N. and C. Spain, less common or absent near eastern seaboard and in SW., absent from Galicia. Portugal, not recorded from southern provinces.

NORDMANNIA ACACIAE   *Sloe Hairstreak*
Range. From Spain across Europe and S. Russia to Asia Minor.   Map 59

N. acaciae   Fabricius 1787   TL: S. Russia   **Pl. 14**
Description. ♂fw 14/16mm, without sex-brand; hw tail on v2 often short; ups dark brown; upf unmarked; uns gc paler brown; unf white pd stripe often faintly marked and broken, darker shade at anal angle in s1b very common; unh white pd line better developed, *marginal lunules in s1a–s3 orange*, that in s2 with *black marginal spot*. ♀ similar, with *black anal tuft*.
Flight. June/July.
Habitat. Rough ground around sloe bushes, from sea-level to 1500m. Larval food plant sloe (*Prunus spinosa*).
Distribution. S. Europe to 48°N, in S. Germany to 51°N, and eastwards to Balkans and Greece. France, north to Rennes, local, common in Jura. Switzerland, local in southern Cantons. S. Germany. Tirol. Italy, widely distributed through Apennines to Lucania. Spain, local but not rare.
Similar species. *N. ilicis* below, larger, uns gc darker; unh submarginal lunules darker red, orange mark in s2 and black spot less prominent; ♀ without black anal tuft.

NORDMANNIA ILICIS   *Ilex Hairstreak*
Range. Europe to S. Sweden, Asia Minor, Lebanon.   Map 60

N. ilicis   Esper 1779   TL: Erlangen, Germany   **Pl. 14**
Description. ♂fw 16/18mm, upf without sex-brand; ups dark brown; upf with or without orange discal mark; uns paler with slightly irregular series of white pd striae, best developed on hw; unh *marginal lunules red* usually *bordered with black internally and externally* and followed by white marginal line. ♀ often larger, markings

brighter, upf with or without orange discal patch; unh red submarginal lunules generally larger.

Flight. June/July.

Habitat. On rough slopes among oaks of various species, from lowlands to 1500m. Larval food plants oaks, usually smaller bushy species.

Distribution. S. and C. Europe to about 58°N, including S. Sweden, widely distributed to Balkans and Greece, but more local and often scarce in its northern range. In Spain local in Cantabrian Mts., Cuenca, Teruel and Guadarrama. Absent from Britain, Corsica, Sardinia, Crete, S. Spain and Portugal.

Variation. On upf the orange discal patch is rare in ♂, inconstant in ♀ in northern and eastern ranges, becoming increasingly common in Provence, Pyrenees, and constant in Cantabrian Mts. and C. Spain in both sexes, f. *cerri* Hübner Pl. 14.

Similar species. *N. acaciae* p. 45, *N. esculi* below, unh series of 5 small discrete red submarginal spots, their black lunules very inconspicuous.

NORDMANNIA ESCULI   *False Ilex Hairstreak*
Range. Restricted to SW. Europe and N. Africa.   Map 61

N. esculi esculi   Hübner 1804   TL: Portugal   **Pl. 14**
Description. ♂fw 15/17mm, resembles *N. ilicis*; upf without sex-brand; unh with *small, discrete bright red submarginal spots* in s1b–s5, only faintly edged black, white marginal line faint beyond v2. ♀ similar, often larger, ups sometimes with indistinct orange pd flush.

Flight. June/July.

Habitat. Lowlands to 1200m on rough ground flying over small sloe bushes. Larval food plant *Quercus* spp.

Distribution. Spain and Portugal, except Galicia and northern coastal districts. France, E. Pyrenees and Provence including Alpes Maritimes. Occurs in Balearic islands.

Variation. In southern localities ♀upf often with slight orange flush accompanied by traces of orange submarginal spots on uph.

N. esculi mauretanica   Staudinger 1892   TL: Morocco   **Pl. 14**
Description. Ups like *N. e. esculi* but uns paler grey-brown, markings absent on fw and nearly so on hw. In some localities there is extensive development of orange ups flush even in ♂.

Flight. May/June.

Habitat. On flowery slopes at 1500–1800m, often common.

Distribution. In Middle Atlas in Morocco, Algeria and Tunisia.

Similar species. *N. ilicis* p. 45.

STRYMONIDIA SPINI   *Blue-spot Hairstreak*
Range. S. and C. Europe to Asia Minor, Lebanon, Iraq and Iran.   Map 62

S. spini   Denis and Schiffermüller 1775   TL: Vienna   **Pl. 14**
Description. ♂fw 14/16mm, ups dark brown; upf sometimes with slight orange discal flush, small oval sex-brand at cell-end; uph orange marginal spots on anal lobe and often in s2; uns paler with white pd stripe firmly marked across both wings; *unh conspicuous blue mark at anal angle*, anal lobe black, two or three orange marginal lunules. ♀ usually larger with markings better defined.

Flight. June/July.

Habitat. Rough places among bushes of *Rhamnus, Prunus*, etc., from lowlands to 1800m, frequent in hilly country. Larval food plant sloe, *Rhamnus* and perhaps other shrubby bushes.
Distribution. S. and C. Europe to 58°N, absent from NW, rare in N. Germany, Czechoslovakia and Poland. Italy, north of Naples. Balearic Islands. Absent from Sicily, Corsica, Sardinia, Elba and Crete.
Variation. In Pyrenees, Spain and Portugal females often have an orange suffusion on disc of fw which may spread widely over both wings, ♀-f. *vandalusica* Lederer Pl. 14, common in S. Spain, rarely well developed in N. and E. Europe.

STRYMONIDIA W-ALBUM *White-letter Hairstreak*
Range. C. Europe to Japan. Map 63

S. w-album Knoch 1782 TL: Leipzig **Pl. 14**
Description. ♂fw 15/16mm, upf with small sex-brand above cell-end; gc dark brown, sometimes with small orange mark on anal lobe of hw; uns brown, with firm white pd line across both wings, on hw directed to v2 with final zig-zag forming *characteristic letter 'W'*, a double line across s1a, four or five orange marginal lunules and a fine white marginal line. ♀ slightly larger, ups paler brown.
Flight. July, at low to moderate altitudes.
Habitat. Near woodlands or isolated trees, visits flowers of bramble, etc. Larval food plants lime, elm and other trees, commonly wych elm in S. England.
Distribution. C. Europe to 60°N, including S. England and Scandinavia. N. Spain and Greece. Absent from Portugal and Mediterranean islands except Sicily.
Similar species. *S. pruni* below.

STRYMONIDIA PRUNI *Black Hairstreak*
Range. W. Europe through Siberia to Korea and Japan. Map 64

S. pruni Linnaeus 1758 TL: Germany (Verity 1943) **Pl. 14**
Description. ♂fw 15/16mm, small sex-brand above cell-end; ups black; uph orange submarginal lunules in s1b–s4; uns gc golden-brown with transverse stripe of black-bordered white striae across both wings; *unh bright orange submarginal band edged internally with conspicuous black spots*, largest at anal angle and often continued on fw, into s1b and s2. ♀ similar, larger, upf often with slight orange discal suffusion.
Flight. End June/July or earlier.
Habitat. Flies near hedges and thickets of blackthorn at low altitudes. Larval food plants *Prunus*, esp. *Prunus spinosa*, plum and rarely other trees.
Distribution. C. Europe to about 58°N, widespread but local. England, only in Midlands. N. Spain. France, from Basses Pyrénées northwards. Zealand and S. Sweden. Italy, only in Po delta. More common in E. Europe in Poland, Romania and Balkans to Bulgaria, Greece, S. Finland, in suitable localities. Absent from Portugal, peninsular Italy and Mediterranean islands.
Similar species. *S. w-album* above, uph without orange marks at anal angle; unh orange submarginal band bordered internally by black lunules which never extend to fw.

CALLOPHRYS RUBI *Green Hairstreak*
Range. From W. Europe and N. Africa across Russia and Asia Minor to Siberia and Amurland. Map 65

C. rubi   Linnaeus 1758   TL: Sweden (Verity 1943)   **Pl. 14**
Description. ♂fw 13/15mm, ups brown to dull grey; uph fringes often slightly undulant and sometimes chequered dark at veins; uns green; unh pd row of small white spots, often incomplete; *frons green; eyes narrowly bordered white.* ♀ similar, ups sometimes paler brown.
Flight. March or later usually in a single brood; a partial second brood has been reported from N. Africa.
Habitat. Rough ground among gorse, heather, broom, etc., from sea-level to 2100m. Larval food plants gorse, broom, ling, *Vaccinium*, etc.
Distribution. Common and widely distributed throughout Europe and N. Africa, including the Mediterranean islands, Canary Islands (Tenerife); probably absent from Orkney and Shetland Isles and Crete.
Variation. Ups generally darker in N., often more ruddy in S. esp. in N. Africa, f. *fervida* Staudinger.
Similar species. *C. avis* below.

CALLOPHRYS AVIS   *Chapman's Green Hairstreak*
Range. Restricted to SW. Europe and N. Africa.   Map 66

C. avis   Chapman 1909   TL: S. France and Morocco   **Pl. 14**
Description. ♂fw 16mm, resembles *C. rubi*; ups brighter reddish-brown; *frons and eye borders foxy-red*; uns white pd line broken only at veins, best marked near costa of hw, often vestigial on fw. ♀ similar.
Flight. April/May, in a single brood.
Habitat. Lowlands, but up to 1500m in N. Africa, flying in bushy places or near isolated strawberry trees. Larval food plant *Arbutus unedo* (Strawberry Tree).
Distribution. France, only E. Pyrenees, Var, Alpes Maritimes. Spain. Portugal. Tangier. Algeria; Khenchela, Zehroun, Algiers.
Variation. In Tunisia smaller and darker, *C. a. barreguei* Dujardin 1972.
Similar species. *C. rubi* above, eyes edged white and scales on front of head green.

TOMARES BALLUS   *Provence Hairstreak*
Range. From Spain and Morocco to Tripolitania, Cyrenaica and Egypt.   Map 67

T. ballus   Fabricius 1787   TL: Spain   **Pl. 16**
Description. ♂fw 14/15mm, apex pointed; ups dark grey with traces of orange submarginal spots on uph in s1b, 2; unf discal area orange-red with black discal and pd spots; *unh green* with grey marginal border. ♀ upf discal area and uph wide marginal band orange-red.
Flight. January/April in a single brood.
Habitat. On rough stony ground at low or moderate levels. Larval food plants possibly *Lotus hispidus*, perhaps other low plants.
Distribution. S. France in Var, Bouches du Rhône, Maritime Alps, E. Pyrenees. Spain, local but widely distributed. Portugal, in mountainous central areas. N. Africa, on coastal plain and foothills of Atlas Mts. in Morocco, Algeria and Tunisia.
Similar species. *T. mauretanicus* below, unh brown or grey.

TOMARES MAURETANICUS *Moroccan Hairstreak*
Range. Restricted to N. Africa. Map 68

T. mauretanicus Lucas 1849 TL: Algeria **Pl. 16**
Description. ♂fw 14–15mm, like *Tomares ballus*, ups smoky-brown, unmarked, or with small red anal mark on uph; unf variable, smoky-grey, usually with an orange patch below cell and black discal and pd spots in series; unh grey to brown, with small dark spots in rather indistinct series. ♀ups orange-red, marginal borders brown, extent of orange uph most variable, uns as in male.
Flight. January/April or later. Flies weakly over barren, stony slopes from sea level to 1500m or more. Larval food plants *Hedysarum pallidum* and *Hippocrepis multisiliquosum*.
Variation. Locally very variable, ♂uph red anal mark may be absent or enlarged. (f. *undulatus* Gerhard), esp. in Middle Atlas, Morocco. In both sexes unf the black spots may be irregular, fused together, or series incomplete, most common in Algeria, perhaps occurring in individual colonies.
Distribution. Morocco, Algeria, Tunisia.

TOMARES NOGELLII *Nogel's Hairstreak*
Range. Eastern Balkans, S. Russia, Syria, Lebanon and N. Iran. Map 69

T. nogellii dobrogensis Caradja 1895 TL: Tulcea (Romania) **Pl. 23**
Description. ♂fw 15–16mm, ups dark brown, unmarked, uns pale grey; unf disc orange with short costal and longer pd rows of black spots; unh with three orange bands, each bordered on both sides by square, black dots, the basal band incomplete. ♀similar.
Flight and **Habitat.** (*T. n. nogellii*) Flies in May/June, usually among low brushwood. Larval food plant *Astragalus ponticus*.
Distribution. This subspecies described from Tulcea, a town in the Romanian Dobrugea on the frontier with the USSR; but no further reports from this area. Reported also from European Turkey (Forster).

LYCAENA HELLE *Violet Copper*
Range. C. and N. Europe across Russia and Siberia to Amurland. Map 70

L. helle Denis and Schiffermüller 1775 TL: Vienna **Pls. 4, 15**
syn: *amphidamas* Esper 1780
Description. ♂fw 12/14mm, upf orange gc almost wholly obscured by *strong violet gloss*, three discal and all pd spots black; uph dark grey with orange submarginal lunules bordered by small black spots, all suffused violet; unf orange-yellow with markings as ups and complete submarginal series; unh gc yellow-grey with small dark spots at base and on disc, complete pd series and prominent orange submarginal band enclosed by proximal and distal black spots, the former bordered internally by white lunules. ♀fw less pointed, markings better defined, without violet suffusion ups.
Flight. End May/October, in one or two broods according to locality.
Habitat. Damp meadows and marshy places from lowlands to 1500m. Larval food plants knot grass (*Polygonum*).
Distribution. C. and N. Europe, local in widely scattered colonies. France, in Doubs, Jura, E. Pyrenees, Mont Dore. Belgium; Ardennes. Switzerland, in NE. on marshes of Jura, Urschweiz, Oberland, etc. Germany, mostly on the peat-mosses of

Bavaria, becoming scarce, absent in north-west Poland. Baltic countries. Czechoslovakia. Fennoscandia, widely distributed to North Cape in a single annual brood; absent from S. Sweden.

LYCAENA PHLAEAS *Small Copper*
Range. Europe and N. Africa through temperate Asia to Japan. Abyssinia. Aden and Uganda. Eastern States of N. America. Map 71

L. phlaeas phlaeas Linnaeus 1761 TL: Westermannia, Sweden **Pl. 15**
Description. ♂fw 12/15mm, ups gleaming reddish-gold with small black spots in cell, the irregular pd series and marginal border black; hw with triangular anal lobe and often a short projection at v2; uph dark grey with red submarginal band from anal lobe to s5, bordered by small black spots on margin; unf gc orange, black markings as on upf, each spot bordered yellow, marginal border grey-brown; *unh grey-brown with small scattered dark spots and inconspicuous red submarginal lunules.* ♀ similar, often larger, fw less pointed.
Flight. February/March and later in two or more broods.
Habitat. Flowery banks from sea level to 1800m. Larval food plants dock and sorrel, also knot grass (*Polygonum*).
Distribution. Europe and N. Africa including Mediterranean and Atlantic islands.
Variation. In hot localities specimens of second and later broods are more or less heavily suffused dark grey on ups, and anal tails of hw are longer, f. *elea* Fabricius, a seasonal form. Small blue spots may occur on uph, f. *caeruleopunctata* Rühl. Rare specimens occur in which ups gc is white or pale golden or the pattern of ups black spots is abnormal.

L. phlaeas polaris Courvoisier 1911 TL: Norwegian Lapland **Pl. 15**
Description. Resembles *L. p. phlaeas* on ups; differs in the pale grey gc of unh with dark spots prominent, esp. the irregular pd series; f. *caeruleopunctata* not uncommon.
Flight and **Habitat.** End June/July, in a single brood.
Distribution. Arctic Europe, Bodö, Saltdalen, Abisko, Porsanger, etc.

L. phlaeas phlaeoides Staudinger 1901 TL: Madeira
Description. Ups as in *L. phlaeas phlaeas*; unh grey-brown with rather obscure darker markings in some specimens, a narrow pale grey pd band is more constantly present, sometimes prominent in fresh specimens. Late broods commonly with marked *elea*-features.
Distribution. Madeira only.
Flight. From March and later.

LYCAENA DISPAR *Large Copper*
Range. From Western Europe across Russia to Amurland. Map 72

L. dispar dispar Haworth 1803 TL: England (Cambridgeshire) **Pl. 15**
Description. ♂fw 18/20mm, ups burnished red-gold with narrow black discoidal bar and black marginal borders; unf orange, row of pd spots almost evenly aligned, small black marginal marks present before the grey marginal border; unh gc pale blue-grey, red submarginal band wide extending from anal angle to v6, and pale-ringed black spots in the usual pattern. ♀ often larger, upf not burnished, discal spots present but without submarginal series, black marginal borders wide; uph black with wide orange submarginal band; uns as in male.

Flight. June/July in a single brood.
Habitat. Marshes and fens. Larval food plants docks, esp. *Rumex hydrolapathum* and *R. aquaticus*.
Distribution. Formerly occurred in England in the fen country of Cambridgeshire and Huntingdonshire. It became extinct about 1850, owing to drainage of the fens and the activities of collectors. Present still in N. Holland, in a few localities in Friesland. By some authors, the Dutch population is ranked as a subspecies (*L. dispar batava* Oberthur 1920).

L. dispar rutila   Werneburg 1864   TL: Berlin   **Pl. 15**
Description. ♂fw 17/18mm, *first brood* in both sexes smaller than *L. d. dispar*; unh gc slightly yellowish-grey, orange submarginal band paler, narrower, not reaching v6. *Second brood* specimens often small, ♂fw 16/17mm, ♀ black markings smaller; unh orange submarginal band narrow and pale.
Flight. May/June and August/September in most lowland localities, a single brood in some northern localities and at higher altitudes.
Habitat. Formerly generally distributed in rough country, in damp meadows and wet ditches from sea level to about 1000m, but becoming increasingly rare throughout Europe. Larval food plants docks (Rumex) of several species, also *Polygonum* and (rarely) *Iris*.
Distribution. France, local in Hte. Marne, Aube, Alsace, Nièvre and Côte d'Or, Gironde etc. Germany, widely distributed near Berlin and northwards to S. Finland. Czechoslovakia, Hungary, Romania, Balkans, esp. near the river Save, Bulgaria and Greece. Italy, still found in marshy places in N. Italy, formerly occurred near Rome.
Similar species. *H. virgaureae* L., unh with white discal spots or band.
Note. In 1927 a small stock of the Dutch Large Copper was introduced to a carefully prepared area at Woodwalton Fen in Huntingdonshire, England. These formed a colony which has been maintained until the present day.

HEODES VIRGAUREAE   *Scarce Copper*
Range. From Europe and Asia Minor through C. Asia to Mongolia.   Map 73

H. virgaureae virgaureae   Linnaeus 1758   TL: Sweden (Verity 1943)   **Pl. 15**
Description. ♂fw 16/17mm, ups gleaming red-gold, unspotted; upf black marginal border widest near apex; uph narrow black marginal border fusing with black spots between veins; unf black spots in usual pattern and marginal border grey; unh yellow-grey with small black spots, *pd spots bordered distally white*, submarginal band ill defined, orange. ♀ups with rather large black spots in usual pattern; uph black spots conspicuous only in pd area; uns resembles ♂.
Flight. July/August in a single brood.
Habitat. Flowery meadows from lowlands to 1500m, attracted to flowers of golden rod. Larval food plants docks (*Rumex*).
Distribution. Common locally from Pyrenees across C. and N. Europe, including Italy, to the Balkans and N. Greece, esp. in mountains. Absent from Britain.
Variation. Generally smaller in N. Europe; at high latitudes in Lapland, f. *oranulus* Freyer, very small, ♂fw 11/13mm, ups yellow-gold; ♀uph suffused dark grey with orange submarginal band. In S. Europe larger, ♂fw 17/19mm.

H. virgaureae montanus   Meyer-Dür 1851   TL: Rhône Glacier,   **Pl. 16**
Switzerland
Description. ♂fw 15/16mm, small, black marginal borders wider; ups sometimes

with small black discoidal spot. ♀ups heavily suffused grey, with usual golden colour sometimes obliterated.
Flight. July/August.
Habitat. Mountains, at high altitudes of 1800m or more, flying on flowery slopes.
Distribution. On the higher groups of the southern Alps from the Dauphiné to Gross Glockner, esp. in Oetztal Alps and Ortler group.

H. virgaureae miegii   Vogel 1857   TL: Guadarrama, C. Spain   **Pl. 15**
Description. ♂fw 17/18mm, large, upf black marginal border wide, black discoidal spot present and also with three or four small black pd spots in s4, 5, 6; uph black marginal spots larger, small pd spots occasionally present. ♀ups gc clear orange-yellow with minimal dark suffusion and prominent black markings.
Flight and **Habitat** as for *H. v. virgaureae*.
Distribution. C. Spain, La Granja, etc., and northwards to southern slopes of Cantabrian Mts., where it merges with *H. v. virgaureae*.
Similar species. *H. ottomanus* below, *T. thetis* p. 55, *L. dispar* p. 50.

HEODES OTTOMANUS   *Grecian Copper*
Range. Southern Balkans, Greece and Asia Minor.   Map 74

H. ottomanus   Lefèbvre 1830   TL: Greece   **Pls. 15, 23**
Description. ♂fw 14/15mm, hw with marginal tooth (♂) or tail (♀) at v2; ups gleaming red-gold like *H. virgaureae*; upf black marginal border widest at apex, small black spots at cell-end and in s4–6; uph black marginal border fused with round black marginal spots between veins near anal angle; uns resembles *L. phlaeas*, gc yellow-grey; *unh broad red submarginal lunules* present in s1a–s5, *no white pd spots*. ♀ups resembles *H. virgaureae*; uns as in ♂.
Flight. March/April and end June/July in two broods.
Habitat. Rough places and flowery meadows at low to moderate levels. Larval food plants not known.
Distribution. Southern Balkans, including Montenegro, Albania and SE. Yugoslavia. In Greece esp. on Mt. Parnassus and south of the Gulf of Corinth, Chalkidike Peninsular and Thrace. Rare south of the Gulf of Corinth.
Variation. Hw tails at v2 more pronounced in *second brood*, in which also unh appears to be more yellow than grey.
Similar species. *H. virgaureae* p. 51, slightly larger and easily recognised by white pd spots on unh.

HEODES TITYRUS   *Sooty Copper*
Range. From W. Europe through Russia and Transcaucasus to Altai Mts.
Map 75

H. tityrus tityrus   Poda 1761   TL: Graz, S. Austria   **Pl. 16**
   syn: *dorilis* Hufnagel 1766; *circe* Denis and Schiffermüller 1775 (invalid homonym)
Description. ♂fw 14/16mm, hw with marked anal lobe; *ups dark grey-brown*, fringes white; upf obscurely marked with darker spots in usual pattern; uph orange lunules in s1b–s3 or 4 vestigial; unf with black spots as above and traces of orange in submarginal area; unh yellow-grey with irregular small black spots, orange submarginal band more definite. ♀upf gc orange with usual pattern of black spots; uph dark brown, orange submarginal band conspicuous and enclosing round black spots *that barely touch margins*; uns resembles ♂ but more brightly marked.

Flight. April/May and August/September in two broods, a partial third brood has been reported from S. Europe.
Habitat. In flowery meadows, usually in lowlands but sometimes to 1500m in S. Europe. Larval food plant dock (*Rumex*).
Distribution. C. and S. Europe to about 54°N. Spain, local in Cantabrian Mts. and Catalonia, e.g., Montseny. Greece, including the Peloponnesos. Absent from Fennoscandia, Britain, Mediterranean islands except Sicily, and S. Spain.

H. tityrus bleusei Oberthur 1884 TL: Escorial and Madrid, Spain.
Description. ♂ups with orange gc as in ♀ and rather large black markings. In second (summer) brood with well-developed tails on hw.
Flight. April and July.
Habitat. Flowery meadows and banks at low altitudes.
Distribution. Known only from C. Spain, uncommon.

H. tityrus subalpinus Speyer 1851 TL: Innsbruck, N. Tirol   **Pl. 16**
Description. Ups dark grey, unmarked except for a darker cell-bar, fringes brilliant white; uns gc pale, rather yellowish-grey with markings as in *H. t. tityrus* but small; ♀ similar but fw more rounded. Forms intermediate between *H. t. tityrus* and *H. t. subalpinus*, with traces of ups markings esp. common in ♀, are not rare. Most colonies can be referred without difficulty to one or the other.
Flight. End June/July in a single brood.
Habitat. Mountain meadows at 1200–2100m occasionally at lower levels.
Distribution. Alps, from Basses Alpes to Hohe Tauern.
Similar species. *T. thersamon* ♀ p. 54, uph marginal black spots fuse with marginal line.

HEODES ALCIPHRON   *Purple-shot Copper*
Range. From W. Europe across Asia Minor to Iran.   Map 76

H. alciphron alciphron Rottemburg 1775 TL: Berlin   **Pl. 16**
Description. ♂fw 16/18mm, ups gleaming reddish-orange heavily suffused violet, but in most specimens gc is clear near costa of hw; upf dark spots in usual pattern, pd row irregular, not always well defined, sometimes absent; uph dark cell-bar and pd spots sometimes vestigial; uns pattern of dark spots more complete on both wings; unh gc pale grey with orange submarginal band. ♀fw broad, less pointed; ups dark brown with *irregular pd row of darker spots*; uph with orange submarginal lunules in s1b–s6; uns markings as in male, but unf gc orange.
Flight. June/July in a single brood.
Habitat. Flowery banks and meadows, lowlands to 900m. Larval food plants dock (*Rumex*).
Distribution. France in Alsace and Jura. Germany, northwards to Baltic coast but absent in NW, Czechoslovakia, Altvater Mt., Brno, etc., and eastwards to Hungary, Romania and Balkans to Greece. Absent from Britain and Fennoscandia.

H. alciphron melibaeus Staudinger 1879 TL: Greece
Description. ♂fw 17/18mm, like *H. a. alciphron* but ups violet suffusion reduced, with pale golden gc slightly veiled by grey suffusion, most marked on fw; usual black markings often scanty or vestigial; uns gc pale grey. ♀ larger, ups brown with usual markings; uph orange submarginal band conspicuous; sometimes traces of orange on upf disc.

Flight and **Habitat.** As for *H. a. alciphron*, common in mountains up to 1500m.
Distribution. Romania and Balkans to Greece; the dominant form in the Near East.

H. alciphron gordius Sulzer 1776 TL: Graubünden, Switzerland **Pl. 16**
Description. Resembles *H. a. alciphron*; ♂ups violet suffusion reduced, black spots large and well defined; uns colour tones brighter. ♀ups gc orange-yellow, fuscous suffusion slight or absent.
Flight. June/August.
Habitat. Mountains of S. Europe, flying at 1200–1800m.
Distribution. The common form in S. Europe. France, in C and S. districts, and on all mountains from Alpes Maritimes to Dolomites. Spain, Portugal, Italy, including peninsular Italy. Absent from Balkans and Mediterranean islands except Sicily.

H. alciphron heracleanus Blachier 1913 TL: High Atlas, Morocco **Pl. 16**
Description. ♂fw 18/19mm, ups pale orange-yellow without violet suffusion. ♀ larger with fw to 21mm, yellow to orange, black markings large and prominent.
Flight. June.
Habitat. High alpine meadows at 2400–2700m.
Distribution. Known only from the High Atlas (Toubkal massif).
Similar species. *P. hippothoe eurydame* (♀ only) p. 56, fw black pd spots in nearly evenly curved row.

THERSAMONIA THERSAMON *Lesser Fiery Copper*
Range. From Italy and E. Europe across W. Asia to Iraq and Iran. Map 77

T. thersamon Esper 1784 TL: Sarepta, S. Russia **Pl. 15**
Description. ♂fw 14/16mm, ups gc rather pale gleaming gold with narrow black marginal borders; upf unmarked; uph discal area slightly dusky, sometimes faintly flushed violet, golden submarginal band enclosing black marginal spots which fuse with black border; unf with spots in usual pattern; unh grey with broken orange submarginal band and small dark spots. ♀ups with usual pattern of black spots complete on both wings; uph often darker, with bright orange submarginal band; uns like ♂.
Flight. April/May and July/August in two broods.
Habitat. Waste places among grass and flowers, lowlands to 1200m. Larval food plants dock and broom (*Rumex, Sarothamnus*).
Distribution. E. Europe, widely distributed but local in Austria, Czechoslovakia, Hungary, Romania and Balkans including Greece and Turkey. Italy; Liguria, Emilia, Lombardy and various localities in the Abruzzi. Reports from NE. Italy need confirmation.
Variation. Specimens of *second brood* usually have a short tail on hw at v2, f. *omphale* Klug.
Similar species. *T. phoebus* below. *H. tityrus* ♀ p. 52.

THERSAMONIA PHOEBUS *Moroccan Copper*
Range. Confined to High Atlas in W. Morocco. Map 78

T. phoebus Blachier 1908 TL: High Atlas, Morocco **Pl. 15**
Description. ♂fw 14mm, ups gc golden; upf with narrow black marginal border and small black spots in usual pattern; uph pd and submarginal spots close together, followed by orange submarginal band and black marginal spots, wing-margin slightly

wavy near pointed anal lobe; unf black spots larger, pale-ringed; unh gc pale yellow-grey with prominent orange submarginal band. ♀ups gc paler, black spots larger; uph slightly suffused fuscous; uns as in ♂.
Flight. May or later with prolonged emergence.
Habitat. Lowlands to 1500m. Larval food plants docks (*Rumex*).
Distribution. W. Morocco, Asni, Marrakesh, etc.
Similar species. *T. thersamon* p. 54, slightly larger, upf ♂ without black spots; ♀unh markings more bold; does not occur in Africa.

THERSAMONIA THETIS *Fiery Copper*
Range. From Greece through W. Asia to Iraq and Iran.   Map 79

T. thetis   Klug 1834   TL: Syria   **Pl. 15**
Description. ♂fw 15/16mm, ups fiery red-gold; upf marginal spots touching narrow black apically expanded border; uph black marginal border narrow with black antemarginal spots between each vein; unf gc pale yellow-grey with black spots in usual pattern; unh pale grey, faintly spotted, with faintly yellow submarginal band. ♀ups with usual markings of black spots; uns as male. In both sexes a filamentous tail may be present at v2 of hw, probably only in second brood, f. *caudata* Staudinger.
Flight. July.
Habitat. Flies at 1500m or more in mountains, attracted by thyme. Larval food plant not known.
Distribution. In Europe only in Greece, Mt. Veluchi, Kaljaccuda, Taygetus, etc., perhaps also in SE. Yugoslavia (Skopje).
Similar species. *H. virgaureae* p. 51, unh with white discal spots.

PALAEOCHRYSOPHANUS HIPPOTHOE *Purple-edged Copper*
Range. W. Europe and through Russia and Siberia to the Amur.   Map 80

P. hippothoe hippothoe   Linnaeus 1761   TL: Sweden (Lowland)   **Pl. 15**
Description. ♂fw 16/17mm, ups rather *dark red-gold with black marginal borders*; upf shot purple along costa and with black discoidal stria; uph very dark and shot purple below cell, traces of orange at anal angle; uns gc grey or yellow-grey with usual markings of small black spots. ♀upf gc paler, less burnished, often suffused dark fuscous, with small black pd spots in nearly even curve; uph black with orange submarginal band enclosing black spots, f. *caeruleopunctata* Rühl, common.
Flight. June/July in a single brood.
Habitat. Damp meadows and bogs from lowlands to 1500m. Larval food plants docks and snakeweed (*Polygonum bistorta*).
Distribution. C. and N. Europe, esp. in mountains, to 66°N. Spain; Cantabrian Mts., Riano, Sierra Mancilla (Burgos), Sierra Moncayo, very local. N. Italy in Po Valley. Recorded from Poland and Romania. Absent from C. and S. Spain, NW. France, S. Alps and peninsular Italy.

P. hippothoe stiberi   Gerhard 1853   TL: Lapland   **Pl. 15**
Description. Resembles *P. h. hippothoe*; ♂ups gc more golden (paler); unf gc orange-yellow with smaller black spots. ♀upf orange-yellow without usual black suffusion, black spots small; uph orange submarginal band more distinct from anal angle to s5.
Flight. July.
Habitat. Coastal districts and mountain valleys.

Distribution. Fennoscandia, in northern districts, from Dovrefjeld to North Cape and N. Finland.

P. hippothoe eurydame Hoffmannsegg 1806 TL: Mountains near Geneva.   **Pl. 15**
  syn: *eurybia* Ochsenheimer 1808
Description. ♂fw 16/17mm, ups differs from *P. h. hippothoe* in brighter orange-golden gc, black wing-borders narrower and without purple reflections, upf discoidal spot vestigial or absent. ♀ups generally completely dusky, orange markings vestigial if present.
Flight. July/August.
Habitat. Alpine meadows from 1500m upwards.
Distribution. Maritime Alps to Oetztal and high Dolomites. Italy, local on higher Apennines southwards to Caserta. Replaced by *P. h. hippothoe* north of Rhône Valley, in Pyrenees and in eastern Alps of Austria. Distinction between *P. h. hippothoe* and *P. h. eurydame* is generally well defined but intermediate forms may occur where they meet.

P. hippothoe leonhardi Fruhstorfer 1917   TL: Rilo Mts., Bulgaria   **Pl. 15**
  syn: *candens* auct.
Description. ♂fw 17/19mm, large, otherwise indistinguishable from *P. h. hippothoe* by external characters but genitalia differ; ups purple reflections usually well marked; upf black discoidal spot present; uph dark area includes s3. ♀ resembles *P. h. hippothoe* ♀, unh fawn-grey, markings inconspicuous.
Flight. End June/July in a single brood.
Habitat. Mountain meadows at 900–1500m. Larval food plants docks.
Distribution. Replaces *P. h. hippothoe* in Balkan countries from Albania and SE. Yugoslavia and Greece. Absent from Peloponnesos. A form of *P. hippothoe*, possibly *P. h. leonhardi*, has been taken in Romania.
Similar species. *Heodes alciphron* p. 53 (♀ only); upf pd row of black spots less regular; unh grey, markings prominent.

LAMPIDES BOETICUS *Long-tailed Blue*
Range. Nearly world-wide in warm countries.   Map 81

L. boeticus Linnaeus 1767   TL: Algeria   **Pl. 17**
Description. ♂fw 15/18mm, fw apex pointed; hw tailed at v2; ups violet-blue with hairy appearance due to numerous androconia, dark marginal border narrow; uph violet-blue; uns gc fawn-grey with transverse white and dark grey stripes; *unh with wide white pd stripe* and small black and peacock-green marginal ocelli in s1c and s2. ♀ups brown, basal and discal areas violet-blue; uns resembles ♂.
Flight. Throughout summer months in succession of broods according to locality.
Habitat. Flowery banks and rough places from lowlands to 1800m or more. Larval food plants Leguminosae, esp. *Colutea*, living in seed-pods.
Distribution. Strongly migratory, resident in S. Europe and N. Africa, ranging N. in late summer to reach France, Belgium, Switzerland, Germany and occasionally England.
Similar species. *S. pirithous* below.

SYNTARUCUS PIRITHOUS *Lang's Short-tailed Blue*
Range. N. Africa and S. Europe to Egypt, Lebanon, Asia Minor and eastwards to India and C. Asia. Map 82

S. pirithous Linnaeus 1767 TL: Algeria **Pl. 17**
syn: *telicanus* Lang 1789
Description. ♂fw 12/13mm, ups blue with narrow dark marginal borders; ups without dark discoidal spot; uph obscure dark marginal spots in s1b, 2; *uns* both wings with light brown *complicated slightly variable pattern of pale transverse stripes*; unh with conspicuous green ocelli with black centres and ringed orange in s1b, 2. ♀ups grey-brown; upf with blue flush over middle third, and dark discal and pd spots; uph a faint blue basal flush and a dark round marginal spot in s2; uns as ♂.
Flight. March and throughout summer.
Habitat. Flowery banks and waste ground, usually at low altitudes. Larval food plants small Leguminosae, broom, etc.
Distribution. S. Europe, esp. coastal regions, including all the larger Mediterranean islands and extending northwards to southern Alpine slopes. Morocco. Algeria. Tunisia.
Similar species. *L. boeticus* p. 56, unh with conspicuous white pd band.

CYCLYRIUS WEBBIANUS *Canary Blue*
Range. Confined to Canary Islands. No map

C. webbianus Brullé 1839 TL: Canary Islands **Pl. 16**
Description. ♂fw 14/15mm, ups deep violet-blue with rather wide black borders; unf gc light orange-brown with slightly darker spots and white subapical mark; unh grey-brown with obscure white discal markings and brilliant white pd band. ♀ups golden-brown with darker marginal borders and discoidal spot, wing-bases flushed blue; uns as in ♂.
Flight. March and later throughout the summer.
Habitat. Open ground from sea-level to 3000m on Tenerife. Larval food plant *Cytisus canariensis* and *Spartocytisus rubigenus*.
Distribution. Canary Islands, on Tenerife, Gran Canary, La Palma and Gomera.

TARUCUS THEOPHRASTUS *Common Tiger Blue*
Range. S. Spain and throughout Africa, Asia Minor, Iraq, Arabia and east to India. Map 83

T. theophrastus Fabricius 1793 TL: Morocco **Pl. 17**
Description. ♂fw 10/11mm, ups blue with fine black marginal lines; upf a dark oblong discoidal spot; uph a small black marginal mark in s2, often also another at anal angle; *uns pd line macular on both wings*. ♀ups brown; upf obscure dark discal markings show through from uns, white pd spot in s4, often another in s5; uph discal spots very obscure, usually with line of grey or white spots in s2–4, dark marginal ocelli often conspicuous, wing-bases slightly flushed blue.
Flight. April/May and later in several broods.
Habitat. Flies around thorn bushes in very hot localities at low altitudes. Larval food plant *Zizyphus vulgaris*, a spiny shrub common in SE. Europe.
Distribution. S. Spain; Cadiz, Jaen, Almeria, Murcia. Morocco, Algeria, Tunisia, usually in lowlands near coast.
Similar species. *T. balkanicus* p. 58, ♂ups with distinct dark discal markings; ♀ups

without white pd spots on fw or hw. *T. rosaceus* below, uns dark pd marks fused into narrow continuous line on both wings.

TARUCUS ROSACEUS *Mediterranean Tiger Blue*

Range. Algeria, Tunisia and desert oases of N. Africa and Arabia, widely distributed in W. Asia to Iraq and Iran. Map 84

T. rosaceus Austaut 1885 TL: Alexandria, Egypt   **Pl. 13**
  syn: *mediterraneae* B-Baker 1917

Description. ♂fw 9/11mm, ups resembles *T. theophrastus* but with faint pinkish tint; upf dark discoidal mark more linear and less conspicuous; unf black pd marks usually fused into *slightly irregular continuous line from v1–7*, slightly broken at crossing of v6; unh pd marks fused into continuous dark line from inner margin to v8. ♀ups resembles *T. theophrastus*; upf blue basal suffusion more extensive with clear white pd marks in s3, 4, 5 and smaller marks behind a row of three dark pd spots; uph white lunules capping black marginal spots much better defined; uns resembles ♂.

Flight. Probably flies throughout summer in Algeria and Tunisia.

Habitat. Lowlands, probably to foothills, but food plant does not extend far into mountains. Larval food plant *Paliurus spina-christi* (Iraq).

Distribution. Tunisia and Algeria (Biskra). Morocco (Agadir).

Similar species. *T. theophrastus* p. 57; *T. balkanicus* below, upf dark discal markings present.

TARUCUS BALKANICUS *Little Tiger Blue*

Range. Coastal regions of N. Africa, Balkans and Asia Minor to Lebanon and Iran. Map 85

T. balkanicus Freyer 1845 TL: 'Turkey' (probably Balkans)   **Pl. 17**

Description. ♂fw 9/11mm, ups gc lilac-blue; *upf with obvious dark discoidal and pd spots*, and dark marginal borders; uph small discoidal stria usually distinct, marginal border dark, often with obscure darker submarginal spots; unh black spots of pd band joined to form a continuous line. ♀ups dark brown, wing-bases flushed blue, discoidal and pd markings obscure on dark gc; upf without white pd spot in s4, 5; uph without white pd spots, marginal ocelli dark, rarely well-formed.

Flight. April/May and later, in two or three broods throughout summer.

Habitat. Flies around bushes of Christ's Thorn in hot localities, at low altitudes in Balkans. Larval food plant *Paliurus spina-christi*.

Distribution. Balkans, widely distributed in hot districts in Dalmatia, Montenegro, Albania and Greece. Romania, reported from Dobrugea. Algeria. Tunisia. Distribution not well known owing to confusion with *T. rosaceus* and *T. theophrastus*. Absent from Peloponnesos.

Similar species. *T. theophrastus* p. 57 and *T. rosaceus* above.

AZANUS JESOUS *African Babul Blue*

Range. Widely distributed in Africa, Egypt, Syria, etc. Map 86

A. jesous Guérin 1849 TL: Abyssinia   **Pl. 16**

Description. ♂fw 11/12mm, ups pale shining blue with rosy reflections and a narrow dark border to both wings; uph dark marginal spot in s2; uns gc pale brown with white transverse striae; unf short brown stripe below costa from base, and white transverse striae; unh short black basal bar and *conspicuous round black spots*, *i.e.* four sub-basal, one on costa at two-thirds, and six sub-marginally in s1c to s6, two ocelli with peacock-green pupils in s1c, 2. ♀ups light brown often with pale suffusion enclosing discoidal spot; uph marginal spots in s1c, 2, larger and darker; uns as in male.

Flight. April and throughout summer.

Habitat. Flies around mimosa bushes at low altitudes. Larval food plants *Acacia*, perhaps also lucerne.

Distribution. Morocco, in western areas.

ZIZEERIA KNYSNA   *African Grass Blue*

Range. Africa, Tropical Asia and Australia; Canary Islands, S. Portugal and S. Spain.   Map 87

Z. knysna knysna   Trimen 1862   TL: Cape Town and   **Pl. 18**
Plettenberg Bay
syn: *lysimon* Hübner 1805 (invalid homonym)

Description. ♂fw 10/12mm, ups violet blue with *wide dark marginal borders*, otherwise unmarked; uns pale fawn with discal and marginal markings in slightly darker shade of fawn. ♀ups brown with restricted and variable patches of blue above inner margins of both wings; uns as in ♂.

Flight. In N. Africa, etc., in two broods, April/June and August, but variable with locality.

Habitat. Moist places beside streams, etc., at low altitudes. Larval food plants *Oxalis, Medicago*, etc.

Distribution. Very local in Portugal and Spain, esp. in coastal areas, but with occasional scattered colonies northwards to Santander. Morocco. W. Algeria. Canary Islands.

Variation. Size of specimens varies slightly in most localities, constantly large in the Canary Islands.

Z. knysna karsandra   Moore 1865   TL: NW. India

Description. Indistinguishable from *Z. k. knysna* except by a small character in the male genitalia.

Flight and **Habitat** as for *Z. k. knysna*.

Distribution. E. Algeria, Tunisia, Sicily and Crete; widely distributed through tropical Asia and most of Australia.

Note. The two subspecies meet in Algeria.

Similar species. *C. lorquinii* p. 62.

EVERES ARGIADES   *Short-tailed Blue*

Range. From Cantabrian Mts. and France across Europe and Asia to Japan.
Map 88

E. argiades   Pallas 1771   TL: Samara, S. Russia (April)   **Pl. 17**

Description. ♂fw 10/15mm, *first brood* ups violet-blue with narrow black marginal borders; uph antemarginal spots sometimes present in s1b–4; uns gc pale grey; unf pd spots in regular series very slightly curved; *unh marginal spots in s1c, s2 both filled orange*. ♀ups black with blue basal suffusion and orange spot at anal angle of hw. *Second brood* (f. *tiresias* Rottemburg) larger, ♂fw 12/15mm, ups darker tone of blue; ♀ups little or no blue basal suffusion but often with orange anal lunules.

Flight. April and later in two or more broods.

Habitat. Flowery banks and meadows, often in damp places, from lowlands to 500m. Larval food plants small Leguminosae, esp. medick, trefoil, etc.
Distribution. From Cantabrian Mts and Pyrenees to 52°N and eastwards through Europe, Sicily and Greece. Reports from Sardinia and Corsica need confirmation. Absent from C. and S. Spain and NW. Europe. Has been taken occasionally in Britain, Holland, N. Germany, Finland, etc., as a vagrant.
Similar species. *E. alcetas* below, unh without orange anal lunules.

EVERES DECOLORATUS   *Eastern Short-tailed Blue*
Range. Restricted to SE. Europe.   Map 89

E. decoloratus   Staudinger 1886   TL: Vienna, Hungary, Bulgaria   **Pl. 17**
   syn: *sebrus* Hübner 1824 (name rejected by ICZN Op. 970)
Description. ♂fw 12/13mm, ups gc bright blue with black marginal borders about 1mm wide and extending along veins; *upf with black discoidal spot*; uns gc very pale grey with small white-ringed spots in the usual pattern; unf spot in s2 of pd series displaced slightly basad; unh markings often vestigial, without orange anal lunules; hw tail at v2 very short. ♀ups both wings black or dark grey, unmarked; uns as in ♂.
Flight. April/September, usually in two broods, but information imperfect.
Habitat. Flowery banks, usually in hilly country, lowlands to 900m. Larval food plant medick (*Medicago lupulina*).
Distribution. Local in Lower Austria, Romania, Croatia, Albania, N. Greece and Bulgaria, probably widely distributed within this area.
Variation. Fresh specimens are brighter blue, but the blue scales wear off and worn specimens look rough and darker, with fuscous scales along veins more obvious.
Similar species. *E. alcetas* below, upf without discoidal spot and black marginal line very narrow, linear.

EVERES ALCETAS   *Provençal Short-tailed Blue*
Range. Spain and across S. Europe to Bulgaria; not recorded from Asia Minor.   Map 90

E. alcetas   Hoffmannsegg 1804   TL: Austria   **Pl. 17**
   syn: *coretas* Ochsenheimer 1808
Description. ♂fw 13/16mm, hw with short tail at v2; ups clear violet-blue, *black marginal lines exceedingly narrow; upf without discoidal spot*; uph an antemarginal black spot in s2; uns gc pearl-grey, spots small, often partly obsolete; unh small black marginal spot in s2 constant. Traces of orange anal lunules may be present in Balkan specimens. ♀ups gc black, unmarked; uns resembles ♂.
Flight. April/September in two or three broods.
Habitat. Flowery banks, lowlands to 900m or more. Larval food plants small Leguminosae esp. *Coronilla varia*.
Distribution. Local in C. Spain and S. France and in scattered colonies throughout southern Europe; northwards to Isère, Rhône valley and southern slopes of Alps; Corsica, across Balkans to Bulgaria. Central and N. Greece.
Similar species. *E. argiades* p. 59; *E. decoloratus* above; *C. argiolus* p. 62; *C. osiris* p. 61 uns without marginal markings.

CUPIDO MINIMUS *Little Blue*
Range. From C. Spain and France through Europe and Asia to Amurland and Mongolia. Map 91

C. minimus minimus Fuessly 1775   TL: Switzerland   **Pl. 17**
syn: Denis and Schiffermüller 1775
Description. ♂fw 10/12mm, *ups dark brown with silver-blue scales* scattered over both wings, often concentrated between veins of fw and over lower half of hw; uns pale grey, sometimes with slightly blue basal flush, with usual markings of small, white-ringed spots; unf pd series nearly straight, parallel with outer margin; unh pd series sinuous, spot in s6 usually displaced basad, a small marginal dot in s2. ♀ similar but blue scales absent on ups.
Flight. End April/September, a single brood appearing late at high altitudes, perhaps two broods in some lowland localities. In England usually a single brood in June.
Habitat. Grassy banks from sea-level to 2200m. Larval food plants various small Leguminosae, feeding upon flowers and seeds.
Distribution. Widely distributed, often common, throughout Europe, esp. on calcareous soils, to 69°N, including Ireland. N. Spain to Cuenca. Absent from S. Spain, Portugal and Mediterranean islands except Sicily.
Variation. The blue scaling on ♂ups may be very extensive or almost, but never quite, absent. Large specimens with fw to 14mm occur at high altitudes among others of average size, f. *alsoides* Gerhard.

C. minimus trinacriae Verity 1919   TL: Palermo, Sicily
Description. ♂fw 8/9mm, ups very dark (black) and without blue scales. ♀ similar.
Flight. April/May. A single brood only has been recorded.
Habitat. Mountainous country from 150–1200m.
Distribution. Sicily in Madonie Mts., Mt. Salvatore (Petralia), Trapani, San Martino della Scala, etc.
Similar species. *Everes*, all species pp. 59–60, hw with short tail; *C. carswelli* p. 62, unh discal spots in s2–5 in a straight row, ups in ♂ with occasional purple-blue scales; *C. osiris* below; *C. lorquinii* p. 62.

CUPIDO OSIRIS *Osiris Blue*
Range. From Spain and Provence through S. Europe and Asia Minor to C. Asia.   Map 92

C. osiris Meigen 1829   TL: not known   **Pl. 17**
syn: *sebrus* auct. Name rejected by ICZN Op. 970.
Description. ♂fw 12/15mm, *ups gc violet-blue*, unmarked, with *narrow black marginal lines*; uns light grey with markings as in *C. minimus*; unh often with slight blue basal flush. ♀ups dark brown sometimes with blue flush upf; uns as in ♂.
Flight. End May and later, in one or two broods.
Habitat. Flowery banks, usually in mountainous country, flying from 500–1800m, rarely at lower altitudes. Larval food plants small Leguminosae, esp. *Onobrychis*, perhaps also *Lathyrus*.
Distribution. N. and C. Spain. France, in Var and N. to Isère, Savoie, also Ardéche, Gard, Hérault and Bouches du Rhône. Switzerland, Valais and Jura. Italy,

Piedmont and Apennines S. to Lucania. Hungary, Romania and Balkans including Albania, Bulgaria and Greece. A local species and often overlooked.
Similar species. *C. minimus* p. 61, ♀ never with violet-blue flush upf; *C. semiargus* p. 80; *Everes* pp. 59–60 all species.

CUPIDO LORQUINII   *Lorquin's Blue*
Range. Restricted to N. Africa, Spain and Portugal.   Map 93

C. lorquinii   Herrich-Schäffer 1847   TL: not stated   **Pl. 17**
Description. ♂fw 11/14mm, *ups violet-blue* with *broad black marginal borders* extending basad along veins, otherwise unmarked; uns small white-ringed dark spots arranged as in *C. minimus*, series sometimes incomplete. ♀ups dark grey, sometimes with a few blue scales.
Flight. May/June in a single brood.
Habitat. Flies over short grass at roadsides, etc., to 1500m. Larval food plants not recorded.
Distribution. S. Spain, local near Malaga, Seville, Granada, etc. Portugal in Estremadura. Morocco. Algeria.
Similar species. *C. minimus* p. 61, gc not violet-blue; *Z. knysna* p. 59, ups marginal borders wider, uns gc fawn-brown with marginal markings present.

CUPIDO CARSWELLI   *Carswell's Little Blue*
Range. Known only from Murcia.   Map 94

C. carsweli   Stempffer 1927   TL: Sierra de Espuna, Spain
Description. ♂fw 11mm, resembles *C. minimus*; ups brown with *a few purple-blue scales near wing-bases*; unh pd spots in s2–5 in straight row. ♀ups dark grey-brown.
Flight. May.
Habitat. Flies over short grass at 1200m.
Distribution. Local in Sierra de Espuna, Murcia.
Similar species. *C. minimus* p. 61. Care should be taken to identify the blue basal scales on ups in *carswelli*, since the relative positions of spots on unh are slightly variable.
Note. Considered to be a local form of *C. minimus* by some authors.

CELASTRINA ARGIOLUS   *Holly Blue*
Range. From N. Africa throughout Europe to C. Asia and Japan; from coast to coast in N. America and southwards to New Mexico.   Map 95

C. argiolus   Linnaeus 1758   TL: England (Verity 1943)   **Pl. 16**
Description. ♂fw 13/17mm, *first brood* ups shining pale sky blue with fine black marginal line slightly expanded at apex of fw; *uns white* with faintly blue shading at wing-bases, marked in the usual pattern with very small black spots often partly obsolete, *unf pd series displaced towards outer margin*, marginal markings obscure if present. ♀ups blue paler, upf dark marginal border includes apex and outer margin, base and discal areas broadly blue. In *second brood* ♀ups darker blue, upf dark border extensive, blue area reduced; uph costa usually dark.
Flight. April/May and July/August in two broods.
Habitat. Common in light woodland from lowlands to 1500m or more. Larval food plants various shrubs and trees esp. ivy, holly and buckthorn.

Distribution. Throughout the region except in N. W. Scandinavia.
Similar species. *E. alcetas* p. 60, distinguished by presence of short tail on hw at v2.

GLAUCOPSYCHE ALEXIS *Green-underside Blue*
Range. From W. Europe across Russia and C. Asia to Amurland. Map 96

G. alexis alexis Poda 1761 TL: Graz, Austria **Pl. 17**
syn: *cyllarus* Rottemburg 1775
Description. ♂fw 13/18mm, ups blue, black marginal borders 1–2mm wide; uns pale grey *without marginal markings*; unf black pd spots variable, usually prominent in a curved series, *large in s2*, diminishing in size to costa; unh basal area green, pd spots usually small, often obsolete. ♀ups brown with variable blue basal flush.
Flight. April/June in a single brood.
Habitat. Flowery banks near woodland among hills and mountains; lowlands to 1200m. Larval food plants *Astragalus, Cytisus* and other small Leguminosae.
Distribution. Widely distributed in W. and N. Europe to 66°N but rare in north. Absent or occasional in N. Germany and Denmark; absent from Britain, SW. Spain, Portugal, Sardinia and Crete.

G. alexis melanoposmater Verity 1928 TL: Aflou, Algeria
Description. ♂fw 13/15mm, ups black marginal borders narrow; unh green flush reduced or absent, black pd spots vestigial or absent. ♀ups basal areas of both wings generally blue.
Flight and **Habitat.** No information.
Distribution. Algeria and Tunisia. Not recorded from Morocco.
Similar species. *G. melanops* below.

GLAUCOPSYCHE MELANOPS *Black-eyed Blue*
Range. Confined to SW. Europe and N. Africa. Map 97

G. melanops melanops Boisduval 1828 TL: Aix-en-Provence
Description. ♂fw 11/13mm, ups resembles *G. alexis*, sometimes paler blue; uns pale brown with *traces of marginal markings; unf black pd spots prominent*; unh narrowly dark grey at base, pd spots small but rarely absent. ♀ups grey-brown to black, usually with basal blue suffusions.
Flight. April/May in a single brood.
Habitat. Heaths and light woodland with broom and heather, rarely above 700m. Larval food plants *Dorycnium, Genista, Lotus*, in the flowers.
Distribution. SE. France in Ardèche, Var, Basses Alpes, Bouches-du-Rhône; E. Pyrenees. Hte Garonne; N. Italy, Liguria.

G. melanops algirica Heyne 1895 TL: Algeria **Pl. 18**
Description. ♂fw 14/16mm, larger, ups dark marginal borders wider; uns marginal markings better defined; unh with faintly marked grey submarginal lunules and antemarginal spots in each space. ♀ups blue basal suffusion generally reduced.
Flight. March/April/May.
Habitat. Among tall broom, to 900m in Spain, to 2000m in N. Africa.
Distribution. C. and S. Spain, Morocco, Algeria, Tunisia. Transitional to *G. m. melanops* in Catalonia.
Similar species. *G. alexis* above, ups very similar; uns gc pale grey and marginal markings absent, unh suffused green except in Algeria.

TURANANA PANAGAEA *Odd-spot Blue*
Range. Greece and Asia Minor (TL of *L. panagaea* Herrich-Schaeffer 1852) to Turkestan. Map 98

T. panagaea taygetica Rebel 1902 TL: Mt. Taygetos, Greece **Pl. 16**
Description. ♂fw 10/11mm, ups blue with black marginal borders about 2mm wide and a small discoidal stria; uns gc light grey-brown; unf with large black pd spots, *spot in s3 esp. large and displaced distad*, a narrow black discoidal stria and marginal markings; unh with basal and pd black spots in series, large marginal spot in s2 and marginal markings. ♀ups brown.
Flight. May/June/July in a single brood.
Habitat. Hilly and mountainous districts at 900–2100m. Larval food plant not known.
Distribution. Greece, on Mt. Chelmos and Taygetos Mts., not below 2000m.

MACULINEA ALCON *Alcon Blue*
Range. From N. Spain and France across Europe to C. Asia. Map 99

M. alcon alcon Denis and Schiffermüller 1775 TL: Vienna **Pl. 18**
Description. ♂fw 17/19mm, ups pale rather dull blue with black marginal borders 1–2mm wide, *otherwise unmarked*; uns gc light brown with darker light-ringed spots arranged in the usual pattern; *unh without blue or green basal dusting*. ♀ups heavily suffused grey-brown, sometimes flushed blue at wing-bases; upf an obscure discoidal spot and small pd spots often present.
Flight. July in a single brood.
Habitat. Damp meadows and marshy places, lowlands to 900m. Larval food plant *Gentiana pneumonanthe*, later in ants' nests.
Distribution. Widely distrubuted but very local in C. Europe. France, esp. in NE. Belgium. Switzerland. Most common in Germany, esp. on moorlands in Bavaria, N. Italy. Denmark and east to Romania and Balkans. N. Greece and northwards to Estland and S. Sweden.

M. alcon rebeli Hirschke 1904 TL: Styrian Alps **Pl. 18**
Description. Like *M. a. alcon*, ♂ups brighter blue, black marginal borders generally narrower and better defined, fringes often slightly chequered; uns gc grey-brown, markings more distinct and usually with slight blue-green flush at base of hw. ♀ups basal areas blue, discoidal and black pd spots distinct.
Flight. End June/July.
Habitat. Meadows and grass slopes at 1200–1800m, sometimes at lower altitudes in France, often in dry localities. Larval food plants *Gentiana cruciata* and *G. germanica*.
Distribution. France, esp. Massif Central and SE. Alps; E. Pyrenees (Aulus). Denmark, very local. Switzerland and, chiefly as a mountain insect, through C. Europe, the Dolomites and Apennines. Spain, known from a few localities near Soria, Teruel and Santander.
Similar species. *M. arion*, uns grey rather than brown, ♂ nearly always with black discal spots upf; unh with wide basal blue-green flush and well-defined discal and marginal markings.
Note. Typical *M. a. alcon* and *M. a. rebeli* are so different that some authors have regarded them as distinct species, in spite of the fact that they are linked by intermediates.

MACULINEA ARION *Large Blue*
Range. From W. Europe across Russia and Siberia to China. Japan. Map 100

M. arion arion Linnaeus 1758 TL: Nuremberg, Germany (Fruhstorfer) **Pl. 18**
Description. ♂fw 16/20mm, ups bright gleaming blue, fringes white, black marginal borders broad; *upf pd series of elongate black spots* variable but rarely absent; uph small black pd spots inconstant; *uns gc grey* to grey-brown with usual markings, fringes chequered; *unh blue-green basal suffusion usually extensive*. ♀ similar, ups black discal markings often larger.
Flight. June/July in a single brood.
Habitat. Rough grassy places with thyme from sea-level to 1800m. Larval food plant thyme (*Thymus serpyllum*), later in ants' nests.
Distribution. Widely distributed in C. Europe to 62°N, including Pyrenees, Balkans and Greece. Very local in S. England; a mountain species in central Spain. Absent from Norway, S. Spain, Portugal and Mediterranean islands except Corsica.
Note. Collecting this species in England is illegal.

M. arion obscura Christ 1878 TL: Zermatt and Liestal, Switzerland **Pl. 18**
Description. Ups pd areas heavily suffused dark grey, markings sometimes nearly obliterated, blue shade present only at wing-bases.
Flight. July.
Habitat. Mountains from 1200m upwards.
Distribution. Predominant form in Alps of SE. France, Switzerland south of Rhône valley and Austria.

M. arion ligurica Wagner 1904 TL: Ligurian coastal region
Description. Often of large size, resembling *M. a. arion*; ups gc pale gleaming blue with black markings crisply defined; uph black marginal spots often present; uns gc pale grey, sometimes yellowish; unh blue-green basal flush reduced. ♀ups black markings generally large, sometimes confluent.
Flight. End June/July.
Habitat. Lowlands to moderate levels.
Distribution. Coastal regions of French and Italian Riviera from Nice to Genoa and inland to Modena and Florence; recorded also from Corsica.
Variation. Broadly speaking blue races occur at low or moderate altitudes, dark forms at higher levels in mountains, but this is not invariable. Variation in the extent of dark suffusion is clinal throughout the whole species, with the two major forms distributed in somewhat haphazard manner, more suggestive of ecological modifications than of geographical subspecies.
Similar species. *M. alcon* p. 64, *M. telejus* below.

MACULINEA TELEJUS *Scarce Large Blue*
Range. From France through C. Europe and Asia to Japan. Map 101

M. telejus Bergsträsser 1779 TL: Hanau, W. Germany **Pl. 18**
  syn: *euphemus* Hübner 1800
Description. ♂fw 16/18mm, ups pale grey-blue, slightly paler in submarginal areas before the rather wide black marginal borders which extend basad along veins; upf black pd spots small, often reduced, sometimes absent; *uns gc pale brown*, usual markings rather faint except pd spots which are black and prominent; *unh without*

blue-green basal flush. ♀ups, wide dusky suffusion along costa and outer margins; upf dark pd spots more constant; uns gc slightly darker shade of brown.
Flight. July.
Habitat. Marshy meadows and moorland from lowlands to 1800m. Larval food plant *Sanguisorba officinalis*, later in ants' nests.
Distribution. Very local in C. Europe to 53°N (Berlin). France, chiefly in NE. Savoie, Isere; Switzerland, not S. of Rhône valley. Italy, in southern foothills of Alps from Susa to Carniola. Absent from Romania and Balkans.
Similar species. *M. arion* p. 65, ups blue gc brighter, with larger black markings, uns gc grey rather than brown, with extensive unh blue flush. *M. nausithous* below, uns cinnamon-brown, no marginal markings.

MACULINEA NAUSITHOUS   *Dusky Large Blue*
Range. From N. Spain and France across C. Europe in widely scattered colonies to the Urals and Caucasus.   Map 102

M. nausithous   Bergsträsser 1779   TL: Hanau, W. Germany   **Pl. 18**
   syn: *arcas* Rottemburg 1775 (invalid homonym)
Description. ♂fw 17/18mm, ups resembles *M. telejus* but gc slightly darker tone of blue, black marginal borders 3mm wide, pd spots often small, partly obscured; *uns cinnamon brown*, black pd spots in complete series but *no marginal markings*. ♀ups dark brown, unmarked, fringes brown; vestigial blue basal flush occasionally present.
Flight. July.
Habitat. Marshy lowlands, often beside lakes. Larval food plant *Sanguisorba officinalis*, later in ants' nests.
Distribution. Very local in C. Europe to 52°N. France, chiefly in NE, Colmar, Ain, Sère. N. Switzerland, Weesen, Berne, etc. Spain, an isolated colony near Soria. More widely distributed in Bavaria and C. Germany, Austria, Hungary and Czechoslovakia. Absent from N. Germany, Denmark, Tirol and Balkans; occurrence in N. Italy and Holland needs confirmation.
Similar species. *M. telejus* p. 65.

IOLANA IOLAS   *Iolas Blue*
Range. From N. Africa and C. Spain through S. Europe and Asia Minor to Iran.   Map 103

I. iolas   Ochsenheimer 1816   TL: Hungary   **Pl. 17**
Description. ♂fw 18/21mm, ups lustrous violet-blue with narrow black marginal borders, otherwise unmarked; uns pale grey; unf discoidal stria present, also a series of black white-ringed *pd spots close to and parallel with outer margin*; unh with blue-grey basal flush and black basal and pd spots, marginal spots usually vestigial on both wings. ♀ups variable, usually blue with wide fuscous marginal borders often extending almost to base on both wings.
Flight. May/June usually in a single brood, a scanty late brood has been recorded in August/September.
Habitat. Rocky places and open woodland from lowlands to 1800m. Larval food plant senna (*Colutea*).
Distribution. Spain, local in Sierra Nevada and Sierra Alta (Albarracin). France, Provence. Switzerland, only in Rhône valley. From Apennines and S. slopes of Alps to Hungary, Romania, Balkans and Greece. Algeria. Not recorded from Morocco.

PSEUDOPHILOTES BATON *Baton Blue*
Range. From Spain across S. and C. Europe to Asia Minor, Iran, Afghanistan and Chitral. Map 104

P. baton baton Bergsträsser 1779 TL: Hanau, Germany **Pl. 17**
Description. ♂fw 10/12mm, *ups light powder blue*; upf narrow marginal borders and discoidal spot black; uph antemarginal spots black; uns gc light grey to grey-brown with prominent dark spots; *unh conspicuous orange submarginal lunules* in s1b–5 surmounted by small black lunules. ♀ups black with variable blue basal flush.
Flight. April/June and July/September in two broods at low levels, a single brood at high altitudes.
Habitat. Flowery banks among thyme, lowlands to 2100m. Larval food plant Gen. 1, *Thymus vulgaris* and *T. serpyllus*; Gen. 2 flowers only of *Lavendula latifolia*, *Saturela* and *Mentha*.
Distribution. Widely distributed in C. Europe to 48°N, southwards to Pyrenees, Cantabrian Mts. and Portugal. Widely distributed in Italy, including Sicily. Corsica.
Variation. Second brood specimens are usually small.

P. baton schiffermuelleri Hemming 1929 TL: Dom Altenberg, Austria
syn: *P. b. vicrama* auct.
Description. Indistinguishable from *P. b. baton* by external characters, but ♂ genitalia differ.
Flight and **Habitat** as for *P. b. baton*.
Distribution. E. Europe to 62°N in Finland, C. Germany, Czechoslovakia; Alto Adige in Italy, Austria and eastwards to Balkans and Greece.
Similar species. *P. bavius* below, uph with orange submarginal lunules.

PSEUDOPHILOTES PANOPTES *Panoptes Blue*
Range. Confined to Spain.
P. panoptes Hübner 1813 TL: Spain. Map 105 **Pl. 17**
syn: *P. baton panoptes* auct.
Description. ♂fw 9/11mm, ups gc slightly deeper blue; uns gc pale brown, dark discal spots clearly white-ringed and marginal markings narrow; unh *orange submarginal lunules vestigial or absent* submarginal and marginal dark lunules very close together. ♀ups dark brown with minimal blue basal flush.
Flight. April/May and July in two broods.
Habitat. Rough ground with thyme, larval food plant, 700–1800m.
Distribution. Replaces *P. b. baton* in C. and S. Spain.
Similar species. *P. abencerragus* below, ♂ups darker (indigo) blue with wing-margins widely suffused dark fuscous, androconia scanty, about twice as long as wide (in *P. baton* abundant, small, rounded).

PSEUDOPHILOTES ABENCERRAGUS *False Baton Blue*
Range. From Spain and Morocco across N. Africa to Egypt and Jordan. Map 106

P. abencerragus Pierret 1837 TL: Morocco **Pl. 17**
Description. ♂fw 9/11mm, resembles *P. baton panoptes*; fringes strongly chequered; ups *gc lustrous dark steel blue*, with dark marginal borders rather widely suffused; upf discoidal spot sometimes outlined white; uph costa broadly grey, antemarginal spots usually distinct; uns gc grey-brown, white-ringed dark spots strongly marked in regular series; unh submarginal and antemarginal markings

close together, sometimes with traces of orange between. ♀ups dark grey with minimal blue basal dusting.
Flight. April/May, perhaps a second brood in summer (not recorded).
Habitat. Rough places among heather (*Erica arborea*), etc., 700–1200m in Spain, to 2000m in N. Africa. Larval food plant *Cleonia lusitanica* (Labiatiae).
Distribution. Morocco, not rare in Middle and High Atlas. Algeria. Tunisia. Portugal, Alemtejo to Serra da Estrela. S. Spain, widely distributed but very local from Aranjuez southwards.
Variation. In African specimens (High Atlas) uns gc slightly paler yellowish-grey than in Spanish specimens.
Similar species. *P. panoptes* p. 67.

PSEUDOPHILOTES BAVIUS *Bavius Blue*
Range. Morocco and Algeria; Hungary, Greece, Asia Minor and S. Russia (*Lycaena bavius* Eversmann 1832 TL: S. Urals). Map 107

P. bavius hungaricus Dioszeghy 1913 TL: 'Hungary' Not figured
Description. ♂fw 12/15mm, fringes white, chequered dark; ups gc violet-blue with broad diffuse fuscous marginal borders; *uph bright orange submarginal lunules in s1c, 2, 3* surrounding black antemarginal spots; uns markings jet-black and prominent; unh gc almost white with wide orange-red submarginal band; androconia abundant. ♀ups suffused black, blue restricted to basal areas; uns as in ♂.
Flight. May, probably a second brood in July/August.
Habitat. Rough flowery places from lowlands to 900m. Larval food plant *Salvia argentea*.
Distribution. Romania, Cluj district (Transylvania). Greece, Mt. Chelmos.

P. bavius fatma Oberthur 1890 TL: Lambessa, Algeria **Pl. 17**
Description. Resembles *P. b. hungaricus*; ♂ups black marginal borders and antemarginal black dots better defined; uph series of orange submarginal lunules prominent and complete from s1b–7. ♀ups blue suffusion extensive.
Flight. April/May. A late brood has not been recorded.
Habitat. Woodland margins with *Salvia* at 1500–1800m.
Distribution. Algeria. Morocco, Middle Atlas, Anosseur, Ifrane, etc.
Similar species. *P. baton* p. 67.

SCOLITANTIDES ORION *Chequered Blue*
Range. From Spain and C. France across Europe and C. Asia to Japan. Map 108

S. orion orion Pallas 1771 TL: E. Russia **Pl. 17**
Description. ♂fw 13–14mm, ups white fringes strongly chequered, wings dull blue with grey discoidal spot, submarginal and marginal markings. ♀ slightly larger, ups markings more extensive; uns both sexes white, markings jet-black, large, hw submarginal band bright orange, prominent.
Flight and **Habitat.** Flies at moderate altitudes in July, among rough vegetation. Larval food plants Stonecrop, *Sedum telepheum* and *S. album*.
Distribution. S. Scandinavia and S. Finland, extending widely eastwards into Russia.

S. orion lariana Fruhstorfer 1910 TL: Lake Como
Description. ♂fw 15–16mm, like *S. orion orion* but upc very dark, blue markings reduced, vestigial or absent, often with dull blue basal flush extending to discoidal

spot, marginal markings usually lost in wide black wing borders. ♀ups black, usually unmarked; uns as in *S. orion orion*.

Flight and **Habitat**. Usually a single emergence in late June–July, flying in rough, stony places from lowlands to altitudes of 1000m.

Distribution. S. Europe to 50°N, from E. Spain across France and Switzerland to Romania, Sicily, the Balkans and Greece.

FREYERIA TROCHYLUS *Grass Jewel*

Range. SE. Europe and widely distributed in tropical and sub-tropical Asia and Africa   Map 109.

F. trochylus Freyer 1844   TL: Turkey   **Pl. 17**
Description. ♂fw 8/9mm, ups gc brown; upf unmarked; uph 2–4 conspicuous orange lunules surmounting dark marginal spots near anal angle; uns pale grey-brown with usual markings; unh orange marginal band in s1c–4 enclosing four round *black ocelli ringed in shining green*. Sexes similar.

Flight. March or later, perhaps with continuous emergence through summer.

Habitat. Barren stony ground from lowlands to moderate altitudes, flying near the ground, fond of settling on stones. Larval food plant heliotrope. Larva said to be attended by ants of the genus *Pheidole*.

Distribution. Greece, Crete and Turkey. Widespread in Africa and Asia.

PLEBEJUS VOGELII *Vogel's Blue*

Range. Confined to Morocco.   Map 110

P. vogelii Oberthur 1920   TL: Taghzeft Pass, Middle Atlas   **Pl. 19**
Description. ♂fw 12/14mm, *ups pale grey-brown with chequered fringes*; upf black discoidal spot large, conspicuous orange submarginal line divided by veins into separate lunules, each enclosed internally and externally by black lunules, a fine white terminal line; uph similar, with very small discoidal stria; unf discoidal and pd spots very large; unh spots small, marginal borders not well defined. ♀ similar, ups often with small bluish-white marks internal to marginal borders.

Flight. August/September, a single brood only is recorded.

Habitat and **Distribution**. Only known from Morocco. It flies in the Middle Atlas near the Taghzeft Pass on rough stony ground at an altitude of 2100m. Larval food plant *Erodium cheiranthifolium*.

PLEBEJUS MARTINI *Martin's Blue*

Range. Confined to Morocco and Algeria.   Map 111

P. martini martini Allard 1867   TL: Algeria   **Pls. 4, 19**
Description. ♂fw 14/15mm, ups resembles *P. p. sephirus*, lavender-blue with fine black marginal lines, otherwise unmarked; *uns gc pale grey-brown* with faint blue-grey basal shade; unf with usual markings, black pd spots prominent; unh markings smaller, *orange submarginal lunules very small*, inconspicuous. ♀ups dark brown with blue basal flush; uph with orange submarginal lunules in s1, 2, 3, 4 (5) and with black marginal spots in s1–4; uns rather brown than grey with marginal markings better developed.

Flight. May, in a single brood.

Habitat. Rough places with heather, etc., at 1500–2100m. Larval food plant not recorded.

Distribution. Algeria, common in east, Lambessa, Batna, Khenchela. Morocco, in Middle and High Atlas and in El Ríf, very local and rare.
Variation. Some Moroccan specimens have large pd spots on unf transitional to *P. m. allardi.*

P. martini allardi Oberthur   TL: Oran, Algeria   **Pl. 4**
Description. On ups resembles *P. m. martini* but uns black discoidal and postdiscal spots greatly enlarged. This was described as a distinct species, but probably correctly placed as a local form of *P. martini.*
Distribution. Only known from Algeria.

PLEBEJUS PYLAON   *Zephyr Blue*
Range. From Spain eastwards with occasional scattered colonies through S. Europe including S. Russia (*Lycaena pylaon* Fischer 1832 TL: Sarepta); more widely distributed in W. Asia to Iran.   Map 112

P. pylaon sephirus Frivaldszky 1835   TL: Slivno, Bulgaria   **Pl. 18**
Description. ♂fw 14/17mm, ups clear violet-blue with *narrow black marginal lines; uph small black antemarginal spot constant in s2*, occasional in s1b, 3, 4; uns gc pale grey-brown; unh with prominent orange submarginal bands bordered proximally with black V-marks, black antemarginal spots *without silver scales.* ♀ups brown; uph two or more orange submarginal lunules each with black antemarginal spot; uns as ♂.
Flight. End May/June according to altitude, in a single brood.
Habitat. Flowery banks from lowlands to 1500m. Larval food plant vetch (*Astragalus*).
Distribution. Bulgaria (Sliven, Pirin Mts.); Albania; Hungary, in a restricted area in the foothills of the Siebenburgen; Romania (Cluj, Temisoara etc.). In Greece, *P. pylaon brethertoni* Brown 1976 ups paler blue, flying at high altitudes on Mt. Parnassos, Mt. Chelmos etc.

P. pylaon trappi   Verity 1927   TL: Simplon   **Pl. 18**
   syn: *lycidas* Trapp 1863 (invalid homonym)
Description. ♂fw 14/17mm, ups gc darker blue with wider black margins; uph three or more black antemarginal spots; uns gc pale grey-brown with usual markings; *unh with well-marked white shade between pd spots and orange submarginal lunules.* ♀ resembles *P. p. sephirus*; ups often with slight blue basal suffusion; uph orange submarginal lunules often vestigial or absent.
Flight. End June/July in a single brood.
Habitat. Sheltered grassy places in mountains at 1200–1500m. Larval food plant vetch (*Astragalus excapus*).
Distribution. S. Switzerland esp. Simplon, Gemmi, Saastal, Zermatt, etc. Savoie Alps. Slightly smaller in Valnontey (Aosta). Val d'Ossola; Merano, large specimens, f. *delattini* Junge.

P. pylaon hespericus   Rambur 1839   TL: Sierra de Alfacar, Andalusia   **Pl. 18**
Description. ♂fw 14/15mm, resembles *P. p. sephirus; ups pale shining blue*; uph with black antemarginal spots in s1–3; uns gc yellow-grey with markings as in *sephirus.* ♀ups paler brown, orange submarginal lunules on hw well marked.
Flight. May.
Habitat. Sheltered places in mountains at 900–1200m. Larval food plant *Astragalus arragonensis.*
Distribution. Spain. Now extinct in Sierra de Alfacar. Teruel, very local at Albar-

racin, etc., also reported from Murcia. In Toledo, Aranjuez etc., slightly larger, fw 16mm, ups blue not quite so pale, f. *galani* Agenjo.

Similar species. *L. idas* p. 72 and *P. argus* below are distinguished by peacock-blue scales in unh submarginal spots; *A. escheri* p. 85, ups blue less violet-tinted and unh white suffusion between pd spots and orange lunules reduced to white streak along v4; uph without black marginal spots.

PLEBEJUS ARGUS *Silver-studded Blue*
Range. Throughout Europe and temperate Asia to Japan. Map 113

P. argus argus Linnaeus 1758 TL: S. Sweden (Verity 1943) **Pl. 19**
  syn: *aegon* Denis and Schiffermüller 1775
Description. ♂fw 12/15mm, resembles *L. idas* Linnaeus, *fore-tibia with strong spine; ups rather deep blue with black marginal borders about 1mm wide*; uph small black marginal spots between veins; uns gc variable, light grey to smoky grey with usual markings of black white-ringed spots and orange submarginal lunules; unh black antemarginal spots with green pupils ('silver-studded'). ♀ups brown with or without orange submarginal lunules and often with blue basal suffusion, fringes white at apex of fw; uns medium brown, white band between pd spots and submarginal markings prominent.
Flight. May or later with two broods in C. Europe, a single brood in N. Europe.
Habitat. Grassy banks and heaths from sea-level to moderate altitudes. Larval food plants Leguminosae, flowers of gorse, broom, bird's foot trefoil, ling, bog bilberry.
Distribution. Europe to 68°N. Not Scotland, Ireland, Sicily, Sardinia, Elba.
Variation. Minor local variation is common. In C. Europe generally the ups black marginal borders often wider, ♀ rarely with blue basal flush, f. *aegon* Denis and Schiffermüller. In England variable, on southern heaths uns darker grey-brown and ♀ without blue ups flush.

P. argus aegidion Meisner 1818 TL: Grimsel Pass, Switzerland
Description. ♂fw 12/13mm ups resembles *P. a. argus* but black marginal borders 3mm wide; uns gc medium grey with usual markings. ♀ups brown, orange submarginal markings often obscure, rarely absent.
Flight. July/August in a single brood.
Habitat. Alpine meadows and grass slopes at 1500m and above.
Variation. Below 1500m in S. Alps distinctive characters often less marked, becoming transitional to *P. a. argus*.
Distribution. Generally distributed in higher Alps.

P. argus hypochionus Rambur 1858 TL: Andalucia **Pl. 19**
Description. ♂fw 14/17mm, fw slightly pointed; ups marginal borders 1–2mm wide but often less where antemarginal black spots are clearly defined; uns gc nearly white with markings conspicuous; unh white band between pd spots and submarginal lunules disappears in pale gc. ♀ups orange submarginal lunules generally large, esp. uph.
Flight. June/July in a single brood.
Habitat. Mountain slopes from 1200m upwards.

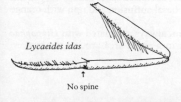

Lycaeides idas

↑
No spine

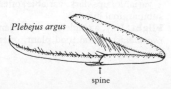

Plebejus argus

↑
spine

Distribution. C. and S. Spain, widely distributed.
Variation. In N. Spain, Cantabrian Mts., Sierra de la Demanda, etc., variable, in some colonies ups brilliant pale blue.

P. argus corsicus Bellier 1862 TL: Corsica **Pl. 19**
Description. ♂fw 13/14mm, ups resembles *P. a. argus* in size and general appearance; uns gc grey-brown with pale markings appearing as white rings with centres scarcely darkened. ♀ups generally with blue basal suffusions; uns slightly darker brown, otherwise resembling ♂.
Flight, Habitat and **Distribution.** In Corsica, rather local in forest clearings, etc., flying in July.
Similar species. *Lycaeides idas* below, *L. argyrognomon* p. 73; in these male foreleg is without tibial spine. *Plebejus pylaon* p. 70.

LYCAEIDES IDAS *Idas Blue*
Range. Europe, Asia and N. America, probably circumpolar in suitable latitudes, but absent from Britain. Map 114

L. idas idas Linnaeus 1761 TL: Sweden **Pls. 18, 19**
Description. ♂fw 14/16mm, like *P. argus*, but fore tibia without spine; ups bright blue, both wings with *characteristic narrow black borders*; uns gc pale grey, often with yellowish tint, but variable, markings generally small and rather inconspicuous; unh black marginal spots with blue-green pupils. ♀ups brown with or without basal blue flush, orange sub-marginal lunules often prominent esp. on uph; uns gc pale brown with markings often larger, orange marginal bands brighter and more extensive.
Flight. June/July with a single brood in N. and C. Europe, usually two broods in S.
Habitat. Rough ground and mountain slopes from lowlands to 1200m. Larval food plants various Leguminosae. The larvae are associated symbiotically with ants, e.g., *Lasius niger*, *Formica cinerea*, etc., and pupate within their nests where they also hibernate.
Distribution. From Spain to the North Cape and eastwards throughout Europe. Absent from Britain, Sicily and smaller Mediterranean islands.
Variation. *L. idas* is widely distributed in W. Europe and many local forms have been described and named. In general the variation shows a clinal series, with intergrading local forms and subspecies not well defined. Size is variable, at low altitudes often large, especially in N. Italy, in the striking form *opulentus* Verity, ♂fw 15/16mm; in the Pyrenees and Alps common but rather local at altitudes of 900–1500m, of moderate size, male ups dark borders narrow, ♀often with blue basal flush, f. *alpinus* Berce Pl. 18 single-brooded; at high altitudes in the Alps smaller, ♂fw 11/13mm, f. *haefelfingeri* Beuret Pl. 19. In arctic regions a similar small form occurs f. *lapponicus* Gerhard Pls. 18, 19. The nominate subspecies *L. i. idas* Linnaeus from S. Sweden is slightly larger than f. *lapponicus*, uns markings larger and better developed.

L. idas calliopis Boisduval 1832 TL: Grenoble
Description. ♂fw 14mm, resembles *L. idas idas*, uns black spots usually very small. ♀ variable, ups dark, variable, often with blue basal suffusion and uph with orange submarginal lunules.
Flight. July, a single brood, lowlands to 1000m, always associated with *Hippophae rhamnoides*, larval food plant, often abundant in a small area around the bushes,

showing no disposition to wander. Larvae symbiotic with ants on the Hippophae.
Distribution. SE France, extending into alpine foothills and to Geneva.

L. idas magnagraeca Verity 1936 TL: Greece (Olympos) **Pl. 22**
Description. ♂fw 16–17mm, ups deep blue, black marginal borders 2mm wide,
veins black; upf black discoidal stria small. Uns pale grey with usual markings; unh
green pupils of submarginal spots very brilliant. ♀ups orange marginal lunules
conspicuous and fused to form a complete band.
Flight and **Habitat.** Flies at 1500m or more in July in a single brood, in mountainous areas.
Distribution. S. Yugoslavia, Mt. Perister, N. Greece, Kalambaka, Mt. Olympos.
Colonies very localized.

This insect was described originally as a form of *Plebejus argus*. A smaller form of
L. idas, lacking the wide, black wing borders, occurs elsewhere in Greece, e.g.
Delphi, Mt. Timphristos etc.

L. idas bellieri Oberthur 1910 TL: Bastelica, Corsica **Pl. 22**
Description. Ups black marginal borders about 1mm wide; uns gc generally pale
yellow-grey with large and prominent markings. ♀ups with blue basal flush on both
wings. A very distinct subspecies.
Flight and **Habitat.** As for *L. i. idas*, flying in July in a single brood, from sea-level –
1200m. Larval food plant not recorded.
Distribution. Corsica, widely distributed, Sardinia, more local.
Variation. In Sardinia male specimens often have ups black wing borders up to
3mm wide.
Similar species. *P. argus* p. 71, usually small and with wider black marginal
borders, uns markings small and unf pd spot in s2 more displaced basad; ♂ *fore-tibia
with terminal spine*; androconial scales more oval in *P. argus*; male genitalia distinctive. *L. argyrognomon* below, large and colour brilliant; unh black chevrons before
orange submarginal lunules nearly flat (larger and sagittate in *idas*).

LYCAEIDES ARGYROGNOMON *Reverdin's Blue*
Range. From France and Switzerland across C. Europe, perhaps also in S. Russia.
Map 115

L. argyrognomon Bergsträsser 1779 TL: Hanau, Germany **Pl. 18**
syn: *ismenias* Meigen 1829 (invalid homonym); *aegus* Chapman 1917.
Description. Closely resembles *L. idas* but often larger; identification by external
characters is difficult and often uncertain, but usually possible by noting the following distinctive features:
  (1) Ups gc in ♂ is very clear bright blue, esp. noticeable in fresh specimens.
  (2) Uns gc in ♂ is usually white, often with a bluish tint.
  (3) Unh the black V-marks proximal to orange submarginal lunules are gently
       curved (sagittate in *idas*). This is probably the most reliable specific character,
       present in both sexes, but not always well defined.
Flight. May/June and July/August, usually in two broods.
Habitat. Flowery banks, from lowlands to 1000m. Larval food plant *Coronilla*.
Distribution. France, mostly in N. and E., Seine-et-Marne, Seine-et-Oise, Marne,
Aisne, Hte Savoie, Isère esp. near Rhône valley. Norway, very local near Oslo;
recorded also from S. Sweden. Switzerland in Jura and near Geneva. Italy, widely

distributed but local. Austria. Absent from Denmark, Britain, NW. and SW. Europe.
Similar species. *L. idas* p. 72; *P. argus* p. 71.

VACCINIINA OPTILETE   *Cranberry Blue*
Range. Central Alps and arctic Europe to Japan and N. America.   Map 116

V. optilete Knoch 1781   TL: Braunschweig, Germany   **Pl. 19**
Description. ♂fw 13/15mm, *ups deep violet-blue* with narrow black marginal lines, otherwise unmarked; uns gc dull grey, usual markings regular, prominent and dark; *unh with blue-scaled red submarginal spot in s2* sometimes also in s1c and s3. ♀ups dark brown with some violet basal suffusion; uph a small orange submarginal spot sometimes present in s2; uns resembles ♂.
Flight. July in a single brood.
Habitat. Moorlands and mountain slopes with *Vaccinium* from lowlands to 2100m. Larval food plant *Vaccinium oxycoccus* (cranberry), esp. the flowers, and other *Vaccinium* species.
Distribution. Fennoscandia and Baltic countries, generally common on *Vaccinium* slopes to North Cape; Denmark; C. Europe, local on peat moorlands in Germany, Czechoslovakia. Alps, present as a high alpine species from Savoie to Grossglockner. Balkans, only in Yugoslavia, Crni Vrh and Schar Planina. Absent from Vosges, Jura, Pyrenees, Apennines, and Julian Alps.
Variation. At high altitudes in Alps and in arctic regions often slightly smaller and with uns markings less prominent; ♀uph orange marginal spot in s2 absent.
Note. *Kretania eurypilos* is no longer regarded as a European species, since its presence in Greece has never been confirmed.

KRETANIA PSYLORITA   *Cretan Argus*
Range. Known only from Crete.   Map 117

K. psylorita Freyer 1845   TL: Mt. Ida, Crete   **Pl. 20**
Description. ♂fw 13mm, ups light brown; upf with or without small orange submarginal lunules; uph with small antemarginal spots surmounted by orange lunules but all markings very faint and small; uns gc very pale brown, unf no spot in cell; *unh pd series strongly curved but all markings very small, and faint*; silver scales sometimes present on the marginal dark spots. ♀ similar, ups and uns yellow submarginal lunules better developed.
Flight. June.
Habitat and **Distribution.** Known only from Crete, flying on Mt. Ida at 1600–1800m, low-flying, associated with a spiny *Astragalus* larval food plant.

EUMEDONIA EUMEDON   *Geranium Argus*
Range. From Cantabrian Mts. and Pyrenees to North Cape and across Europe and Asia to the Pacific.   Map 118

E. eumedon Esper 1780   TL: Erlangen, W. Germany   **Pl. 20**
syn: *chiron* Rottemburg 1775 (invalid homonym)
Description. ♂fw 14/16mm, ups dark brown, unmarked; uns grey to grey-brown with usual markings; unf no spot in cell, pd series in s1b–5 in straight row but often

incomplete, marginal markings variable; unh with blue basal suffusion, *a short white streak along v5* from discoidal spot to pd spots, submarginal orange lunules often inconspicuous. ♀ larger, uph generally with traces of orange marginal lunules near anal angle; uns all markings well developed.

Flight. June/July in a single brood.

Habitat. Hilly or mountainous country, lowlands to 2400m. Larval food plants *Geranium*, esp. *G. pratense.*

Distribution. Spain, in Cantabrian Mts. France, Pyrenees, Massif Central, Jura; widely spread from Alps to N. Cape; peninsular Italy and Sicily; Balkans. Absent from Portugal, S. Spain, NW. Europe (including Denmark) and Mediterranean islands except Sicily.

Variation. In SE. Europe often large, uns gc brownish (yellow-brown) rather than grey, orange submarginal lunules and other markings all well developed. In arctic regions usually small, unh markings inconspicuous, f. *borealis* Wahlgren, similar in Alps at high altitudes. The unh white streak may be absent, f. *fylgia* Spangberg, usually found flying with typical specimens, rare in W. Europe but more common and sometimes confusing in Balkans.

ARICIA AGESTIS *Brown Argus*

Range. N. Spain and eastwards across Europe to Iran, W. Himalayas, Siberia and Amurland. Map 119

A. agestis agestis Denis and Schiffermüller 1775 TL: Vienna **Pl. 19**
  syn: *astrarche* Bergsträsser 1779; *medon* Hufnagel 1776 (invalid homonym)

Description. ♂fw 12/14mm, *ups dark brown with orange marginal lunules usually in complete series*; upf discoidal spot dark; uns variable, often grey or grey-brown, with black white-ringed discoidal and pd spots and series of bright orange-red submarginal spots; unf lacking basal spot; unh pd spot in s6 displaced basad, a white mark on v4. ♀ similar, fw less pointed, often slightly larger.

Flight. April or later, usually in 2 annual broods but often 3 broods in S. Europe.

Habitat. Heaths and open places from lowlands to 900m. Larval foodplants rockrose and various Geraniaceae, e.g. Stork's Bill (*Erodium*).

Distribution. S. and C. Europe to about 56°N lat., including England and S. Scandinavia. Widely distributed esp. on calcareous soils. Absent from S. and C. Spain, Portugal, Balearic Islands and Ireland.

Variation. In S. Europe including Sardinia, Corsica, Elba, Greece and Malta ups orange marginal lunules often larger, f. *calida* Bellier.

A. agestis cramera Eschscholtz 1821 TL: Canary Islands **Pl. 19**
  syn: *canariensis* Blachier 1889

Description. ♂fw 11/13mm. Like *A. a. agestis*, ups series of orange *marginal lunules complete*; uns variable, usually grey (first brood) or brown (second brood). ♀ slightly larger.

Flight. April or later in two or more broods. Habitat, rough ground and rocky slopes from sea level to 1800m or more. Larval food plants *Sarothamnus, Trifolium* etc.

Distribution. Portugal, Spain, widely distributed to foot-hills of Pyrenees; Balearic Islands, Morocco; Algeria; Canary Islands, on Tenerife, Gomera and La Palma.

  A. a. cramera differs from *A. a. agestis* by a small character in the male genitalia. Considered specifically distinct by some authors.

Similar species. *A. a.allous* and *A.a.montensis.*

ARICIA ARTAXERXES   *Mountain Argus*
Range. From Morocco, Sicily and the Balkans to Fennoscandia and eastwards to the
Altai Mts. in several subspecies.   Map 120

A. artaxerxes artaxerxes   Fabricius 1793   TL: Anglia (Scotland)   **Pl. 19**
Description. ♂fw 11/12mm, narrow, pointed; ups orange marginal lunules reduced
in number, series incomplete, sometimes absent, *discoidal spot white*; uns gc grey,
markings in usual pattern but all spots white, sometimes with vestigial black pupils,
orange submarginal lunules in complete series on both wings. ♀ similar, ups orange
submarginal lunules slightly larger.
Flight. Late June/July in a single brood.
Habitat. Sheltered moorland localities. Larval food plant Rock Rose.
Distribution. Scotland, in Fife, Forfar, etc. and in local colonies to Cromarty Firth
and Sutherland; occasional in England in Durham and Lancashire.
Variation. In N. England small, ups orange lunules reduced but upf often without
the white discoidal spot which may appear in about 10% of individuals, more
commonly in ♀; uns spots usually with small black pupils, f. *salmacis* Stephens. Rare
individuals with upf white discoidal spot have been reported from various localities
in S. England and in S. Sweden, outside the range of this subspecies.

A. artaxerxes allous   Geyer 1837   TL: Alps of Provence   **Pl. 19**
   syn: *inhonora* Jachontov 1909
Description. Like *A. agestis*; ♂fw 12/14mm, ups dark brown; upf unmarked or with
small orange submarginal lunules in incomplete series; uph orange marginal lunules
commonly present in s1c, s2 and s3 but variable; fringes not chequered; uns pale
grey-brown with markings as in *A. agestis*. ♀ similar, fw apex less pointed.
Flight. June/July/August in a single brood.
Habitat. A mountain butterfly in C. Europe flying at 1200–2100m; at lower altitudes north of the Alps, a lowland species in the far north.
Distribution. Pyrenees and Alps of C. Europe extending northwards through
Fennoscandia far into the Arctic and eastwards to Sicily and Greece. Absent from
the Tatra and Carpathians.
Variation. Small and usually with greatly reduced or absent ups markings in the far
north (*inhonora* Jachontov). Large races with ♂fw 14/16mm occur in Denmark,
S. Sweden, Poland, etc., flying at low altitudes, and there perhaps indistinguishable
from *A. a. montensis* described below.

A. artaxerxes montensis   Verity 1928   TL: Andalusia   **Pl. 19**
   syn: *montana* Heyne 1895 (invalid homonym) *nevadensis* Oberthur 1910 (invalid
   homonym).
Description. Like *A. a. allous* but larger, ♂fw 14/16mm, upf orange submarginal
lunules reduced or absent; uph submarginal orange lunules usually present; unh pale
yellow-grey, sometimes inclining to brown, pd spot in s6 often very slightly displaced basad. ♀ups paler brown, large orange marginal lunules in complete series on
both wings; uns gc inclined more to brown.
Flight. June/July in a single brood.
Habitat. A mountain butterfly in N. Africa and in SW. Europe, flying on flowery
slopes at 900–2200m.
Distribution. Morocco, Algeria and Tunisia in Atlas Mts. Spain, widely distributed on mountains. France, in Pyrenees and Massif Central and thence to
SW. Alps. Less Common in Jura and Vosges. Yugoslavia and Greece.

Variation. In N. Spain, Pyrenees and SW. Alps often smaller, when distinction from *A. a. allous* may be difficult or impossible.

A. a. montensis is considered specifically distinct by some authors.

ARICIA MORRONENSIS   *Spanish Argus*
Range. Confined to Spain.   Map 121

A. morronensis   Ribbe 1910   TL: Mt. Morron, Murcia   **Pl. 19**
    syn: *idas* Rambur 1840 (invalid homonym); *ramburi* Verity 1929
Description. ♂fw 13/15mm, *apex of fw not pointed*, outer margin convex, fringes lightly chequered; ups brown; upf dark discoidal spot sometimes ringed white; uph vestigial orange marginal lunules in s2, 3; uns pale coffee-brown with usual markings of small white-ringed dark spots; *unh pd spot in s6 displaced basad*; small inconspicuous orange-yellow submarginal lunules present on both wings. ♀ similar.
Flight. May and July/early August in two broods.
Habitat. Rough stony slopes at 2000m in S. Spain, to 900–1200m farther north. Larval food plant not recorded.
Distribution. Spain, widely distributed but always extremely local in isolated colonies, Sierra Nevada, Sierra de Espuna, Sierra Priete, Casayo, Ordesa, etc.
Variation. Different colonies vary slightly in size, development of orange ups lunules, etc; northern specimens are larger.
Similar species. *A. artaxerxes* p. 76, apex of fw more pointed, ups orange submarginal lunules more numerous; uns submarginal lunules orange-red.

ARICIA ANTEROS   *Blue Argus*
Range. Balkan Peninsula and eastwards to Iran.   Map 122

A. anteros   Freyer 1839   TL: Constantinople   **Pl. 19**
Description. ♂fw 15/16mm, *ups gleaming pale blue* with black marginal borders about 2mm wide; orange submarginal lunules generally prominent on both wings; *upf a small black discoidal spot*; uph small round antemarginal spots usually present; uns gc pale grey-brown with usual markings; unf no spot in cell; unh spot in s6 slightly displaced basad, with gap before spot in s5. ♀ups brown, orange submarginal spots usually present on hw, sometimes also on fw; upf discoidal spot black; uns gc brown or yellow-brown. Androconia present on upf in ♂.
Flight. June/early July in a single brood.
Habitat. Mountains, flying over rough flowery slopes, commonly at 900–1500m, rarely at lower levels. Larval food plant not known.
Distribution. Bulgaria, in Rila and Rhodope Mts. Albania. Yugoslavia, Velebit Mts., and through Croatia to Dobrugea but scarce and local in northern Balkans. Greece.
Similar species. *P. eros* p. 93 and *P. eroides* p. 93, on ups resemblance is close but discoidal spots absent, unf with spot in cell; unh pd spots in regular series, no gap between spots in s5 and s6.

PSEUDARICIA NICIAS   *Silvery Argus*
Range. Pyrenees and SW. Alps, Finland and Russia.   Map 123

P. nicias nicias   Meigen 1830   TL: Rhetian Alps (Verity 1943)   **Pl. 19**
    syn: *donzelii* Boisduval 1832
Description. ♂fw 11/12mm, *ups pale silvery blue* with wide fuscous marginal

borders; upf discoidal spot very small, uph often absent; unh gc pale grey with usual markings small, sometimes incomplete or indistinct, marginal markings vestigial if present, pd spot in s6 slightly if at all displaced basad, a wedge-shaped white mark wide distally along v4. ♀ups brown with light brown fringes; uns resembles ♂. Androconia present on upf in ♂.

Flight. July in a single brood.

Habitat. Mountains at 900–1500m in S. Europe. Larval food plants *Geranium*, esp. *G. silvaticum* and *G. pratense*, meadow cranes-bill.

Distribution. E. Pyrenees and S. Alps of France, Switzerland and eastwards to Stilfserjoch and Franzenshohe.

P. nicias scandica   Wahlgren 1930   TL: Sweden

Description. ♂fw 12/13mm, slightly larger than *P. n. nicias*; ups blue areas brighter and better defined on both wings, dark wing borders narrower. ♀ not seen.

Flight and **Habitat.** Flies in July/August at moderate altitudes in the mountains.

Distribution. Local and uncommon between 60° and 65° in S. Finland and E. Sweden. More widely distributed eastwards in Russia.

Similar species. *A. glandon* below, larger, unh markings without a white streak along v4; *A. damon* p. 81, much larger, ups ♂ brilliant blue, unh gc brown with white streak along v4 extending to base.

ALBULINA ORBITULUS   *Alpine Argus*
Range. Alps and Norway to C. Asia.   Map 124

A. orbitulus   de Prunner 1798   TL: Piedmont, N. Italy   **Pl. 19**
    syn: *pheretes* Hübner 1805

Description. ♂fw 12/14mm, ups gc shining sky-blue with black marginal lines, otherwise unmarked; uns gc grey; unf usual markings reduced and inconspicuous, sometimes absent, no spot in cell, discoidal and pd spots small, white-ringed, spot in s1b absent, *no marginal markings; unh spots white without black pupils*, large, pd series broken, spots in s4 and s5 displaced distad, pd spots often elongate oval, marginal markings vestigial. ♀ups brown often with slight blue basal suffusion; uns gc light brown with variable markings as in ♂.

Flight. July/August in a single brood.

Habitat. High alpine meadows from 1700m upwards. Larval food plants *Astragalus alpinus* and *A. frigidus*.

Distribution. Basses Alpes to Savoie and eastwards to Grossglockner, on nearly all high mountains. Norway in Jotunfjeld and Dovrefjeld flying at 900–1200m. Sweden in Jämtland. Absent from Carpathians, Karawanken Mts. and Balkans.

Variation. Markings on uns are variable individually but racial variation is not marked.

AGRIADES GLANDON   *Glandon Blue*
Range. Sierra Nevada, Pyrenees, Alps and N. America.   Map 125

A. glandon glandon de Prunner 1798   TL: W. Alps (Col du Glandon?)   **Pl. 20**
    syn: *orbitulus* Esper 1800 (invalid homonym)

Description. ♂fw 13/15mm, ups shining pale greenish-blue with wide ill-defined *fuscous marginal borders* which often suffuse broadly across fw and less often across costal area of hw, discoidal spots small if present; uph sometimes with small brown antemarginal spots; unf gc pale grey-brown, cell-spot, discoidal and pd spots black, *marginal markings grey, obscure*; unh with large white discoidal spot, basal and pd spots usually well defined, except spots in s4, 5, often small and without black pupils, small yellow submarginal lunules rarely absent in s2 (3). ♀ often small, ups brown; uns resembles ♂ but gc darker and markings better defined.

Flight. July/August in a single brood.

Habitat. Mountains at 1800–2400m flying over short grass slopes. Larval food plants *Androsace, Soldanella* (Primulaceae).

Distribution. Pyrenees and Basses Alpes through C. and S. Alps to Gross Glockner.

Variation. Size and extent of ups fuscous suffusion vary slightly, with darkest races at very high altitudes. In the Bavarian Alps, f. *alboocellatus* Osthelder, unh spots mostly without black pupils, perhaps better graded as a subspecies. In ♀ and more rarely in ♂upf discoidal and pd spots may be ringed white.

A. glandon zullichi Hemming 1933 TL: Sierra Nevada **Pl. 20**
syn: *nevadensis* Zullich 1928 (invalid homonym)
Description. ♂fw 12mm, resembles *A. g. glandon*; ups brown with restricted blue basal suffusion, discoidal spots present on both wings; uph submarginal lunules present but obscure in s1b–6; uns gc pale brown; unh pd spots in s6, 7 with brown pupils, remaining spots represented by elongate white chevrons just proximal to submarginal lunules.

Flight. July/August.

Habitat and Distribution. E. Sierra Nevada flying at 2400m. Habitat appears to be very restricted.

A. glandon aquilo Boisduval 1832 TL: North Cape Map 304 **Pl. 20**
Description. ♂fw 10/11mm, *ups smooth shining pale grey* with slightly blue flush shading into narrow brown outer marginal borders, discoidal spots very small, marginal markings faint or absent; uns pale grey, markings as in *A.g.glandon*; unf submarginal spots dark and usually complete; unh markings white, rarely with vestigial black pupils, pd spots joined to submarginal lunules to form long white stripes. ♀ups brown with pale submarginal markings and vestigial pd spots on fw in some specimens; uns resembles ♂.

Flight. End June/July.

Habitat. Sheltered grassy places at low altitudes. Larval food plant *Astragalus alpinus*.

Distribution. Arctic Norway, local near coast from 66°N to North Cape, e.g., Tromsö, Saltdalen, Porsanger. N. Finland, Kilpisjärvi.

Similar species. *A. pyrenaicus* below, ♂ups pale silvery grey with narrow dark marginal borders; in both sexes unf submarginal spots black (grey in *glandon*). *P. nicias* p. 77.

A. g. aquilo is sometimes regarded as a distinct species.

AGRIADES PYRENAICUS *Gavarnie Blue*
Range. Cantabrian Mts., Pyrenees; Balkans and N. Caucasus Map 126

A. pyrenaicus pyrenaicus Boisduval 1840 TL: Pyrenees **Pl. 20**
Description. ♂fw 13/14mm, ups *pale silvery grey* with narrow black marginal lines; upf discoidal spot small, black and round; unf resembles *A.g.glandon* but pd spot in s6 displaced slightly basal, s3–5 *black submarginal lunules*; unh basal and pd spot in s7

white but often with black pupils, remaining discal and pd spots white without black pupils, outer margin white with small yellow lunule in s2. ♀ups brown, uph often with traces of submarginal pale lunules; uns as in ♂.
Flight. July.
Habitat. Flies over grass slopes at 1800m or more. Larval food plant *Androsace villosa*.
Distribution. Htes Pyrénées, Cauterets, Gavarnie, etc. Absent from Andorra and E. Pyrenees.

A. pyrenaicus asturiensis Oberthur 1910   TL: Picos de Europa   **Pl. 20**
Description. Ups gc slightly paler grey, black marginal lines preceded by obscure white marks between veins; uph usually with white submarginal lunules and small black antemarginal spots. ♀upf discoidal spot white-ringed, larger, and pale marginal marks small; uph submarginal lunules more prominent; uns resembles ♂.
Flight and **Habitat** as for *A. p. pyrenaicus*.
Distribution. Cantabrian Mts. on Picos de Europa, not recorded elsewhere.

A. pyrenaicus dardanus Freyer 1844   TL: Turkey (Balkans?)   **Pl. 20**
Description. ♂fw 11/12mm, ups grey-blue gc more extensive, fuscous marginal borders narrow; markings resemble those of *A. g. glandon* but unh pd spots in s4, 5 vestigial or absent.
Flight and **Habitat** as for *A. glandon*.
Distribution. In Europe ♀ known only from Vran Planina and Cvrstnica in Hercegovina.
Similar species. *A. glandon* p. 78.

CYANIRIS SEMIARGUS   *Mazarine Blue*
Range. Morocco and throughout temperate Europe and Asia to Mongolia.
Map 127

C. semiargus semiargus Rottemburg 1775   TL: Saxony, Germany   **Pl. 19**
   syn: *acis* Denis and Schiffermüller 1775
Description. ♂fw 14/17mm, ups dull violet-blue, ill-defined black marginal borders 1–2mm wide, somewhat diffused basad along veins; uns gc pale grey-brown with blue basal flush; *unf* without spot in cell, discoidal stria and *pd spots present but marginal markings absent*; unh markings as on unf with additional basal spot in s7, traces of marginal markings near anal angle sometimes present. ♀ups brown, unmarked; uns gc brown, markings as in ♂.
Flight. End June/July/August in a single brood depending upon altitude.
Habitat. Flowery meadows and alpine slopes from sea-level to 1800m; will congregate in scores at wet places on paths. Larval food plants *Trifolium, Anthyllis, Melilotus, Armeria*, etc; larva hibernates when small.
Distribution. Widely distributed and often common throughout W. Europe to 68°N, but local in mountains and often rare in Spain and Portugal. Morocco, very local in High Atlas and Middle Atlas, flying at 2100–2400m. Now extinct in Britain. Records from Corsica and Sardinia need confirmation.

C. semiargus parnassia Staudinger 1870   TL: Mt. Parnassus
Description. ♂fw 15mm, differs from *C. s. semiargus* in its small size, upf dark marginal border narrow, almost linear, unh an obscure orange submarginal lunule present in s1c in about ⅓ of specimens. Staudinger remarks that in occasional specimens the orange lunule may be prominent (*ganz roth*), and present on ups. ♀uph orange obscure lunule in s1c present in about half the specimens, but unh is

constant and better defined, often with vestigial grey submarginal spots to s3.

Flight and **Habitat.** May/early June in mountains at 1300–1500m or more.

Distribution. Mt. Parnassos, Mt. Timphristos. Perhaps widely distributed in C. Greece. In N. Greece only nominate *C. semiargus* has been seen.

In his account of *parnassia*, Staudinger refers to the obvious relationship to *Cyaniris helena*.

Similar species. *Cupido osiris* p. 61, ups gc similar but black marginal borders linear and well defined; uns gc pale grey (more brown in *semiargus*) with smaller markings; unf pd spots in nearly straight row. *C. helena* below.

CYANIRIS HELENA   *Greek Mazarine Blue*

Range. Greece, Asia Minor, Lebanon and Iraq.   Map 128

C. helena   Staudinger 1862   TL: Mt. Taygetos, S. Greece   **Pl. 19**

Description. ♂fw 13/14mm, resembles *C. semiargus*; ups violet-blue with narrow black marginal borders; *uph sometimes with traces of orange lunules near anal angle*; uns gc pale grey; unf a small discoidal stria, pd spots small, in nearly straight row close to indistinct submarginal and marginal markings; unh with blue basal suffusion, pd spots in very even curved series close to *orange submarginal lunules* at least *in s1c to s3*. ♀ups brown, sometimes with blue basal suffusion, upf with orange lunules in s1b to 3; uph with 3 to 5 orange marginal lunules in s1c to s4 or 5 often forming a band; uns as in ♂.

Flight. June/July, in a single brood.

Habitat. Mountains at 1200–1500m. Larval food plant *Trifolium, Anthyllis*.

Distribution. Greece, recorded from Mt. Chelmos, Zachlorou, Kalavryta, Taygetos Mts.

Similar species. *C. semiargus* above, unh without orange submarginal band.

Note. *C. helena* is a striking little butterfly often ranked as a subspecies of *C. semiargus*.

Note. Species of the genera *Lysandra* and *Agrodiaetus*, especially *A. ripartii* and its close relatives (Anomalous Blues), form a most confusing complex. It is known that further species have been recognised and await publication of their descriptions and names, so the following account should be considered as provisional.

AGRODIAETUS IPHIGENIA   *Chelmos Blue*

Range. Greece (Peloponnesos), Asia Minor, S. Russia   TL: Tokat   Map 129

A. iphigenia nonacriensis   Brown 1976   TL: Mt. Chelmos, Greece   **Pl. 22**

Description. ♂fw 16mm, ups bright shining blue, both wings with narrow, black marginal lines, fringes white; uns pale yellow-grey with usual pattern of black spots, unh a white stripe along v4 firmly marked, pd spots small, marginal lunules vestigial. ♀ups brown, unmarked, uns pale yellow-brown, markings as in ♂.

Flight and **Habitat.** Flies in July on rough ground at 500–1500m, on mountain slopes.

Distribution. Greece, only known from Mt. Chelmos (Peloponnesos).

AGRODIAETUS DAMON   *Damon Blue*

Range. From Spain locally through S. and C. Europe, including Estland, Russia and Armenia to Altai Mts.   Map 130

A. damon   Denis and Schiffermüller 1775   TL: Vienna   **Pl. 21**

Description. ♂fw 15/17mm, ups gc pale shining blue with wide fuscous margins

which extend basad along veins, no sex brand; unf gc yellow-grey with simple markings of discoidal stria and five or six pd spots all dark and white-ringed; *unh* slightly darker, more brown, with a *firm narrow pale stripe from base along v4* nearly to margin, basal and pd markings small or vestigial. ♀ usually slightly smaller; ups gc brown, often with a few blue scales on thorax and at wing-bases; uns gc café-au-lait with markings as in ♂.
Flight. July/August in a single brood.
Habitat. Usually in mountains on calcareous soils, from valleys to 2100m. Larval food plant sainfoin (*Onobrychis*).
Distribution. Widely distributed in Europe in scattered localised colonies. Spain, N. and C. France, in C. Pyrenees, Lozère, Provence to Savoie, thence through C. Europe to 56°N at Riga. In Balkans recorded from Dalmatia, Bosnia and Macedonia, Greece. Rare in S. Italy; absent from S. Spain, Portugal and Mediterranean islands.
Variation. There is considerable variation in size and colour, forming local races of which the best defined are:
A. d. ultramarina Schawerda from Estonia. A large form with ♂fw up to 19mm, ups colour rather deep blue, fuscous basal extensions along the wing veins quite prominent.
A. d. noguerae de Sagarra TL: Noguerra (Spain, Catalonia). A small form, ♂fw 13–16mm, ♂ ups blue of pale tone, recorded by Manley from Bronchales and appearing as a geographical race quite widespread in Teruel, flying at 3500–5500ft.

AGRODIAETUS DOLUS *Furry Blue*
Range. Confined to SW. Europe and Italy.   Map 131

A. dolus dolus Hübner 1823   TL: Maritime Alps (Verity 1943)   **Pl. 21**
Description. ♂fw 17/19mm, *ups gc very pale blue* with fuscous marginal borders; base of fw with extensive *pale brown androconial* area which appears slightly rough; uph with fuscous marginal shades between veins; uns gc pale yellow-grey; unf pd spots conspicuous; unh standard markings often incomplete, the white streak along v4 sometimes indistinct. ♀ups brown, veins lined darker; uph with darker marginal spots between veins; uns gc darker brown than ♂; fringes pale.
Flight. Mid-July/August in a single brood.
Habitat. Hilly or mountainous districts from low levels to 1800m. Larval food plant sainfoin and lucerne (*Onobrychis* and *Medicago sativa*).
Distribution. France, in Provence, very local in Var, Alpes Maritimes, Bouches du Rhône, etc. Spain (Catalonia).

A. dolus vittatus Oberthur 1892   TL: Lozère, France
Description. ♂fw 16/17mm, slightly smaller than *A. d. dolus*, ups gc pale grey with extensive fuscous suffusion along all veins, suffused blue at wing-bases only; uns gc pale grey-brown, deeper in tone on hw where white streak along v4 is clearly defined. ♀uns medium brown, considerably darker than in *A. d. dolus*.
Flight. Mid-July/August in a single brood.
Habitat. Rough ground at low levels.
Distribution. Lozère, Aveyron, Florac, Mende, Peyreleau, Balsièges, etc.

A. dolus virgilius Oberthur 1910   TL: Sulmona, Abruzzi   **Pl. 21**
Description. ♂fw 16/17mm, ups gc white, with narrow fuscous marginal lines somewhat shaded basad and along veins, extensive basal androconial area rough and brown, thorax and wing-bases blue; uph gc white with fuscous marginal line and variable fuscous marginal shading, veins lined dark esp. v6 and v7, dark ante-

marginal spots vestigial, base flushed blue; uns gc very pale cream, unh white streak along v4 rarely definite. ♀ resembles *A. d. dolus*, uns slightly darker brown; unh white streak usually absent.

Flight and **Habitat** as for *A. d. dolus*.

Distribution. Peninsular Italy, Bologna, Sulmonia, l'Aquila, Sorrento, Roccaraso, Mt. Majella, Monti Sibillini, Lucania, Puglia, etc., with minor variation in different colonies.

Similar species. *A. damon* p. 81.

AGRODIAETUS AINSAE *Forster's Furry Blue*
Range. Restricted to northern Spain. Map 132

A. ainsae Forster 1961 TL: Ainsa, N. Spain
Description. ♂fw 15/16mm, small, ups gc pale shining blue shading to white, indistinguishable from *A. dolus* except by small size.
Flight and **Habitat.** As for *A. dolus*.
Distribution. N. Spain, recorded from Ainsa, Jaca, Huesca, Burgos.
Note. *A. ainsae* is distinguished specifically from *A. dolus* by its lower chromosome number.

AGRODIAETUS ESCHERI *Escher's Blue*
Range. S. Europe and Morocco. Map 137

A. escheri escheri Hübner 1823 TL: Var, S. France (Verity 1943) **Pl. 21**
syn: *agestor* Godart 1824
Description. ♂fw 17/19mm, *ups deep sky-blue*, fw costa and veins often paler, with fine black marginal lines; *hw fringe half chequered*, outer margin appears slightly wavy; uns gc grey with standard markings; unh with blue basal suffusion. ♀ups brown; series of *orange submarginal lunules generally complete and prominent*, some times missing on fw; uph marginal blue scaling rare; uns gc brown with bold markings as in ♂. Unf without cell-spot.
Flight. End June/July in a single brood.
Habitat. From lowlands to 1800m, generally in mountainous districts. Larval food plants *Astragalus*.
Distribution. Spain and Portugal, generally distributed in mountainous districts. France, in C. and E. Pyrenees, Provence to Savoie and Hautes Alpes, Cantal, Lozère, Bouches du Rhône, Lot and Charente Inf. Switzerland, only in Rhône valley and Alps of Valais, Tessin and perhaps farther east. Italy, generally common in Alps of Piedmont and Ligurian Apennines and E. to Alto Adige (Bolzano, etc.).

A. escheri splendens Stefanelli 1904 TL: Florence
Description. ♂fw 15/17mm, ups gleaming pale sky blue; uns gc pale grey with small markings. ♀ups orange submarginal lunules well developed.
Flight. End June/early July.
Habitat. Rocky places with flowers at altitudes of 300m or little more.
Distribution. Ligurian and Emilian Apennines, sometimes flying with more typical specimens, Florence, Genoa, Portofino, Arquarta Scrivia, Reggio, etc., in some colonies small, ♂fw 15/16mm, f. *altivolans* Verity Pl. 21.

A. escheri dalmaticus Speyer 1882 TL: Dalmatia **Pl. 13**
syn: *olympena* Verity 1936
Description. ♂fw 17/20mm, large, gc sky blue paler than in *A. e. escheri*, black marginal border 1–2mm wide, not linear; uns gc paler, nearly white. ♀ resembles *A. e. splendens*.

Flight and **Habitat.** Flies in June at moderate levels in hilly country.
Distribution. Dalmatia, Hercegovina, Blagai, Stolác. Greece, Drama, Mt. Olympus, Mt. Parnassos, Mt. Chelmos, Taygetos Mts. Widespread in mountains of N. Greece.

A. escheri ahmar Le Cerf 1932 TL: Djebel Ahmar, Morocco
Description. ♂fw 14/15mm, small, ups rather dull, pale blue; uns markings as for *A. e. escheri*, complete but not prominent. ♀ups brown, marginal lunules pale yellowish; unh marginal markings not well developed.
Flight and **Habitat.** Flies in June, among mountains at 1800m or more.
Distribution. Middle Atlas, Morocco, Djebel Ahmar and Tizi n'Tskine.
Similar species. *L. bellargus* p. 91, fw fringes chequered, unf with spot in cell. *A. thersites* below, smaller, ups gc violet-blue, unh pd spots smaller; ♀uph without full series of orange submarginal lunules. *Plebejus pylaon* p. 70.

AGRODIAETUS AMANDA *Amanda's Blue*
Range. From N. Africa and Spain widely distributed in Europe and W. Asia to Iran. Map 138

A. amanda amanda Schneider 1792 TL: S. Sweden **Pl. 20**
syn: *icarius* Esper (after 1792)
Description. ♂fw 16/19mm, ups gc sky blue; *upf margin widely suffused with fuscous which extends basad along veins*; uph with dark marginal line extending basad along veins, sometimes with obscure antemarginal dark spots; uns gc pale dove grey with blue basal flush; unf usual markings rather small, no spot in cell and marginal markings obscure; unh pd markings rather small, generally with orange submarginal lunules in s1c, 2, 3 followed by small dark antemarginal spots from s1c–7. ♀ups medium brown, often with extensive blue basal suffusion; uph orange submarginal lunules with marginal black spots in s1c–3; uns gc darker grey-brown, otherwise as in ♂.
Flight. End June/July in a single brood.
Habitat. Flowery banks, etc., from lowlands to 1500m in southern Europe; associated with larval food plant, tufted vetch (*Vicia cracca*). Hibernates as small larva.
Distribution. Absent from NW. Europe, Venezia Giulia and Carniola: otherwise widely distributed but local to 65°N, especially in mountains.
Variation. Local variation is not marked. Females widely suffused with blue are common in Scandinavia, rare in the Alps and Pyrenees, f. *isias* Frühstorfer.

A. amanda abdelaziz Blachier 1905 TL: Atlas Mts., Morocco **Pl. 20**
Description. ♂ups blue gc slightly paler with slightly silvery tone; uns markings small; unh orange lunules in anal area vestigial or absent. ♀ups brown with large orange-yellow marginal lunules on both wings and a slight general orange suffusion in some specimens.
Flight and **Habitat.** Flies June, in a single brood, on mountain meadows at 1800–2200m.
Distribution. Morocco, Middle and High Atlas. Algeria.
Similar species. The large size and slightly dusky gleaming pale blue ups and dove-grey lightly marked uns are unlike any other species.

AGRODIAETUS THERSITES *Chapman's Blue*
Range. N. Africa and S. Europe to Lebanon, Asia Minor, Iran and Thian Shan. Map 139

A. thersites Cantener 1834 TL: Vosges, etc., NE. France **Pl. 20**
Description. ♂fw 13/16mm, resembles *P. icarus* but *androconia numerous*, ups

bright blue generally with slightly violet tint, fringes white, not chequered; uns gc light grey to brown; unf no spot in cell, otherwise with usual markings; orange submarginal lunules generally well developed on both wings; unh blue basal flush usually well marked in early specimens, often absent in late broods, usual markings complete with white mark on v4. ♀ups brown, sometimes with blue basal suffusion; uph orange submarginal lunules present, often absent upf; uns gc light brown with markings as in ♂, white streak along v4 often conspicuous.

Flight. May and later in two or more broods.

Habitat. Flowery meadows esp. fields of sainfoin (*Onobrychis*), larval food plant, from lowlands to 1500m.

Distribution. N. Africa, in Middle Atlas and High Atlas, flying there at 1500–1800m. Europe, widely distributed but local to 50°N. Not recorded from Mediterranean islands (except Sicily) or from Algeria.

Variation. In some localities females often have a slight ups basal blue flush.

Similar species. *Polyommatus icarus* p. 92, wing-markings and colour are nearly identical but on unf *P. icarus* has a spot in the cell, sometimes very small. The male androconia on upf in *A. thersites* produce a slightly furry appearance which is not present in *P. icarus*. *A. escheri* p. 83. *P. dorylas* p. 87.

The following species include small, brown butterflies with specific characters poorly defined. To aid identification they are recorded here in two groups, depending upon the presence or absence of a white stripe on the hindwing underside. This arrangement, including little more than names and localities is to be considered provisional.

UNDERSIDE OF HINDWING WHITE STRIPE PRESENT

AGRODIAETUS ADMETUS *Anomalous Blue*
Range. E. Europe and Asia Minor.   Map 133

A. admetus   Esper 1785   TL: Hungary   **Pl. 21**
Description. ♂fw 15/19mm, ups brown, unmarked, base and discal areas of fw covered by *patch of hairy androconial scales*; uns gc pale brown, submarginal markings definite; unf without spot in cell, discoidal stria and pd spots black, pale ringed, marginal spots paler brown, faint; unh usual markings present, *sometimes with wedge-shaped white pd mark on v4*. ♀ often smaller, ups gc paler, smooth brown; uph generally with obscure orange marginal lunules near anal angle; uns markings brighter and better developed than in ♂.

Flight. End June/July in a single brood.

Habitat. Hot rocky slopes, at low or moderate altitudes. Larval food plant sainfoin (*Onobrychis*).

Distribution. Hungary. Czechoslovakia. Romania, Dobrudscha. Bulgaria, Karlovo. SE. Yugoslavia, Skopje. Greece, Parnassus, Taygetos Mts. Usually very local in widely scattered colonies.

Similar species. *A. ripartii* p. 86; *A. fabressei* below.

AGRODIAETUS FABRESSEI *Oberthur's Anomalous Blue*
Range. Confined to central Spain.   Map 134

A. fabressei fabressei   Oberthur 1910   TL: Albarracin, C. Spain   **Pl. 22**
Description. ♂fw 17/18mm, resembles *A. admetus* but differs in more pointed fw; uns brown gc darker café-au-lait, discal markings bolder, marginal markings fainter;

outer margin of hw not evenly rounded but with a slight bulge at v5, 6. ♀ smaller, unh often with short wedge-shaped white mark on v4.
Flight. End June/August.
Habitat. Hot rocky mountain slopes at 900–1200m. Larval food plant *Onobrychis*.
Distribution. C. Spain in Province of Teruel, Albarracin, Noguera, etc.

A. fabressei agenjoi Forster 1965 TL: Spain (Catalonia)
Anjenjo's Anomalous Blue
Description. Uns discal markings well defined but marginal markings not well developed.
Flight and **Habitat.** Flies in late July/August at low altitudes, colonies extremely localized.

A. f. humedasae Toso & Balleto 1979 TL: Cogne, N. Italy *Piedmont Anomalous Blue*
Description. A relatively large form, ups dark brown, uns marginal markings often absent in males, but developed in females.
Flight and **Habitat.** Flies in August over sub-alpine meadows at 800m and over.

AGRODIAETUS AROANIENSIS *Grecian Anomalous Blue*
Range. Greece, Mainland and Peloponnesos Map 135

A. aroaniensis Brown 1976 TL: Mt. Chelmos, Greece **Pl. 22**
Description. ♂fw 14/16mm, like *A. ripartii*, ups dark brown, unmarked, fw apex pointed, unf pd spot in s1b often double, uns pale yellow-brown, unh white longitudinal stripe vestigial or absent, pd series of dark spots often incomplete, marginal markings vestigial or absent. ♀ similar.
Flight and **Habitat.** Flies in July/August at 700–1800m, over flowery meadows.
Distribution. N. and C. Greece, Drama etc., Mt. Chelmos, Mt. Timphristos etc. Probably widely distributed in mountainous country.
Similar species. *A. admetus; A. fabressei.* Originally described as a subspecies of *A. alcestis,* Zerny, of Lebanon and Turkey, in which unh a white stripe is prominent.

UNDERSIDE OF HINDWING WHITE STRIPE ABSENT

AGRODIAETUS RIPARTII *Ripart's Anomalous Blue*
Range. From Spain in widely separated colonies across S. Europe to Asia Minor. Map 136

A. ripartii ripartii Freyer 1830 TL: Spain **Pl. 21**
Description. ♂fw 14/17mm, resembles *A. admetus;* ups brown, unmarked; upf basal areas covered by rough hairy patch of androconial scales; uns pale yellow-grey with usual discal markings of white-ringed dark spots, *marginal markings vestigial or absent;* unh with narrow pale stripe from base of wing along v4. ♀ smaller, ups gc slightly paler; uph often with orange lunules near anal area; uns darker grey-brown, markings bolder esp. unf pd spots; unh white streak conspicuous, slightly expanded distally, marginal markings usually absent; fringes dark.
Flight. End July/August.
Habitat. Hot rocky slopes with rough vegetation, lowlands to 900m or more, often flying with *A. admetus* in E. Europe. Larval food plant *Onobrychis* esp. *O. saxatilis.*
Distribution. Spain, Jaca. France, in Alpes Maritimes and Basses Alpes. Italy, near Oulz in N. Piedmont, Lucania. Bulgaria, Sliven, Karlovo. SE. Yugoslavia, Prilep, Skopje. Albania. Absent from Hungary.

A. r. pelopi   Brown 1976   TL: Mt. Chelmos, Peloponnesos.
Description. Like *A. r. ripartii*, ♂fw 16/17mm, uns pale grey, often shaded yellowish; unh a white stripe extends along v4 almost to margin, narrow, not conspicuous. ♀ smaller, fw 15mm, unh white stripe well defined. A small distinctive character present in ♂-genitalia.
Flight and **Habitat.** Flies from 800m upwards, usually in stony places. July/early August.
Distribution. Greece, Mt. Chelmon, Mt. Taygetos, Mt. Timphristos.
Similar species. *A. aroaniensis* Brown; *A. admetus* Esper etc. The relationships of the brown *Agrodiaetus* are most complicated. Their distinctive chromosome numbers give important indications of specific rank.

NEOLYSANDRA COELESTINA   *Pontic Blue*
Range. Greece and eastwards across N. Turkey and S. Russia to the Caucasus.
Map 140

N. c. hera Eckweiler & Schurian 1980   TL: Mt. Chelmos, S. Greece   **Pl. 22**
Description. ♂ups deep blue, marginal borders 2–3mm wide, black, otherwise unmarked, fringes white; uns pale grey-brown; unf discoidal and pd black white-ringed spots in complete series; unh *gleaming blue-green basal suffusion* extending to end of cell, discoidal spot and pd spots in complete and regular series, as on fw, submarginal markings absent. ♀ ups brown, vestiges of yellow marginal lunules present at anal angle of hw, otherwise unmarked; unh with yellow submarginal lunules in short series.Larval food plant *Vicia dalmatica*.
Flight. June, in Greece, on mountains at 1200–1500m.
Distribution. In Europe known only from the Peloponnesus, Greece.
Similar species. *C. semiargus*, p. 80.

PLEBICULA DORYLAS   *Turquoise Blue*
Range. From Spain through S. Europe to Asia Minor.   Map 141

P. dorylas   Denis and Schiffermüller 1775   TL: Vienna   **Pl. 20**
   syn: *argester* Bergsträsser 1779; *hylas* Esper 1793 (invalid homonym)
Description. ♂fw 15/17mm, ups *gleaming pale blue*, the narrow black marginal lines extending slightly basad along veins; uns gc pale olive-buff to grey with usual markings; unf no spot in cell, *margins broadly white, antemarginal markings vestigial*; unh markings small on slightly darker gc, a wedge-shaped white mark on v4. ♀ups brown, sometimes with blue basal suffusion, orange submarginal lunules usually present on hw, rare on fw; uns gc brown with markings as in ♂.
Flight. May/July and August/September in two broods at low levels, a single brood in July/August at high altitudes.
Habitat. Flowery slopes and meadows commonly at 900–1500m. Larval food plants *Melilotus, Trifolium, Thymus, Anthyllis*.
Distribution. S. and C. Europe to Baltic. Very local in Spain, Cuenca, Burgos, etc.; more widely distributed from Pyrenees through Alps to Carpathians, Balkans and Greece; local in S. Sweden, Latvia and Lithuania. Reported from Sicily. Absent from NW. Europe, S. Italy and Mediterranean islands except Sicily.
Variation. There is slight individual variation in the shade of blue on ♂ups. Local variation is not well marked.
Similar species. In *A. thersites* p. 84, ♀uns marginal markings well developed. *P. golgus* p. 88, *P. nivescens* p. 88.

PLEBICULA GOLGUS *Nevada Blue*
Range. Confined to S. Spain.   Map 142

P. golgus Hübner 1813   TL: S. Spain   **Pl. 20**
Description. ♂fw 13/15mm, resembles *P. dorylas* but smaller; fw apex pointed, *ups gc deeper blue* with fine black marginal lines; uns gc yellow-grey; unf white marginal band enclosing antemarginal small dark spots; unh yellow lunules vestigial, antemarginal spots small. ♀ups brown; uph with or without small orange submarginal lunules; uns gc darker yellow-grey with markings better developed, orange submarginal lunules present on both wings.
Flight. July.
Habitat and **Distribution.** Known only from Sierra Nevada, flying at altitudes of 2100–2400m.
Similar species. *P. dorylas* p. 87, ups gc pale blue; uns gc pale grey, marginal markings vestigial in white marginal band.

PLEBICULA NIVESCENS *Mother-of-Pearl Blue*
Range. Confined to Spain.   Map 143

P. nivescens Keferstein 1851   TL: Sierra de Alfacar   **Pl. 20**
Description. ♂fw 15/18mm, resembles *P. dorylas; ups pale shining silvery-grey;* upf marginal border dark grey 1–2mm wide; uph black marginal lines preceded by dark grey antemarginal spots; uns gc very pale grey, hw yellowish with markings as in *P. dorylas*, but submarginal markings sometimes more distinct. ♀ups brown with broad orange-yellow lunules generally well developed on both wings; uns as in ♂ but gc yellow-grey.
Flight. June/July in a single brood.
Habitat. In mountains at 900–1800m. Larval food plants not recorded.
Distribution. Spain, local but widely distributed from Granada to Catalonia and Leon, extending to Pyrenees at Aulus. Absent from W. Spain.
Similar species. *P. dorylas* p. 87, ♂ups definitely blue; ♀ best identified by association with ♂. *L. albicans* p. 91, unf with spot in cell in both sexes.

PLEBICULA ATLANTICA *Atlas Blue*
Range. Confined to Morocco.   Map 144

P. atlantica Elwes 1905   TL: High Atlas, Morocco   **Pl. 20**
Description. ♂fw 14/17mm, ups resembles *P. dorylas, ups very pale sky blue;* upf black marginal border about 1mm wide; uph antemarginal black spots usually present; unf gc yellow-grey, pd spots very large, in tight curve; unh markings quite small, sometimes incomplete. ♀ups gc brown, slightly suffused orange, submarginal orange lunules very large and coalesced to form continuous bands on both wings, small black antemarginal spots present on uph; uns as in ♂.
Flight. End May/June and August/September in two broods, *second brood* specimens small, ♂fw 13/14mm.
Habitat. Stony slopes and dry scrub areas at 2100–2400m. Larval food plant not known.
Distribution. Morocco, Middle Atlas on Taghzeft Pass, High Atlas on Toubkal Massif.
Similar species. There is no similar species in Morocco.

MELEAGERIA DAPHNIS   *Meleager's Blue*

Range. From southern France across S. Europe to Lebanon, Syria and Iran.   Map 145

M. daphnis   Denis and Schiffermüller 1775   TL: Vienna   **Pls. 20, 21**
syn: *meleager* Esper 1779

Description. ♂fw 18/19mm, *outer margin of hw slightly scalloped between v2 and v3;* ups light shining blue with narrow black marginal borders, otherwise unmarked; uns gc pale grey, hw slightly darker, usual markings present with basal and discal spots black, marginal markings grey; unf no spot in cell; unh without orange submarginal lunules. ♀hw more deeply scalloped; ups deeper blue with dark discoidal spot, costal and marginal borders dark; uph with antemarginal spots; uns gc light brown with markings as in ♂, a white wedge-shaped pd mark on v4.
Flight. June in a single brood.
Habitat. Warm flowery slopes from lowlands to 1300m. Larval food plants species of *Orobus, Thymus, Astragalus.*
Distribution. France, in Cevennes, Provence and Dauphiné. Switzerland, esp. Rhône valley. Italy, widely distributed in mountainous areas of Piedmont, southern slopes of Alps, peninsular Italy and Sicily. Spain, local in NE. In E. Europe more widely distributed to 50°N or beyond. Absent from Pyrenees, Portugal and Mediterranean islands except Sicily.
Variation. A ♀ form in which ups is dark grey with markings obscurely outlined in blue-grey, f. *steeveni* Treitschke Pl. 20, is common in some districts.

LYSANDRA CORIDON   *Chalk-hill Blue*

Range. Europe including S. Russia (Ukraine).   Map 146

L. coridon coridon   Poda 1761   TL: Graz, Austria   **Pl. 21**
Description. ♂fw 15/18mm, fringes strongly chequered; ups gc pale silvery blue; upf with fuscous marginal borders 2–3mm wide; uph black marginal line narrow, antemarginal spots round; uns standard markings all present; unf gc pale grey; unh gc tinted brown with slight blue-green basal suffusion, markings less conspicuous than on fw, orange submarginal lunules often small and pale, the wedge-shaped white mark along v4 extending to submarginal lunules. ♀ups brown, sometimes with blue suffusion; uns brown, markings as in ♂.
Flight. July/August in a single brood.
Habitat. Grass banks from sea-level to 1800m, restricted to chalk and limestone country. Larval food plants various Leguminosae, e.g., vetches and trefoils, esp. *Hippocrepis comosa*; larva hibernates when small.
Distribution. From Pyrenees northwards to Baltic coast in Germany thence generally distributed in calcareous areas through S. and C. Europe from S. England to Sorrento in peninsular Italy and Balkans (rare and local). Absent from Ireland, NW. Germany, Denmark, Scandinavia, C. and S. Spain, Portugal and Mediterranean islands. Recently recorded from Corsica, *L. c. nufrellensis* Schurian 1977.
Variation. Slight local variation occurs in size, intensity of markings and in shade of blue gc. In females ups blue suffusion is common and very extensive in some areas, f. *syngrapha* Keferstein, rare in the Alps.
Note. It is difficult to decide upon the correct taxonomic treatment of the blue Spanish forms of *Lysandra*, including *caelestissima* Verity, *asturiensis* Sagarra, and others with differing shades of blue. Careful examination has failed to show any

constant differences from *L. coridon* in biology, in anatomical characters or in chromosomal patterns. A special study of the situation was made by the late Hubert de Lesse, who concluded that the different variants were best regarded as local colour forms of *L. coridon*, which is probably present in the NE (Catalonia), but not elsewhere in Spain in its usual paler greyish form so widely distributed in W. Europe. De Lesse's conclusions are accepted in this book, and the blue forms are included under the general heading of *Lysandra c. caelestissima*.

L. coridon caelestissima   Verity 1921   TL: C. Spain, Albarracin   **Pl. 21**
Description. ♂fw 15/18mm, like *L. coridon coridon* but ups is sky-blue; upf dark marginal border about 1mm wide, but slightly suffused, obscuring black antemarginal spots; uph marginal border linear; uns like *L. c. coridon*. ♀ usually slightly smaller, ups brown.
Flight. Late July/August in a single brood.
Habitat. Flowery mountain slopes up to 1600m or more.
Distribution. Montes Universales in Teruel and Cuenca (Albarracin, Bronchales, Tragacete etc.).
Variation. Several slightly different forms have been described. These include f. *asturiensis* Sagarra 1924, blue shade less brilliant, widely distributed in N. Spain; f. *burgalesa* Agenjo, at Burgos ♂ deep blue with broad, dark wing-borders; f. *manleyi* de Lesse, at Jaca ♂ pale blue, fuscous wing-borders narrower, many ♀ of f. *syngrapha*. A slightly different form *caerulescens* flies with *caelestissima* near Bronchales. It is often slightly larger, ups a pale, faded blue, upf with wide, grey marginal borders like *L. arragonensis* which occurs in the same district. It is a hybrid between these two butterflies.

L. c. graeca   Ruhl 1895   TL: Greece, not illustrated, no map.
Description. ♂ups pale grey with strong yellowish reflections; uns very pale, with usual markings but black spots reduced in size.
Distribution. Widespread on the mountains of Central Greece, Mt. Parnassos, Pindus Mts. etc. flying at moderate altitudes. An outstanding form. Specimens from S. Italy (Puglia) are rather similar.

LYSANDRA HISPANA   *Provence Chalk-hill Blue*
Range. Confined to SE. France, N. Italy and NE. Spain.   Map 147

L. hispana   Herrich-Schäffer 1852   TL: Spain   **Pl. 21**
   syn: *rezneciki* Bartel 1905
Description. ♂fw 16/18mm, very similar to *L. coridon*, not easily distinguishable without data; *ups pale blue-grey, slightly yellowish in oblique light*; upf discoidal stria minute if present, fuscous borders variable, sometimes wide with included *vestigial pale submarginal lunules*, often preceded by a paler area of gc; uns boldly marked esp. on hw. ♀ups brown, indistinguishable from *L. coridon* without accompanying ♂; *syngrapha*-like forms of the female have not been recorded.
Flight. April/May and September in two broods.
Habitat. Grassy banks and foothills at low levels, not above 900m. Larval food plant *Hippocrepis comosa*.
Distribution. France in E. Pyrenees, Aude, Hérault, Ardèche, Drôme, Basses Alpes, Var and Alpes Maritimes. Spain in Catalonia, esp. env. of Barcelona. Italy, in Liguria and Emilia to Florence and Siena.
Similar species. *L. coridon* p. 89, emerges in July/August, between broods of *L. hispana; L. albicans* below.

LYSANDRA ALBICANS   *Spanish Chalk-hill Blue*
Range. Confined to Spain and N. Africa.   Map 148

L. albicans albicans   Herrich-Schäffer 1851   TL: Spain   **Pls. 13, 21**
Description. ♂fw 18/21mm, ups *palest silky grey*, thorax and wing-bases faintly blue; upf fuscous *marginal border broad, often double* and enclosing marginal spots vaguely ringed with pale grey; uph fuscous marginal spots conspicuous; unf gc white with standard markings small; unh gc variable, brown, yellowish or white, markings often small and faint. ♀ups brown, often with small discoidal spots, orange submarginal lunules usually present before dark antemarginal spots on both wings and sometimes preceded by grey-white markings; uns brown, boldly marked in standard pattern.
Flight. July/August in a single brood.
Habitat. Rocky slopes and rough grass, etc., at 900–1500m. Larval food plants not recorded.
Distribution. Spain, except W. Spain, local but not rare from Malaga, Granada, Bailen, Toledo, Albarracin, Burgos, to Jaca, etc. Absent from Portugal.
Variation. Ups gc varies considerably, very pale and nearly without blue basal flush in S. Spain; farther N. and at higher altitudes more grey than white and uns darker, unh esp. pale brown, f. *arragonensis* Gerhard Pl. 13. These colour variants appear to form a clinal series.

L. albicans berber   Le Cerf 1932   TL: Middle Atlas
Description. ♂fw 16/18mm, small and ups very pale, with well-marked dusky marginal borders; uns very pale. ♀ups brown, undistinguished.
Flight. August.
Habitat. Mountains at 1500–2300m.
Distribution. Morocco, recorded from Kasr-el-Kebir, Timesmout, Tameghilt, Moussah ou Salah, all in Middle Atlas; not recorded from High Atlas.
Similar species. *L. coridon* p. 89, ♂ups definitely blue; *L. hispana* p. 90, only in NE. Spain, generally smaller, ♂ups grey gc slightly more suffused blue but distinction difficult without data, first brood over before *albicans* begins to fly; females of both species lack the small pale grey discal and marginal markings generally present in ♀ *albicans*. *P. nivescens* p. 88.

LYSANDRA BELLARGUS   *Adonis Blue*
Range. Europe including Russia to Iraq and Iran.   Map 149

L. bellargus   Rottemburg 1775   TL: W. Germany   **Pl. 21**
syn: *adonis* Denis and Schiffermüller 1775
Description. ♂fw 14/17mm, *ups shining vivid sky blue* with fine black marginal lines, fringes white, chequered black; uph with small black antemarginal spots; uns gc light-brown to grey-brown with standard markings complete; unh with blue-green basal flush; ♀ups brown, often with blue suffusion, rarely extensive; uph orange submarginal lunules often conspicuous, sometimes present also on fw; uns gc darker brown, markings as in ♂, but blue basal suffusion reduced or absent.
Flight. May/June and July/August in two broods in most localities.
Habitat. Meadows, etc., from lowlands to 1800m, restricted to calcareous areas. Larval food plant horse-shoe vetch (*Hippocrepis*), and various other small Leguminosae.
Distribution. Widely distributed in S. and C. Europe to 55°N and to Latvia, local

in S. England, rare in S. Spain. Absent from Ireland and Mediterranean islands except Majorca.

Variation. Racial variation is not marked; minor individual variation with fusion or absence of uns spots is not very uncommon. In rare females blue ups suffusion may be complete except on marginal borders, f. *ceronus* Esper.

Similar species. *L. coridon* p. 89, in ♀ only; blue scales or suffusion on ups pale silvery. *A. escheri* p. 85, ♀.

Note. In some localities where *L. coridon* and *L. bellargus* occur on the same ground rare specimens have occurred in which the blue ups gc is paler, intermediate in shade between these species, f. *polonus* Zeller. Nine such specimens examined by de Lesse had variable chromosome numbers (52–70) with abnormal meiosis patterns, and there seems little doubt that some at least of these pale forms are hybrids between *L. coridon* and *L. bellargus*.

LYSANDRA PUNCTIFERA　　*Spotted Adonis Blue*
Range. Confined to Morocco and Algeria.　Map 150

L. punctifera　Oberthur 1876　TL: Lambessa, Algeria　　　　　**Pl. 21**
　　syn: *punctigera* Oberthur 1909

Description. ♂fw 15/18mm, ups bright gleaming sky blue, resembling *L. bellargus; uph antemarginal black spots free, conspicuous*; uns gc brown with small blue basal flush, standard markings conspicuous esp. on fw but orange submarginal lunules rather small. ♀ups gc brown, blue suffusion often present, sometimes extensive; uns as in ♂. Fringes white, strongly chequered black in both sexes.

Flight. May/June and September/October, second brood very small.

Habitat. Flowery banks at 1500–1800m in Middle Atlas, to 2200m in High Atlas. Larval food plant not recorded.

Distribution. Morocco, Algeria.

Similar species. None in Africa.

POLYOMMATUS ICARUS　　*Common Blue*
Range. From Canary Islands and temperate N. Africa throughout Europe and temperate Asia.　Map 151

P. icarus　Rottemburg 1775　TL: Saxony, Germany　　　　**Pls. 4, 19**
Description. ♂fw 14/18mm, size variable; ups *androconia absent*, gc light violet-blue with fine black marginal lines; uns gc grey with blue-green basal flush, markings well developed; *unf with spot in cell and second basal spot below this in s1b*, frequent pd spots in regular sinuous curve and orange submarginal lunules more or less developed; unh with all usual markings and white flash on v4 beyond pd spot. ♀ups brown, often flushed blue, orange submarginal lunules generally in complete series across both wings; uph with black antemarginal spots between veins; uns gc brown, all markings better developed.

Flight. April or later in two or three broods in S. Europe, a single brood in June/July in the far north.

Habitat. Meadows and open spaces, lowlands to 1800m or more. Larval food plants small Leguminosae, esp. trefoil, vetches and clovers.

Distribution. N. Africa, Canary Islands, all Europe to North Cape and all Mediterranean islands; one of the commonest and most ubiquitous butterflies, flying in the High Atlas to 2400m.

Variation. Seasonal variation is sometimes well marked late broods being small and pale. Individual variation (aberrations) causing the loss or fusion of markings on uns are not uncommon.
Similar species. *Agrodiaetus thersites* p. 86, markings on both surfaces are nearly identical but on unf there is no spot in cell and on upf androconia are abundant (absent in *icarus*). *P. icarus* does occur without a spot in cell on unf but rarely, f. *icarinus* Scharfenberg. *P. eros* below, ♂ups pale silvery blue; ♀ smaller, ups blue basal scaling, if present, paler.

POLYOMMATUS EROIDES   *False Eros Blue*
Range. Poland and Czechoslovakia to Balkans and Asia Minor.   Map 152

P. eroides   Frivaldsky 1835   TL: Balkans   **Pl. 20**
Description. ♂fw 15/18mm, ups gleaming sky blue with *black marginal borders about 2mm wide*; uph with round antemarginal spots against dark border in s1c–s5; uns closely resembles *P. icarus*. ♀ups brown with slightly grey tint, without blue suffusion, orange submarginal lunules variable; uns gc brown, markings as in ♂.
Flight. End June/July in a single brood.
Habitat. Mountainous country at 1200–1800m.
Distribution. E. Prussia, Czechoslovakia, N. Poland and Balkans in Bulgaria (Pirin Mts.), Albania and S. Greece (Peloponessos).
Similar species. *P. eros* below.

POLYOMMATUS EROS   *Eros Blue*
Range. Pyrenees, Alps and Apennines to C. Asia.   Map 153

P. eros   Ochsenheimer 1808   TL: Alps of Tirol etc.   **Pl. 20**
Description. ♂fw 13/14mm, ups pale shining blue with *black marginal borders wide*; uns resembles *P. icarus* closely, unh with blue basal suffusion darker. ♀ups medium brown, often with light-blue basal suffusion; submarginal orange lunules and antemarginal dark spots very variable, rarely well developed; uns gc grey-brown with markings as in ♂, blue basal suffusion reduced.
Flight. July/August in a single brood.
Habitat. Mountains, on grass slopes at 1500–2400m, usually at alpine levels in Pyrenees and Alps, but from 1200m in Apennines. Larval food plants Leguminosae including *Oxytropis* and *Astragalus*.
Distribution. France on the higher mountains of Cantal (Mont Ventoux) etc., Pyrenees and from Maritime Alps eastwards through the Alps to the Grosser Glockner. In Spain, only in Catalonia. Local on the Apennines from 1200m upwards. Occasionally recorded from the Balkans (Trebevic etc.). Absent from the Carpathians. In S. Greece, *P. eros menelaos* Brown 1976, larger, ♂fw 14/17mm, markings as in *P. e. eros*. Flies in late June/July on the Taygetos, Mts. from 1200m upwards.
Similar species. *P. eroides* above; *P. icarus* p. 92.

RIODINIDAE

Grote 1895

Closely related to the Lycaenidae, but differing in important respects; male fore-leg greatly reduced, useless for walking. An extensive family which reaches its maximum development in the American tropics. In the Old World it is represented by a few genera in tropical Asia and Africa, and in Europe by a single species.

HAMEARIS LUCINA   *Duke of Burgundy Fritillary*
Range. From C. Spain widely distributed through S. and C. Europe to C. Russia. Map 154

H. lucina   Linnaeus 1758   TL: England (Verity 1943)   **Pl. 24 ♀; Pl. 31 ♂**
Description. ♂fw 14/17mm, ups gc dark brown to black with small fulvous spots arranged in transverse series, well-marked on fw, on hw sometimes nearly obliterated by extension of dark gc; unf cinnamon-brown, basal markings as on ups; unh discal band and marginal area cinnamon-brown, *basal and pd spots white in transverse series.* ♀ similar.
Flight. May and August in two broods in southern range, a single brood in May/June in north.
Habitat. A lowland species, usually in woodland clearings, rarely to 1200m. Larval food plants cowslips and primroses.
Distribution. Throughout C. Europe to 60°N, including England, S. Sweden and Baltic countries, but local. Spain, local, from Guadarrama northwards. Rare in Italy except on southern Alpine slopes. Balkans and N. Greece. Absent from S. Spain, Ireland and Mediterranean islands excepting Sicily.
Variation. Northern races are small, ♂fw 13/14mm; southern races often larger, especially in N. Italy with ♂fw 16/17mm, f. *praestans* Verity Pl. 24. In *second brood* often with extended dark markings f. *schwingenschussi* Rebel Pl. 31.

LIBYTHEIDAE

Boisduval 1840

Rather small butterflies allied to the *Nymphalidae*, recognisable by the prominent tooth on the outer margin of the fore-wing, and by the great length of the palpi. They are migrants, and although the total number of species is small, they have become established on every continent and often occur on remote islands.

LIBYTHEA CELTIS *Nettle-tree Butterfly*

Range. From S. Europe and N. Africa through Asia Minor and Siberia to Chitral, Formosa and Japan. Map 155

L. celtis Laicharting 1782 TL: Bolzano, S. Tirol **Pl. 32**
Description. Palpi project nearly four times the length of the head. ♂fw 17/22mm, ups dark brown with orange-brown markings; upf a small white subapical mark on costa; unh neutral brown or grey with darker stripe along median vein, white mark often present at base of v4. ♀ similar. Markings are very constant.
Flight. June or later until hibernation, hibernated examples again in March/April. A notable migrant species.
Habitat. Low altitudes to 500m near trees of *Celtis australis*, the larval food plant, but in late summer vagrants occur at much higher altitudes.
Distribution. Spain, S. France from Pyrenees to Basses Alpes, occasionally in Haute Provence. Corsica and Sardinia. Italy. Sicily, Austria, Hungary, Slovakia, Yugoslavia, Greece and Algeria.
Note. The butterflies disappear into a long hibernation in August/September until the following March/April, when they fly again and eggs are laid, which produce the single annual brood.

NYMPHALIDAE

Swainson 1827

This large family contains many of the best known European butterflies, such as the Tortoiseshells and Purple Emperor. They are conspicuously coloured and often common. In both sexes the fore-legs are small, densely hairy ('brush-footed'), useless for walking, the middle and hind legs normal.

CHARAXES JASIUS   *Two-tailed Pasha*
Range. From Mediterranean coastal districts across Abyssinia (*C. j. epijasius* Reiche) and into equatorial Africa as *C. jasius saturnus* Butler.   Map 156

C. jasius   Linnaeus 1766   TL: Barbaria (Algeria)   **Pls. 23, 25**
Description. ♂fw 38/41mm, ups rich dark brown; upf with wide yellow-brown marginal border and vestigial pd spots; uph, marginal border continued, edged black, blue proximal spots in s1c–s4; uns basal area with elaborate pattern of spots and stripes outlined in white. ♀ similar, larger.
Flight. May/June and August/September in two broods.
Habitat. From sea-level to 500m. Larval food plant *Arbutus*.
Distribution. Mediterranean coastal districts from Greece westwards, including the larger islands. France, penetrates to Lozère, Cevennes, E. Pyrenees, not common. Italy, abundant locally on western coast, absent from Adriatic coast. Spain and Portugal, local in March and October in coastal areas. Balearic Is. N. Africa, local and uncommon near coasts in Morocco and Algeria; more common in Tunisia.

APATURA IRIS   *Purple Emperor*
Range. W. Europe and across temperate Asia to China.   Map 157

A. iris   Linnaeus 1758   TL: Germany, England   **Pl. 25**
Description. ♂fw 31/37mm, outer margin rounded at v6; tip of antenna black; ups gc almost black, flushed brilliant iridescent blue; upf discal and pd spots white, *black spot in s2 obscure*; uph oblique discal band white; uns brightly variegated with chestnut-brown, olive grey, etc.; unf pd fulvous mark enclosing a blue-pupilled ocellus in s2; unh *white discal band with straight inner edge*, tapering towards anal angle. ♀ larger, ups without blue flush and white markings larger.
Flight. July/August in a single brood.
Habitat. Flies around tree-tops in old-established woodlands from sea level to 900m. Larval food plants willow and sallow, esp. *Salix caprea*, also *S. aurita* and *S. cinerea*.
Distribution. N. Portugal. Spain in Guadarrama and Cantabrian Mts. From Basses Pyrénées across C. Europe, including S. England, Denmark and Baltic countries to 60 N including NW Greece. Migrant in Finland. Absent from Scandinavia and from much of southern Europe, including peninsular Italy.
Variation. In a rare but recurrent form, ups white markings are nearly or quite absent, f. *iole* Denis and Schiffermüller.
Similar species. *A. ilia* below.

96

APATURA ILIA   *Lesser Purple Emperor*
Range. From C. and S. Europe to the Ural Mts. and again in E. Asia.   Map 158.

A. ilia ilia   Denis and Schiffermüller 1775   TL: Vienna   **Pl. 25**
Description. ♂fw 32/35mm, resembles *A. iris* with similar blue flush on ups in males; outer margin of fw with blunt angle at v6; apex of antenna brown; upf discal markings white, a *well-defined pd orange-ringed spot in s2*; uph discal band white; unh inner margin of dull discal band not straight, a small dark spot present at base of cell. ♀ larger, pale markings larger. In nearly all localities and in both sexes dimorphic, upperside pale markings often yellow-brown (f. *clytie* Denis and Schiffermüller), but apical spots on fore-wing remain white. Extent of brown marking is variable, sometimes suffused over whole upperside. One or other colour may preponderate in a given colony, f. *clytie* is rare in C. Italy, Spain and Portugal.
Flight. May/June and August/September in two broods in southern localities; a single brood in July in northern range. No seasonal variation has been reported.
Habitat. Light woodland at moderate altitudes. Larval food plants willows, poplar, etc., esp. *P. tremula* and *P. nigra*.
Distribution. Portugal; Geres. N. Spain, France; widely distributed from Pyrenees to Jura and Vosges. Belgium. Switzerland, rare in south. Germany to Romania. Absent from NW. Europe, England and Mediterranean islands.

A. ilia barcina   Verity 1927   TL: Antoni de Vilamajor, Catalonia   **Pl. 22**
Description. ♂ like *A. i. ilia* but ups differs slightly in more complete white markings; upf white spot present in s1a and sometimes with obscure pale submarginal spots; uph white discal band wide at costa, outer edge straight, band tapering, directed to inner margin, pale submarginal spots often well defined; uns gc sandy-buff, markings white as on ups. ♀ larger, ups gc brown, white markings slightly larger, blue flush absent. Form *clytie* occurs rarely.
Flight and **Habitat** as for *A. i. ilia*.
Distribution. Catalonia, NE. Spain, esp. in Province of Barcelona. In C. Italy somewhat similar.
Similar species. *A. iris* p. 96, in which upf black spot in s2 is usually obscured by dark ground-colour.

APATURA METIS   *Freyer's Purple Emperor*
Range. SE. Europe including N. Greece and in China, Korea and Japan.   Map 159

A. metis metis   Freyer 1829   TL: Pecs (Fünfkirchen), Hungary
                                                        Pl. 22 ♀; Pl. 25 ♂
Description. Like *A. ilia* f. *clytie*, the dark nominate form figured by Freyer is extremely rare in Europe. ♂fw 30/32mm, upf orange submarginal band enlarged in spaces 5, 6, 7; pd dark spot in s2 small; uph the rounded pd spots almost always well defined in *A. ilia* are represented in *A. metis* by a dark band enclosing an orange spot in s2 which often has a small, dark pupil, and a second smaller orange spot in s3.
Flight and **Habitat** as for *A. ilia*. European larval food plants include a narrow-leaved *Salix* not identified; in Japan several species of *Salix* and *Populus* are acceptable.
Distribution. Austria, Hungary, Bulgaria.

LIMENITIS POPULI *Poplar Admiral*

Range. From C. Europe through C. Asia to Japan.   Map 160

L. populi   Linnaeus 1758   TL: Sweden (Verity 1950)   **Pl. 25**
Description. ♂fw 35/40mm, ups dark grey-brown with white spots, often indistinct, in cell and in pd areas, and with *orange-red and black submarginal spots*; uns *gc orange*, all markings better defined in white or blue-grey; unh with double row of dark pd spots. ♀ often larger, ups white markings much larger, uph with prominent white discal band.
Flight. June/July.
Habitat. Open woodland, from sea-level to 1000m. Larval food plants aspen and other kinds of poplar.
Distribution. C. Europe to 66°N, often common. In SE France, rare or occasional in Drôme and Vaucluse, also in Macedonia and Bulgaria. Absent from W. France, Pyrenees, Spain, Portugal, Britain, peninsular Italy and Greece.
Variation. Absence in ♂ of white markings on upf (except three apical spots), common in some localities, f. *tremulae* Esper.

LIMENITIS REDUCTA *Southern White Admiral*

Range. From S. and C. Europe across W. Asia to Syria, Caucasus and Iran.   Map 161

L. reducta schiffermuelleri   Higgins 1932   TL: Carniola   **Pl. 26**
  syn: *rivularis* auct. *anonyma* Lewis 1872 (rejected by I.C.Z.N., Opinion 562) *camilla* auct.
Description. ♂fw 23/27mm, ups gc blue-black, a submarginal series of small black spots edged blue on both wings; upf a prominent white spot in cell; uns gc reddish-brown; unh pale grey basal band and broad white central band followed by *single row of dark pd spots*. ♀ similar.
Flight. May or later in two or three broods in S. Europe, a single brood in July in N. Switzerland.
Habitat. Light woodland or bushy places, from lowlands to tree-line. Larval food plant honeysuckle (*Lonicera*).
Distribution. All S. Europe to 50°N. Rare in N. and W. France. Absent from Crete.
Similar species. *L. camilla* below, unh with double row of dark pd spots.

LIMENITIS CAMILLA *White Admiral*

Range. C. Europe and across Russia and C. Asia to China and Japan.   Map 162

L. camilla   Linnaeus 1763   TL: Germany   **Pl. 26**
  syn: *sibilla* Linnaeus 1767
Description. ♂fw 26/30mm, white cell-spot faint or absent; uns markings varied blue-grey, white and tawny-brown; unh pd area tawny-brown with *double series of small black spots*; base and inner margin light grey. ♀ similar.
Flight. June/July.
Habitat. Flies in woodland from lowlands to 900m. Larval food plant honeysuckle (*Lonicera*).
Distribution. C. Europe to 56°N, including S. England and S. Sweden. Very local in N. Spain and N. Portugal. Italy in Apennines south to 42°N. Absent from SE. France, S. Italy and Mediterranean islands.
Similar species. *L. reducta* above.

NEPTIS SAPPHO *Common Glider*
Range. E. Europe, from Salzburg across Russia and C. Asia to Japan. Map 163

N. sappho Pallas 1771 TL: Volga, S. Russia **Pl. 26**
  syn: *aceris* Esper 1783; *hylas* auct.
Description. ♂ and ♀fw 22/24mm, upf a narrow white stripe through cell with triangular mark beyond, both clearly marked; *uph discal and pd white bands present*; unh cinnamon red, broken pd band wider.
Flight. May/June and July/September.
Habitat. A lowland species flying in woodlands. Larval food plant *Lathyrus verna* (vetchling).
Distribution. E. Europe, esp. S. Hungary, N. Yugoslavia (Croatia) and Romania, but extending westwards to Salzburg and Gorizia; N. Greece.
Similar species. *N. rivularis* below, uph with single white transverse band.
Note. *N. sappho* is commonly associated with Fenton's Wood White, *Leptidea morsei*, which has a similar distribution and the same food plant in W. Europe.

NEPTIS RIVULARIS *Hungarian Glider*
Range. From Piedmont in scattered colonies through Russia to C. Asia and Japan. Map 164

N. rivularis Scopoli 1763 TL: Graz, Austria **Pl. 26**
  syn: *lucilla* Schiffermüller 1775
Description. ♂ and ♀fw 25/27mm, upf white stripe in cell vestigial; uph *a single oblique white discal band* crossed by black veins; uns cinnamon-brown, unh sometimes with traces of submarginal lunules.
Flight. June/early July.
Habitat. Light woodland, lowlands to 900m. Larval food plants *Spiraea*.
Distribution. From Salzburg through Danube countries to Balkans and Bulgaria; S. Alps from Piedmont (Susa) in scattered colonies in southern alpine valleys, eastwards to NW. Yugoslavia (Gradisca).
Similar species. *N. sappho* above.

NYMPHALIS ANTIOPA *Camberwell Beauty*
Range. From W. Europe across temperate Asia and N. America. Map 165

N. antiopa Linnaeus 1758 TL: Sweden (Verity 1950) **Pl. 27**
Description. ♂fw 30/34mm, ups dark purple with wide cream-yellow marginal borders (white after hibernation), preceded by small blue spots. ♀ similar.
Flight. June/July or later and again in spring after hibernation.
Habitat. Open country but generally among hills or mountains. Larval food plants forest trees, willows, birch, etc.
Distribution. Europe, rarely common, most frequent in south but ranges north through Fennoscandia to North Cape. Occurs in Britain as a rare vagrant. Absent from S. Spain and Mediterranean islands.
Variation. In spite of the vast range of this species, geographical variation is practically non-existent.

NYMPHALIS POLYCHLOROS *Large Tortoiseshell*
Range. From N. Africa across S. and C. Europe and Asia Minor to the Himalayas. Map 166

N. polychloros polychloros   Linnaeus 1758   TL: Sweden (Verity 1950)   **Pl. 27**
Description. ♂fw 25/32mm, ups orange-brown with black markings and dark marginal borders enclosing pale lunules; uph with blue lunules internal to dark border; uns basal areas brown to blue-black, pd areas paler. ♀ similar. In both sexes *hair covering palpi and legs very dark brown or black*.
Flight. A single brood in June/July with long flight period, flying again in spring after hibernation.
Habitat. Light woodland, lowlands to 1500m. Larval food plants elms, willows and other trees.
Distribution. W. Europe, including southern Fennoscandia, S. England and Mediterranean islands. Absent from Ireland.

N. polychloros erythromelas   Austaut 1885   TL: Nemours, Algeria
Description. Size and markings as in *N. p. polychloros*; ups gc bright fulvous-red; uns very dark, basal areas and marginal borders generally black.
Flight and **Habitat** as in *polychloros*; recorded by Oberthur in August.
Distribution. Morocco, Algeria, Tunisia, mostly in Atlas Mts, flying at 1500–1800m.
Similar species. *N. xanthomelas* below, hair covering middle and hind-legs dull buff; does not occur in W. Europe.

NYMPHALIS XANTHOMELAS   *Yellow-legged Tortoiseshell*
Range. E. Europe and through C. Asia to China and Japan.   Map 167

N. xanthomelas   Denis and Schiffermüller 1775   TL: Vienna   **Pl. 27**
Description. ♂fw 30/32mm, like *N. polychloros*; marginal angles slightly more pronounced; ups orange-brown; uph black border before blue marginal lunules slightly wider with inner margin less well defined. ♀ similar. In both sexes *legs and often palpi are dull brown or buff*.
Flight. July/September in a single brood and again in spring after hibernation.
Habitat. A lowland species in E. Europe flying usually near willow trees in which the silken larval nests are conspicuous. Larval food plants willows, more rarely other forest trees.
Distribution. Romania, Bulgaria, N. Yugoslavia, Hungary, Poland, E. Germany, Czechoslovakia, Lower Austria and Baltic countries, but rare in its western range. Occasional records, probably of vagrant specimens, from Sweden, Finland, Denmark, Greece, etc.
Similar species. *N. polychloros* above.

NYMPHALIS VAU-ALBUM   *False Comma*
Range. From E. Europe across temperate Asia to China and Japan; also in S. Canada and northern United States, where it is known as *N, j-album* Boisduval and Leconte.   Map 168

N. vau-album   Denis and Schiffermüller 1775   TL: Vienna   **Pl. 27**
syn: *N. l-album* Esper 1781
Description. ♂fw 30/33mm, ups resembles *N. polychloros* but *with prominent white costal marks near apex of fw and on hw*; uns usually yellow-brown with darker marbling; unh a small j-shaped white mark at cell-end. ♀ similar, uns pale markings predominantly grey.
Flight. July/September and again in spring after hibernation.

Habitat. A lowland species, most often in flowery meadows bordering woodland. Larval food plants forest trees, elm, beech, poplar, sallow, etc.
Distribution. Rare and local in E. Europe, most frequent in Romania, esp. Retezat Mts. and Banat, also Bulgaria. Reported occasionally from other Danube countries westwards to 16°E and from S. Finland, Sweden and Baltic countries; probably vagrants.
Similar species. *N. polychloros* p. 99 and *N. xathomelas* p. 100, both lacking the white costal mark on uph.

INACHIS IO *Peacock Butterfly*

Range. From W. Europe through temperate Asia to Japan. Map 169

I. io Linnaeus 1758 TL: Sweden (Verity 1950) **Pl. 27**
Description. ♂fw 27/29mm, size variable; ups chocolate-brown with *'peacock eye' ocellate marks on each wing*, impossible to confuse with any other butterfly. ♀ similar, slightly larger.
Flight. July or later and again in spring after hibernation.
Habitat. Flowery banks and gardens from lowlands to 1800m. Larval food plant nettle, more rarely other low plants.
Distribution. W. Europe to 60°N, including all the larger islands of the Mediterranean. Absent from Crete, S. Greece and N. Africa.

VANESSA ATALANTA *Red Admiral*

Range. Azores, Canary Islands, N. Africa and through Europe and Asia Minor to Iran. N. America to Guatemala. Haiti and New Zealand (probably introduced). Map 170

V. atalanta Linnaeus 1758 TL: Sweden (Verity 1950) **Pl. 27**
Description. ♂fw 28/31mm, ups black; upf with *unbroken red band across cell to anal angle* and white apical markings; uph red marginal border in s2–5; unh dark brown with confused markings. ♀ similar.
Flight. May to October; in S. Europe hibernated specimens appear in spring.
Habitat. Flowery banks, gardens, etc., from lowlands to 1800m. Larval food plants nettle (*Urtica*); more rarely thistles.
Distribution. Throughout W. Europe to 62°N, more rarely to Arctic Circle probably on migration. Morocco, Algeria, Tunisia. Canary Islands. Azores.
Note. North of the Alps, and in England, survival of hibernating specimens through winter is probably extremely rare. The abundant second brood in England in late summer is due to the arrival in spring of immigrants from S. Europe or N. Africa.
Similar species. *V. indica* below.

VANESSA INDICA *Indian Red Admiral*

Range. Canary Islands and Madeira; India (TL of *Papilio indica* Herbst 1794), China, Japan and Korea. No map

V. indica calliroe Hübner 1808 TL: Canary Islands (Kirby 1904)
  syn: *vulcania* Godart 1819; *occidentalis* Felder 1862; *callirhoe* Millière 1867
Description. ♂fw 27/29mm, like *V. atalanta*; upf *red band wider*, its lower border *broken by black gc*; unh dark with confused cryptic markings. ♀ similar.
Flight. May/June or later in a succession of broods.
Habitat. Flowery banks, woodland borders, etc. Larval food plants not recorded.

Distribution. Madeira. Canary Islands, widely distributed and often common, probably absent from Fuerteventura and Lanzarote. Absent from the Azores.
Similar species. *V. atalanta* above, upf red band narrower, unbroken.
Note. *V. indica* is not known from any locality between the Canary Islands and India. In the western *calliroe* on ups, the red markings are bright carmine and the short band of three white spots runs from the costa at a right angle. In the oriental *indica*, the red markings tend to buff and the white costal band is oblique. Confusion about the name of this taxon arose because Hübner gave 'China' as the locality for the specimen he figured, whereas it must have come from the Canary Islands or from Madeira.

CYNTHIA CARDUI *Painted Lady*
Range. Cosmopolitan, except S. America.   Map 171

C. cardui   Linnaeus 1758   TL: Sweden (Verity 1950)   **Pl. 27**
Description. ♂fw 27/29mm, ups rosy-buff; upf with small white spots at apex but not in s2; uph small black pd spots in s2–6 without pupils; unh pd area slightly darker than basal and discal areas and enclosing *five rather small ocelli*. ♀ similar.
Flight. In S. Europe from April onwards, may fly in any month in Africa. In N. Europe, including Britain, immigrants appear in May–June, followed by a new brood in summer.
Habitat. Flowery banks and mountain sides from lowlands to 1800m or more. Larval food plants thistles and nettles, rarely other plants.
Distribution. In Britain and in much of Europe only as an immigrant, rare in Ireland; has been recorded from Iceland.
Similar species. *C. virginiensis* below, unh pd ocelli in s2 and s5 very large.

CYNTHIA VIRGINIENSIS *American Painted Lady*
Range. Canary Islands and Madeira; throughout temperate N. America to Guatemala and Cuba.   No map

C. virginiensis   Drury 1773   TL: New York   **Pl. 27**
    syn: *huntera* Fabricius 1775
Description. ♂fw 20/25mm, size variable; ups resembles *V. cardui* but gc is orange-buff without rosy flush; upf white spot present in s2; uph pd spots in s2 and s5 enlarged to blue-pupilled ocelli; *unh pd ocelli in s2 and s5 very large* in well-defined darker pd band. ♀ similar.
Flight. June or later.
Habitat. Flowery places, generally in mountains. Larval food plants various Compositae, in America esp. *Gnaphalium* species.
Distribution. Canary Islands; Gran Canary, Gomera, La Palma, Tenerife. Rare vagrants occasional in SW. Europe, especially in Portugal.
Similar species. *C. cardui* above.

AGLAIS URTICAE *Small Tortoiseshell*
Range. From W. Europe across Russia and Asia to Pacific coast.   Map 172

A. urticae urticae   Linnaeus 1758   TL: Sweden (Verity 1950)   **Pl. 27**
Description. ♂fw 22/25mm, ups gc red with black markings; upf with small black

pd spots in s2 and 3; *uph basal area black*; unh basal area dark brown, pd area paler with dark marginal border. ♀ similar, slightly larger.
Flight. May or later in one or more broods; a single brood in N. Europe; hibernated specimens often appear in March/April.
Habitat. Flowery places from sea-level to 2100m, frequent as a migrant on high mountains. Larval food plant nettles.
Distribution. All W. Europe to North Cape; absent from N. Africa and Atlantic islands.

A. urticae ichnusa Hübner 1824 TL: not stated   **Pl. 27**
Description. Resembles *A. u. urticae* but ups gc is brighter red and upf black spots in s2 and 3 are absent or obsolescent.
Flight and **Habitat** as for *A. u. urticae*.
Distribution. Corsica and Sardinia with characters constant.
Similar species. *N. polychloros* p. 99, uph base fulvous, with black costal mark.

POLYGONIA C-ALBUM *Comma Butterfly*
Range. From N. Africa across Europe to China and Japan.   Map 173

P. c-album Linnaeus 1758 TL: Sweden (Verity 1950)   **Pl. 26**
Description. ♂fw 22/24mm, ups orange-brown with darker markings; unh c-mark at cell-end. *First brood* (f. *hutchinsoni*) markings and uns marbling very bright in ♂ and ♀. *Second brood* markings duller; ♀unh very dark brown, markings obscure, with marked greenish tints.
Flight. June and end July/August in two broods; hibernated specimens fly in March/April.
Habitat. Flowery meadows, margins of woodland, gardens, etc, from lowlands to 1800m. Larval food plants nettles, willow, hop and various trees.
Distribution. W. Europe to 66°N, including larger Mediterranean islands. N. Africa; Morocco, Algeria, Tunisia, not uncommon in Atlas Mts. Absent from Balearic Islands and Crete.
Similar species. *P. egea* below.

POLYGONIA EGEA *Southern Comma*
Range. Provence and across S. Europe, Syria and Asia Minor to Iran.   Map 174

P. egea Cramer 1775 TL: Istanbul and Izmir   **Pl. 26**
Description. ♂fw 22/23mm; *first brood* ups yellow-brown with small darker brown markings; uns confused brown markings on yellow ground, with bands of minute dark striae in pd areas; unh a small white y-mark on discoidal vein. ♀ similar. *Second brood* (f. *j-album* Esper) ups slightly darker, more fulvous brown with darker markings, uns darker, markings grey-brown.
Flight. May/June and August/September in two broods; again in spring after hibernation.
Habitat. Hot, dry stony valleys, around cliffs, etc., rarely above 1200m. Larval food plant principally pellitory (*Parietaria*), more rarely nettles and various trees.
Distribution. Widely distributed in SE. France and in Italy. Common in SE. Europe to 46°N including Mediterranean islands, but absent from N. Africa, Portugal and Spain with Balearic Islands.
Similar species. *P. c-album* above, unh with white c-mark at cell-end.

ARASCHNIA LEVANA   *Map Butterfly*
Range. From Portugal and Spain across Europe and Asia to Japan.   Map 175

A. levana   Linnaeus 1758   TL: Germany   **Pl. 26**
Description. ♂fw 16/19mm; *first brood* (f. *levana* Linnaeus) ups yellow-brown with irregular black markings; upf yellow pd mark on costa and small white pd spots in s2–4 and at apex; unh dark red-brown with confused markings, white veins and cross-lines. ♀ similar. *Second brood* (f. *prorsa* Linnaeus) ups black, discal bands pale yellow or white, broken on upf at v4; uns as in f. *levana*; ♀ similar.
Flight. May/early June and August/September; first brood flies in April in some districts and a third brood may occur, partly overlapping.
Habitat. Light woodland from lowlands to 900m. Food plant nettles. The larvae live gregariously.
Distribution. C. and E. Europe to Baltic coast. France, common in N. and C. districts southwards to Pyrenees. Very local but extending its range in N. Spain and N. Portugal; in C. Europe generally distributed north of the Alps, but rare in Switzerland and in N. Balkans. Absent from Britain, SE. France, Italy and S. Balkans.
Variation. Forms intermediate between *levana* and *prorsa* are not uncommon.

PANDORIANA PANDORA   *Cardinal*
Range. From Canary Islands, through N. Africa, S. Europe and S. Russia to Iran and Chitral.   Map 176

P. pandora   Denis and Schiffermüller 1775   TL: Vienna   **Pl. 29**
   syn: *maja* Cramer 1776
Description. ♂fw 32/40mm, ups fulvous, more or less shaded with greenish-grey suffusion; upf sex-brands along v2 and 3 prominent; unf *discal area rose-red, apex green*; unh green with irregular sub-basal and narrow pd silver stripes and small white pd dots. ♀ larger with increased green-grey suffusion; unh silver stripes and dots better defined.
Flight. June/July in Europe; N. Africa in May/June and August/September in two broods.
Habitat. Flowery meadows from lowlands to 1200m in Europe, to 1800m in N. Africa; visits thistles, flowering lime trees, etc. Larval food plants violets, esp. *V. tricolor*, rarely rue.
Distribution. S. France, extending northwards in Atlantic coastal districts to Morbihan. Italy and Sicily, becoming rare along southern slopes of Alps. Corsica and Sardinia. Spain and Portugal, common in mountains. More widely distributed in E. Europe from Greece through Balkans to Austria, Hungary and Czechoslovakia. Common in Morocco, Algeria and Tunisia. Canary Islands, Tenerife, La Palma, Gomera; Balearic Islands and Crete.
Similar species. *A. paphia* below.

ARGYNNIS PAPHIA   *Silver-washed Fritillary*
Range. From W. Europe and Algeria across temperate Asia to Japan.   Map 177

A. paphia paphia   Linnaeus 1758   TL: Sweden (Verity 1950)   **Pl. 28**
Description. ♂fw 27/35mm, ups bright fulvous with black spots and striae; upf sex-brands conspicuous along v1–4; *unf pale fulvous-yellow*; unh greenish-grey with transverse silver discal and pd stripes, pd area mottled silver and lilac-grey with

darker markings. ♀ occurs in two forms: ♀ f. *paphia* Linnaeus, like ♂, but ups fulvous duller, black markings large; unh silver markings as in ♂. ♀ f. *valesina* Esper pl. 28, ups pale grey with extensive greenish suffusion; uns dark markings and silver stripes as in f. *paphia*; behaves genetically as a dominant to ♀ f. *paphia*.
Flight. End June to August.
Habitat. Flies in woodland clearings from lowlands to 1400m. Larval food plants mostly violets, rarely *Rubus idaeus* and other low plants.
Distribution. Europe to 63°N, Balkans and Greece. Absent from S. Spain, Morocco and Crete. The ♀ form *valesina* occurs sporadically, common in some localities, elsewhere absent as in Ireland or rare, e.g. in Britain.
Variation. In N. and C. Italy and in Spain, f. *anargyria* Staudinger, silver stripes on unh obsolescent, other markings unchanged.

A. paphia immaculata Bellier 1862   TL: Corsica   **Pl. 28**
Description. Resembles *A. p. paphia*; unh markings greatly reduced but with general gleaming golden suffusion; pd area slightly darker with spots larger and better defined. ♀ similar, f. *valesina* not uncommon.
Flight and **Habitat** as for *A. p. paphia*.
Distribution. Corsica, Sardinia, Elba, Giglio, replacing *A. p. paphia*. In Sicily, and elsewhere near the Mediterranean coast, forms of *paphia* transitional to *immaculata* have been reported.

A. paphia dives Oberthur 1908   TL: Lambessa, Algeria
Description. ♂fw 34/36mm, large, ups boldly marked; unh markings well defined, most often without silver stripes, which are replaced by greenish-buff, but variable. ♀ larger, fw to 40mm, variable, tendency to *valesina*-colour uncommon.
Flight. June/July.
Habitat. Wooded valleys at 1200–1500m.
Distribution. Algeria, in mountains near Lambessa, Djebel Aures, Kabylia, Khenchela, Sgag. Absent from Morocco.
Similar species. *P. pandora* p. 104, unf discal area rosy red.

ARGYRONOME LAODICE   *Pallas's Fritillary*
Range. From Baltic countries, Poland and Hungary across Asia to W. China and Japan.   Map 178

A. laodice Pallas 1771   TL: S. Russia   **Pl. 29**
Description. ♂fw 27/29mm, ups bright fulvous with bold black markings; upf with sex-brand on v1 and 2; unh basal half light olive-green with brown markings, separated sharply by white striae from lilac-brown pd area, without silver spots. ♀ups paler fulvous-yellow, upf with white subapical costal spot.
Flight. July/August.
Habitat. Flies in woodland clearings at lowland levels. Larval food plants violets, esp. *V. palustris*.
Distribution. SE. Finland, Lithuania, E. Poland, E. Prussia, NE. Slovakia, Hungary, Romania.

MESOACIDALIA AGLAJA   *Dark Green Fritillary*
Range. From W. Europe and Morocco across Asia to China and Japan.   Map 179

M. aglaja aglaja Linnaeus 1758   TL: Sweden (Verity 1950)   **Pl. 29**
   syn: *charlotta* Haworth 1802

Description. ♂fw 24/29mm, ups markings of usual Argynnid pattern; uph pd spot in s4 small; unh gc yellow-buff with green overlay, all spots silver, *pd series absent*. ♀ ups gc slightly paler.

Flight. June/July.

Habitat. Flowery meadows and heaths with violets, from lowlands to tree-line. Larval food plants violets; persicaria (*Polygonum*) also recorded.

Distribution. W. Europe from Mediterranean to North Cape, including British Isles. Absent from Crete and Mediterranean islands except Sicily.

Variation. Dark suffusion ups may be marked in some districts, e.g. Bavaria and Orkneys, esp. in ♀.

M. aglaja lyauteyi   Oberthur 1920   TL: Azrou, Morocco   **Pl. 29**

Description. ♂fw 30/33mm, large, ups gc paler yellow-buff with enlarged black markings; uns green suffusion more extensive and colour more intense, esp. over hw. ♀ups gc pale buff with greenish reflections, fw 35mm.

Flight. June/early July.

Habitat. Forest clearings at 1500–1800m.

Distribution. Morocco, in Middle Atlas; Azrou, Ain Leuh, Ifrane, etc. Not recorded from High Atlas, nor from Algeria.

Similar species. *F. niobe* p. 107; *F. adippe* below; in both unh submarginal spots, silver-pupilled, are distinctly separate from the large discal spots.

FABRICIANA ADIPPE *High Brown Fritillary*
Range. From N. Africa and W. Europe across temperate Asia to Japan.   Map 180

F. adippe adippe   Denis and Schiffermüller 1775   TL: Vienna   **Pl. 28**
   syn: *cydippe* Linnaeus 1761 (rejected name)

Description. ♂fw 25/31mm, ups bright fulvous; upf sex-brands on v2 and 3 thick; uph a fringe of long hair along v7; unh gc buff with darker shading and *reddish silver-pupilled pd spots*, small or absent in s4. ♀ similar, uph hair fringe along v7 absent. This subspecies occurs in two forms which may fly together: f. *adippe* Schiffermüller pl. 28, unh basal, discal and other spots brilliant silver; f. *cleodoxa* Ochsenheimer pl. 28, unh spots obscurely outlined against buff gc but without silver, except the pupils of pd series.

Flight. June/July in a single brood.

Habitat. Woodland clearings and meadows, from sea-level to tree-line, frequent in mountainous country. Larval food plant violets.

Distribution. All Europe except Arctic regions, Ireland, Spain (but see *F. a. chlorodippe* below), Portugal and the Mediterranean islands other than Sicily.

F. adippe chlorodippe   Herrich-Schäffer 1851   TL: Spain   **Pl. 28**

Description. ♂ups resembles *F. a. adippe*; uph hair fringe pronounced; unh gc olive-green, all spots fully silvered. ♀ similar, uph hair fringe absent.

Flight. June/early July.

Habitat. Flowery banks, woodland or heaths in mountains from 1000m.

Distribution. Portugal. Spain south of Pyrenees and Cantabrian Mts., often common.

Variation. Unh green restricted to basal suffusion, spots without silver except pd series, outlined in brown, f. *cleodippe* Staudinger Pl. 28.

   The relative abundance of the forms *adippe* (with silver spots on unh) and *cleodoxa* and *cleodippe* (without silver spots) varies greatly from place to place. In northern and north-eastern Europe f. *adippe* is common, and f. *cleodoxa*, extremely rare in Britain, Belgium and Denmark, is rare in Fennoscandia. In northern and central France, Germany, Austria and N. Switzerland f. *cleodoxa* is less rare but still uncommon. On the southern slopes of the Alps the position is reversed, f. *cleodoxa* often preponderating in S. Switzerland, N. Italy and along the chain of the Appenines. In Sicily f. *adippe* appears to be absent. In the Pyrenees f. *cleodoxa* is common, but in Spain f. *cleodippe* (also without silver spots) is rare, especially in S. Spain, and the silver-spotted f. *chlorodippe* much more common. In Hungary, Romania and the Balkans f. *cleodoxa* becomes progressively more common until in Greece it apparently replaces f. *adippe* entirely.

Similar species. *F. niobe* below, often smaller and unh cell usually includes small yellow spot with black central point, unh veins black near outer margin; upf ♂ sex-brands often thin. *M. aglaja* p. 105.

FABRICIANA NIOBE *Niobe Fritillary*
Range. From W. Europe through Russia and Asia Minor to Iran.   Map 181

F. niobe niobe Linnaeus 1758   TL: Sweden (Verity 1950)   **Pl. 59, Pl. 29**
Description. ♂fw 23/30mm, ups as in *F. adippe*; upf slender sex-brands along v2 and 3 in N. and C. Europe, often absent in SW.; uph black pd spot small in s4, small or absent in s6; unh often flushed green near base with or without silver spots. *The small yellow spot below median vein near base of cell generally enclosing a minute black point* and black-lined veins are important specific characters. ♀ups black markings often heavy and more or less suffused dark grey.
Flight. June/July.
Habitat. Meadows and subalpine pastures to tree-line. Larval food plants violets, more rarely plantains.
Distribution. W. Europe, esp. in mountains, to 62°N. Local or occasional in NW. France, absent from Britain, Corsica, Sardinia and Crete.
Variation. In C. and S. Spain upf sex-brands may be absent. In many districts the species occurs in two forms, that may fly together, similar to those of *F. adippe*: f. *niobe* Linnaeus pl. 29, unh basal, discal and other spots brilliant silver; f. *eris* Meigen pl. 29, unh spots without silver, but outlined in black or brown against pale buff gc. Intermediate specimens with spots partly filled with silver are not uncommon. In most localities f. *niobe* is uncommon or rare, far outnumbered by f. *eris*. Form *niobe* is more common in females than in males, probably more common at low altitudes than in mountains. Form *niobe* is more common than f. *eris* in parts of C. France (Auvergne) and in C. Italy (Abruzzi), and in these and doubtless in other localities it may form about 70% of the population. No series exclusively of f. *niobe* has been seen from any locality. South of the Pyrenees the population appears to consist entirely of f. *eris*, and this is the situation also in the Asiatic range.

F. niobe auresiana Fruhstorfer 1908   TL: Djebel Aures, Algeria   **Pl. 28**
    F. adippe auresiana auct.
Description. ♂ resembles *F. a. chlorodippe*; ups sex-brand absent; uph hair fringe sparse; unh gc deeper green, silver spots often small, sometimes obsolescent. ♀ similar.
Flight. June/early July.
Habitat. Open woodlands and heaths at 1500–1800m, common locally.
Distribution. Morocco. Algeria.

Variation. In High Atlas, flying at 2700m, small, ♂fw 25/26mm, f. *astrifera* Higgins. A *cleodippe*-like form has not been recorded from N. Africa.
Similar species. *F. adippe* p. 106; *M. aglaja* p. 105.

FABRICIANA ELISA *Corsican Fritillary*
Range. Confined to Corsica and Sardinia. Map 182

F. elisa Godart 1823 TL: Corsica and Sardinia **Pl. 29**
Description. ♂fw 23/26mm, ups gc bright fulvous, black markings mostly small, but upf pd spots well developed in s2, 3, 5 and 6, sex-brand absent; *unh spots all small and silver*, except pd row of white-pupilled brown spots. ♀ slightly larger, ups gc paler with somewhat reduced markings.
Flight. June/July.
Habitat. In light woodland and heathland areas from 900m upwards. Larval food plant violets.

ISSORIA LATHONIA *Queen of Spain Fritillary*
Range. W. Europe, N. Africa and Canary Islands, and across C. Asia to Himalayas and W. China. Map 183

I. lathonia Linnaeus 1758 TL: Sweden (Verity 1950) **Pl. 29**
Description. ♂fw 19/23mm, fw without sex-brand, outer margin concave below v5; hw angled at v8 and anal angle often produced; uph with grey basal suffusions; *unh silver spots mostly very large.* ♀ similar.
Flight. February/March or later, in two or three broods throughout summer in the south, single brooded at higher latitudes.
Habitat. In rough places and meadows from sea-level to 2100m or more. Larval food plant violets.
Distribution. N. Africa and S. Europe, thence northwards to 64°N or beyond, occasional in Britain but resident in S. Sweden. Canary Islands; Tenerife, La Palma, Gomera.
Note. The butterfly is a notable migrant. It is said to hibernate as an egg, larva or imago according to local conditions.

BRENTHIS HECATE *Twin-spot Fritillary*
Range. From SW. Europe to Russia, Asia Minor, Iran and C. Asia. Map 184

B. hecate Denis and Schiffermüller 1775 TL: Vienna **Pl. 30**
Description. ♂fw 18/22mm, ups pd and submarginal black spots in regular and complete series on both wings; unh veins lined dark brown on buff gc, basal marks and spots of discal band all outlined brown or black; *pd and submarginal series of black spots both complete*, double marginal lines distinct. ♀ similar, ups often suffused fuscous.
Flight. End May/June.
Habitat. Rough ground and open slopes from 600/1500m. Larval food plant *Filipendula vulgaris*.
Distribution. In S. France, very local to 46°N, esp. in Var and Alpes Maritimes etc. Spain, widely distributed among mountains. Italy, locally common in valley of the Po, local and rare in Peninsular Italy. More general in E. Europe, in Czechoslovakia, Hungary, Austria and southwards to the Balkans, Greece, usually in scattered colonies. Absent from Pyrenees, Portugal and Mediterranean islands.

Similar species. *B. daphne* below; *B. ino* below; both have a single row of small dark pd spots on unh.

BRENTHIS DAPHNE *Marbled Fritillary*

Range. SW. Europe through Russia and C. Asia to China and Japan. Map 185

B. daphne Denis and Schiffermüller 1775 TL: Vienna **Pl. 30**
Description. ♂fw 21/26mm, ups resembles *B. hecate*, upf spots of pd series uneven, small in s1 and s4, large in s2 and s3; unh veins and spots of discal band lined rather light brown against gc of yellow-buff, broad pd area marbled lilac-brown with markings rather obscure, *base of s4 mostly brown*. ♀ similar, ups gc paler.
Flight. June/early July.
Habitat. Warm valleys, rarely to 1200m, often visits flowers of bramble. Larval food plants violets and bramble.
Distribution. S. Europe to 46°N in west, farther east extending to Austria, Czechoslovakia and Hungary, common in Balkans and Greece. Absent from S. Spain, Portugal and Mediterranean islands except Sicily.
Similar species. *B. ino ino* below; *B. hecate* p. 108.

BRENTHIS INO *Lesser Marbled Fritillary*

Range. C. and N. Europe and through temperate Asia to N. China and Japan. Map 186

B. ino ino Rottemburg 1775 TL: Halle, Germany **Pl. 32**
  syn: *parsthenie* Bergsträsser.
Description. ♂fw 17/20mm, smaller than *B. daphne*, ups black markings more linear, black marginal borders generally entire and continuous; unh *base of s4 usually yellow-buff*, pd spots and ocelli irregular. ♀ similar, slightly larger, ups often suffused fuscous with violet sheen in fresh specimens.
Flight. June/July.
Habitat. In marshy meadows and damp places, lowlands to 1500m. Larval food plants principally meadowsweet, raspberry and great burnet.
Distribution. C. and N. Europe from Cantabrian Mts., Pyrenees and Alps to North Cape. Peninsular Italy, only in Calabria. Balkans, not rare, including Albania and Bulgaria. C. Spain, local in Teruel. Absent from Portugal, Britain and Mediterranean islands.
Similar species. *B. daphne* above, larger, unf black pd spots large in s2 and s3; unh base of s4 mostly brown. *B. hecate* p. 108.

BOLORIA PALES *Shepherd's Fritillary*

Range. Alpine levels from Cantabrian Mts. and Pyrenees, Alps, to C. Asia, W. Himalaya Mts. Map 187

B. pales pales Denis and Schiffermüller 1775 TL: Vienna **Pl. 33**
Description. ♂fw 17/19mm, ups gc bright fulvous; upf *discal markings macular (not linear)*; uph black basal suffusion includes cell; unf *black markings scanty*, shadowy; unh brightly variegated, basal and pd areas generally dark red, yellowish discal band not conspicuous, spot in s4 and marginal spots silver, a yellow area from margin in s3. ♀ upf gc sometimes paler.
Flight. July/August.

Habitat. From tree-line on mountains, flying over slopes of grass or *Vaccinium* to levels of 2400m or more. Larval food plant violets, esp. *V. calcarata.*
Distribution. E. Alps, Bavaria, N. Tirol and Dolomites, Austria, Tatra Mts. Carpathians and Julian Alps.

B. pales palustris Fruhstorfer 1909   TL: Zermatt, Switzerland   **Pl. 31**
Description. ♂fw 16/18mm, small, ups gc paler, yellowish; upf black discal markings thin; unh variable, sometimes nearly uniform red with obscure markings. ♀ generally similar, sometimes paler with slightly grey tint near wing-margins.
Flight and **Habitat** as for *B. p. pales.*
Distribution. S. Alps, from Alpes Maritimes to Ortler and Brenner. Apennines, local on a few high peaks, Gran Sasso, Monte Majella, etc. Balkans, on most high mountains, Rila and Pirin, Prenj, Durmitor and in Albania. North of Rhône valley less typical, often transitional to *B. p. pales.* Absent from Jura and Vosges.
Variation. At high levels in southern Alps often very small, upf markings linear, unh brightly coloured.
Similar species. *B. napaea* below, often larger, ups gc paler, upf markings more linear; ♀ ups more or less suffused grey. *B. graeca* p. 111, only in SW. Alps and Balkans; ups gc orange-yellow with macular black markings, unf black spots present, unh colours pale. *B. aquilonaris* p. 111, unf black spots well developed.

B. pales pyrenesmiscens Verity 1932   TL: Gèdre, Htes Pyrénées   **Pl. 31**
Description. ♂fw 18/20mm, ups gc orange-yellow with macular black markings; uph black basal suffusion less extensive, cell clear; unf *black markings variable,* generally small and scanty; unh markings not brilliant, yellowish, sometimes with distinctly greenish tints. ♀ups often paler, sometimes with slight general dusky suffusion.
Flight. End June/July.
Habitat. From 1500m upwards on grass slopes, etc.
Distribution. Pyrenees and Cantabrian Mts. on most higher slopes from Mt. Canigou to Picos de Europa, widely distributed on northern slopes of Pyrenees, more local on southern slopes.
Similar species. No similar species occurs in C. Pyrenees. In E. Pyrenees only *B. napaea* below occurs, very locally in the Cambre-d'Aze region.

BOLORIA NAPAEA *Mountain Fritillary*
Range. E. Pyrenees, Alps and Fennoscandia to North Cape, eastwards to Altai Mts. and Amurland, probably extending throughout arctic Asia; Alaska and Wyoming.   Map 188

B. napaea Hoffmannsegg 1804   TL: Alps of Tirol   **Pl. 31**
Description. ♂fw 17/21mm, resembles *B. pales; ups gc fulvous yellow or pale buff;* upf *black markings linear,* discal series composed of confluent striae; uph black basal suffusion extensive; *unf black markings greatly reduced or absent;* unh pale or sandy red and yellow with little contrast, but sometimes brighter and darker in eastern Alps. ♀ generally larger, ups more or less suffused grey, often with violet reflections; unh pale, tinted green near base.
Flight. July/August.
Habitat. Near or above tree-line in mountains, often in damp places, rarely above 1800m. Larval food plant alpine bistort (*Polygonum viviparum*).
Distribution. S. Alps from Alpes Maritimes to Hohe Tauern, often common. N. of

Rhône valley from Bernese Alps to Bavaria, Innsbruck, etc., more local, often scarce. E. Pyrenees on French and Spanish slopes, extremely local on Cambre d'Aze, Val d'Eyne, Carlitte, etc. Fennoscandia, widely distributed from Hardanger Fjeld at 60°N to North Cape, usually small, f. *frigida* Warren Pl. 31. Absent from Styrian Alps, Tatra, Carpathians and Balkans.
Similar species. *B. pales palustris* p. 110, in W. Alps has rather linear black markings on ups, but unh is more brightly coloured than in any form of *napaea* and the females are not suffused with grey. *B. pales pyrenesmiscens* p. 110, in E. Pyrenees is larger, black markings ups larger and more macular, unf with some black spots. *B. aquilonaris* below; *B. graeca* below.

BOLORIA AQUILONARIS   *Cranberry Fritillary*
Range. Fennoscandia and C. Europe on Vaccinium moors to Altai Mts. and Siberia.   Map 189

B. aquilonaris   Stichel 1908   TL: Gellivare, Sweden   **Pl. 31**
    syn: *arsilache* Knoch 1781 (invalid homonym).
Description. ♂fw 16/17mm; ups gc bright fulvous red; upf *black basal and discal spots prominent*, esp. in s1b, shaped like the letters V-V lying horizontally with apices joined; uph black basal suffusion covers cell; unf black spots well developed; unh gc sandy-red with darker areas, discal band not well defined, pd area red, usual yellow marginal mark in s3 small or absent; spot in s7, spots at apex of cell, in s1c near anal angle, and the six marginal spots all silver. ♀ often with slightly dusky suffusion.
Flight. June/early July.
Habitat. On bogs and in swampy places where larval food plant grows, from lowlands to 1800m depending upon latitude. Larval food plant cranberry (*Vaccinium oxycoccus*).
Distribution. Fennoscandia and Baltic countries to North Cape, usually common in suitable localities. More widely dispersed on *Vaccinium* bogs in Poland, Czechoslovakia, Austria, Germany (often common near Bavarian lakes), Jura, Vosges, Denmark, Belgium (in Ardennes) and France in the Massif Central. A few colonies are known at high altitudes in Switzerland, in Grisons and Engadin.
Variation. In Scandinavia small in arctic region; large with ♂fw 21mm or more in some localities in S. Sweden, Germany and France, f. *alethea* Hemming Pl. 31.
Similar species. *B. napaea* p. 110, ups black markings thin, linear, unf black markings absent. *B. pales* p. 109; *B. graeca* below.

BOLORIA GRAECA   *Balkan Fritillary*
Range. Confined to Balkans and SW. Alps.   Map 190

B. graeca graeca   Staudinger 1870   TL: Mt. Veluchi, Greece   **Pl. 31**
Description. ♂fw 18/20mm, hw anal angle slightly produced and margin more *sharply angled at v8* than in the other three species of *Boloria*; ups clear orange-fulvous; uph black suffusion does not include apex of cell; unf black spots small but *pattern over discal area complete*; unh yellowish with red and green marbling, discal band not well defined, silver spots present at cell-apex, in s7 and s1c, along outer margin and near costal angle, pd spots ocellate and prominent. ♀ups gc paler; unh greenish marbling more definite.
Flight. From first week of July.
Habitat. In subalpine meadows at altitudes of 1500m or over.

Distribution. C. and N. Greece on Mts. Smolikas, Perister, Parnassos and others near Drama and Florina. Absent from Peloponnesos.

B.graeca balcanica Rebel 1903   TL: Rila Mts., Bulgaria   **Pl. 31**
Description. ♂fw 16/17mm. Like *B. graeca* but smaller, unf black spots less prominent and unh ocellar pd spots well defined.
Distribution. This small form appears to replace *B. g. graeca* in most Balkan countries. It also appears in S. E. France (*B. b. tendensis* Higgins) on the Col di Tenda at 1500m and locally northwards. Above the Col another small form, probably *B. pales palustris* is present at about 2000m.
Flight. July at 1700m or more.
Similar species. *B. pales* p. 109; *B. napaea* p. 110, unf black markings greatly reduced; *B. aquilonaris* p. 111, gc bright reddish-fulvous with black markings heavy on both surfaces, not known from localities where *B. g. graeca* occurs.

PROCLOSSIANA EUNOMIA *Bog Fritillary*
Range. A few scattered colonies in W. Europe, Fennoscandia, Russia and Siberia to Amurland; in N. America from Labrador to Alaska and along Rocky Mts. to Colorado.   Map 191

P. eunomia eunomia Esper 1799   TL: Kaliningrad (Königsberg)   **Pl. 32**
  syn: *aphirape* Hübner 1799/1800
Description. ♂fw 20/23mm, ups gc clear fulvous yellow with neat markings; unh gc sandy-yellow, basal spots, discal band and marginal spots all gleaming yellow, subbasal and narrow pd bands fulvous, pd spots in form of *small black circles filled white or pale yellow*. ♀ups often with some fuscous suffusion.
Flight. June/early July.
Habitat. Wet meadows and marshy places from lowlands to 1500m. Larval food plant bistort (*Polygonum bistorta*), *Vaccinium*, etc.
Distribution. Very local in widely separated colonies. France, Vosges, E. Pyrenees. Belgium, Hertogenwald. Italy, only Alto Adige (Val Venosta). On moors and mosses in Germany. Austria and Czechoslovakia; not uncommon. Balkans, only Bulgaria.

P. eunomia ossiana Herbst 1800   TL: not stated   **Pl. 32**
Description. ♂fw 16/18mm, small, with dusky suffusion extending over ups; unh brightly marked, pale basal, discal and marginal spots white or gleaming silver.
Flight. End June/July.
Habitat. Rough moorlands and arctic bogs in lowlands.
Distribution. Fennoscandia, ups fuscous suffusion well marked from 65°N to North Cape, a common species on the tundra. Intermediate forms brightly marked on uns but without heavy dusky suffusion on ups, are common in S. Scandinavia and in Baltic countries.

CLOSSIANA EUPHROSYNE *Pearl-bordered Fritillary*
Range. From W. Europe across Asia to Amurland and Kamschatka.   Map 192

C. euphrosyne Linnaeus 1758   TL: Sweden (Verity 1950)   **Pl. 30**
Description. ♂fw 19/23mm, ups markings very like *C. selene*; unh sandy-red including basal area of cell, discal band yellow, but *central spot in s4*, basal spot in s1c and marginal spots are all *bright silver* and prominent. ♀ similar.

Flight. April/May and July/August in southern areas, second brood often scanty; a single brood in N. Europe and at high altitudes in south.
Habitat. In light woodland from lowlands to 1800m. Larval food plant principally *Viola*.
Distribution. Widely distributed throughout Europe to North Cape, including Britain, N. and C. Spain and Portugal. Very local in Ireland, absent from Mediterranean islands except Sicily.
Variation. The markings are constant over an enormous area. In high mountains and in northern range ups often slightly darker, ♀ with fuscous suffusion, f. *fingal* Herbst Pl. 30.
Similar species. *C. selene* p. 113, unh large round black spot in cell, all spots in discal band yellowish or silvery. *C. thore borealis* p. 115.

CLOSSIANA TITANIA   *Titania's Fritillary*
Range. From W. Europe, including the Alps and S. Finland to Kentei and Altai Mts. in Siberia. Also in N. America, across Canada from Quebec to Alaska, thence along Rockies to New Mexico.   Map 193

C. titania titania   Esper 1793   TL: 'Sardinia' (i.e. Piedmont)   **Pl. 30**
Description. ♂fw 21/23mm, ups clear orange-fulvous with delicate black markings; unh marbled brown or yellowish, the six ocellate pd spots often joined to *marginal series of long V-shaped chevrons*. ♀ larger, ups gc paler; unh paler, yellowish, sometimes with greenish tints.
Flight. End June/July.
Habitat. In light woodland or forest clearings at 1200–1500m. Larval food plants *Viola, Polygonum*.
Distribution. Italy, in Cottian Alps, esp. Crissolo, Oulz. France; Isère, Auvergne, esp. on Mt. Mézenc, Col de Mayrand, etc. Very similar in Baltic countries and S. Finland, *C. t. rossica* Hemming.

C. titania cypris   Meigen 1828   TL: Bavaria and Switzerland   **Pl. 30**
syn: *amathusia* Esper 1784 (invalid homonym)
Description. ♂fw 21/24mm, ups gc fiery fulvous with heavy black markings; unh marbled purple-brown, yellow, etc., discal band pale and uneven. ♀ larger, gc ups paler.
Flight and **Habitat** as for *C. t. titania*.
Distribution. Through central and southern Alps to Bavaria and Austria. Yugoslavia, more local, Trebević, Durmitor, Maklen Pass; Transsylvania.

CLOSSIANA SELENE   *Small Pearl-bordered Fritillary*
Range. From W. Europe eastwards across N. and C. Asia to Korea; widely distributed in N. America (*C. myrina* Cramer).   Map 194

C. selene   Denis and Schiffermüller 1775   TL: Vienna   **Pl. 30**
Description. ♂fw 18/21mm, closely resembles *C. euphrosyne*; ups gc orange-fulvous with few distinctive markings; uph round black spot usually present in cell; unh *yellow spot at cell base followed by round black spot*, gleaming metallic texture of discal band variable, sometimes absent, marginal spots yellow or silvered, pd spots dark, largest in s2 and s5. ♀ similar.
Flight. April/May and July/August in southern localities, the second brood often scanty; June/July in single brood in N. Europe and at high altitudes.

Habitat. Woodland margins or clearings from lowlands to 1800m. Larval food plant violets.
Distribution. Widely distributed throughout W. Europe, including all Fennoscandia, Britain, E. Pyrenees to Andorra; N. and W. Spain to Sierra de Guadarrama; N. Portugal. Absent from Htes and Basses Pyrénées, SE France, Ireland, peninsular Italy, Greece and Mediterranean islands.
Variation. Upperside colour tones may be darker with more extensive black markings in extreme north, f. *hela* Staudinger Pl. 20.
Similar species. *C. euphrosyne*; *C. thore* p. 115.

CLOSSIANA CHARICLEA *Arctic Fritillary*
Range. Arctic Europe, Greenland, boreal America, probably circumpolar.
Map 195

C. chariclea   Schneider 1794   TL: Lapland   **Pl. 32**
Description. ♂fw 16/18mm, ups gc fulvous with extensive black suffusion from wing-bases, esp. over hw; upf black discal markings fused into continuous band; unh gc red-brown with paler pd area, *discal band pale with spots prominent and mostly silvered*, small basal and marginal spots also silver. ♀ similar.
Flight. End June/July, depending upon weather.
Habitat. Dry tundra and hillsides at 300m or more, well above valley levels. Larval food plant unknown.
Distribution. Fennoscandia, not south of 68°N, esp. Porsanger, Kilpisjärvi, Enontekiö, etc. The species has been taken at 81°42′N, probably farther north than any other butterfly.
Similar species. *B. freija* below, which may fly with *C. chariclea*, lacks prominent pale discal band on unh.

CLOSSIANA FREIJA *Frejya's Fritillary*
Range. From Scandinavia and Baltic countries across N. Siberia to Japan, boreal N. America and locally in western mountains to Colorado.   Map 196

C. freija   Thunberg 1791   TL: Sweden   **Pl. 32**
Description. ♂fw 18/22mm, upf black discal spots united to form an irregular discal band; uph black basal suffusion extensive; unh marbled light and dark brown with white markings, including white spot at base of s1c, white marks on costa in s7 and at base of s4 and seven white marginal spots, *prominent dark zig-zag marks in s1b, 1c, 2 and 3*. ♀ similar.
Flight. May to June, depending much upon weather.
Habitat. Moors, mountain heaths and tundra. Larval foodplants cloudberry (*Rubus chamaemorus*) and bog bilberry (*Vaccinium uliginosum*).
Distribution. Fennoscandia from 60°N to North Cape, widely distributed but more local in SE. Finland; reported also from Estonia.
Similar species. *C. chariclea* above; *C. polaris* p. 115, unh with numerous white marks.

CLOSSIANA DIA *Weaver's Fritillary*
Map 197

C. dia   Linnaeus 1767   TL: Austria   **Pl. 32**
Description. ♂fw 16/17mm, margin of *hw sharply angled at v8*; ups black markings

large; unh gc violet-brown, discal band with prominent spots in s1c, s4, s7 and six marginal spots, all silver, *pd spots dark, prominent*. ♀ similar.
Flight. April/May and throughout summer in two or three broods.
Habitat. Light woodland, heaths, etc., from lowlands to 900m, frequent in hilly districts. Larval food plants *Viola, Rubus* and other low plants.
Distribution. Europe from France, Belgium, Holland, eastwards through Switzerland to Romania, Balkans and northern Greece; rare or occasional in N. Germany, Lithuania and Estonia; uncommon in S. Europe, but occurs in SW. Alps, E. Pyrenees, Cantabrian Mts. and Catalonia (Montseny). Absent from Britain and Mediterranean islands.

CLOSSIANA POLARIS *Polar Fritillary*
Range. Circumpolar, in boreal regions of Europe, Asia, Greenland and N. America. Map 198

C. polaris Boisduval 1828 TL: North Cape **Pl. 32**
Description. ♂fw 18/19mm, ups gc fulvous yellow; upf discal black spots fused into continuous irregular band; uph black suffusion covers basal and discal areas; unh mottled light and dark brown with *many small white marks in basal and discal areas*, white marks before each pd spot and seven white marginal marks. ♀ similar.
Flight. End June/July.
Habitat. On dry tundra and rough slopes above valley levels. Larval food plant possibly *Dryas octopetala*.
Distribution. Fennoscandia, not south of 68°N, esp. Petsamo, Maalselv, Pallastunturi, etc., very local and rare.
Similar species. *C. freija* p. 114.

CLOSSIANA THORE *Thor's Fritillary*
Range. From N. Europe and Alps through Russia and N. Asia to Japan mostly as *C. t. borealis* and nearly related forms. Map 199

C. thore thore Hübner 1803 TL: Alps of Tirol **Pl. 32**
Description. ♂fw 20/23mm, ups fulvous almost obscured by black suffusion, markings indistinct; uph pd spots and marginal border generally fused into a wide black marginal band; unh gc brown, *discal band dull yellow*, pd and marginal markings gleaming lead-coloured. ♀ larger, ups black suffusion less dense.
Flight. End June/July.
Habitat. Flies at 900–1500m, often near spruce woods. Larval food plant *Viola*.
Distribution. Restricted to Alps. Switzerland, local north of Rhône valley and in Graubünden. Germany, Bavarian and Allgäuer Alps. Austria, Arlberg, N. Tirol, Carinthia. Italy, Dolomites, esp. Canazei. E. Finland (f. *carelia* Valle).

C. thore borealis Staudinger 1861 TL: Lapland **Pl. 32**
Description. ♂fw 19/20mm, small, ups gc yellow-fulvous, only slightly clouded darker; uph pd spots large; unh light brown markings indistinct without metallic marginal markings. ♀ similar, often larger.
Flight. End June/July.
Habitat. At low levels in birch zone in hilly country.
Distribution. Scandinavia, in mountainous districts, not south of 62°N, Abisko, Altenfjord, Inari, Saltdalen.

Similar species. *C. euphrosyne* p. 112, unh markings distinct, discal spot in s4 silvered. *C. selene* p. 113, unh basal and discal markings silvered.

CLOSSIANA FRIGGA   *Frigga's Fritillary*

Range. From Scandinavia across N. Asia, including Altai and Tarbagatai Mts. N. America, widely distributed in Canada and extending through Rocky Mts. to Colorado.   Map 200

C. frigga   Thunberg 1791   TL: Lapland   **Pl. 32**
Description. ♂fw 20/23mm, ups gc orange-fulvous, black markings heavy and regular; uph with wide basal and discal black suffusions; unh gc red-brown, discal band pale with white spots in s1c, s4 and s7; pd area paler lilac-tinted, pd markings not well defined. ♀ larger.
Flight. End June/July.
Habitat. At low levels on wet bogs and moors in mountain valleys. Larval food plant cloudberry (*Rubus chamaemorus*).
Distribution. Fennoscandia, not south of 60°N, most frequent in far north, esp. Dalecarlia, Maalselvdal, Abisko, etc., locally common. Recorded from Estonia and Latvia.

CLOSSIANA IMPROBA   *Dusky-winged Fritillary*

Range. N. Europe, N. America from Labrador to Alaska, Novaya Zemlya. No records available from boreal Asia.   Map 201

C. improba   Butler 1877   TL: Arctic America   **Pl. 32**
Description. ♂fw 15/17mm, *ups yellow-grey, markings indistinct*, almost obliterated by fuscous suffusion; unh pale brown, discal band pale with white marks in s4 and s7 well defined, costa narrowly white. ♀ similar.
Flight. July.
Habitat. On dry mountain slopes and hill-tops from 400–1000m. Larval food plant unknown.
Distribution. Fennoscandia, not south of 66°N, Abisko, on Mt. Nuolja at 900–1100m, Altevand, N. of Kilpisjärvi at 400m.

MELITAEA CINXIA   *Glanville Fritillary*

Range. From W. Europe and Morocco through Russia and W. Asia to Amurland.   Map 202

M. cinxia cinxia   Linnaeus 1758   TL: Sweden (Verity 1950)   **Pl. 34**
Description. ♂fw *first brood* 16/20mm, *second brood* smaller; ups gc dull fulvous with complete black pattern; uph with a *black spot in each segment of sub-marginal band in s1c–s5*; unh yellow submarginal band with internal border of *proximally concave black lunules*, black marginal spots small. ♀ larger, ups black markings often heavier, sometimes with grey suffusion.
Flight. May/June and August/September in two broods in S. Europe; a single brood at high altitudes and in north.
Habitat. Flowery meadows from lowlands to 1800m or more. Larval food plants commonly plantain, more rarely hawkweed, knapweed (*Centaurea*), etc.
Distribution. S. and C. Europe, widely distributed to 60°N, flying at high altitudes in S. Alps. Local in N. and C. Spain, in S. Spain recorded from Murcia. Morocco

and Algeria, local in Middle Atlas at 1500–1800m. Absent from Britain except in Isle of Wight, and absent from Mediterranean islands except Sicily.
Variation. At high levels in the Dauphiné Alps some specimens are small, ups with gc pale and heavily marked, transitional to *M. c. atlantis*.

M. cinxia atlantis le Cerf 1928   TL: High Atlas, Morocco   **Pl. 34**
Description. ♂fw 17/19mm, ups gc pale yellow with heavy black markings. ♀ slightly larger.
Flight and **Habitat.** End June/early July, at altitudes of 2400m or more. A second brood is not recorded.
Distribution. Morocco in the High Atlas.
Similar species. *M. arduinna* below.

MELITAEA ARDUINNA   *Freyer's Fritillary*
Range. Extreme SE. Europe through S. Russia (TL of *Papilio arduinna* Esper 1784) and Asia Minor to Iran and central Asia.   Map 203

M. arduinna rhodopensis   Freyer 1836   TL: 'Turkey' (Macedonia)   **Pl. 34**
Description. ♂fw 21/23mm, like *M. cinxia* but larger, ups bright fulvous; unh orange marginal band with large black spots in each segment, its inner border formed of *black lunules, flat or outwardly concave*, in s1c–4; thin semilunes between veins at margin. ♀ larger, ups black markings heavier.
Flight. May/June, only a single brood recorded in Europe.
Habitat. In mountainous areas, flying in flowery places at 1200m or more. Larval food plant uncertain, perhaps *Centaurea*.
Distribution. Very local in SE. Europe. SE. Yugoslavia; Bitola, Katlanova, Selenokova. NW. Greece (Florina etc.). Bulgaria, Burgas. Romania, Tultscha.
Similar species. *M. cinxia* p. 116, smaller, fw narrower, unh black proximal lunules of orange marginal band concave inwardly.

MELITAEA PHOEBE   *Knapweed Fritillary*
Range. From Europe and N. Africa across C. Asia to N. China.   Map 204

M. phoebe phoebe   Denis and Schiffermüller 1775   TL: Vienna   **Pls. 24, 33**
Description. ♂fw *first brood* 20/24mm, *second brood* often smaller; ups gc generally bright fulvous with solid black margins; *upf marginal lunule in s3 much the largest*; uph orange submarginal band well defined, usually without enclosed black spots; unh each segment of yellow submarginal band enclosing a round red spot, a single row of orange marginal lunules, black marginal lunules joined to form a continuous wavy line. ♀ often larger.
Flight. End April or later and July or later in two or three broods at low levels, a single brood in July in mountains.
Habitat. Flowery meadows and slopes, lowlands to 1600m. Larval food plants knapweed (*Centaurea*), more rarely plantain.
Distribution. C. and S. Europe to 50°N, (58° in Estonia), except Spain and Portugal.
Variation. Mountain races in the S. Alps are generally large, f. *alternans* Seitz, heavily marked and brightly variegated with yellow and fulvous. Late broods in S. Europe may be very small with ♂ fw 19mm or less, ups black markings reduced, f. *pauper* Verity pl. 24, as in Italy, Sicily, etc.

118   NYMPHALIDAE

M. phoebe occitanica   Staudinger 1871   TL: 'Iberia'   **Pl. 33**
Description. ♂fw 22/25mm, ups gc paler fulvous-yellow, the darker reddish-fulvous discal markings and submarginal bands producing a bright colour-contrast; black wing-markings may be heavy in mountainous localities.
Flight and **Habitat** as for *M. p. phoebe.*
Distribution. Spain, south of the Cantabrian Mts., and Portugal.
Variation. The full characters of *occitanica* are developed in the second brood, esp. in S. Spain, Granada, etc. First brood specimens (April) in which colour contrast is less marked are not greatly different from those of southern alpine localities. In all localities and in both broods there is considerable individual variation.

M. phoebe punica   Oberthur 1876   TL: Lambessa, Algeria   **Pl. 33**
Description. ♀fw 17/18mm, small, ups gc yellowish, black markings not heavy but discal spots upf well developed; unh gc gleaming white. ♀ similar.
Flight. May/June and September in two broods.
Habitat. Flowery slopes from 1000–2100m.
Distribution. Algeria, Lambessa, Batna, Geryville. Morocco, Azrou, Ifrane and High Atlas at 2500m, slightly larger, f. *gaisericus* Hemming.
Similar species. *M. aetherie* below, uph orange submarginal band not well defined.

MELITAEA AETHERIE   *Aetherie Fritillary*
Range. Confined to N. Africa, Iberian Peninsula and Sicily.   Map 205

M. aetherie aetherie   Hübner 1826   TL: not stated   **Pl. 33**
Description. ♂fw 21/23mm, resembles *M. phoebe*; ups black markings reduced; upf discal spots small, pd spots often absent, submarginal and marginal markings complete, marginal lunule in s3 large; uph basal and discal markings small or absent, *orange submarginal band not defined*; unh submarginal band with a large round red spot in each segment. ♀ similar, ups grey suffusion on fw and over posterior area of hw common.
Flight. Late April/July. A second brood has not been recorded.
Habitat. In open woodland and flowery meadows at low levels. Larval food plant not known.
Distribution. Very local in S. Spain, Cadiz, Chiclana, Algiceras, etc. Portugal, Val da Rosal.

M. aetherie algirica   Rühl 1892   TL: Algeria   **Pl. 33**
Description. Resembles *M. a. aetherie*, but unf black discal spots are generally prominent. ♀ups heavily suffused dark grey except the anterior half of hw.
Flight and **Habitat.** End May/June, flying at 1500–2600m.
Distribution. Local in Morocco, Algeria; in Tunisia it is said to fly at lower altitudes. Sicily, local in northern mountains.
Similar species. *M. phoebe* p. 117.

MELITAEA DIDYMA   *Spotted Fritillary*
Range. From S. and W. Europe and N. Africa to Russia, C. Asia, Turkestan and Amdo; also Tripolitania to Fezzan and Tibesti.   Map 206

This widely distributed butterfly occurs in Europe in a variety of biotopes from sea-level to over 1800m. Its colonies show marked local variation, often confused by the presence of two or three annual broods, each with distinctive character. The variation is best regarded as clinal, and the seasonal differences suggest that, in part at least, the basis is ecological. There is little evidence of the development of true geographical races, which is not surprising in a species with such a wide and continuous distribution. Nevertheless, it is possible to distinguish a northern 'European' form, a southern 'Mediterranean' form and an 'Alpine' form, but descriptions can apply only to average specimens, for intermediates occur nearly everywhere and defy analysis.

M. didyma didyma   Esper 1779   TL: Bavaria   **Pl. 33**
Description. ♂fw 18/21mm, ups gc tawny red, black markings irregular and heavy, pd spots usually present; unh *basal orange band irregular but continuous, marginal black spots always round.* ♀ often larger, ups gc paler, esp. upf, with variable grey suffusion rarely quite absent.
Flight. May or later in one or two or even three broods.
Habitat. Flowery meadows from lowlands to 600m, common in hilly districts. Larval food plants principally plaintains and toadflax.
Distribution. C. Europe to 55°N, esp. in NW. France. Belgium, Ardennes. N. Switzerland, Germany and Austria. Absent from Britain, Holland, Denmark and much of NW. Germany.

M. didyma meridionalis   Staudinger 1870   TL: Mt. Parnassus, Greece   **Pl. 33**
Description. ♂fw 20/22mm, large, ups gc rich fulvous-red; pd spots rarely indicated. ♀ variable, ups usually heavily suffused dark grey, except anterior area of hw.
Flight. June/July, usually in a single brood.
Habitat. Most typical on subalpine meadows at 900–1500m. At lower altitudes ♀ generally with less grey ups suffusion.
Distribution. The usual form in mountains of C. and S. Europe and foothills of Alps, Pyrenees, Apennines and Balkans.

M. didyma occidentalis   Staudinger 1861   TL: Albarracin, Spain (Verity 1950)
                                                                         Pls. 24, 33
Description. ♂fw 20mm, or more, size variable; ups gc paler fulvous to yellow-buff; black markings, often small, pd spots rarely present; unh orange basal band usually broken into several spots. ♀ similar, generally larger and without grey ups suffusion.
Flight. May and later in two or three annual broods.
Habitat. Open places and meadows from lowlands to 900m in Europe, to 2100m in N. Africa.
Distribution. S. Europe, in low-lying warm southern districts, most typical in late summer broods in Spain, Portugal, Italy, Hungary and coastal areas of Balkans. N. Africa, local on northern slopes of Atlas Mts. at 900–2100m. Absent from Mediterranean islands except Sicily.
Variation. Late broods may be small, ♂fw 15/17mm, ups pale yellow-buff with black markings reduced, f. *dalmatina* Staudinger Pl. 24, in hot, low-lying localities in August/September, esp. in Italy and Balkans.
Similar species. *M. trivia* p. 120, unh black marginal spots triangular. *M. deserticola* below, easily confused in N. Africa, unh orange basal spots separated and bordered prominently in black.

MELITAEA DESERTICOLA   *Desert Fritillary*
Range. N. Africa. In Atlas Mts., esp. southern slopes and in desert oases; Tripolitania, Fezzan; Egypt, Lebanon and Transjordan.   Map 207

M. deserticola   Oberthur 1876   TL: Algeria   **Pl. 33**
Description. ♂fw *first brood* 18/20mm, resembles *M. didyma*, but ups gc pale buff, with small but bold black markings; upf pd spots absent, unh gc white, *basal orange band completely broken up, each spot edged black*, pd orange band with double black proximal border in s2–s5. ♀ similar.
Flight. March/April and later. Second broods almost certainly, and perhaps third broods also occur in N. Africa, but have not been specifically recorded.
Habitat. Flies in hot valleys up to 1800m in Atlas Mts. Larval food plants unknown.
Distribution. Morocco, in High Atlas, Ourika, Amizmiz. Middle Atlas. Algeria, Mecheria, Biskra, Laghouat. Tunisian Sahara.
Similar species. *M. didyma* above.

MELITAEA TRIVIA   *Lesser Spotted Fritillary*
Range. From S. Europe through S. Russia and W. Asia to Iran, Pakistan and Baluchistan.   Map 208

M. trivia trivia   Denis and Schiffermüller 1775   TL: Vienna   **Pl. 33**
Description. ♂fw *first brood* 17/19mm, *second brood* 14/16mm, resembles *M. didyma*; ups gc orange-yellow (*didyma* orange-red); orange marginal lunules complete in regular series and fully enclosed by darker border; uph pd black spots often prominent; *unh marginal black spots nearly always triangular* (round in *didyma*); in hw lower dc vein present (absent in *didyma*). ♀ larger, ups sometimes slightly flushed fuscous.
Flight. May/June and July/August in two broods.
Habitat. Flowery banks and rough ground to 1500m. Larval food plant mullein (*Verbascum thapsus*).
Distribution. E. Europe from Balkans to Czechoslovakia. Italy, Lake Garda, and rarely in warm valleys in Alto Adige and E. Emilia; very local in Apennines and Calabria.
Variation. First brood generally large, ♂fw to 22mm in Balkan Mts., esp. mountains of Bulgaria and Macedonia, Greece, f. *fascelis* Esper Pl. 33.

M. trivia ignasiti   Sagarra 1926   TL: Portugal   **Pl. 33**
Description. ♂fw 17/18mm, ups gc paler orange-yellow, markings sharply defined and without fuscous suffusion, yellow marginal lunules free, not enclosed in dark border. ♀ similar, larger.
Flight and **Habitat** as for *M. t. trivia*; there is little difference between broods.
Distribution. Italy, only recorded from Susa district, N. Piedmont. Spain, common in northern and central districts, Catalonia, Cantabrian Mts., Cuenca, Sierra de Guadarrama. Portugal, Serra da Estrela.
Similar species. *M. didyma* p. 118.

MELITAEA DIAMINA   *False Heath Fritillary*
Range. From N. Spain through C. Europe to 62°N and across central and north-central Asia to Amur, principal colonies in mountains.   Map 209

M. diamina diamina   Lang 1789   TL: Augsburg   **Pl. 33**
  syn: *dictynna* Esper 1779 (invalid homonym)

Description. ♂fw 19/21mm, ups wings dark, esp. uph, obscuring much of fulvous gc, marginal spots when present often pale; unh gc pale, markings orange-brown, submarginal band enclosing in each segment *a pale spot with darker mark external to it; double marginal lines filled yellow*. ♀ similar, uph markings often pale yellow to white.
Flight. End May/July in a single brood.
Habitat. Grass banks and damp alpine meadows from lowlands to 1800m. Larval food plants principally species of plantain, *Veronica* and cowwheat (*Melampyrum*).
Distribution. France and C. Europe to 62°N, including N. Italy, Yugoslavia and Bulgaria. In Hautes and Basses Pyrénées mostly transitional to following subspecies. Absent from peninsular Italy, Britain, Mediterranean islands and Greece.

M. diamina wheeleri Chapman 1910 TL: Reazzino, N. Italy
Description. Like *M. d. vernetensis* but smaller, ♂fw 16–18mm, ups bright fulvous, black markings well defined, lacking black suffusion. Unh markings chestnut-brown. ♀ similar.
Flight. May/June and July/August in two broods.
Distribution. Local in warm lowland valleys in Ticino, Bergamasker Alps, Alto Adige, Val Degano etc.
Similar species. Resemblance to *M. athalia, M. aurelia* and *M. britomartis* may be confusing.

M. diamina vernetensis Rondou 1902 TL: Vernet-les-Bains, E. Pyrenees **Pl. 35**
Description. ♂fw 17/19mm, ups black suffusion absent, resembles *M. athalia*; upf prominent club-shaped discal spot generally present in s1b; unh resembles *M. d. diamina* but markings in paler tones with small dark spot in each lunule of orange submarginal band in s1b–s4, these spots often far from obvious.
Flight and **Habitat** as for *M. d. diamina*.
Distribution. E. Pyrenees, esp. Mt. Canigou, Porta, etc. Spain, Cantabrian Mts., Picos de Europa, Pajares.

M. diamina codinai Sagarra 1932 TL: Tortosa, NE. Spain
Description. ♂fw 17/18mm, small, ups resembles *M. d. vernetensis* and *M. athalia*, ups without dusky suffusion, upf dumb-bell shaped discal black spot in s1b large; unh dark points in submarginal lunules vestigial or absent. ♀ similar or slightly larger.
Flight. May and July/August, in two annual broods.
Distribution. Spain, in Catalonia, very local, Planolas, Santa Fe, Tortosa.
Similar species. *M. athalia* p. 122, uph generally less suffused black, unh without vestigial dark spots in orange submarginal band. In *M. diamina vernetensis* ups colour and markings resemble *athalia* very closely. *M. britomartis* p. 125, size smaller than *diamina*, ups wing markings well defined (less black suffusion), unh spots in submarginal band less well formed; confusion with *M. d. wheeleri* is possible.
Note. *M. diamina* in most of its external characters agrees best with the species of the genus *Mellicta*, but in its genitalia is very similar to *M. cinxia* in the genus *Melitaea*.

MELLICTA ATHALIA   *Heath Fritillary*
Range. From W. Europe through Russia and temperate Asia to Japan.   Map 210

   This butterfly is the commonest and most widespread species of the genus, as well as the most variable. In W. Europe it occurs mainly in two subspecies, *athalia* Rottemberg and *celadussa* Fruhstorfer, superficially similar but with clearly defined characters in the male genitalia. The subspecific frontier between these varies in width from 30 to 100 miles and is indicated on the map by a white line along which all grades of intermediates occur.

M. athalia athalia   Rottemburg 1775   TL: Paris   **Pl. 35**
   syn: *neglecta* Pfau 1945
Description. ♂fw 18/20mm, ups black markings often heavy; unf yellow marginal lunules irregular and with *heavy black internal border in s2 (and s3)*, pd markings often vestigial or absent, marginal band pale. ♀ often larger, ups sometimes suffused fuscous.
Flight. May or later, sometimes a second brood in August/September.
Habitat. Flowery meadows from lowlands to 1500m. Larval food plants are species of plantain and cow-wheat, more rarely other low plants.
Distribution. Europe north of the Alps, including S. Scandinavia and S. England, and all eastern Europe. Absent from Peloponessos.

M. athalia boris   Fruhstorfer 1917   TL: Sliven, Rumelia   **Pl. 35**
Description. Markings upf are very regular, with wide, dark wing-borders. In ♀ characters not always well defined; in ♂ often more marked with extension of black suffusion invading all basal area of hind-wing. In some areas dark ups suffusion may be very extensive in both sexes, f. *satyra* Higgins Pl. 35.
Flight and **Habitat** as for *M. a. athalia*.
Distribution. Bulgaria.

M. athalia norvegica   Aurivillius 1888   TL: Dovrefjeld, Norway   **Pls. 31, 35**
Description. ♂fw 17/18mm, small, ups markings very regular and complete, upf discal spots often emphasised; unf marginal lunules vestigial. ♀ similar.
Flight. End June/July in a single brood.
Habitat. Moorlands from low levels to 900m.
Distribution. Norway, esp. on fjelds, Jotunheim, Hardanger, Dovrefjeld and extending to North Cape. Sweden. Finland in suitable localities.
Variation. In some districts in Fennoscandia upf postdiscal and submarginal black bands widely separated, leaving a wide fulvous space, f. *lachares* Fruhstorfer Pl. 35.

M. athalia celadussa   Fruhstorfer 1910   TL: Maritime Alps   **Pl. 31, 35**
   syn: *pseudathalia* Reverdin 1921
Description. Resembles *M. a. athalia* in size and general appearance, but genitalia are distinct. On ups gc generally bright fulvous, black markings thin. ♀ups fuscous suffusion uncommon.
Flight. June/July and August/September.
Distribution. SW. Europe and southern Alps eastwards to Venice, and south through Italy to Sicily; absent from Mediterranean islands.
Variation. In S. Europe specimens of late broods may be very small with thin black markings, f. *tenuicola* Verity (Pl. 31), easily confused with *M. parthenoides*. A local race, f. *nevadensis* Oberthur (Pl. 35), occurs in the Sierra Nevada, ups gc pale yellow-buff, upf with prominent dumb-bell shaped black spot in s1b, recalling *M. deione*.

M. athalia biedermanni Querci 1932 TL: Serra da Estrela, Portugal **Pl. 35**
Description. ♂fw 21/23mm, a very large form, ups black markings often thin, but upf discal band usually emphasised. ♀ larger.
Distribution. Portugal, Serra da Estrela. Spain, in Province Leon, large transitional forms occur in Sierra de Guadarrama, Sierra de Gredos, etc.
Similar species. Confusion may arise between *M. athalia* in its various forms and any other species of the genus except *M. asteria*. Identification of *M. athalia* depends largely upon noting the absence of the specific characters of these other species, and especially the presence in *M. athalia* of the well-developed dark internal border to the submarginal lunules in s2 (s3) on unf.

MELLICTA DEIONE *Provençal Fritillary*
Range. Confined to SW. Europe and N. Africa. Map 211

M. deione deione Geyer 1832 TL: Aix-en-Provence **Pl. 34**
Description. ♂ *first brood* 19/22mm, *second brood* 16/19mm. Resembles *M. athalia*; ups gc clear orange-yellow with thin black markings; upf last discal spot in *s1b often dumb-bell shaped* (not constant); unf yellow marginal lunules in s2 (3) *with minimal black proximal shade*, if any; unh discal and sub-marginal bands clear orange, the latter often with round, reddish spot in each space; terminal segment of palpi viewed from below fulvous (grey or slightly yellow in *athalia*). ♀ commonly with paler gc in cell and in pd area, producing a little colour contrast.
Flight. May/June and August/September in two broods.
Habitat. On flowery meadows from low levels to 1500m, usually in mountainous districts. Larval food plants *Linaria*, *Antirrhinum sempervirens*.
Distribution. Spain and Portugal, widely distributed. S. France, widely distributed from Provence to Briançon, Auvergne, Cevennes, Pyrenees, esp. E. Pyrenees.

M. deione berisalii Ruhl 1891 TL: Simplon (error) **Pl. 34**
Description. Size and general appearance as in *M. d. deione*; ups gc darker fulvous, black markings heavier, esp. dark marginal borders, which almost obliterate uph marginal lunules; unh vivid orange discal and submarginal bands contrast strongly with pale gc, black marginal lunules slightly enlarged, veins more distinctly black. ♀ similar; ups colour contrast little developed.
Flight and **Habitat** as for *M. d. deione*, now rare at Martigny. Larval food plants toadflax (*Linaria vulgaris* and *L. minor*).
Distribution. SW. Switzerland and in Rhône valley, Martigny, Saillon, etc. Also in Italy, Piedmont, local near Oulz. S. Tirol, in Eisaktal above Bolzano with characters somewhat intermediate to *M. d. deione*.

M. deione rosinae Rebel 1910/1911 TL: Cintra (S. Portugal) **Pl. 23**
Description. Gen. 1, ♂fw 23mm, ups bright, warm fulvous, slightly darker than *M. d. berisalii*, black markings heavier; unf yellow marginal lunules not well defined. ♀ larger, fw 23–24mm, ups black markings extended, unf marginal lunules better defined, internally bordered black. Gen. 2, similar but smaller, ♂fw 19–20mm. ♀ more variable.
Flight. April and July in two broods.
Distribution. Only seen from S. Portugal, esp. from Serra da Monchique in the Algarve; Sintra.

M. deione nitida Oberthur 1909 TL: Algeria **Pl. 34**
Description. ♂fw 18/20mm, fw apex more rounded; ups gc paler fulvous yellow, lightly marked, black marginal lines clearly double. ♀ similar.
Flight. May, no record of a second brood.
Habitat. Probably flies in mountains at altitudes of 1200–1500m, but there is no precise information.
Distribution. Algeria, in Middle Atlas, Tlemcen, Sebdou. Morocco, not recorded from High Atlas Mts., but probably flies in El Rif.
Similar species. *M. athalia* p. 122, in which unf black pd crescent in s2 is conspicuous (usually absent in *M. deione*).

MELLICTA VARIA *Grisons Fritillary*
Range. Confined to Alps and Apennines. Map 212

M. varia Meyer-Dür 1851 TL: Graubünden Alps **Pl. 35**
Description. ♂fw 15/17mm, ups gc bright fulvous; upf large black spot in s1b often dumb-bell shaped with *distal margin vertical* (oblique in *M. parthenoides*); unf a black streak to base of wing in s1b; uph pd area often clear fulvous, occasionally with included black spots; at high altitudes unh gc generally white. ♀ similar, ups often suffused grey.
Flight. End June/August in a single brood.
Habitat. Flies over short grass from 1800m upwards, rarely at 1400m in Apennines and Basses Alpes. Larval food plant gentians.
Distribution. From Maritime Alps to Savoie and Drôme and through S. Swiss and Italian Alps to Brenner, Landeck and Rieserferner Group. Apennines, local, esp. Gran Sasso, Monte Livata (Sulmona) at 1400m. Sibillini Mts. Absent from Pyrenees, Carpathians, Balkans.
Variation. A larger form, f. *piana* Higgins, ♂fw 17/19mm, occurs as low as 1400m in the Maritime Alps and Abruzzi Mts Pl. 35.
Similar species. In SW. Alps only, *M. varia* overlaps the distribution of *M. parthenoides* below, which generally flies at lower levels and has ups markings thinner and more regular. *M. aurelia* below (subalpine), which also occurs in the same area is usually small, with broader wings and ups markings more complete. *M. athalia* p. 122, larger with ups markings less regular.

MELLICTA PARTHENOIDES *Meadow Fritillary*
Range. Confined to W. Europe. Map 213

M. parthenoides Keferstein 1851 TL: Soucy, France **Pl. 34**
  syn: *parthenie* Godart 1819 (invalid homonym)
Description. ♂fw 16/18mm, ups black markings regular with delicately drawn lines and striae; *upf black discal spots often emphasised, linear discal spot in s1b oblique* (distinction from *M. varia*); uph discal area clear orange-yellow. ♀ often larger, ups with grey suffusion and wider submarginal bands which are sometimes deeper orange; unf black markings resemble *M. varia* with heavy basal mark but pd area clear.
Flight. May/June and August/September in two broods at low levels, a single brood in June/July at high altitudes.
Habitat. Flies in foothills and mountains from 500–2100m. Larval food plants plantain, scabious, *Melampyrum*, etc.
Distribution. SW. Europe. France, from Paris to Jura Mts. and Pyrenees; Bavaria,

very local in SW. districts only. Switzerland, probably confined to SW. in Rhône valley, Tessin, Jura. Italy, only in Maritime Alps, Fenestrelle, Limone Piemonte. Widely distributed in Spain and Portugal.
Variation. Small specimens, ♂fw 15/16mm, are common in late broods. In the C. Pyrenees, f. *plena* Verity is slightly dusky, flying to 2100m and single brooded, with deceptive resemblance to *M. aurelia*.
Similar species. *M. varia* p. 124; *M. athalia* p. 122, ups black markings heavier and irregular.

MELLICTA AURELIA *Nickerl's Fritillary*
Range. C. and E. Europe to Urals, Caucasus and C. Asia.   Map 214

M. aurelia   Nickerl 1850   TL: Erlangen, Germany   **Pl. 34**
   syn: *parthenie* Borkhausen 1788 (invalid homonym)
Description. ♂fw 14/16mm, ups *black markings regular and complete* with tendency to dusky suffusion; unf pd spots variable, sometimes strongly marked; *unh double marginal lines sometimes filled yellow and slightly darker than adjacent lunules*; chequered cilia predominantly pale yellow or white. ♀ similar.
Flight. June/July depending upon altitude, partially double-brooded in some southern localities.
Habitat. Flowery meadows, moorlands, etc., from lowlands to 1500m. Larval food plants plantain, *Veronica* and *Melampyrum*.
Distribution. Hautes Alpes and through NE. France to Ardennes. Bavaria, esp. on peat-moors. Switzerland, including Valais, Czechoslovakia, Austria, Hungary and Balkans; becomes more rare in N. Germany. Italy, rare south of River Po. Absent from SW. and C. France, peninsular Italy, Spain, Portugal and Pyrenees.
Variation is slight apart from occasional individual abnormal wing-markings.
Similar species. *M. britomartis* below, usually slightly larger, darker, and has unh double marginal lines filled dark yellow; unf black markings rarely incomplete. The chequering of the fringes may also help. Dissection may be necessary for identification. *M. athalia* p. 122, black markings less regular, esp. unf.

MELLICTA BRITOMARTIS *Assmann's Fritillary*
Range. C. Europe and through C. Asia to Transbaical and Korea.   Map 215

M. britomartis   Assmann 1847   TL: Breslau, Germany   **Pl. 34**
Description. ♂fw *first brood* 17/18mm, *second brood* often very small. Resembles *M. aurelia*, generally slightly larger; ups strongly marked; unf gc darker fulvous; unh orange submarginal lunules often with *dark brown proximal border*, sometimes with traces of included darker spots within each lunule, which are rarely present in *M. aurelia*; double marginal lines *filled yellow or brown*; fringes chequered predominantly dark in most specimens. ♀ similar.
Flight. May and August in two broods in S. Europe, a single brood in northern range.
Habitat. Heaths and flowery places at low altitudes. Larval food plants plantain and *Veronica*.
Distribution. Italy, very local near Oulz, Turin, and here and there in valley of the River Ticino, esp. Galliate, Turbigo, etc. Commoner in E. Europe, often flying with *M. aurelia*, esp. in Danube countries, Bulgaria, Romania, Hungary; Poland, esp. Wroclaw (Breslau); Germany, Berlin; recorded also from S. Sweden; Slovenia (Mt. Nanos).

Similar species. *M. aurelia* p. 125; *M. diamina* p. 120, small second brood specimens of *M. d. wheeleri* may be confusing. Identification should be confirmed by examination of the male genitalia in specimens from any locality where *M. britomartis* is not already known to occur, since it may fly with *M. aurelia* and with *M. athalia*.

MELLICTA ASTERIA   *Little Fritillary*
Range. Confined to Alps.   Map 216

M. asteria   Freyer 1828   TL: Chur, Switzerland   **Pl. 34**
Description. ♂fw 14/15mm, ups wing-bases heavily suffused black, pd and submarginal orange markings generally clear; unh gc pale yellow to white, veins black, markings well defined, *a single black marginal line*. ♀ similar, ups less heavily suffused fuscous.
Flight. July.
Habitat. Flies over short grassy slopes at 2100–2400m. Larval food plant unknown.
Distribution. Restricted to eastern Alps from Chur to Gross Glockner, esp. Albula Pass, Guarda and Brenner. Reported also from the Niederer Tauern near Turrach.

HYPODRYAS MATURNA   *Scarce Fritillary*
Range. From Europe north of Alps across Russia to Ala Tau and Altai Mts.
Map 217

H. maturna   Linnaeus 1758   TL: not stated   **Pl. 36**
Description. ♂fw 21/23mm, ups gc red; upf with cream-white spots on costa, often also in cell; uph white spots in series beyond cell-end, and prominent broad red pd bands; uns marginal borders red; *unf submarginal lunules, irregular in size, largest in s3*. ♀ usually larger.
Flight. May/June.
Habitat. A lowland species flying in open woodland, often at valley bottoms, attracted by blossoms of privet. Larvae before hibernation live in nests on ash, poplar or beech, after hibernation singly on plantain, scabious, *Veronica*, etc.
Distribution. Paris (Ozoir), and eastwards through Germany, Austria, S. Fennoscandia, Hungary, Romania and Yugoslavia, esp. Bosnia and Slavonia, Bulgaria, Albania and NW. Greece.
Similar species. *H. intermedia* below, ups more uniform red-brown, pd red bands less prominent; unf submarginal lunules more regular. *H. cynthia* ♀ p. 127, which nearly always has small black spots in unh submarginal band.

HYPODRYAS INTERMEDIA   *Asian Fritillary*
Range. From Alps of Savoie to Julian Alps, Altai Mts., Amur (TL of *M. intermedia* Ménétriès 1859), Sutschan and Korea.   Map 218

H. intermedia wolfensbergeri   Frey 1880   TL: Maloja Pass, Engadine   **Pl. 36**
    syn: *ichnea* auct. (misidentification)
Description. ♂fw 19/21mm, ups gc uniformly yellow-brown with red cell-marks and pd bands, black lattice pattern uniform and rather heavy; uns gc paler, yellowish, marginal lines yellow-brown, unf lightly marked, submarginal black lunules regular; *unh pale discal band enclosing a thin black line*. ♀ similar, larger, ups markings often paler, esp. yellowish costal spots of fw and pd spots of hw.
Flight. Eng June/July. Life cycle lasts two years.

Habitat. Mountains at 1500–1600m, often in light spruce woodland. Larval food plants *Lonicera*.
Distribution. Southern Alps, from Savoie to Julian Alps, esp. Pralognan, Saas-Fé, Preda, Bergün, Albula, Dolomites and Triglav.
Similar species. *H. maturna* p. 126, unf submarginal lunules irregular, flies at low altitudes north of main alpine chain, distribution does not overlap that of *H. intermedia*. *H. cynthia* below (♀ only), resemblance extremely close but unh pale yellow discal band without enclosed thin black line.

HYPODRYAS CYNTHIA *Cynthia's Fritillary*
Range. Confined to Alps, and mountains of Bulgaria.   Map 219

H. cynthia cynthia Denis and Schiffermüller 1775   TL: Vienna   **Pl. 36**
Description. ♂fw 19/21mm, ups pd bands red on *white* gc, but partly obscured by black suffusion; uph a black spot enclosed in each segment of red pd band; unh yellowish with orange-brown markings. ♀ resembles *H. intermedia*, ups gc *uniform orange-brown* with light black markings; uns resembles ♂, but unh pale pd band clear yellow-buff *without enclosed thin black line*.
Flight. End May/July depending upon altitude.
Habitat. On mountain heaths with juniper and *Vaccinium* from 400–2100m. At highest levels generally small but brightly marked. Larval food plants plantain (*P. alpina*), lady's mantle (*Alchemilla*).
Distribution. Bavaria, Austria, widely distributed. Bulgaria in Rila Dagh and Pirin, flying at 2100m or over.

H. cynthia alpicola Galvagni 1918   TL: Brenner, Tirol   **Pl. 36**
Description. ♂fw 16/20mm, slightly smaller than *H. c. cynthia*, ups black suffusion more extensive, upf red pd bands often nearly obliterated and on uph reduced to small round spots. ♀ slightly larger, black suffusion ups less extensive.
Flight. Late June/early August.
Habitat. Above tree-line on high mountains, usually at 1800–2400m, attracted by low juniper bushes.
Distribution. From Maritime Alps and Savoie to Brenner and Oetztal, with intermediate forms in eastern range.
Variation. Extreme forms occur in the Maritime Alps with maximum extension of dark suffusion in ♂ups, ♀ups gc paler, sometimes with grey-white markings.
Similar species. *H. intermedia* p. 126, close resemblance in females.

HYPODRYAS IDUNA *Lapland Fritillary*
Range. Boreal Scandinavia, Caucasus, Altai Mts., Sajan Mts. in widely scattered local colonies.   Map 220

H. iduna Dalman 1816   TL: Sweden   **Pl. 36**
Description. ♂fw 18/19mm, ups gc pale yellowish with black markings and *broad orange-red cell-marks and pd bands*, double marginal lines filled orange; uns markings similar but better defined and without black suffusion. ♀ similar.
Flight. End June/July according to weather; butterflies emerge with onset of summer.
Habitat. Mountain sides and moorland at moderate altitudes, or near tree-line, often in light woodland with *Vaccinium*. Larval food plants not recorded.

Distribution. Fennoscandia, from 64°N to North Cape, esp. Abisko, Maalselv, Porsanger, etc. Always local, commonest in far north.

EURODRYAS AURINIA Marsh Fritillary
Range. W. Europe, Russia, Asia Minor and across temperate Asia to Korea. Map 221

This species and *E. desfontainii* differ in several ways from the preceding species. On uns the narrow coloured marginal band is replaced by the more usual black dots; black spots are always prominent in the red pd band of hw.

E. aurinia aurinia Rottemburg 1775   TL: Paris   **Pl. 36**
Description. ♂fw 17/19mm, ups gc yellow-buff, cell-spots and pd bands orange-red, black markings variable; *uph with dark spots in each segment of pd orange band* in s1a to 6; uns paler, gc yellow-grey with light orange-brown bands, often pale with little colour contrast; *unf without prominent pd black spots.* ♀ generally larger, otherwise similar.
Flight. May/June.
Habitat. Very varied, bogs, flowery meadows, grassy banks, boggy margins of lakes, moors, etc., from lowlands to 1500m. Larval food plants plantain, scabious, more rarely other low plants.
Distribution. All C. and E. Europe, including Britain, Balkans and Fennoscandia, to 62°N. Absent from Mediterranean islands. Rare in peninsular Italy.
Variation. Individual differences and abnormal patterns are common, and even the characteristic features of a colony may vary from year to year. *E. a. aurinia* extends across Russia and far into Siberia with relatively slight geographical variation.

E. aurinia provincialis Boisduval 1828   TL: Provence, France
Description. ♂fw 19/22mm, often large, ups gc yellow-buff, pd bands little darker than gc with reduced colour contrast and thin black lattice pattern; unh pale, sometimes sandy-yellow overall with black markings obsolescent.
Flight. End April/May.
Habitat. Flowery banks and meadows at about 600m.
Distribution and **Variation.** France, only in Basses Alpes, Bouches du Rhône, Gironde and Var. N. Italy, a few colonies near Lake Como, small and paler, f. *comacina* Turati 1910, flying at about 1000m. Yugoslavia, esp. Dalmatia, in a large form, f. *rotunda* Roeber 1926.

E. aurinia beckeri Herrich-Schäffer 1851   TL: Cadiz   **Pl. 36**
Description. ♂fw 20/23mm, ups gc reddish-fulvous with or without yellow discal and pd markings, black lattice pattern often heavy; upf black marginal lines often single, marginal lunules large; ups pd red band wide and submarginal black spots large; unh gc pale yellow-grey, coloured bands bright orange, wide, black-edged, colour contrast brilliant. ♀ similar, sometimes very large.
Flight. End May/June.
Habitat. On rough ground, often among mountains, from lowlands (Gibraltar) to 1500m. Larval food plants honeysuckle (perhaps also plantain, *Centaurea*, *Centranthus*).
Distribution. Portugal. Spain, widely distributed from Malaga and Granada to Catalonia; in Cantabrian Mts. transitional to *E. a. aurinia*. Morocco, common in Middle Atlas and El Rif, flying at 1500–1800m Algeria.

Similar species. *E. desfontainii* below, easily distinguished by series of black pd spots on unf.

E. aurinia debilis Oberthur 1909 TL: E. Pyrenees Map 222 **Pl. 36**
syn: *merope* de Prunner (invalid homonym)
Description. ♂fw 15/17mm, ups gc yellow, discal spots and submarginal bands orange-red; uns paler, gc yellow-grey with black markings reduced, often vestigial. ♀ often larger with fw to 19mm.
Flight. End June/July.
Habitat. Flies over grass slopes, usually at levels of 1800m and upwards, sometimes down to 1300m (Bavaria, Carnic Alps). Larval food plants gentian, *Primula viscosa*.
Distribution. E. Pyrenees, Basses Alpes to Hte Savoie and eastwards through the Alps to Bavarian Alps and Hohe Tauern (Gr. Glockner). Absent from Pyrenees west of Ariège, from Jura, Carpathians and Balkans.
Variation. Brightly coloured in the E. Pyrenees, but at high altitudes in central Alps, ups with gc paler and black markings extended, often widely suffused fuscous but variable f. *glaciegenita* Verity Pl. 36.

EURODRYAS DESFONTAINII *Spanish Fritillary*
Range. Confined to N. Africa, Spain and E. Pyrenees. Map 223

E. desfontainii desfontainii Godart 1819 TL: Algeria **Pls. 32, 36**
Description. ♂fw 20/24mm, fw apex rounded, ups gc red with paler discal and transverse bands; upf small yellow spots in red pd band, dark marginal border enclosing yellow lunules; *unf black pd spots prominent*, other markings as on ups, gc sandy-red. ♀ similar.
Flight. May/early June.
Habitat. Flies at 1500–1800m on warm slopes among *Cistus*, etc., in Middle Atlas. Larval food plant in Algeria *Knautia.*
Distribution. Morocco. Algeria. Not recorded from Tunis. Specimens from Morocco are especially brilliant, f. *gibrati* Oberthur Pl. 32, local but not uncommon.

E. desfontainii baetica Rambur 1858 TL: Andalusia **Pl. 36**
Description. Resembles *E. d. desfontainii*; ups gc paler red, cell-marks and pd bands yellow-buff and marginal lunules distinct; uns gc paler, often yellowish; unf black discal spots prominent, esp. near costa; unh markings mostly vestigial.
Flight and **Habitat** as for *E. d. desfontainii* but flies at 600–1200m.
Distribution. In S. and E. Spain; Granada, Ronda, etc., and in widely separated colonies northwards to Catalonia and E. Pyrenees (Sournia).
Variation. Different colonies show well-marked racial features. One illustrated is f. *zapateri* Higgins (Pl. 36) TL: Albarracin, Teruel, smaller, ups orange-fulvous; unh gc yellow with markings well defined by black striae.

PLATE 1

PLATE 2

1. **Archon apollinus**   *False Apollo*   20
   ♀. Uph with six large red, black and blue submarginal spots.

2. **Zerynthia cerisyi**   *Eastern Festoon*   20
   Outer margin of hw deeply scalloped, short tail at vein 4.

   2a. *Z. c. ferdinandi* ♂. Ups dark discal markings scanty on both wings.
   2b. *Z. c. cretica* ♀. Ups dark markings more extensive on both wings.
   See also Pl. 23.

3. **Zerynthia polyxena**   *Southern Festoon*   19
   Upf lacking red spots in cell and at cell-end; no vitreous window.

   3a. *Z. p. polyxena* ♂. Ups dark markings not extensive; uph postdiscal yellow band wide.
   3b. *Z. p. polyxena* ♀. Slightly larger, markings as in ♂.
   3c. *Z. p. cassandra* ♂. Ups dark markings extensive; uph postdiscal
   yellow band narrow.

4. **Zerynthia rumina**   *Spanish Festoon*   19
   Upf red spots present in cell and at cell-end; vitreous window near
   apex. ♀ ground-colour pale yellow or (f. *canteneri*) brownish.

   4a. *Z. r. rumina* f. *honoratii* ♀. All red areas greatly extended.
   4b. *Z. r.* f. *medesicaste* ♂. Uph red basal spot present.
   4c. *Z. r. africana* f. *canteneri* ♀. Very large, ground-colour buff.
   For typical *Z. r. africana* (♀) see front endpaper.

PLATE 3

1. Parnassius phoebus   *Small Apollo*   21
Antennae white, broadly ringed dark grey; ♂ uph lacks postdiscal
markings, red ocelli prominent.

   1a. *P. p. sacerdos* f. *cardinalis* ♀. Ups dark markings extensive; uph red
     ocelli united by black bar.
   1b. *P. p. sacerdos* ♂. Ups less heavily marked; uph red ocelli smaller.

2. Parnassius mnemosyne   *Clouded Apollo*   22
Small, ups without red markings.

   2a. *P. m. athene* ♂. Ups black markings scanty; upf grey apical area
     enclosing small white spots.
   2b. *P. m. mnemosyne* ♀ f. *melaina*. Ups black markings more complete,
     extensively suffused dark grey.

3. Parnassius apollo   *Apollo*   20
Antennae white narrowly ringed pale grey; ♂ uph with grey postdiscal
and marginal markings; red ocelli prominent.

   3a. *P. apollo* f. *rhodopensis* ♂. Upf lacking grey discal suffusion, uph
     ocelli large, red.
   3b. *P. apollo* f. *hispanicus* ♀. Upf with grey discal suffusion, all dark
     markings more extensive; uph ocelli orange-yellow. Red ocelli are
     much more common.

See front endpaper for *P. a.* f. *bartholomaeus*.

PLATE 4

1. Pieris brassicae *Large White* 23
Upf with extensive black apical border from costa down outer margin
to vein 3.

   1a. *P. b. brassicae* first brood ♀. Upf with round black spots in spaces
      1b and 3, apical black border powdered grey; unh grey.
   1b. *P. b. brassicae* second brood ♂. Upf lacks black discal spots, apical
      border black; unh yellow lightly powdered grey.
   1c. *P. b. cheiranthi* ♀. Large, fw black discal spots large and united on
      both surfaces.
   1d. *P. b. cheiranthi* ♂. Large, upf lacks black discal spots; uns as in ♀.

2. Lycaena helle *Violet Copper* 49
   ♀. Ups not suffused violet, markings well defined. For ♂ **see Pl. 15.**

3. Polyommatus icarus *Common Blue* 92
   ♀. Ups brown, wing-bases flushed blue; uns pale brown. For ♂ **See
Pl. 19.**

4. Plebejus martini *Martin's Blue* 69

   4a. *P. m. martini* ♀. Ups brown, wing-bases flushed blue; uns brown,
      markings small. For ♂ **see Pl. 19.**
   4b. *P. m. allardi* ♀. Ups like *P. m. martini* ♀; uns markings larger.

1c

4a

2

1a

1d

4b

3

1b

PLATE 5

1. **Artogeia ergane**   *Mountain Small White*   25
   Unf without black markings but discal spot shows through from ups.

   1a.   ♂. Upf often with round black spot in space 3 (variable).
   1b.   ♀. Upf as in ♂ but with additional black spot in space 1b.

2. **Artogeia mannii**   *Southern Small White*   24
   Upf apical black mark extending down outer margin to vein 4.

   2a.   First brood ♂. Small, apical mark small; unh heavily powdered
         with dark scales.
   2b.   First brood ♀. Upf dark scales extend along veins to connect black
         spot in space 3 with outer margin; additional black mark present
         in space 1b.
   2c.   Second brood ♂. Ups black markings larger; upf spot in space 3
         tends to connect along veins to outer margin, appearing moon-
         shaped.
   2d.   Second brood ♀. Ups all markings intense black and larger.

3. **Artogeia rapae**   *Small White*   24
   Upf apical mark grey, extending further along costa than down outer
   margin, spot in space 3 not connected with outer margin.

   3a.   First brood ♂. Upf apical grey mark small, not well defined; unh
         powdered with dark scales.
   3b.   Second brood ♀. Upf apical mark and dark spots black, better
         defined; unh yellowish, dark shading slight.

4. **Artogeia krueperi**   *Krueper's Small White*   27

   4a.   Second brood ♂. Upf with apical mark broken between veins, and
         dark costal bar before apex; unh dark costal mark at vein 7, basal
         area pale.
   4b.   First brood ♀. Upf black markings larger; unh basal area dark,
         greenish.

1 a

1 b

2 a

2 b

2 c

2 d

3 a

3 b

4 a

4 b

PLATE 6

1. Artogeia napi   *Green-veined White*   25

Upf with or without black spot in space 3; apical mark broken, composed of grey expansions on veins along outer margin; unh veins lined green or grey. **See also Pl. 13.**

1a.-1d. *A. n. napi.* In ♀ ups white, lacking general fuscous suffusion but wing-bases powdered grey.

1a. *A. n. napi* first brood ♂. Upf veins faintly lined grey near outer margin, unh ground-colour yellow, veins strongly lined green.

1b. *A. n. napi* first brood ♀. Ups more heavily marked; upf with black spots in spaces 1b and 3; unh as in ♂.

1c. *A. n. napi* second brood ♂ f. *napaeae.* Upf veins not lined grey, black spot in space 3 constant; unh ground-colour faintly yellow, veins partly lined grey (variable).

1d. *A. n. napi* second brood ♀ f. *napaeae.* Ups veins slightly or not at all lined black, other black markings well-defined; uns as in ♂.

1e. *A. n. adalwinda* ♂. Small, ups black markings greatly reduced; unh veins strongly marked on yellowish ground-colour.

1f. *A. n. bryoniae* ♂. Ups veins lined grey, marginal dark markings distinct; unh ground-colour yellowish. For ♀ see **Pl. 13.**

1g. *A. n. flavescens* f. *subtalba* ♂. Ups dark markings reduced; unh ground-colour white, veins lined grey.

1h. *A. n. flavescens* ♀. Ups yellowish ground-colour prominent, fuscous suffusion extensive, veins lined grey.

1i. *A. n. segonzaci* ♂. Large, upf black spot in s3 prominent; unh ground-colour yellowish, veins broadly lined greenish.

1j. *A. n. segonzaci* ♀. Large, upf black spots in spaces 1b, 3 and 5, veins lined grey in post-discal areas.

1a

1b

1c

1d

1e

1f

1g

1h

1i

1j

PLATE 7

1. Euchloe simplonia ♂   *Dappled White*   28
Upf black costal mark rarely extends along fw costa; mark wide in both
sexes.

2. Euchloe insularis ♀   *Corsican Dappled White*   29
Small, unf costal mark narrow.

3. Euchloe ausonia   *Mountain Dappled White*   28
Upf black costal mark extends along fw costa.

    3a. *E. a. ausonia* ♂. Upf mark often narrow and angled.
    3b. *E. a. ausonia* ♀. Ups black markings extended.

4. Pontia chloridice   *Small Bath White*   27
Unh with rather irregular continuous white postdiscal band; white
marginal marks between veins regular and elongate.

    4a. Second brood ♂. Ups black submarginal markings little devel-
        oped.
    4b. First brood ♂. Ups black submarginal markings present on both
        wings.

5. Pontia daplidice   *Bath White*   27
Unf with black postdiscal spot in slb; unh with isolated round white
spot in cell.

    5a. Second brood ♂. Upf lacks postdiscal black spot in slb; unh green
        ground-colour mixed with yellow.
    5b. First brood ♀. Ups black markings more extensive; unh ground-
        colour deep green.

6. Pontia callidice   *Peak White*   28
Unh elongate white mark in cell followed by row of white postdiscal
chevrons.

    6a. ♂. Upf black markings scanty; uph unmarked.
    6b. ♀. Upf black submarginal markings well developed; uph dusky
        grey with black submarginal lunules.

7. Colotis evagore nouna ♂   *Desert Orange Tip*   33
Upf apex red; unh ground-colour sandy-yellow or pinkish.

PLATE 8

1. **Euchloe tagis**   *Portuguese Dappled White*
   Like *E. ausonia* **(Pl. 7)** but hw costa evenly rounded at vein 8.
   1a. *E. t. tagis* ♂. Unh ground colour greenish with few small white
       spots. ♀ similar, often slightly larger.
   1b. *E. t. bellezina* ♀. Unh white markings larger and more numerous.
       Southern France. **See also Pl. 1** and *E. t. castellena.*
2. **Elphinstonia charlonia**   *Greenish Black-tip*   31
   2a. *E. c. charlonia* ♂. Small, yellow; upf apex broadly dark brown.
   2b. *E. c. penia* ♀. Larger, ground-colour slightly paler.
3. **Euchloe falloui**   *Scarce Green-striped White*   30
   ♂. Unf black discoidal spot small, lacks central white mark. ♀ slightly
   larger, otherwise similar, costa not striated.
4. **Euchloe belemia**   *Green-striped White*   30
   Like *Euchloe falloui*, but unf discoidal spot includes a slender white
   line.
   4a. *E. b. belemia* first brood ♂. Unh ground-colour dark green, white
       stripes clearly defined.
   4b. *E. b. belemia* second brood ♂. Unh ground-colour paler, yellowish,
       white stripes not clearly defined. **See also Pl. 1.**
5. **Euchloe pechi**   *Pech's White*   30
   ♂. Small; unh ground-colour green with small white discoidal spot.
6. **Anthocharis cardamines**   *Orange Tip*   31
   Ground-colour white; unh with mottled green markings.
   6a. ♂. Upf with broad orange-red apical patch.
   6b. ♀. No orange apical patch upf; apex rounded, grey apical border
       lacks distinct white spots (distinction from *Euchloe ausonia*, **Pl. 7**).
7. **Anthocharis belia**   *Morocco Orange-tip*   31
   Like *A. cardamines* but unh ground-colour yellow with markings
   reticulate.
   7a. *A. b. euphenoides* ♂. Ups yellow; upf with orange apical patch.
   7b. *A. b. euphenoides* ♀. Ups white, upf apex powdered orange; unh
       yellow, markings as in ♂.
   7c. *A. b. belia* ♂. Like *A. b. euphenoides* but unh reticulate markings
       grey or reddish-grey, usually obscure.
   7d. *A. b. belia* ♀. Ups as in *A. b. euphenoides* ♀; unh yellow, markings as
       in ♂.
8. **Anthocharis damone**   *Eastern Orange-tip*   32
   Like *A. cardamines* but unh yellow, with mottled green markings.
   8a. *A. d. damone* ♂. Ups yellow; upf with orange apical patch.
   8b. *A. d. damone* ♀. Ups white, lacking upf orange apical patch.
9. **Anthocharis gruneri**   *Gruner's Orange-tip*   32
   Like *A. cardamines* but small; unh green, with irregular white spots.
   9a. *A. g. gruneri* ♂. Ups pale yellow; upf with orange apical patch.
   9b. *A. g. gruneri* ♀. Ups white; upf grey apical mark wide, extending to
       vein 2, discoidal grey spot large, extending to costa.

PLATE 9

1. Colias phicomone   *Mountain Clouded Yellow*   34
Hw yellow discoidal spot well defined, generally prominent on both
surfaces.

> 1a. ♂. Ups usually heavily suffused dark grey except the submarginal
> spots or band; unh bright yellow, basal and discal areas lightly
> suffused grey.
> 1b. ♀. Ups greenish-white, lacking dark suffusion; unh as in ♂.

2. Colias nastes werdandi   *Pale Arctic Clouded Yellow*   34
Hw discoidal spot very small or vestigial on both surfaces.

> 2a. ♂. Ups pale greenish-yellow; upf veins finely lined black; unh
> greenish-grey with light marginal markings.
> 2b. ♀. Ups greenish-white, dark markings more extensive; unh as in ♂.

3. Colias palaeno   *Moorland Clouded Yellow*   34
Ups black marginal borders unspotted; unh discoidal spot small, black
or white, submarginal spots absent.

> 3a. *C. p. palaeno* ♂. Ups ground-colour very pale yellow.
> 3b. *C. p. palaeno* ♀. Ups ground-colour clear greenish-white.
> 3c. *C. p. europome* ♂. Ups ground-colour bright yellow; upf discoidal
> spot often black.
> 3d. *C. palaeno* ♀-form *illgneri*. Ups bright yellow; upf inner border of
> dark margin irregular, not well defined.

4. Zegris eupheme   *Sooty Orange-tip*   33
Upf with broad dark apical area enclosing small orange patch; unh
yellow, with reticulate pattern in dark grey-green.

> 4a. *Z. e. meridionalis* ♂. Upf orange apical patch well developed.
> 4b. *Z. e. meridionalis* ♀. Ups orange apical patch small or vestigial.

1a
1b
2a
2b
3a
3b
3c
3d
4a
4b

PLATE 10

In the species figured on this and the following plate males and females differ so greatly that it is not possible to give specific characters that cover both sexes.

MALES. Uph with oval sex-brand in space 8 except in *C. chrysotheme*; unf discal area yellow except 1a.

1a. Colias libanotica heldreichii   *Greek Clouded Yellow*   35
Large; ups dusky orange with faintly rosy reflection, marginal dark borders crossed by yellow veins; uns yellow-green, unf yellow discal area vestigial or absent.

2a. Colias chrysotheme   *Lesser Clouded Yellow*   35
Small; ups orange-yellow, marginal dark borders crossed by yellow veins; uph sex-brand absent.

3a. Colias myrmidone   *Danube Clouded Yellow*   36
Ups bright orange-yellow, marginal dark borders not crossed by veins; uph pale submarginal spots present internal to narrow black border.

4a. Colias crocea   *Clouded Yellow*   36
Ups deep yellow; upf marginal dark border crossed by yellow veins at least near apex; uph lacks pale submarginal spots internal to dark marginal border.

FEMALES. Often polymorphic, orange or greenish-white.

1b. Colias libanotica heldreichii. Fw apex pointed; unh smooth pale   35
blue-green, white discoidal spot small.
2b. Colias chrysotheme. Small, fw apex pointed; upf costa broadly   35
greenish-grey; white form not known.
3b., 3c. Colias myrmidone. Like *C. crocea* but uph large pale sub-   36
marginal spots are present in regular series. 3c., ♀-form *alba*,
greenish-white.
4b., 4c. Colias crocea. Uph pale submarginal spots irregular in size,   36
series usually incomplete. 4c., ♀-form *helice*, greenish-white, uph
suffused grey.

1a   1b

2a   2b

3a   3b

4a   3c

4b   4c

150

PLATE 11

MALES.

1a. Colias hyale   *Pale Clouded Yellow*   37
Pale yellow; fw pointed, apex broadly dark grey; uph discoidal spot
pale orange.

2a. Colias australis   *Berger's Clouded Yellow*   38
Differs from *C. hyale* in more brilliant tone of yellow ground-colour;
fw less pointed and dark markings slightly less extensive; uph discoidal spot larger, bright orange.
Identification of *Colias hyale* and *C. australis* may be difficult when
specific characters are not well marked. **See pp. 37-8.**

3a. Colias balcanica   *Balkan Clouded Yellow*   37
Like *C. myrmidone* **(Pl. 10)** but larger, ups ground-colour reddish-
orange.

4a. Colias hecla sulitelma   *Northern Clouded Yellow*   37
Small, ups orange, discoidal spot small; uph sex-brand absent.

5. Colias erate   *Eastern Pale Clouded Yellow*   38
Ups ground-colour bright butter-yellow.

FEMALES.

1b. Colias hyale. Like ♂ but ground-colour greenish-white; uph lacks   37
grey suffusion (distinction from *C. crocea* ♀).

2b. Colias australis. Greenish-white, markings as in ♂.   38
Distinctive characters of these two species are often less well-
developed in females and identification may be very difficult.

3b.,3c. Colias balcanica. Like *C. myrmidone* **(Pl. 10)** but larger; ups   37
(3c.) deeper shade of orange; upf dark basal shade usually well-
marked. 3b. ♀-form *rebeli*, ups greenish-white.

4b. Colias hecla sulitelma. Small; ups pale spots in grey marginal   37
borders large and prominent; upf veins lined grey; white form not
known.

PLATE 12

1. Gonepteryx rhamni   *Brimstone*   39

   1a.   ♀. Uns pale green; unf sometimes with faintly yellow streak through cell.

   1b.   ♂. Ups both wings sulphur-yellow.

2. Gonepteryx farinosa   *Powdered Brimstone*   41

   ♂. Upf bright yellow with scaling slightly rough; uph yellow distinctly paler.

3. Gonepteryx cleopatra   *Cleopatra*   39

   3a.   *G. c. cleobule* ♂. Upf deep orange; hw yellow. ♀ ups yellow slightly suffused orange.

   3b.   *G. c. palmae* ♀. Ups white with faint orange flush over hw and fw costa.

   3c.   *G. c. palmae* ♂. Ups yellow with faint orange flush over fw.

   3d.   *G. c. cleopatra* ♀. Greenish white; unf with pale yellow streak through cell.

   3e.   *G. c. cleopatra* ♂. Ups yellow; upf with deep orange-red flush from base to postdiscal area. **See also Pl. 23.**

PLATE 13

1a   1b   1c

2a   2b   2c

3a   5a   3b

4a   5b

4b   6   8

4c   7   9

PLATE 14

1. **Nordmannia ilicis**   *Ilex Hairstreak*   45
   1a. *N. i. ilicis* ♂. Ups fw dark brown; unh red submarginal spots
   black-bordered internally and externally; no sex-brand.
   1b. *N. ilicis* f. *cerri* ♀. Upf postdiscal area orange.

2. **Nordmannia esculi**   *False Ilex Hairstreak*   46
   2a. *N. e. esculi* ♂. Unh red spots smaller, without black borders.
   2b. *N. e. mauretanica* ♀. Unh grey, markings vestigial.

3. **Nordmannia acaciae**   *Sloe Hairstreak*   45
   3a. ♂. Like *N. ilicis*; unh orange submarginal lunules enclosing black
   spots near anal angle; no sex-brand.
   3b. ♀. Apex of abdomen with black hair tuft.

4. **Strymonidia spini**   *Blue-spot Hairstreak*   46
   4a. ♂. Anal angle black with blue spot above. Sex-brand present.
   4b. *S. s.* ♀-f. *vandalusica*. Ups postdiscal areas broadly orange.

5. **Strymonidia w-album**   *White-letter Hairstreak*   47
   ♂. Unh white postdiscal line forming W-mark in anal area. Sex-brand
   present. ♀ similar, often larger.

6. **Strymonidia pruni**   *Black Hairstreak*   47
   ♀. Uph with orange submarginal lunules in spaces 1c–4; unh orange
   submarginal band bordered internally with black spots. ♂. smaller,
   upf without orange flush, sex-brand present.

7. **Callophrys rubi**   *Green Hairstreak*   47
   ♂. Frons green, eyes bordered white.

8. **Callophrys avis**   *Chapman's Green Hairstreak*   48
   ♂. Like *C. rubi*; frons red, eyes bordered red.

9. **Thecla betulae**   *Brown Hairstreak*   44
   9a. ♀. Upf with postdiscal orange band.
   9b. ♂. Upf dark brown with or without vestigial orange mark.

10. **Laeosopis roboris**   *Spanish Purple Hairstreak*   45
    10a. ♂. Upf base and disc blue.
    10b. ♀. Like ♂ but upf blue at base only.

11. **Quercusia quercus**   *Purple Hairstreak*   44
    11a. *Q. q. quercus* ♂. Ups violet-blue with narrow black marginal
    borders; uns with postdiscal white lines, anal spots orange.
    11b. *Q. q. iberica* ♀. Ups blue restricted to fw in space 1b. and cell;
    uns markings vestigial.

158

PLATE 15

1a 1b 1c

3a 3b 3c

3e 3d 3f

4b 4a 7

5 8a

9a 6a 8b

9b 6b 2

PLATE 16

162

PLATE 17

PLATE 18

1. **Zizeeria knysna**   *African Grass Blue*   59
   ♂. Ups violet blue, margins broadly brown; uns markings small; ♀ ups brown; uns as in ♂.

2. **Glaucopsyche melanops**   *Black-eyed Blue*   63
   G. m. algirica ♂. Ups blue; unf postdiscal spots large, submarginal markings present. ♀ ups brown, wing-bases suffused blue.

3. **Lycaeides idas**   *Idas Blue*   72
   3a. *L. i.* f. *alpinus* ♀. Ups brown, submarginal lunules yellow (variable); uns pale brown; unf lacks cell-spot; unh marginal spots near anal angle with blue-green scales.
   3b. *L. i.* f. *alpinus* ♂. Ups blue, black marginal line narrow; uns ground-colour pale grey, markings as in ♀.
   3c. *L. i.* f. *lapponicus* ♂. Small, like *L. i. alpinus*; uns ground-colour darker grey, markings small. ♀ ups brown, often with blue basal suffusions; uns as in ♂. **See also Pl. 19 and Pl. 22.**

4. **Lycaeides argyrognomon**   *Reverdin's Blue*   73
   ♂. Ups deep blue; unh ground-colour pale blue-grey; (male genitalia distinctive). ♀ brown, wing-bases usually blue.

5. **Plebejus pylaon**   *Zephyr Blue*   70
   5a. *P. p. hespericus* ♂. Ups pale gleaming blue; uns pale grey; unh spots at anal angle black, lacking green scales. ♀ ups brown; uns pale brown, otherwise as in ♂.
   5b. *P. p. sephirus* ♀. Like *L. idas* ♀; orange submarginal lunules well developed.
   5c. *P. p. trappi* ♂. Larger; ups deeper blue; uns as in *P. p. hespericus*; unf no cell-spots; unh pale postdiscal band usually prominent.

6. **Maculinea alcon**   *Alcon Blue*   64
   6a. *M. a. alcon* ♂. Ups pale blue; uns brown, lacking blue basal shade; unh no spot at base of space 1c.
   6b. *M. a. alcon* ♀. Ups brown, blue basal flush small if present.
   6c. *M. a. rebeli* ♀. Ups brown, wing-bases rather widely blue.
   6d. *M. a. rebeli* ♂. Like *M. a. alcon* but ups bright blue; uns ground-colour pale grey-brown, unh often with small blue basal flush.

7. **Maculinea telejus**   *Scarce Large Blue*   65
   7a. ♂. Ups pale blue, brown borders wide, black postdiscal spots present; unh brown, no blue-green basal flush.
   7b. ♀. Ups darker blue, postdiscal black spots larger.

8. **Maculinea arion**   *Large Blue*   65
   8a. *M. a. obscura* ♂. Ups heavily suffused grey-brown except over basal areas; unh with spot at base of space 1c.
   8b. *M. a. arion* ♂. Ups blue, no brown suffusion.

9. **Maculinea nausithous**   *Dusky Large Blue*   66
   ♂. Ups very dark, fringes brown; uns coffee-brown. ♀. ups brown, otherwise similar.

166

PLATE 19

168

PLATE 20

1. **Agriades glandon**   *Glandon Blue*   78
   1a. *A. g. glandon* ♂. Ups greenish blue; unf submarginal markings vestigial; unh most ocelli with black pupils.
   1b. *A. g. glandon* ♀. Ups brown; unh gc brown, markings as in ♂.
   1c. *A. g.* f. *alboocellatus* ♂. Unh white markings mostly lack pupils.
   1d. *A. g. aquilo* ♂. Ups pale grey-blue; unh white markings large.
   1e. *A. g. zullichi* ♂. Small; unh white spots mostly lack pupils.

2. **Agriades pyrenaicus**   *Gavarnie Blue*   79
   2a. *A. p. pyrenaicus* ♂. Unf submarginal black spots distinct.
   2b. *A. p. asturiensis* ♂. Unf black markings larger.
   2c. *A. p. asturiensis* ♀. Ups pale brown; markings grey.
   2d. *A. p. dardanus* ♂. Small with fewer dark spots.

3. **Eumedonia eumedon**   *Geranium Argus*   74
   3a. *E. e. eumedon* ♂. Unh white postdiscal stripe on vein 5.
   3b. *E. e. eumedon* f. *borealis* ♂. Unh, white stripe on vein 5 vestigial or absent.

4. **Kretania psylorita**   *Cretan Argus*   74
   ♂. Ups brown; uph marginal lunules pale yellow; uns markings very small.

5. **Plebicula dorylas**   *Turquoise Blue*   87
   ♂. Ups sky-blue; uns margins white.

6. **Plebicula atlantica**   *Atlas Blue*   88
   6a. ♂. Ups like *P. dorylas*, but paler blue; uns as in ♀.
   6b. ♀. Ups brown, orange lunules very large.

7. **Plebicula nivescens**   *Mother-of-Pearl Blue*   88
   ♂. Ups shining pale silver-grey; uns as in *P. dorylas*.

8. **Plebicula golgus**   *Nevada Blue*   87
   ♂. Small, ups deep sky blue; uns pale grey-brown

9. **Agrodiaetus thersites**   *Chapman's Blue*   86
   ♂. Like *Polyommatus* **(Pl. 19)** but ups more violet and unf without black cell-spot. ♀ like *P. icarus* **(Pl. 4)** but uns as in *thersites*.

10. **Agrodiaetus amanda**   *Amanda's Blue*   86
    10a. *P. a. amanda* ♂. Large; uns pale grey, markings small.
    10b. *P. a. amanda* ♀. Uph submarginal lunules incomplete.
    10c. *P. a. abdelaziz* ♀. Ups submarginal lunules complete.

11. **Polyommatus eroides**   *Balkans Blue*   93
    ♂. Ups shining sky-blue, dark borders 2 mm. wide; unf with black spot in cell. ♀ ups brown

12. **Polyommatus eros**   *Eros Blue*   93
    ♂. Small; ups gleaming sky blue; borders 1 mm.; ♀ ups brown.

13. **Meleageria daphnis**   *Meleager's Blue*   89
    13a. ♂. Hw outer margins slightly scalloped.
    13b. *M. d. daphnis* ♀-f. *steeveni*. Ups brown with markings grey. **See also Pl. 21.**

PLATE 21

1. Agrodiaetus escheri *Escher's Blue* **See also Pl. 13.** 83
1a. *P. e. escheri* ♂. Bright blue, black marginal line narrow; uns boldly marked; unf no cell-spot.
1b. *P. e. escheri* ♀. Ups brown, orange marginal lunules prominent.
1c. *P. e. splendens* f. *altivolans* ♂. Smaller, ups paler blue.

2. Meleageria daphnis *Meleager's Blue* 89
♀. Ups blue; hw scalloped. **For ♂ see Pl. 20.**

3. Lysandra bellargus *Adonis Blue* 91
♂. Bright blue, fringes chequered; unf black cell-spot present. ♀ ups brown; uns as in ♂ but ground-colour darker. (Rarely, as in figure, unf cell-spot minute or absent.)

4. Lysandra punctifera *Spotted Adonis Blue* 92
♂. Like *L. bellargus*; ♂ uph marginal black spots prominent.

5. Lysandra coridon *Chalk-hill Blue* 89
5a. *L. c. coridon* ♂. Ups pale silvery-blue. ♀ brown.
5b. *L. c. coridon* ♀-f. *syngrapha*. Ups blue, borders brown; uph often with orange spots.
5c. *L. c. asturiensis* ♂. Ups brighter blue.
5d. *L. c. caelestissima* ♂. Like *L. bellargus* but ♂ ups paler sky-blue.

6. Lysandra albicans *Spanish Chalk-hill Blue* **See also Pl. 13.** 91
L. a. albicans ♂. Large: ups grey-white with darker marginal markings uns markings small. ♀ brown.

7. Lysandra hispana *Provence Chalk-hill Blue* 90
7a. ♂. Like *L. coridon*; ups silvery-blue, sometimes slightly yellowish.
7b. ♀. Like *L. coridon*; ups brown.

8. Agrodiaetus damon *Damon Blue* 81
♂. Ups pale shining blue; unh with firm white strips in space 4. ♀ brown, uns as in ♂.

9. Agrodiaetus dolus *Furry Blue* 82
9a. *A. d. virgilia* ♂. Ups grey-white; upf with wide discal brown suffusion. ♀ ups brown; markings as in ♂.
9b. *A. d. dolus* ♂. Like *A. d. virgilia* but ups pale blue.

10. Agrodiaetus admetus *Anomalous Blue* 85
♂. Uns with postdiscal and submarginal markings

11. Agrodiaetus ripartii *Ripart's Anomalous Blue* 86
♂. Unh with long pale stripe submarginal markings absent. ♀ similar but smaller.

1a

1c

1b

3

4

2

5d

5c

6

5a

7a

7b

5b

9a

10

8

9b

11

172

PLATE 22

1. Apatura metis *Freyer's Purple Emperor* 97
A. m. metis ♀, Hungary. Ups gc yellow-buff, markings grey-brown.
European specimens of both sexes almost always show marked clyteoid
characters. **See also Pl. 25.**

2. Apatura ilia *Lesser Purple Emperor* 97

2a. *A. i. barcina* ♂, Catalonia, gen.l. Uph white discal band is broad
and regular.
2b. *A. i. barcina* ♀, Catalonia, gen.l. Ups white markings as in ♂, gc
grey-brown. **See also Pl. 25.**

3. Agrodiaetus aroaniensis *Grecian Anomalous Blue* 86
♂, Greece, Peloponnesos. Unh lacks white median stripe, submarginal
markings vestigial or absent.

4. Lycaeides idas *Idas Blue* 72

4a. *A. i. magnagraeca* ♂, Macedonia. Large, ups veins blackened near
wide black marginal borders.
4b *A. i. bellieri* ♀, Corsica. Small, uns all markings strongly developed. **See also Pl. 18.**

5. Agrodiaetus iphigenia *Chelmos Blue* 81
A. i. nonacriensis ♂, Greece, Mt. Chelmos. Ups shining sky-blue, unh
white median stripe well defined.

6. Neolysandra coelestina *Pontic Blue* 87
N. c. coelestina ♂, Greece, Mt. Chelmos. Like *Cyaniris semiargus*, ups
darker shade of blue; unh green basal area more extensive.

7. Agrodiaetus fabressei *Oberthur's Anomalous Blue* 85

7a. *A. f. fabressei* ♂, C. Spain, Albarracin. Small, unh median white
stripe absent, markings not strongly developed.
7b. *A. f. agenjoi* ♂, N. Spain, Catalonia. Larger, unh usual markings
well developed but white median stripe lacking.

PLATE 23

1. **Charaxes jasius**   *Two-tailed Pasha*   96
   ♂, SE France. Normal upperside markings. **See also Pl. 25.**

2. **Gonepteryx cleopatra**   *Cleopatra*   39
   G. c. maderensis ♂, Madeira. Upf pale yellow marginal border narrow;
   unh yellow (f. *italica* Gerhard). **See also Pl. 12.**

3. **Heodes ottomanus**   *Grecian Copper*   52
   ♀, Greece, Parnassus, gen. 2. 'Tail' on hw at v2 prominent, black
   markings well developed. **See also Pl. 15.**

4. **Zerynthia cerisyi**   *Cretan Festoon*   20
   Z. c. cretica ♂, Crete. Like *Z. c. cerisyi* but small, hw outer margin little
   scalloped, lacking 'tail' at v4. **See also Pl. 2.**

5. **Tomares nogellii**   *Nogel's Hairstreak*   49
   T. n. dobrogensis, Dobrugea, Tulcea. Unh grey with narrow orange
   bands.

6. **Coenonympha leander**   *Russian Heath*   314
   C. l. orientalis ♂, Greece, Pindus Mts. Unh presents a pale yellow band
   before the prominent submarginal ocelli. **See also Pl. 57.**

7. **Mellicta deione**   *Provençal Fritillary*   123
   M. d. rosinae, gen. 1, Portugal, Serra da Monchique. Large, ups gc
   bright orange-fulvous, Black pattern heavily marked. **See also Pl. 34.**

PLATE 24

1. **Danaus chrysippus**   *Plain Tiger*   321
   ♂. Ups veins not darkened; uph with small sex-brand on vein 2.
   ♀ similar but lacking sex-brand.

2. **Danaus plexippus**   *Milkweed* or *Monarch*   321
   ♂. Ups veins darkened; uph sex-brand on vein 2, very small. ♀ similar
   but lacks sex-brand.

3. **Kirinia roxelana**   *Lattice Brown*   320
   3a. ♂. Fw narrow, distorted by sex-brands; unh with 5 large, 2 small
        postdiscal ocelli.
   3b. ♀. Fw shape normal; upf with pale apical markings; unh as in ♂.

4. **Melitaea didyma**   *Spotted Fritillary*   118
   M. d. occidentalis f. *dalmatina* ♂. Small, ups pale buff with small
   markings. **See also Pl. 33.**

5. **Melitaea phoebe**   *Knapweed Fritillary*   117
   M. phoebe f. *pauper* ♂. Small, ups uniform pale fulvous with thin dark
   markings. **See also Pl. 33.**

6. **Hamearis lucina**   *Duke of Burgundy Fritillary*   94
   First brood ♀. Large, ups markings well defined, dark suffusion slight
   (f. *praestans*). **For ♂ see Pl. 31.**

PLATE 25

1. **Apatura iris** *Purple Emperor* 96
   ♂. Ups with bright purple gloss; upf dark postdiscal spot in space 2 inconspicuous. ♀ ups grey-brown, no purple gloss, white markings larger.

2. **Apatura ilia** *Lesser Purple Emperor* 97
   Ups like *A. iris* but dark spot in space 2 conspicuous, ringed orange. ♀ like *A. iris* ♀, often tinted yellowish.

   2a. *A. i. ilia* ♂. Ups discal markings white.
   2b. *A. i. ilia* f. *clytie* ♂. Ups discal markings yellow-brown.
   See also Pl. 22.

3. **Apatura metis** *Freyer's Purple Emperor* 97
   ♂ Small, uph ocellar marginal dark spots reduced to narrow lunular band. **See also Pl. 22.**

4. **Limenitis populi** *Poplar Admiral* 98
   ♂. Ups dark with white and orange markings. ♀ similar but ups white markings larger.

5. **Charaxes jasius** *Two-tailed Pasha* 96
   ♂. (Underside only.) Hw with two short tails; ups dark brown with wide fulvous borders. ♀ similar, larger. **See also Pl. 23.**

PLATE 26

1. Polygonia egea *Southern Comma*   103
First brood ♂. Unh white discoidal mark very small, shaped like letter 'y'. Sexes similar.

2. Polygonia c-album *Comma Butterfly*   103
Unh white discoidal mark larger, shaped like letter 'C'.

    2a. First brood ♂ (f. *hutchinsoni*). Ups ground-colour bright fulvous; uns markings in rather pale tones of brown, buff, etc. Sexes similar.
    2b. Second brood ♂. Ups darker; uns strongly marked in brown, buff, green, etc.
    2c. Second brood ♀. Uns very dark, markings obscure, mixed with green and very dark brown.

3. Araschnia levana *Map Butterfly*   104
Ups variable seasonally; uns with pale linear markings.

    3a. First brood ♂. Ups fulvous with black markings. Sexes similar.
    3b. Second brood ♂ (f. *prorsa*). Ups black with prominent white discal markings.
    3c. Second brood ♀ (f. *prorsa*). Ups like ♂ but with small fulvous postdiscal markings.

4. Neptis sappho *Common Glider*   99
♂. Uph with white discal band and postdiscal spots; unh without black postdiscal spots. Sexes similar.

5. Neptis rivularis *Hungarian Glider*   99
♂. Uph with single white discal band; unh without black postdiscal spots. Sexes similar.

6. Limenitis camilla *White Admiral*   98
♂. Unh with 2 rows of dark postdiscal spots. ♀ similar.

7. Limenitis reducta *Southern White Admiral*   98
♂. Unh with single row of dark postdiscal spots. ♀ similar.

1

2 b

2 a

2 c

3 b

3 a

3 c

4

6

5

7

PLATE 27

1. Aglais urticae   *Small Tortoiseshell*   102
Ups red with black and yellow markings and blue submarginal
lunules; uph with wide dark basal area. ♀ similar.

1a.   *A. u. urticae* ♂. Upf with black postdiscal spot in spaces 1b, 2, 3.
1b.   *A. u. ichnusa* ♂. No black postdiscal spots on upf.

2. Cynthia virginiensis   *American Painted Lady*   102
♂. Unh with very large submarginal ocelli in spaces 2 and 5. ♀ similar.

3. Cynthia cardui   *Painted Lady*   102
♂. Unh with 5 small submarginal ocelli. ♀ similar.

4. Vanessa indica vulcania   *Indian Red Admiral*   101
♂. Upf red transverse band irregular, broken by black ground-colour.
♀ similar.

5. Vanessa atalanta   *Red Admiral*   101
♀. Red transverse band intact, of even width throughout. ♂ similar.

6. Nymphalis xanthomelas   *Yellow-legged Tortoiseshell*   100
♂. (Upperside only.) Ups inner edges of dark wing-borders indistinct; fore-legs buff; uns as in 7 but darker. ♀ similar.

7. Nymphalis vau-album   *False Comma*   100
♂. Bright white marks present near apex of fw and on costa of hw. ♀
similar.

8. Nymphalis polychloros   *Large Tortoiseshell*   99
♂. (Upperside only). Ups inner edges of dark wing-borders sharply
defined; fore-legs black; uns as in 7 but darker. ♀ similar.

9. Nymphalis antiopa   *Camberwell Beauty*   99
♂. Ups purple with wide cream-coloured border on both wings. ♀
similar.

10. Inachis io   *Peacock*   101
♂. Ups with large 'peacock eye' on each wing. ♀ similar.

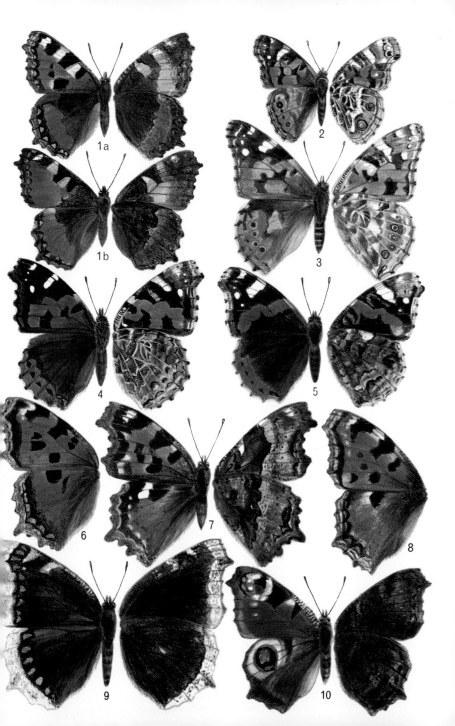

PLATE 28

1. Fabriciana adippe   *High Brown Fritillary*   106
Unh with small silver-pupilled postdiscal spots.

    1a. *F. a. adippe* ♂. Unh ground-colour buff; basal, discal and marginal
    spots filled silver.
    1b. *F. a. chlorodippe* ♀. Unh yellow-green, all spots present and filled
    silver. ♂ similar.
    1c. *F. a. cleodippe* ♂. Unh buff with green basal suffusion; spots paler
    buff, *not* filled silver.
    1d. *F. a. cleodoxa* ♂. Unh pale buff, spots (except postdiscal series) *not*
    filled silver. ♀ similar.

2. Fabriciana niobe   *Niobe Fritillary*   107
F. n. auresiana ♂. Unh green, spots filled silver but some basal spots
missing. ♀ similar, larger. **See also Pl. 29 and Pl. 59.**

3. Argynnis paphia   *Silver-washed Fritillary*   104
Unh greenish with transverse bands and outer margin silvery.

    3a. *A. p. paphia* ♂. Upf with thick sex-brands along veins 1–4, other
    black markings rather small.
    3b. *A. p. paphia* ♀. Ups black markings larger and complete.
    3c. *A. p. immaculata* ♀. Unh suffused greenish-gold and markings
    obscure. Ups gc yellow-grey (♀-form *valesina*).

1a

1b

2

1c

3a

1d

3b

3c

PLATE 29

1. **Mesoacidalia aglaja**   *Dark-green Fritillary*   105
Unh with silver basal, discal and marginal spots, but no postdiscal
spots.

   1a. *M. a. aglaja* ♂. Unh yellow-buff with green markings. ♀ ups often
   suffused grey.
   1b. *M. a. lyauteyi* ♂. Large, ups more heavily marked; unh green
   suffusion more extensive. ♀ larger, ups paler fulvous.

2. **Fabriciana niobe**   *Niobe Fritillary*   107
Like *F. adippe* **(Pl. 28)** but unh with a small silver or buff spot in centre
of cell which often encloses a small black point (see 2b); small postdiscal spots present. ♀ ups clouded with grey suffusion. **See also Pl. 28.**

   2a. (Uns only.) *F. niobe* ♂. Unh all spots filled or pupilled with silver.
   ♀ similar.
   2b. (Uns only.) *F. niobe* f. *eris* ♂. Unh all spots buff except the small
   postdiscal spots. ♀ similar. **See also Pl. 59.**

3. **Fabriciana elisa**   *Corsican Fritillary*   108
♂. Unh with numerous small silver spots. ♀ similar, larger.

4. **Issoria lathonia**   *Queen of Spain Fritillary*   108
♂. Unh with distinctive large silver spots. ♀ similar.

5. **Argyronome laodice**   *Pallas's Fritillary*   105
♀. Upf with small white costal mark near apex; unh base olive-yellow,
distal area brown. ♂ similar.

6. **Pandoriana pandora**   *Cardinal*   104
Unf ground-colour rosy-red.

   6a. ♂. Unh green with silver striae near costa.
   6b. ♀. Unh green with wavy transverse silver stripes; upf without
   sex-brands.

PLATE 30

1. Brenthis hecate   *Twin-spot Fritillary*

   1a. ♂. Unh with two rows of black postdiscal spots.
   1b. ♀. Similar, ups sometimes suffused grey.

2. Brenthis daphne   *Marbled Fritillary*

   2a. ♂. Unh with single row of black postdiscal spots, base of space 4
      usually brown (yellow in *B. ino* **(Pl. 32)**
   2b. ♀. Similar, usually larger.

3. Clossiana euphrosyne   *Pearl-bordered Fritillary*
Unh central spot in yellow discal band silver.

   3a. *C. euphrosyne* ♂. Ups clear fulvous, markings slender.
   3b. *C. euphrosyne* f. *fingal* ♀. Smaller, ups black markings heavier.

4. Clossiana selene   *Small Pearl-bordered Fritillary*
Unh spots of discal band uniformly yellow or silver.

   4a. *C. selene* ♂. Ups black markings slender.
   4b. *C. selene* f. *hela* ♀. Ups black markings heavier.

5. Clossiana titania   *Titania's Fritillary*

   5a. *C. t. titania* ♂. Ups orange-fulvous, black markings slender; unh
      colour contrast not striking. ♀ similar.
   5b. *C. t. cypris* ♂. Ups bright fiery fulvous, black markings larger; unh
      brightly marked in purple-brown, yellow, etc.

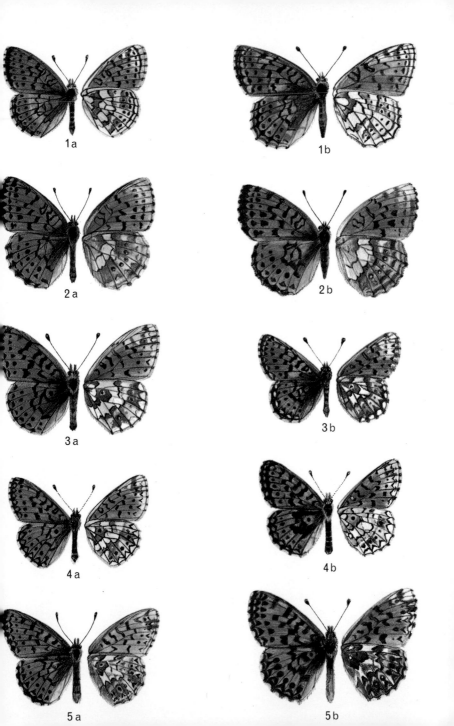

1a

1b

2a

2b

3a

3b

4a

4b

5a

5b

PLATE 31

1. Boloria napaea   *Mountain Fritillary*   110
Ups ground-colour fulvous with thin black markings; unf black markings scanty or vestigial.

   1a. *B. napaea* f. *frigida* ♂. Small, unh markings well defined; ♀ rarely
        heavily suffused grey.
   1b. *B. napaea* ♀. Ups usually heavily suffused dark grey; unh brightly
        variegated with yellow, greenish, red-brown, etc.; uph black basal
        shade rarely extends to cell-end.
   1c. *B. napaea* ♂. Ups ground-colour fulvous yellow.

2. Boloria pales   *Shepherd's Fritillary*   109
Like *B. napaea*; ups black pattern more macular, discal spots firmly
marked; unf black spots vestigial or absent.

   2a. *B. p. pales* ♀. Ups black markings heavy; uph black basal shade
        extends widely to cell-end, often includes body groove.
   2b. *B. p. pales* ♂. Ups clear bright fulvous; uph black basal shade as in
        ♀; unh markings lack greenish reflections.
   2c. *B. p. palustris* ♂. Small, ups markings less macular; unf black spots
        sometimes better developed.
   2d. *B. p. palustris* ♀. Ups often slightly paler, otherwise similar to ♂.
   2e. *B. p. pyrenesmiscens* ♂. Ups markings macular; uph black basal
        shade reduced; unf black markings present.

3. Boloria graeca   *Balkan Fritillary*   111
Hw outer margin strongly angled at vein 8; unf black markings well
developed.

   3a. *B. g. graeca* ♂. Unh with 6 round postdiscal spots well defined.
   3b. *B. g. tendensis* ♀. Ups paler fulvous-yellow.

4. Boloria aquilonaris   *Cranberry Fritillary*   111
Unf black markings complete; unh red postdiscal area invading usual
yellow mark in space 3 and postdiscal ocelli well defined.

   4a. *B. aquilonaris* ♂. Upf marks strongly angled in space 1b.
   4b. *B. aquilonaris* ♀. Ups often with faint violet gloss.
   4c. *B. aquilonaris* f. *alethea* ♀. Large.

5. Mellicta athalia   *Heath Fritillary*   122

   5a. *M. a. norvegica* ♂. Small, ups black reticulate pattern very regu-
        lar. ♀ similar. **See also Pl. 35.**
   5b. *M. a. celadussa* f. *tenuicola* ♂. Small, ups pale, black markings thin
        and incomplete. **See also Pl. 35.**

6. Hamearis lucina   *Duke of Burgundy Fritillary*   94
Second brood ♂. Ups fulvous spots partly obscured by extension of
black ground-colour. **See also Pl. 24.**

1a

2a

2c

1b

2b

2d

1c

5a

3a

5b

2e

4b

3b

4a

6

4c

PLATE 32

1. **Proclossiana eunomia**   *Bog Fritillary*   112
   Unh with six white-centred postdiscal ocelli.
   1a. *P. e. eunomia* ♂. Ups ground-colour clear fulvous; unh pale discal
       spots and marginal lunules yellow. ♀ ups often slightly fuscous.
   1b. *P. e. ossianus* ♂. Ups slightly suffused fuscous; unh marginal
       lunules silvered. ♀ often darker and more heavily suffused fus-
       cous.

2. **Brenthis ino**   *Lesser Marbled Fritillary*   109
   ♂. Ups like *B. daphne* (**Pl. 30**) but smaller and black marginal lines
   continuous; unh base of space 4 yellow. ♀ similar, ups sometimes
   suffused fuscous.

3. **Clossiana polaris**   *Polar Fritillary*   115
   ♂. Unh with many small white markings. ♀ similar.

4. **Clossiana frigga**   *Frigga's Fritillary*   116
   ♂. Unh with conspicuous white costal and discal marks set in deep
   brown. ♀ similar.

5. **Clossiana thore**   *Thor's Fritillary*   115
   5a. *C. t. thore* ♂. Ups with very extensive black markings; unh yellow
       discal band conspicuous. ♀ similar.
   5b. *C. t. borealis* ♂. Ups ground-colour pale fulvous, less heavily
       marked; unh markings pale, not well defined. ♀ similar.

6. **Clossiana freija**   *Freya's Fritillary*   114
   ♂. Unh with prominent zig-zag brown postdiscal line in spaces 1, 2, 3.
   ♀ similar.

7. **Clossiana chariclea**   *Arctic Fritillary*   114
   ♀. Unh with prominent pale discal band. ♂ similar.

8. **Clossiana improba**   *Dusky-winged Fritillary*   116
   ♂. Small, ups dusky, markings not well defined; unh like *C. frigga*.
   ♀ similar.

9. **Clossiana dia**   *Weaver's Fritillary*   114
   ♂. Hw outer margin sharply angled at vein 8; unh marbled with
   purple-brown. ♀ similar.

10. **Eurodryas desfontainii**   *Spanish Fritillary*   129
    ♀. Uns suffused brick-red; unf with prominent discal band of black
    spots; unh markings clearly defined by black striae (f. *gibrati*). **For** ♂
    see Pl. 36.

11. **Libythea celtis**   *Nettle-tree Butterfly*   95
    ♂. Palpi very long; wings sharply angled. ♀ similar.

PLATE 33

1. **Melitaea phoebe**   *Knapweed Fritillary*   117
   Upf orange marginal lunule in space 3 very large; a most variable
   species, ♀ ups sometimes suffused dark grey.
   1a. *M. p. phoebe* second brood ♂. Ups fulvous ground-colour
   moderately constant in tone across both wings.
   1b. *M. p. phoebe* f. *alternans* ♂. Ups brightly marked with alternating
   bands of yellow and bright fulvous ground-colour, black markings
   heavy.
   1c. *M. p. punica* ♂. Small; upf black discal spots prominent but
   postdiscal area almost unmarked; unh ground-colour pale cream
   to white.
   1d. *M. p. occitanica* second brood ♂. Ups brightly marked, ground-
   colour pale buff, postdiscal bands orange-red, black markings
   thin. **See also Pl. 24.**

2. **Melitaea aetherie**   *Aetherie Fritillary*   118
   Ups like *M. phoebe*, postdiscal areas of both wings almost unmarked in
   ♂. Sexes differ. Females very variable.
   2a. *M. a. algirica* ♂. Ups bright fulvous without colour contrast.
   2b. *M. a. algirica* ♀. Ups heavily suffused dark grey except the costal
   area of hw.

3. **Melitaea didyma**   *Spotted Fritillary*   118
   Ups black markings macular, discrete; unh ground-colour pale yellow,
   marginal black spots round. ♀ very variable.
   3a. *M. d. occidentalis* second brood ♂. Ups ground-colour bright
   fulvous, black markings scanty. ♀ generally similar with larger
   black markings. **See also Pl. 24.**
   3b. *M. d. didyma* first brood ♂. Ups tawny red ground-colour bright;
   black markings larger, including postdiscal spots. ♀ ups often
   powdered grey.
   3c. *M. d. meridionalis* first brood ♀. Ups ground-colour obliterated by
   grey suffusion except the costal area of hw. ♂ ground-colour
   reddish-fulvous, ups markings usually almost complete.

4. **Melitaea trivia**   *Lesser Spotted Fritillary*   120
   Unh marginal spots triangular; in hw lower discocellular vein always
   present. Sexes similar, ♀ often larger, slightly variable.
   4a. *M. t. trivia* second brood ♂. Ups ground-colour fulvous yellow,
   black markings rather heavy.
   4b. *M. t. trivia* f. *fascelis* first brood ♂. Large, ground-colour darker
   and black markings heavier.
   4c. *M. t. ignasiti* second brood ♂. Small, ground-colour paler, black
   markings, smaller.

5. **Melitaea deserticola**   *Desert Fritillary*   120
   ♂. Ups like *M. didyma*; unh ground-colour white, basal orange markings broken up, each spot bordered with black. ♀ similar.

1a

1b

1c

1d

2a

2b

3a

3b

3c

4a

4b

4c

5

PLATE 34

1. Melitaea cinxia   *Glanville Fritillary*   116
Uph with 4 or 5 round black spots in submarginal band; unh marginal
spots small, discrete; fringes chequered. Sexes similar, ♀ often larger.

1a. *M. c. cinxia* first brood ♀. Ups fulvous yellow.
1b. *M. c. atlantis* first brood ♂. Ups pale buff, markings intense black.

2. Melitaea arduinna   *Freyer's Fritillary*   117
M. a. rhodopensis ♂. Ups like *M. cinxia*, larger, ups fulvous red; unh
marginal black lunules joined. ♀ often larger, ups yellowish and black
markings heavier.

3. Mellicta deione   *Provençal Fritillary*   123
Upf discal spot in space 1b, dumb-bell shaped (inconstant): unf black
inner border of orange marginal lunule in space 2, vestigial or absent.

3a. *M. d. deione* first brood ♂. Ups clear orange-yellow.
3b. *M. d. deione* first brood ♀. Large, ups colour contrast strong.
3c. *M. d. berisalii* first brood ♀. Ups darker, black markings heavy,
black marginal borders wider.
3d. *M. d. nitida* first brood ♂. Ups orange-yellow; uph discal area
almost unmarked. **See also Pl. 23.**

4. Mellicta parthenoides   *Meadow Fritillary*   124
Ups black pattern regular; upf black discal spot in space 1b oblique;
uph postdiscal area often unmarked (inconstant); unf postdiscal area
unmarked.

4a. *M. parthenoides* first brood ♂. Ups ground-colour clear fulvous.
4b. *M. parthenoides* ♀. Ups black markings heavier with slight colour
contrast.
4c. *M. parthenoides* f. *plena* ♂. Ups darker, black markings heavier.

5. Mellicta britomartis   *Assman's Fritillary*   125
♂. Like *Mellicta aurelia*; unh orange submarginal lunules bordered
internally by dark band. Identification may entail dissection. ♀ similar.

6. Mellicta aurelia   *Nickerl's Fritillary*   125
6a. ♂. Like *M. britomartis*, usually slightly smaller; unf black postdiscal markings often complete; unh orange submarginal lunules
bordered internally by grey.
6b. ♀. Like ♂; often slightly larger and ups fulvous paler.

7. Mellicta asteria   *Little Fritillary*   126
♂. Small; unh marginal black line single.

PLATE 35

1. **Mellicta athalia**   *Heath Fritillary*   122
   Unf black inner border of yellow marginal lunules in spaces 1b, 2 (3)
   usually well developed. A most variable species.

   1a. *M. a. athalia* first brood ♂. Ups black markings regular and well
        defined.
   1b. *M. a. boris* f. *satyra* ♂. Ups black markings greatly extended.
   1c. *M. a. boris* ♂. Ups black markings regular, marginal black borders
        wider.
   1d. *M. a. norvegica* f. *lachares* ♀. Ups black markings thin, postdiscal
        fulvous band wide. **See also Pl. 31.**
   1e. *M. a. celadussa* ♂. Ups like *M. a. athalia*, but often brighter. The
        genitalia show subspecific characters.
   1f. *M. a. celadussa* ♀. Ups rather brightly marked with slight colour
        contrast. **See also Pl. 31.**
   1g. *M. a. biedermanni* ♂. Large, ups ground-colour bright fulvous,
        black discal spots prominent.
   1h. *M. a. celadussa* f. *nevadensis* ♂. Ups ground-colour pale orange-
        yellow, black markings thin.

2. **Melitaea diamina**   *False Heath Fritillary*   120
   Unh orange lunules of the submarginal band each enclose a small
   round spot; marginal line orange on both wings.

   2a. *M. d. diamina* ♂. Ups black markings heavy; uph base and discal
        areas black.
   2b. *M. d. diamina* ♀. Ups postdiscal and marginal spots usually pale.
   2c. *M. d. vernetensis* ♀. Like *M. athalia*, but ups without dark
        suffusion; unh marginal line pale, yellowish, but submarginal dark
        spots usually distinct.

3. **Mellicta varia**   *Grisons Fritillary*   124
   Upf discal black mark in space 1b. almost vertical (oblique in *M.
   parthenoides*); unf postdiscal area unmarked. ♀ ups often suffused grey.

   3a. *N. varia* f. *piana* ♂. Large, upf postdiscal markings present; unh
        discal band very pale.
   3b. *M. varia* ♂. Smaller, ups postdiscal areas unmarked; unh discal
        band yellowish (or white).

1a   1g

1h   1f

1c   1b

1d   2a

1e   2c

3a   3b   2b

PLATE 36

1. Eurodryas aurinia   *Marsh Fritillary*   128
Unf markings obscure, lacking black discal spots; unh submarginal
band with a black spot in each space; unh margin pale; fringes not
chequered. Sexes alike. ♀ larger. Very variable.

   1a. *E. a. debilis* f. *glaciegenita* ♂. Ups heavily suffused dark grey.
   1b. *E. a. debilis* ♂. Small; ups brightly marked in orange-red on
      yellowish ground-colour, black markings heavy.
   1c. *E. a. debilis* ♀. Like ♂ but larger.
   1d. *E. a. aurinia* ♂. Ups yellow with orange-brown bands and spots,
      black markings reduced and lacking dusky suffusion.
   1e. *E. a. aurinia* ♀. Ups pale yellow with reddish bands and spots;
      black markings increased.
   1f. *E. a. beckeri* ♂. Large, hw submarginal band wide with large black
      spots.

2. Hypodryas iduna   *Lapland Fritillary*   127
♂. Ups ground-colour pale yellowish with orange-red spots and bands;
hw sub-marginal band lacks black spots. Sexes similar.

3. Eurodryas desfontainii   *Spanish Fritillary*   129
E. d. baetica f. *zapateri* ♂. Like *E. aurinia* but unf black discal spots
prominent.
For ♀ see Plate 32.

4. Hypodryas cynthia   *Cynthia's Fritillary*   127
Unh marginal line orange; submarginal band includes small black
spots.

   4a. *H. cynthia* ♂. Ups white with red spots and black markings.
   4b. *H. c. alpicola* ♀. Ups red-brown, spots and bands little or not at all
      darker; unh pale discal band includes fine black cross-lines in
      spaces 5, 6, 7; unf pale marginal lunules in regular series.

5. Hypodryas maturna   *Scarce Fritillary*   126
♂. Ups black markings heavy; ground-colour red with prominent
bands and small pale spots; unf pale marginal lunules irregular; unh
marginal line orange. Sexes similar.

6. Hypodryas intermedia   *Asian Fritillary*   126
H. i. wolfensbergeri ♀. Ups like *H. cynthia* ♀; unh pale postdiscal band
includes a fine black line running from costa to anal angle, marginal
line orange. Sexes similar.

1a

1b

1c

1d

1e

1f

2

3

4a

4b

5

6

PLATE 37

1 a

1 b

1 c

2

3 a

4 a

3 b

4 b

PLATE 38

1. Melanargia galathea   *Marbled White*   256

   1a. *M. g. lachesis* f. *duponti* ♂. Ups black markings reduced.
   1b. *M. g. lucasi* ♂. Unf with grey area beyond white cell-mark. **See
   also Pl. 37.**

2. Melanargia occitanica   *Western Marbled White*   258
Ups like *M. ines* **(Pl. 37)**; upf cell-bar at or beyond centre of cell; unh
veins lined in brown. ♀ similar, larger.

   2a. *M. o. occitanica* ♂. Uph ocelli conspicuous; unh with fine brown
   line in space 1b.
   2b. *M. o. pelagia* ♂. Small, like *M. o. occitanica* but upf with circular
   mark at cell-end often filled with blue.
   2c. *M. o. pherusa* ♂. Ups black markings reduced; uph ocelli small or
   absent in form *plesaura* (figured).

3. Melanargia larissa   *Balkan Marbled White*   258
Ups wing-bases extensively suffused with black, which may extend to
apex of cell.

   3a. *M. l. larissa* ♂. Ups black markings very dense and extensive.
   3b. *M. l. herta* ♀. Ups not heavily marked; upf thin black cell-bar not
   covered by basal suffusion.

4. Erebia eriphyle   *Eriphyle Ringlet*   276
E. e. tristis ♀. Ups medium brown, orange markings well developed;
uns paler. **For ♂ see Pl. 48.**

5. Erebia manto   *Manto Ringlet*   277
E. m. constans ♂. Black, and unmarked on both surfaces. ♀ unf sometimes with vestigial fulvous markings. **See also Pls. 48, 49 and 54.**

6. Erebia euryale   *Large Ringlet*   275
E. e. adyte ♀. Unh postdiscal band grey-white. **See also Pl. 46.**

1b

1a

2b

2c

3b

2a

3a

4

5

6

PLATE 39

1. **Hipparchia fagi**   *Woodland Grayling*   260
   Large, fw over 33 mm;

   1a. ♂. Upf densely suffused grey-brown; uph postdiscal pale band obscure.
   1b. ♀. Upf pale postdiscal band better defined; uph white postdiscal band wide.

2. **Hipparchia alcyone**   *Rock Grayling*   261
   Like *H. fagi* but smaller, fw 33 mm or less, variable.

   2a. *H. a. alcyone* ♂. Ups like *H. fagi* but pale postdiscal bands yellowish and better defined.
   2b. *H. a. alcyone* ♀. Ups pale postdiscal bands well defined, yellowish on fw, white on hw.
   Note. It is not always possible to distinguish between *H. fagi* and *H. alcyone* without dissection. See comparative table pp. 260–1.

3. **Hipparchia syriaca**   *Eastern Rock Grayling*   261
   H. syriaca serrula ♂. Fw apex pointed, markings as in *H. fagi* ♂.

4. **Hipparchia ellena**   *Algerian Grayling*   262
   Like *H. alcyone*; ups postdiscal bands white and well-defined; uns dark basal areas make strong contrast with white postdiscal bands.

   4a. ♂. Fw apex pointed.
   4b. ♀. Fw apex more rounded; postdiscal markings better developed; upf with ocellus in space 2.

PLATE 40

1. **Hipparchia azorina** *Azores Grayling* 264
Small, ups dusky, unh white postdiscal band strongly angled.

   1a. ♀. Uph postdiscal markings white and well defined.
   1b. ♂. Smaller, uph postdiscal markings yellowish, obscure.

2. **Hipparchia aristaeus** *Southern Grayling* 263
Ups very variable; specific characters in male genitalia.

   2a. *H. a. aristaeus* ♂. Ups brown, suffused orange; uph with wide orange postdiscal band.
   2b. *H. a. aristaeus* ♀. Ups bright orange-brown markings extensive.
   2c. *H. a. algirica* ♂. Ups lacks orange suffusion; postdiscal markings orange-yellow.
   2d. *H. a. maderensis* ♂. Ups dusky brown, markings obscure.
   2e. *H. a. maderensis* ♀. Ups orange-yellow markings well defined, resembles *H. semele cadmus* (fig. 3c). **See also Pl. 59.**

3. **Hipparchia semele** *Grayling* 262
Ups variable; specific characters in male genitalia.

   3a. *H. s. semele* ♂. Small; ups grey-brown with yellowish postdiscal areas well defined.
   3b. *H. s. cadmus* ♂. Larger, ups dark grey-brown, postdiscal markings greatly reduced, submarginal area of hw bright orange; unh white postdiscal band conspicuous.
   3c. *H. s. cadmus* ♀. Larger; ups yellow postdiscal markings more extensive; unh marbled light and dark grey.

1a

1b

2c

2a

3a

2b

3b

2d

3c

2e

PLATE 41

1. **Neohipparchia statilinus**   *Tree Grayling*   265
   Upf ocelli usually blind; hw outer margin slightly scalloped, fringes
   paler. Unh very variable.

   1a. *N. s. statilinus* ♂. Ups very dark, markings obscure; unh smooth
      brown, discal band indicated by irregular dark lines.
   1b. *N. s. statilinus* ♀. Ups postdiscal areas paler, markings better
      defined; unh grey, markings vestigial.
   1c. *N. s. sylvicola* ♂. Unh grey-brown, markings obscure.

2. **Neohipparchia fatua**   *Freyer's Grayling*   265
   Like *N. statilinus* but larger; unh densely striated and irrorated with
   dark scales, margin deeply scalloped.

   2a. *N. f. fatua* ♂. Ups very dark; uph dark submarginal lunules well
      defined.
   2b. *N. f. fatua* ♀. Ups ocelli ringed yellow, markings more complete.

3. **Neohipparchia powelli**   *Powell's Grayling*   266
   ♂. Ups lacks yellow markings; unh veins conspicuously lined pale
   grey.

4. **Pseudotergumia wyssi**   *Canary Grayling*   267
   Ups ocelli usually blind; unf with rather prominent pale mark in space
   2; hw outer margin deeply scalloped, fringes white, chequered.

   4a. *P. w. wyssii* ♂. Fw pointed; ups medium brown, markings obscure;
      unh ground-colour yellowish-grey, white postdiscal band promi-
      nent.
   4b. *P. w. wyssii* ♀. Upf with pale postdiscal markings in space 2 and on
      costa, white spots in spaces 3, 4 larger; uns as in ♂.
   4c. *P. w. bacchus* ♀. Fw less pointed; ups dark brown, postdiscal
      markings better developed; unh as in *P. w. wyssi* but darker.

PLATE 42

1. Chazara briseis   *The Hermit*   267

   1a.   ♂. Upf costa pale yellow-grey; unh grey basal area bounded by
         dark mark on costa.
   1b.   ♀. Unh pale brown, markings obscure, heavily dusted with fine
         dark striae.

2. Chazara prieuri   *Southern Hermit*   268

   2a.   *C. prieuri* ♂. Upf with buff flash in cell; unh white postdiscal band
         followed by saggitate dark markings.
   2b.   *C. prieuri* ♀. Upf lacks buff flash in cell; unh marbled dark grey,
         brown, etc.
   2c.   *C. prieuri* ♀-form *uhagonis*. Ups white markings replaced by
         orange-brown.

3. Neohipparchia hansii   *Austaut's Grayling*   266

   3a.   ♂. Ups medium brown; upf with white-pupilled ocelli in spaces 2,
         5, and white spots in spaces 3, 4, in obscurely yellow postdiscal
         band; unh postdiscal band pale grey.
   3b.   ♀. Like ♂ but ups markings better defined.

4. Pseudotergumia fidia   *Striped Grayling*   266

   4a.   ♂. Ups grey-brown, ocelli inconspicuous; unh with striking dark
         zig-zag lines.
   4b.   ♀. Ups markings better defined.

PLATE 43

1. **Arethusana arethusa**   *False Grayling*   274
   Ups medium brown with orange-yellow postdiscal markings; ♂ up
   with single blind apical ocellus.

   1a. *A. a. arethusa* ♂. Ups orange postdiscal markings vestigial; unh
   brown with obscure paler postdiscal band.
   1b. *A. a. arethusa* ♀. Larger; ups postdiscal orange markings slightly
   better developed.
   1c. *A. a. boabdil* ♂. Ups obscurely marked; unh strongly marked with
   white postdiscal band and white veins.
   1d. *A. a. dentata* ♀. Ups with well developed orange postdiscal bands;
   unh veins lined with pale grey.

2. **Brintesia circe**   *Great Banded Grayling*   274
   ♂. Large, ups almost black; upf with single blind ocellus and white
   interrupted postdiscal band. ♀ similar, larger.

3. **Lopinga achine**   *Woodland Brown*   320
   ♂. Ups with large yellow-ringed blind ocelli on both wings. ♀ similar,
   ocelli slightly larger.

4. **Aphantopus hyperantus**   *Ringlet*   305
   ♂. Ups almost black, ocelli obscure; unh paler, ocelli prominent,
   yellow-ringed, white pupilled, absent in space 4. ♀ ups paler, ocelli
   usually larger; uns yellow-brown.

5. **Berberia abdelkader**   *Giant Grayling*   273
   ♀. Upf outer margin pale yellow-grey (form *nelvai*); unh veins pale
   yellowish, transverse lines obscure. **For ♂ see Pl. 44.**

PLATE 44

1. Satyrus actaea *Black Satyr* 272

    1a. ♂. Ups dark brown (black), upf with single apical ocellus and sex-brand below cell; unh basal area bordered pale grey.

    1b. ♀. Ups paler brown; upf apical ocellus often ringed orange-yellow, a small ocellus in space 2 often present.

2. Satyrus ferula *Great Sooty Satyr* 272

    2a. ♂. Ups very dark brown (black), upf with 2 ocelli, sex-brand absent; unh basal area bordered pale grey.

    2b. ♀. Ups paler brown; upf ocelli strongly ringed orange or set in orange postdiscal band; unh pale brown, markings obscure.

3. Minois dryas *The Dryad* 273

    3a. ♂. Ups very dark brown; upf with 2 small blue-pupilled ocelli; hw outer margin scalloped.

    3b. ♀. Ups paler brown; upf ocelli large; hw outer-margin deeply scalloped.

4. Berberia abdelkader *Giant Grayling* 273

    ♂. Ups ocelli blue-pupilled, with small blue spots between; unh brown with dark pale-edged postdiscal line and pale marginal markings. **For ♀ see Pl. 43.**

PLATE 45

PLATE 46

1. Erebia euryale   *Large Ringlet*   275
Fringes chequered; ♂ upf lacks sex-brand; markings very variable.

  1a. *E. e. euryale* ♂. Ups with small blind ocelli in fulvous postdiscal
     bands; uns ocelli white-pupilled; unh dark, ocelli very small,
     fulvous-ringed.
  1b. *E. e. euryale* ♀. Ups markings paler, ocelli white-pupilled; unh
     dark basal area followed by pale band enclosing ocelli.
  1c. *E. e. ocellaris* ♂. Ups fulvous markings reduced to narrow rings
     round small blind ocelli. ♀ similar.
  1d. *E. e. adyte* ♂. Ups with white-pupilled ocelli in fulvous postdiscal
     bands.
  1e. *E. e. adyte* ♀. Ups like male, but more brightly marked; unh
     postdiscal band wide, yellow or white. **See also Pl. 38.**

2. Erebia ligea   *Arran Brown*   275
Fringes chequered; upf with sex-brand below median vein.

  2a. *E. l. dovrensis* ♂. Ups like *E. euryale*; unh with white costal mark
     before obscure postdiscal band.
  2b. *E. l. ligea* ♂. Large; ups ocelli white pupilled; unh very dark, white
     postdiscal band strongly developed.
  2c. *E. l. ligea* ♀. Ups more brightly marked; unh brown with paler
     postdiscal band and white costal stripe.

3. Erebia lefebvrei   *Lefèbvre's Ringlet*   294

  3a. *E. l. astur* ♂. Ups black; upf with very small white-pupilled apical
     ocelli, and minute white points in space 2 and uph near margin;
     uns markings similar. ♀ unh grey.
  3b. *E. l. lefebvrei* ♂. Ups black with white-pupilled ocelli close to
     margins; upf ocelli weakly fulvous-ringed. ♀ similar but more
     birghtly marked.

PLATE 47

1. **Erebia flavofasciata**   *Yellow-banded Ringlet*   278
   ♂. Unh with yellow postdiscal band enclosing small ocellar spots. ♀
   paler, markings better defined.

2. **Erebia mnestra**   *Mnestra's Ringlet*   288
   ♂. Upf ocelli absent (or very small), no sex-brand; unh cinnamon-
   brown, unmarked. ♀ upf with twin apical ocelli; unh often with pale
   grey postdiscal band.

3. **Erebia aethiopella**   *False Mnestra Ringlet*   288
   Uph with fulvous postdiscal band; ♂ with sex-brands below median
   vein.

   3a. *E. a. aethiopella* ♂. Upf with very small white-pupilled apical
   ocelli; unh brown, dusted with scattered white scales.

   3b. *E. a. aethiopella* ♀. Like ♂ but more brightly marked and ocelli
   larger.

   3c. *E. a. rhodopensis* f. *sharsta* ♂. Upf ocelli larger (sometimes present
   on hw); unh brown or grey. ♀ more brightly marked.

   3d. *E. a. rhodopensis* ♂. Ups more brightly marked with larger ocelli;
   hw postdiscal ocelli present on both surfaces.

4. **Erebia sudetica**   *Sudeten Ringlet*   281

   4a. *E. s. liorana* ♂. Unh with 5 to 6 orange postdiscal spots in regular
   graded series. ♀ unh ground-colour yellow-brown.

   4b. *E. s. sudetica* ♀. Unh postdiscal spots larger, separated only by
   brown veins.

5. **Erebia melampus**   *Lesser Mountain Ringlet*   281
   ♂. Like *E. sudetica* but unh orange postdiscal spot in space 4 displaced
   slightly basally, series irregular. ♀ similar, unh paler.

6. **Erebia claudina**   *White Speck Ringlet*   278

   6a. ♂. Unh brown with 6 or 7 minute white submarginal points
   between veins.

   6b. ♀. Ups paler brown; uph with 4 larger submarginal white points;
   unh pale yellow-grey.

7. **Erebia gorge**   *Silky Ringlet*   287
   Upf with gleaming silky texture; male sex-brands present.

   7a. *E. g. gorge* ♂. Upf fulvous-red postdiscal bands well developed;
   twin apical ocelli prominent; uph with or without postdiscal ocelli;
   unh dark grey marbled paler, dark discal band sometimes present.
   ♀ fringes chequered, unh much paler.

   7b. *E. g. ramondi* ♂. Like *E. g. gorge* but on hw white-pupilled postdiscal ocelli prominent on both surfaces. **For** ♀ **see Pl. 54.**

   7c. *E. g. erynis* f. *carboncina* ♂. Small, upf ocelli greatly reduced (or
   absent); unh very dark. **See also** *E. g. erynis* **Pl. 54.**

   7d. *E. g. triopes* ♂. Like *E. g. ramondi* but upf with 3 united ocelli.

   7e. *E. g. gorge* f. *gigantea* ♂. Like *E. g. gorge* but larger, unh usually
   dark.

8. **Erebia oeme**   *Bright-eyed Ringlet*   298
   E. o. lugens ♂. Ups black, ocelli reduced to vanishing point; uns with
   small blind ocelli present on both wings. ♀ similar. **See also Pl. 50.**

224

PLATE 48

1. Erebia eriphyle   *Eriphyle Ringlet*   276
  1a. *E. e. eriphyle* ♂. Unf discal area orange-brown; uph postdiscal
     orange spot in space 4 prominent.
  1b. *E. e. tristis* ♂. Like *E. e. eriphyle*; ups fulvous markings brighter
     and more extensive. **For ♀ see Pl. 38.**

2. Erebia manto   *Yellow-spotted Ringlet*   277
  E. m. pyrrhula ♂. Small, with obscure fulvous elongate marks on both
  wings. ♀ similar. **See also Pls. 38, 49, 54.**

3. Erebia pharte   *Blind Ringlet*   280
  3a. *E. p. pharte* ♂. Ups broken fulvous postdiscal bands lack included
     black spots. ♀ paler, unh broadly yellowish. **See also Pl. 54.**
  3b. *E. p. eupompa* ♂. Larger, upf fulvous postdiscal bands wide. **For ♀
     see Pl. 54.**

4. Erebia christi   *Rätzer's Ringlet*   280
  4a. ♂. Like *E. epiphron* but unh postdiscal band slightly paler, ocelli
     represented by small black spots.
  4b. ♀. Upf orange postdiscal band wider; unh pale grey-brown,
     4 small dark spots in pale postdiscal area.

5. Erebia epiphron   *Mountain Ringlet*   278
  Unh ground-colour uniform brown, with or without 3 small postdiscal
  ocelli.
  5a. *E. e. epiphron* f. *silesiana* ♂. Upf fulvous postdiscal band wide,
     enclosing 4 blind ocelli; uph 3 blind ocelli ringed fulvous.
  5b. *E. e. epiphron* f. *silesiana* ♀. Like ♂ but more brightly marked; upf
     post-discal ocelli usually with white pupils.
  5c. *E. e. aetheria* ♂. Upf fulvous band dull, narrow, and generally
     lacking ocellus in space 3; hw usually with small postdiscal ocelli.
  5d. *E. e. aetheria* ♀. Ups paler brown; upf ocelli larger, sometimes
     with white pupils.
  5e. *E. e. aetheria* f. *nelamus* ♂. Markings almost obsolete on both
     surfaces.
  5f. *E. e. fauveaui* ♂. Like *E. e. silesiana* but all markings less bright;
     upf generally with 4 blind postdiscal ocelli.
  5g. *E. e. orientalis* ♂. Upf fulvous postdiscal band narrow, enclosing
     twin apical ocelli; uph with 3 ocelli, all with minute white pupils. ♀
     similar with larger ocelli.
  5h. *E. e. mnemon* ♂. Upf markings dull, reduced, but usually with
     4 black spots in the fulvous band.

6. Erebia disa   *Arctic Ringlet*   283
  ♂. Uph unmarked. ♀ similar, ups slightly paler.

7. Erebia embla   *Lapland Ringlet*   283
  ♂. Uph with 3 or rarely 4 blind postdiscal ocelli. ♀ nearly similar.

1a 1b 2

3a 4a 4b

3b 5d 5c

5a 5b 5e

5f 5g 5h

6 7

PLATE 49

1. Erebia pandrose   *Dewy Ringlet*   301
♂. Upf with dark transverse discal line; unh ground-colour grey, discal band defined by two irregular dark lines. **For ♀ see Pl. 54.**

2. Erebia sthennyo   *False Dewy Ringlet*   301
♂. Upf discal markings indistinct; unh pale grey, almost unmarked.

3. Erebia manto   *Manto Ringlet*   277

3a.   ♂. Ups fulvous bands well developed, enclosing small black points between veins; unh with wide yellowish marks in spaces 4, 5 and 6.
3b.   ♀. Ups ground-colour paler brown; unh basal and discal markings yellow, elongate. **See also Pls. 38, 48, 54.**

4. Erebia meolans   *Piedmont Ringlet*   299

4a.   *E. m. meolans* ♂. Ups brightly marked; unh very dark, postdiscal area faintly paler; ocelli small or absent. **For ♀ see Pl. 54.**
4b.   *E. m. bejarensis* ♂. Large, ups fulvous bands wide, bright, ocelli conspicuous.
4c.   *E. m. valesiaca* ♂. Small, ups fulvous markings reduced; unf fulvous band short.

5. Erebia triaria   *de Prunner's Ringlet*   282
♂. Upf with 3 apical ocelli in series; unh very dark, rough, with obscure black transverse markings (distinction from *E. meolans*). ♀ unh paler brown, darker discal band defined.

6. Erebia aethiops   *Scotch Argus*   282

6a.   *E. a.* f. *caledonia* ♂. Small, ups fulvous markings reduced; unh with 3 small white spots in paler postdiscal band. **For ♀ see Pl. 54.**
6b.   *E. a. aethiops* ♀. Fringes slightly chequered; ups brightly marked; unh pale grey, brown discal band wide.

7. Erebia scipio   *Larche Ringlet*   295

7a.   ♂. Upf with twin apical ocelli in fulvous band; unf discal area chestnut-red; unh dark chestnut brown, unmarked.
7b.   ♀. Ups paler, more brightly marked; unh pale grey.

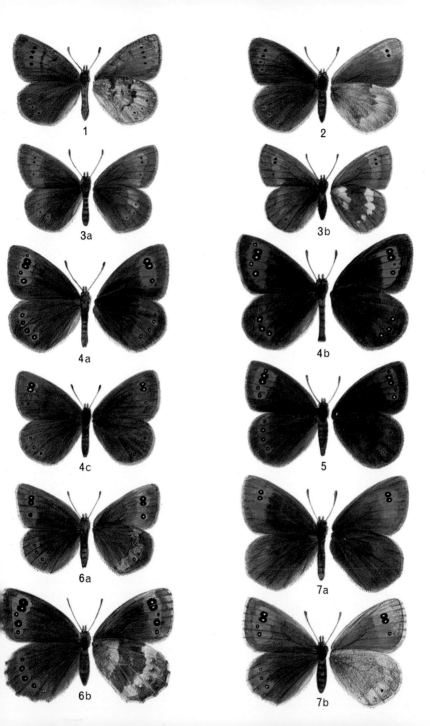

PLATE 50

1. **Erebia polaris**   *Arctic Woodland Ringlet*   285
   ♂. Unh red-brown (contrasting with smooth uniform grey-brown of
   E. medusa); postdiscal area faintly paler. ♀ unh markings better
   defined.

2. **Erebia epistygne**   *Spring Ringlet*   289
   ♂. Upf postdiscal band pale yellow; unf ground-colour red-brown. ♀
   similar.

3. **Erebia oeme**   *Bright-eyed Ringlet*   298

   3a. *E. o. oeme* ♂. Ups fulvous markings small, pupils of ocelli gleaming
       white; tip of antenna black (distinction from *E. medusa*). **See also
       Pl. 47.**
   3b. *E. o. spodia* ♀. Ups ocelli very large with brilliant white pupils; unh
       ground-colour yellowish-brown.

4. **Erebia montana**   *Marbled Ringlet*   297

   4a. *E. m. goante* ♂. Upf fulvous band rather narrow; unh ground-
       colour very dark, marbled white and sprinkled with white scales.
   4b. *E. m. montana* ♀. Ups paler, brightly marked; unh brightly marb-
       led dark on pale grey; fringes slightly chequered; veins white.

5. **Erebia medusa**   *Woodland Ringlet*   284

   5a. *E. m. medusa* ♂. Ups markings orange-yellow; unh uniform
       smooth brown; tip of antenna brown (distinction from *E. oeme*). ♀
       similar, brighter. **See also Pl. 54.**
   5b. *E. m. hippomedusa* ♂. Small, ups dark brown, ocelli very small,
       ringed fulvous. ♀ similar.

6. **Erebia gorgone**   *Gavarnie Ringlet*   289

   6a. ♂. Ups dark, upf postdiscal band red-brown, male sex-brand
       conspicuous; unh with distinctly paler postdiscal band.
   6b. ♀. Ups paler, ocelli larger; unh marbled yellow-grey, veins lined
       paler.

7. **Erebia melas**   *Black Ringlet*   294
   Uph ocelli, when present, are near outer margin.

   7a. *E. m. leonhardi* ♂. Ups black ocelli lack fulvous circles; uph ocelli
       indicated by small white spots between veins.
   7b. *E. m. leonhardi* ♀. Ups dark brown, upf apical ocelli large, widely
       ringed fulvous; unh base dark with paler postdiscal area.

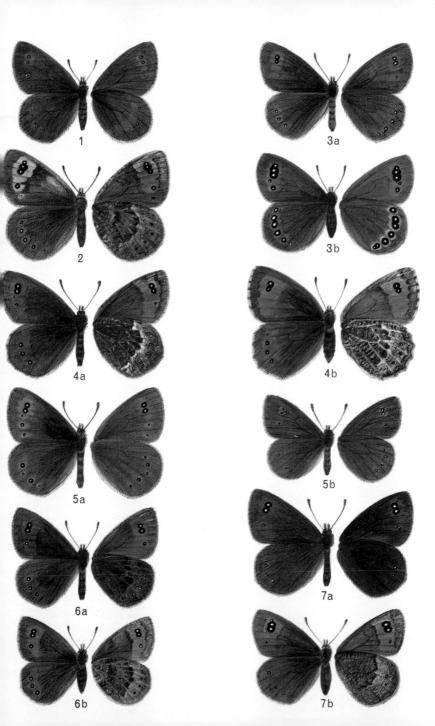

PLATE 51

1. Erebia neoridas   *Autumn Ringlet*   298

    1a. ♂. Fw short; upf fulvous band wide near costa, tapering below; unh medium brown, postdiscal area paler.

    1b. ♀. Ups paler, more brightly marked, fringes slightly chequered; unh paler.

2. Erebia zapateri   *Zapater's Ringlet*   298

    2a. ♂. Small; upf wide postdiscal band orange-yellow; uph dark, ocelli vestigial or absent.

    2b. ♀. Like ♂, more brightly marked; uns all markings paler.

3. Erebia pluto   *Sooty Ringlet*   286

    3a. *E. p. alecto* ♂. Ups black; upf twin white-pupilled apical ocelli small.

    3b. *E. p. alecto* ♀. Ups dark brown; unf discal area rufous-brown; unh grey; markings variable, often vestigial.

    3c. *E. p. velocissima* ♀. Ups red postdiscal bands with white-pupilled ocelli present on both wings.

    3d. *E. p. pluto* ♂. Ups both wings black, unmarked.

    3e. *E. p. oreas* ♂. Ups with wide postdiscal band, ocelli absent.

    3f. *E. p. oreas* ♀. Ups like ♂ but paler; unh with fulvous postdiscal band.

4. Erebia palarica   *Chapman's Ringlet*   300

♂. Large, unh dark brown with grey marbling and rather 'rough' surface (distinction from *E. meolans*).

PLATE 52

1. Erebia alberganus   *Almond-eyed Ringlet*   285

   1a. *E. a. tyrsus* ♂. Lanceolate orange postdiscal spots large on both surfaces, white pupilled ocelli small. ♀ similar, uns suffused yellow.

   1b. *E. a. alberganus* ♂. Ups orange postdiscal oval spots smaller, less bright, uns markings much smaller but ocelli retain white pupils.

   1c. *E. a. phorcys* ♂. Large, like *E. a. tyrsus* but unh postdiscal spots pale yellow, and ocelli lightly tinged orange.

   1d. *E. a. alberganus* f. *caradjae* ♂. Small, fulvous markings inconspicuous, lanceolate on unf only.

2. Erebia ottomana   *Ottoman Brassy Ringlet*   292

   2a. *E. o. bulgarica* ♂. Large, unh silvery postdiscal band enclosing 3 round black ocellar spots.

   2b. *E. o. balcanica* ♀. Ups postdiscal markings orange-yellow, brown ground-colour paler; unh pale yellow-grey, markings obscure.

   2c. *E. o. tardenota* ♂. Smaller, unh dove-grey banded with brown.

3. Erebia cassioides   *Common Brassy Ringlet*   290

   3a. ♂. Fw pointed; upf fulvous band short, twin apical ocelli prominent; uph postdiscal ocelli present.

   3b. ♀. Ups paler; ocelli well developed on both wings; unh yellowish-grey marbled brown. **See also Pl. 54.**

4. Erebia nivalis   *de Lesse's Brassy Ringlet*   292
   ♂. Fw not pointed; upf fulvous band extends into cell; unh bright blue-grey marbled darker grey.

5. Erebia tyndarus   *Swiss Brassy Ringlet*   290

   5a. ♀. Fw short, not pointed; upf ocelli very small; uph lacks ocelli.

   5b. ♂. Like ♀ but brighter; upf ocelli small; uph lacks ocelli.

6. Erebia hispania   *Spanish Brassy Ringlet*   291

   6a. *E. h. hispania* ♂. Large; upf postdiscal band orange with large twin ocelli. ♀ unh yellowish, darker markings better defined.

   6b. *E. h. rondoui* ♂. Like *E. h. hispania* but smaller; upf orange postdiscal band wider; uns grey, usually with darker postdiscal line. ♀ ups more brightly marked; unh dark postdiscal line prominent.

7. Erebia calcaria   *Lorkovic's Brassy Ringlet*   292
   ♂. Fw short; upf very dark, ocelli small; unh grey with dark postdiscal line and small dark submarginal marking.

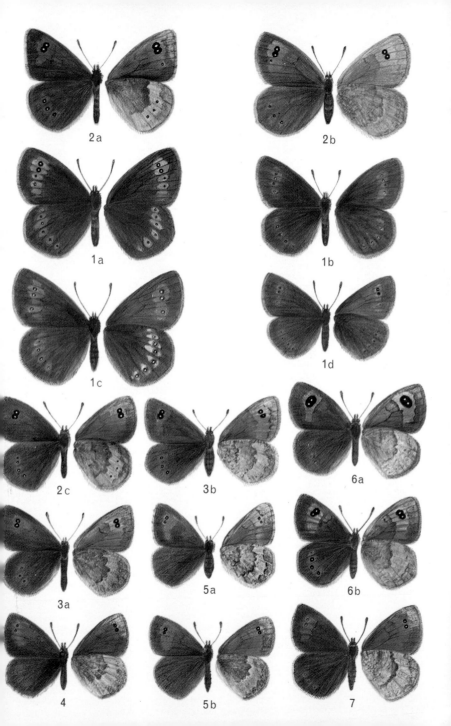

2a 2b

1a 1b

1c 1d

2c 3b 6a

3a 5a 6b

4 5b 7

PLATE 53

1. Erebia pronoe   *Water Ringlet*   293

> 1a. *E. p. pronoe* ♂. Ups fulvous bands well developed; unh violet-grey with wide dark-brown discal band.
> 1b. *E. p. pronoe* ♀. Smaller, ups paler; unh yellow-brown with pale grey postdiscal band.
> 1c. *E. p. vergy* ♂. Ups fulvous markings vestigial; uns as in *E. p. pronoe.*
> 1d. *E. p. vergy* ♀. Ups paler brown, ocelli and fulvous bands vestigial or absent; unh ground-colour yellowish-brown.

2. Erebia styria   *Styrian Ringlet*   295

> 2a. *E. s. styria* ♂. Ups black, fulvous markings restricted, white ocellar pupils brilliant; unh smooth dark brown, postdiscal area slightly paler, ocelli small.
> 2b. *E. s. styria* ♀. Ups brightly marked; unh postdiscal area pale grey, ocelli prominent.
> 2c. *E. s. morula* ♂. Small; ups fulvous postdiscal markings narrow, ocelli greatly reduced.

3. Erebia styx   *Stygian Ringlet*   296

> 3a. *E. s. styx* ♂. Ups like *E. s. stiria*; ups fulvous markings slightly more extensive; unh dark brown marbled paler.
> 3b. *E. s. styx* ♀. Ups paler, fringes slightly chequered; unh yellow-brown, with dark marbling, ocelli small or absent.
> 3c. *E. s. trentae* ♂. Large; ups very dark, fulvous markings narrow; uph ocelli often prominent; unh postdiscal band marbled pale grey. **For ♀ see Pl. 54.**

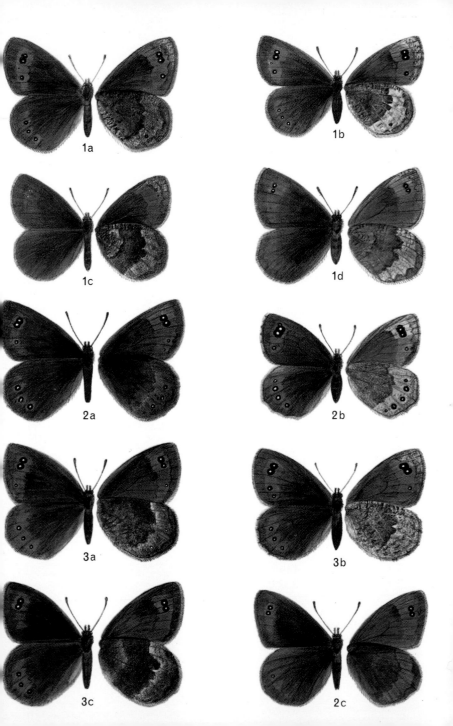

1a
1b
1c
1d
2a
2b
3a
3b
3c
2c

PLATE 54

1. **Erebia manto**   *Manto Ringlet*   277
   E. m. manto ♀-form *bubastis*. Unh basal and postdiscal markings
   white on pale yellow-grey ground-colour. **See also Pls. 38, 48, 49.**

2. **Erebia serotina**   *Descimon's Ringlet*   280
   ♂. Upf fulvous-red postdiscal band narrow; apical ocelli very small,
   blind; unh postdiscal area paler.

3. **Erebia gorge**   *Silky Ringlet*   287
   3a. *E. g. erynis* ♂. Upf tawny bands wide, lacking ocelli; unh dark,
       postdiscal area paler. **See also Pl. 47.**
   3b. *E. g. ramondi* ♀. Uph submarginal ocelli prominent; brightly
       marked. **For ♂ see Pl. 47.**

4. **Erebia medusa**   *The Woodland Ringlet*   284
   E. m. psodea ♀. Ups postdiscal bands yellow, wide, crossed by dark
   veins; uph with 5 or 6 ocelli. **See also Pl. 50.**

5. **Erebia styx**   *The Stygian Ringlet*   296
   E. s. trentae ♀. Ups ocelli large, prominent; unh pale grey, brightly
   marbled darker, discal band well defined. **For ♂ see Pl. 53.**

6. **Erebia meolans**   *The Piedmont Ringlet*   299
   E. m. meolans ♀, Ups like ♂ **(Pl. 49)** but paler, more brightly marked;
   unh brown, postdiscal band pale grey.

7. **Erebia phegea**   *Dalmatian Ringlet*   301
   E. p. dalmata ♂. Upf twin ocelli large, oblique, smaller postdiscal
   ocelli present in all other spaces of both wings.

8. **Erebia cassioides**   *Common Brassy Ringlet*   290
   8a. *E. c.* f. *pseudomurina* ♂. Ups like *E. c. cassioides* **(Pl. 52)**; unh grey,
       markings vestigial.
   8b. *E. c. arvernensis* ♀. Like *E. c. cassioides* **(Pl. 52)**, but larger; unh
       yellowish.

9. **Erebia pandrose**   *The Dewy Ringlet*   301
   E. pandrose ♀-form *roberti*. Unh discal band and marginal markings
   dark brown. **See also Pl. 49.**

10. **Erebia pharte**   *The Blind Ringlet*   280
    10a. *E. pharte eupompa* ♀. Ups medium brown, yellow markings
         conspicuous; uns flushed yellow. **See also Pl. 48.**
    10b. *E. pharte phartina* ♂. Small, markings very obscure on both
         surfaces. **See also Pl. 48.**

11. **Erebia aethiops**   *Scotch Argus*   282
    E. a. f. *caledonia* ♀. Small; unh brown, pale postdiscal band yellowish.
    See also Pl. 49.

PLATE 55

1. Hyponephele maroccana   *Moroccan Meadow Brown*   303

    1a. *H. m. maroccana* ♂. Upf with fulvous postdiscal area, sex-brand narrow; hw outer margin slightly wavy; unf apical ocellus large.

    1b. *H. m. maroccana* ♀. Upf fulvous area extending to wing-base; unf ocelli large.

    1c. *H. m. nivellei* ♂. Small, like *H. m. maroccana*, upf narrow sex-brand prominent. ♀ like *H. m. maroccana* ♀ but smaller.

2. Hyponephele lycaon   *Dusky Meadow Brown*   304

    2a. ♂. Upf ground-colour grey-brown, slightly tinted yellow, sex-brand narrow; hw outer margin scalloped; unf apical ocellus not large.

    2b. ♀. Upf like *H. maroccana* ♀; hw outer margin scalloped; unf ocelli smaller.

3. Hyponephele lupina   *Oriental Meadow Brown*   304

    3a. *H. l. lupina* ♂. Upf ground-colour distinctly yellowish (when fresh), lacking defined fulvous area, sex-brand wide, conspicuous; hw outer margin scalloped; unf apical ocellus small.

    3b. *H. l. mauretanica* ♀. Upf ocelli broadly ringed pale fulvous which rarely extends to basal area; hw outer margin deeply scalloped; unf ocelli small; black discal mark in space 1b.

4. Maniola jurtina   *Meadow Brown*   302

    4a. *M. j. jurtina* ♂. Upf with single small white-pupilled apical ocellus, usually without fulvous postdiscal area, sex-brand large, diffuse; unh grey-brown with small blind ocelli in spaces 2, 5.

    4b. *M. j. jurtina* ♀. Upf fulvous postdiscal area well defined, often extending towards wing-base; unh base brown followed by pale postdiscal band, ocelli absent.

    4c. *M. j. hispulla* ♀. Large, ups fulvous areas extended; upf ocellus large; unh very brightly marked.

PLATE 56

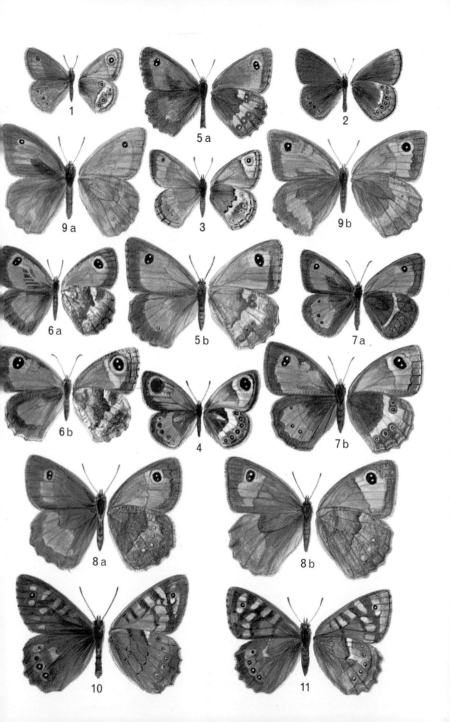

PLATE 57

PLATE 58

1. Coenonympha pamphilus   *Small Heath*   309

    1a.   *C. p. pamphilus* ♂. Ups yellow-buff with narrow grey borders (distinction from *C. tullia*); unh base dark, postdiscal area paler, ocelli obscure.

    1b.   *C. p. pamphilus* f. *lyllus* ♀. Unf oblique postdiscal bar well defined; unh sandy yellow, base slightly darker. **See also Pl. 56.**

2. Coenonympha dorus   *Dusky Heath*   311

    2a.   *C. d. dorus* ♂. Upf dusky; uph fulvous postdiscal area enclosing ocelli in spaces 1–4 in curved series.

    2b.   *C. d. dorus* ♀. Upf lacks dusky shading; uph as in ♂.

    2c.   *C. d. bieli* ♂. Ups very dark; unh markings subdued, ocelli small and pale.

    2d.   *C. d. fettigii* ♂. Unh grey, markings almost obsolete, all ocelli present but minute.

3. Coenonympha corinna   *Corsican Heath*   310
C. c. corinna ♂. Small; ups bright fulvous; unh fulvous postdiscal area bounded by irregular yellowish line, ocelli vestigial except prominent ocellus in space 6. ♀ similar.

4. Coenonympha elbana   *Elban Heath*   310
C. Elbana ♂. Unh pale postdiscal band more regular, ocelli well developed. ♀ similar.

5. Pseudochazara geyeri   *Grey Asian Grayling*   270
♂. Ups grey, markings slightly darker; unh with series of V-marks in submarginal area.

6. Pseudochazara beroe   Asiatic. **For** *P. graeca* **see Pl. 59.**

7. Pseudochazara atlantis   *Moroccan Grayling*   268
♂. Ups with wide orange postdiscal areas. ♀ upf dark basal area often extends along vein 4.

8. Pseudochazara hippolyte   *Nevada Grayling*   268
P. h. williamsi ♂. Like *P. graeca*; ups pale postdiscal bands well defined. ♀ Upf dark basal area extends along vein 4.

9. Hipparchia neomiris   *Corsican Grayling*   262
♂. Ups dark brown with broad fulvous postdiscal bands on both wings. ♀ similar.

1a

2c

2d

1b

2a

2b

3

5

4

6

7

8

9

PLATE 59

PLATE 60

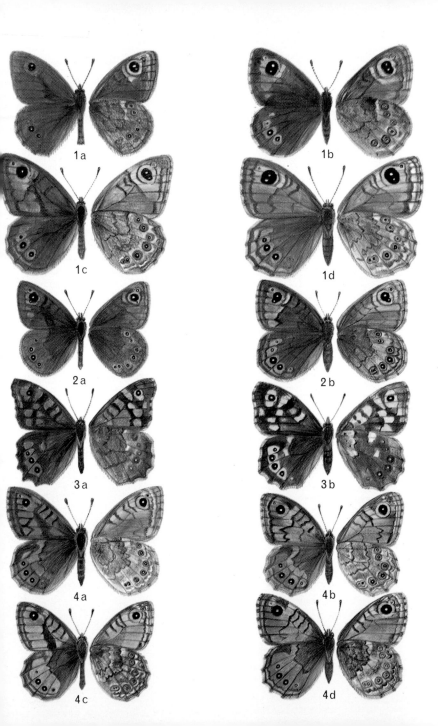

1a

1b

1c

1d

2a

2b

3a

3b

4a

4b

4c

4d

PLATE 61

PYRGUS Upf postdiscal white spots in spaces 4 and 5 displaced outwards; costal fold present in ♂.

1. **Pyrgus malvae** *Grizzled Skipper* 322
♂. Uph postdiscal spots clearly defined. ♀ simlar.

2. **Pyrgus alveus** *Large Grizzled Skipper* 323
2a. *P. a. alveus* ♂. Uph postdiscal spots usually small or absent.
2b *P. a. centralhispaniae* ♂. Uph pale markings more extensive.
2c *P. a. numidus* ♂. Large; ups markings large and complete.
2d. *P. a. alveus* ♀. Ups yellowish; upf white markings very small.
2e. *P. a. scandinavicus* ♂. Unh discal band usually complete.

3. **Pyrgus warrenensis** *Warren's Skipper* 325
♂. Very small; upf white markings minute.

4. **Pyrgus foulquieri** *Foulquier's Grizzled Skipper* 324
♂. Resembles *P. a. centralhispaniae*; uph pale markings large.

5. **Pyrgus armoricanus** *Oberthur's Grizzled Skipper* 324
5a. *P. a. armoricanus* ♂. Small; uph pale discal mark often prominent.
5b. *P. a. maroccanus* ♂. Larger; ups markings larger.

6. **Pyrgus onopordi** *Rosy Grizzled Skipper* 326
♂. Unh 'signe de Blachier' in space 1c **(See text).**

7. **Pyrgus carlinae** *Carline Skipper* 325
7a. *P. c. carlinae* ♂. Unh ground-colour often reddish, prominent
marginal pale mark in space 4/5. **See fig., p. 328.**
7b. *P. c. carlinae* ♀. Ups yellowish, white markings small.
7c. *P. c. cirsii* ♂: Upf white cell-spot rectangular. **See fig., p. 328.**

8 **Pyrgus serratulae** *Olive Skipper* 325
8a. *P. serratulae* ♂. Unh gc olive- to grey-green.
8b. *P. serratulae* f. *major* ♂. Larger; unh gc often dark.
8c. *P. serratulae* ♀. Ups white markings small or obsolete.

9. **Pyrgus carthami** *Safflower Skipper* 327
♂. Uph white post-discal spots in regular series. ♀ similar.

10. **Pyrgus sidae** *Yellow-banded Skipper* 327
10a. *P. s. sidae* ♂. Large, unh bands bright yellow.
10b *P. s. occiduus* ♂. Smaller, unh bands paler yellow.

11. **Pyrgus centaureae** *Northern Grizzled Skipper* 329
♂. Unh ground-colour dark, veins lined white.

12. **Pyrgus andromedae** *Alpine Grizzled Skipper* 328
♂. Unh with white streak and round spot in space 1c.

13. **Pyrgus cacaliae** *Dusky Grizzled Skipper* 328
♂. Upf white spots very small.

1

2 a

3

5 a

9

2 b

6

10 a

2 c

7 c

10 b

4

7 a

11

2 d

7 b

12

2 e

8 a

13

5 b

8 b

8 c

252

PLATE 62

254

PLATE 63

SATYRIDAE

Boisduval 1833

This is a very large cosmopolitan family of grass-feeders, highly developed in the temperate regions of the Old World, the species occurring on open meadows, mountain slopes or light woodland, wherever their food plants can grow. In western Europe only seven or eight species of the genera *Oensis* and *Erebia* are truly boreal, but there is a remarkable concentration of alpine species in the Pyrenees, Alps and Balkan mountains. The family is best represented in the warmer parts of Europe and it accounts for almost one-third of the butterfly fauna of the area. The species are generally of medium size, but some of the largest European butterflies are included in the Satyridae. There is a strong family likeness throughout the family, wings usually some shade of brown, varying from black to fulvous and yellow-buff, but white with black markings in the aberrant genus *Melanargia*. Characteristic markings are the postdiscal ocelli, the ocellus on the fore-wing in s5 is especially constant, often set in a paler mark or band.

MELANARGIA GALATHEA   *Marbled White*
Range. N. Africa across Europe to Caucasus and N. Iran.   Map 224

M. galathea galathea   Linnaeus 1758   TL: Germany (Verity 1953)   **Pl. 37**
Description. ♂fw 23/26mm, *upf cell without isolated black cross-bar*, white cell-patch occupying basal two-thirds only; unh markings black, ocelli enclosed in fuscous submarginal band broken at s4, dark discal band wide on costa at s7. ♀ larger, fw to 28mm, unh markings usually yellowish-brown with gc pale yellow.
Flight. June/July
Habitat. Anywhere in grassy places, from sea-level to 1500m. Larval food plants various grasses, e.g. *Phleum, Agropyron*, etc.
Distribution. Throughout W. Europe, except south-west, northwards to S. England and in Germany to Baltic coast; Lithuania; Estland; doubtfully recorded from Denmark. In SE. France partially replaced by *M. g. lachesis* in Aude, Gard, Hérault, Ariège, Bouches-du-Rhône and E. Pyrenees, but recorded from all these. Present also in Cantabrian Mts. and locally on southern slopes of Pyrenees. Completely replaced by *M. g. lachesis* south of Pyrenees and Cantabrian Mts.
Variation. Recurrent abnormal wing markings include f. *galene* Ochsenheimer, in which unh ocelli are absent, and ♀ f. *leucomelas* Esper, in which the unh gc is plain white, unmarked, a common form in many localities but rare in the north. In S. Italy and Balkans black markings more extensive, f. *procida* Herbst (Pl. 37), with corresponding reduction in white markings, sometimes associated with yellow ground-colour.

M. galathea lachesis   Hübner 1790   TL: Languedoc (S. France)   **Pl. 37**
Description. ♂fw 25/28mm, slightly larger than *M. g. galathea*; ups markings less heavy, esp. basal and discal markings, often vestigial; upf white cell-patch extending in a sharp point to cell-end, black mark at cell-end much reduced; unh markings grey, dark central band narrow on costa in s7. ♀ often larger.

Variation. ♀f. *cataleuca* Staudinger, equivalent of the *leucomelas* form of *M. g. galathea*, with unh plain white, is common.

Flight and **Habitat** as for *M. g. galathea*. Larval food plant *Lamarckia aurea*.

Distribution. SE. France as recorded above, not east of the Rhône. Spain and Portugal, generally distributed south of Pyrenees and Cantabrian Mts. This subspecies is accorded specific rank by many authors. The distributional frontiers between *lachesis* and *galathea* are well defined and along them rather uncommon intermediate forms occur, esp. f. *duponti* Reverdin pl. 38, with black markings reduced on both surfaces.

M. galathea lucasi Rambur 1858 TL: Bougie, Algeria   **Pl. 38**
Description. ♂fw 26/28mm, ups black markings heavy; white cell-patch extended, separated from cell-end by a small grey spot; unf cell closed distally by a black bar shortly before cell-end; unh black central band narrow on costa in s7. ♀ larger, unh slightly yellowish, with larger ocelli with blue pupils. No *leucomelas*-like form of the ♀ has been recorded from Africa.
Flight. June/early July.
Habitat. Local in grassy places in Atlas Mts., flying at 900–2100m.
Distribution. Algeria, Morocco and Tunis. The usual form in Morocco is slightly larger than that of Algeria with heavier black markings.
Similar species. *M. russiae* below, cell of fw crossed by dark line.
Note. The three butterflies *M. g. galathea*, *M. g. lachesis* and *M. g. lucasi*, form an easily recognisable group within the genus *Melanargia*, consisting of what might be termed a superspecies and three semispecies. These are graded species by some authors.

MELANARGIA RUSSIAE *Esper's Marbled White*
Range. Spain, Portugal and SE. France, and in widely scattered colonies across Italy and the Balkans to S. Russia, Transcaucasus and W. Siberia. Map 225

M. russiae russiae Esper 1784 TL: Volga, SW. Russia   **Pl. 37**
    syn: *suwarovius* Herbst 1796
Description. ♂fw 26mm, ups black markings delicate and complete (see *M. r. cleanthe* below). Occurred formerly in Pusta Peszer, Hungary, but is now extinct in that locality. It is unlikely that it occurs anywhere in W. Europe to-day.

M. russiae cleanthe Boisduval 1833 TL: Basses Alpes   **Pl. 37**
Description. ♂fw 26/30mm, ups with delicate complete black markings; upf black cell-end mark enclosing a white spot; *cell crossed by zig-zag black bar*; uph black central band continuous across s4; *unh pattern firmly outlined in black* with spaces filled pale grey; submarginal ocelli distinct, not enclosed in fuscous spaces. ♀ups black markings slightly more extensive, unh with yellow flush.
Flight. July.
Habitat. Dry stony places in hilly districts, to 1500m local.
Distribution. France, in Provence, Gironde, E. Pyrenees; in Aveyron and Lozère small. Spain, not uncommon in N. and C. mountains. Portugal, reported from Serra da Estrela.

M. russiae japygia Cyrillo 1787 TL: S. Italy   **Pl. 37**
Description. ♂fw 25/27mm, black markings ups heavier, individually somewhat variable; uns distinction from *M. r. cleanthe* less definite. ♀ups black markings often tend to grey, unh yellowish.

Flight. July.
Habitat. Mountains, very local at 900–1500m.
Distribution. Italy, from Bolognola southwards in Apennines, Puglia, Lucania, in Sicily slightly larger (rare), e.g. Fonte Larocca, Palermo, Monte Madonie.
Variation. At high levels in Abruzzi often darker. Also in Macedonia and Albania, a few colonies closely resembling the Italian forms reported near Lake Ochrid.
Similar species. *M. larissa herta* below; *M. galathea* p. 256.

MELANARGIA LARISSA *Balkan Marbled White*
Range. Perhaps confined to SE. Europe, but several closely allied species or subspecies widely distributed in W. Asia to Iran.   Map 226

M. larissa larissa   Geyer 1828   TL: Cres (Cherso Is.), Istria   **Pl. 38**
Description. ♂fw 25/30mm, ups black markings heavy, *basal areas of both wings suffused dark fuscous* which may cover cell; *upf cell crossed by fine black line from between v2 and v3*; uph cell obscured by dark basal area; uns resembles *M. russiae*, unh basal area faintly grey, central band unbroken in s4. ♀ usually larger, uns fw apex and hw slightly yellow.
Flight. June/July.
Habitat. Rocky slopes, lowlands to moderate altitudes.
Distribution. Bulgaria, Greece, Albania, SE. Yugoslavia. Replaced in Dalmatia by following subspecies.

M. larissa herta   Geyer 1828   TL: Dubrovnik (Ragusa)   **Pl. 38**
Description. Resembles *M. l. larissa* but all black markings greatly reduced, esp. in pd areas; ups grey basal suffusion present on both wings; uph ocelli well defined. ♀ wing-markings grey, on unh often vestigial.
Flight and **Habitat** as for *M. l. larissa*.
Distribution. Occurs in the Karst regions of Dalmatia and Montenegro; unstable in some populations and forms intermediate between *M. l. herta* and *M. l. larissa* sometimes occur.
Similar species. *M. russiae japygia* p. 257, uph cell always white.

MELANARGIA OCCITANICA *Western Marbled White*
Range. Restricted to SW. Europe and N. Africa.   Map 227

M. occitanica occitanica   Esper 1793   TL: Toulouse   **Pl. 38**
   syn: *psyche* Hübner 1800; *syllius* Herbst 1796
Description. ♂fw 25/28mm, upf two small apical ocelii, black mark at cell-end encloses blue centre, cell crossed by irregular black line; *uns veins lined brown*; unf discal markings black; unh cell closed by double oblique lines directed to v4, ocelli conspicuous, pupils blue, *marginal chevrons long and acute-angled*, longitudinal black line present in s1b. ♀ similar, uns often with heavy brown suffusion.
Flight. End May/June/July, depending upon altitude, etc.
Habitat. Mountainous rocky country, lowlands to 1500m.
Distribution. France, E. Pyrenees, Var, Bouches du Rhône, Maritime and Basses Alps; Italian coastal areas at Capo Mele, Capo Berta, etc.; Spain, widely distributed southwards to Sierra Nevada, but local. Portugal, near Gerez, Coimbra. Reported from Corsica.

M. occitanica pelagia   Oberthur 1911   TL: Sebdou, Algeria   **Pl. 38**
Description. ♂fw 23/25mm, size variable, often small; ups markings more delicate; base of s3 upf clear white, black bar across cell fully separate from cell-end markings.

Flight and **Habitat** as for *M. o. occitanica*.
Distribution. Algeria, in Oran, esp. Sebdou, Geryville, etc. Morocco, local in Middle Atlas, esp. Anosseur, Djebel Hebri, etc., sometimes larger and more heavily marked. Not recorded from Tunisia.

M. occitanica pherusa Boisduval 1833 TL: Sicily **Pl. 38**
Description. ♂fw 25/27mm, ups black markings reduced; upf mark at cell-end usually enclosing a blue spot, base of s3 always white; uph discal field whiter, ocelli small, sometimes absent (f. *plesaura* Bellier Pl. 38), unh veins delicately lined pale brown.
Flight. May/June.
Habitat. Mountains at 600–900m.
Distribution. Confined to Sicily, very local, recorded from Lupo, San Martino, Palermo, etc. This subspecies is given specific rank by some authors.
Similar species. *M. ines* below, unh veins lined black.
Note. In N. Africa, from Morocco eastwards, there is a clinal change in wing markings. Specimens from Morocco are scarcely separable from those from Spain, but in Algeria (Oran) the ups markings are somewhat reduced, and upf the blue discoidal spot is often larger (*M. o. pelagia* Ob.); in Sicily (*M. o. pherusa* Bdv.) many specimens are like the Algerian form, but ups reduction in black markings is often striking (f. *plesaura*). Between Sicily and Italy the cline is interrupted, but the Italian *M. arge* is clearly a member of this series.

MELANARGIA ARGE *Italian Marbled White*
Range. Restricted to peninsula Italy. Map 228

M. arge Sulzer 1776 TL: Kingdom of Sicily (which in 1776 included most of the Apennines) **Pl. 37**
Description. ♂fw 25/26mm, resembles *M. occitanica* but more lightly marked; upf black bar across cell incomplete, mark at cell-end reduced, usually circular, enclosing white and blue scales; unh ocelli more prominent, more brightly coloured, their black circles distinct, veins lined dark brown (black), longitudinal dark line present in s1b; unf markings scanty, *marginal chevrons short, right-angled.* ♀ often larger, otherwise similar.
Flight. May/early June.
Habitat. Hills and mountains, flying in small localised colonies from quite low altitudes to over 1200m.
Distribution. Peninsular Italy, from Gran Sasso southwards to Reggio and Gargano peninsula.
Similar species. *M. ines* below, unh without dark longitudinal line in s1b; does not occur in Italy.

MELANARGIA INES *Spanish Marbled White*
Range. Spain and Portugal, Morocco, Algeria, Tunisia and Cyrenaica. Map 229

M. ines Hoffmannsegg 1804 TL: 'Calabria' (error for Cantabria) **Pl. 37**
Description. ♂fw 23/25mm, resembles *M. occitanica* and *M. arge*; upf a broad black bar crossing middle of cell, blue-pupilled ocelli prominent; unf *marginal chevrons obtuse-angled*, nearly lunulate; unh without longitudinal dark line in s1b, fine black striae present along costa in s8. ♀ slightly larger, unh gc often yellowish.
Flight. April/May/June, depending upon altitude.

Habitat. Rocky slopes with grass, usually in mountainous districts at altitudes of 900–1200m.
Distribution. Spain, a common species in central and southern districts. Portugal. Tunisia. Morocco. Algeria.
Variation. Unusually large specimens with ♂fw to 27mm, occur at low altitudes in western Morocco. In Middle and High Atlas at altitudes of 2100m or more, the black markings of ups are extensive, f. *jehandezi* Oberthur Pl. 37.
Similar species. *M. occitanica* and *M. arge* above.

HIPPARCHIA FAGI *Woodland Grayling*
Range. From France across C. Europe and Balkans to S. Russia.   Map 230

H. fagi   Scopoli 1763   TL: Carniola   **Pl. 39**
    syn: *hermione* Linnaeus 1764
Description. ♂fw 33/38mm, ups dark grey-brown; upf pale yellowish pd band suffused fuscous and enclosing small pd ocelli in (s2), s5; uph pd band better defined, usually white, often with small ocellus in s2, *outer edge of dark basal area nearly straight* or gently curved; unf pd band white or faintly yellowish near apex, dark basal area not sharply angled at v4; unh pd band white, becoming darker near outer margin, the whole irrorated with dark scales and striae. ♀ larger, ups pd bands paler and better defined, often slightly yellow near apex of fw.
Flight. July/August.
Habitat. Among trees or bushes, often rests upon tree-trunks, lowlands to 900m. Larval food plants grasses, esp. *Holcus*.
Distribution. C. and S. Europe to 52°N and including Bulgaria and Greece. Absent from NW. France, C. and S. Spain, Portugal, N. Germany, Fennoscandia and Mediterranean islands except Sicily.
Similar species. *H. alcyone* p. 261:

H. fagi and *H. alcyone*: comparative table of characters

These two species may fly together and often occur in the same districts. Identification may be difficult, especially in the Balkans. Distinctive external characters are contrasted in the following Key, but variation is great and no external character is entirely reliable.

Size
    Length of forewing over 33mm   *fagi*
    Length of forewing under 33mm   *alcyone*
        This simple rule will apply to most specimens
Markings
    Upf pd band in ♂ clouded and suffused fuscous   *fagi*
    Upf pd band in ♂ well defined, yellowish   *alcyone*
    Upf pd band in ♀♀ white, or faintly yellow near apex   *fagi*
    Upf pd band in ♀ decidedly yellowish   *alcyone*
    Upper edge of dark basal area
        (a) nearly straight or evenly curved, with bulge at v3 & 4 pointing
             near anal angle   *fagi*
        (b) irregular with bulge pointing to margin above anal angle *alcyone*
Jullien organ
    Three to five large rods on each side   *fagi*
    Eight to eleven smaller rods on each side   *alcyone*

Habitat

Lowlands, rarely above 1200m *fagi*

Flies at altitudes up to 1800m *alcyone*

Distribution

Absent from Fennoscandia, Germany, central and southern Spain and Portugal. Present in NE. Spain *fagi*

Much more widespread, including Norway, Germany, Spain and Morocco *alcyone*

HIPPARCHIA ALCYONE *Rock Grayling*

Range. W. and C. Europe and Morocco east to Ukraine. Map 231

H. alcyone alcyone Denis & Schiffermüller 1775 TL: Vienna **Pl. 39**
syn: *aelia* Hoffmannsegg 1804

Description. Like the Woodland Grayling but more variable, usually small, ♂fw often less than 33mm, ups dark grey with white or yellowish pd bands. ♀ often larger, ups pale pd bands more prominent, usually yellowish. Uns like *H. fagi*, basal areas dark, unh pd areas often brightly marked.

Flight and **Habitat.** June–July, usually a mountain species in the south, flying among steep rocks to 1500m or more. In N. Europe very local at low altitudes on moorlands or in woodlands.

Distribution. Common in Spain, Portugal, Pyrenees and western Alps, spreading north to Lithuania, S. Norway, and east to Slovakia and Austria, but absent from Bavaria, Hungary, E. Alps, Dolomites. Replaced in the Balkans by *H. syriaca* Standinger.

H. alcyone caroli Rothschild 1933 (June) TL: Morocco
syn: *natasha* Hemming 1933 (Dec.)

Description. In both sexes similar to European *H. a. alcyone* but distinguished by a small character in the ♂–genitalia.

Flight and **Habitat.** Not rare in the Middle Atlas, flying in July on barren, stony slopes at 1600m or more.

Distribution. Occurs only in Morocco on the Middle Atlas. Its presence on the High Atlas needs confirmation.

Similar species. *H. fagi* p. 260; see comparative table of characters.

HIPPARCHIA SYRIACA *Eastern Rock Grayling*

Range. SE. Europe, Asia Minor, Lebanon, S. Caucasus (Borjom) Map 232

H. syriaca serrula Fruhstorfer 1908 TL: Dalmatia (Dubrovnik) **Pl. 39**

Description. ♂fw 31–33mm, ups dark grey, pale pd bands present but partly obscured by dark suffusion; uns brightly marked, pale bands usually prominent across both wings; ups pale bands not obscured, white or yellowish; unh marbled, markings confused.

By external characters probably indistinguishable from the Woodland Grayling, which often flies in the same localities with *serrula*. Anatomical characters are well defined and distinctive in both sexes.

Flight and **Habitat.** Late June and July, occurs in rocky places or light woodland, from sea level to 1000m or more. Larval food plants not known.

Distribution. Yugoslavia (Dalmatia, Montenegro, Macedonia). Greece.

HIPPARCHIA ELLENA   *Algerian Grayling*
Range. Confined to Algeria and Tunisia.   Map 233

H. ellena   Oberthur 1894   TL: Bône, Algeria   **Pl. 39**
Description. ♂fw 30/34mm, ups gc very dark, *pd bands clear white, narrow*, inner border slightly irregular; upf ocelli well developed in s2 and s5; unh outer border of dark basal area straight below v5. ♀ups white bands wider, upf ocelli larger; unh dark basal area more mottled grey, white pd band wide.
Flight. End June/July/August.
Habitat. Among oak and cedar trees from 1600m upwards.
Distribution. Algeria. Tunisia at lower levels.
Similar species. *H. alcyone caroli* p. 261, upf pd bands suffused fuscous.

HIPPARCHIA NEOMIRIS   *Corsican Grayling*
Range. Confined to Corsica, Sardinia and Elba.   Map 234

H. neomiris   Godart 1824   TL: Corsica   **Pl. 58**
Description. ♂fw 23/25mm, ups gc brown with wide orange-yellow pd bands; upf apex suffused fuscous; unh white pd band narrow. ♀upf fuscous clouding less marked.
Flight. June/July.
Habitat. Mountains at 900–1800m on Corsica and Sardinia, at lower levels on Elba.

HIPPARCHIA DELATTINI   *Delattin's Grayling*
Range. Known at present from S. Yugoslavia and Greece.   Map 235

H. delattini   Kudrna 1975   TL: Pristina (Bosnia)
Description. ♂fw 27–28mm, like *H. aristaeus senthes*, wing markings somewhat variable, probably indistinguishable by external characters but male genitalia are distinctive.
Flight and **Habitat.** Occurs in June and early July, flying over barren areas at 500m or more.
Distribution. Not well understood. In Europe confined to Bosnia and Greece.

HIPPARCHIA CRETICA   *Cretan Grayling*
Range. Confined to Crete.   Map 236

H. cretica   Rebel 1916   TL: Crete
Description. ♂fw 26–29mm. In both sexes like *H. semele cadmus* (not known from Crete). Most specimens are large, ♂ups markings not prominent. ♀ brightly marked and with yellowish basal suffusion over both wings. Male genitalia are distinctive.
Flight and **Habitat.** Flies from late May/June, from about 400m upwards. Often common by roadsides.
Previously treated (1970) as a subspecies of *H. semele*.

HIPPARCHIA SEMELE   *Grayling*
Range. W. and C. Europe and through S. Russia. Little is known about the eastern distribution.   Map 237

H. semele and its close allies form a difficult complex, represented in W. Europe by *H. semele*, with large male genitalia, and by *H. aristaeus*, in which the genitalia are smaller. These two species resemble one another very closely. Both occur in Sicily, probably also in S. Italy, but otherwise their distributions do not overlap.

H. semele semele Linnaeus 1758   TL: Europe (Sweden, Verity 1953)   **Pl. 40**
Description. ♂fw 21/25mm, fringes pale, chequered brown; ups gc brown; upf with prominent sex-brand below median vein, yellow pd band often poorly defined, suffused and interrupted along veins by gc, enclosing ocelli in s2 and s5; uph *orange submarginal area broadly broken by veins* and enclosing small ocellus in s2; unh cryptic, marbled light and dark grey, darker basal area generally defined and followed by pale grey or white pd band. ♀ larger, ups yellow markings more extensive with less dusky suffusion; unh markings more uniformly mottled and pale pd band poorly developed.
Flight. July/August.
Habitat. Open heaths and rough hillsides from sea-level to moderate altitudes; fond of settling in full sun on bare ground. Larval food plants various grasses, *Deschampsia, Agropyron*, etc.
Distribution. Southern Fennoscandia, Britain, N. Germany, Czechoslovakia and N. France.

H. semele cadmus Fruhstorfer 1908   TL: Valais, Switzerland   **Pl. 40**
Description. ♂fw 27/30mm, larger, ups dusky suffusion more extensive; upf yellow pd band vestigial or confined to a few yellow scales around ocelli; uph orange submarginal markings usually bright; unh dark basal area and white pd band conspicuous. ♀ larger, ups brightly marked, with yellow areas around ocelli often forming a broken pd band.
Flight. End May or later.
Habitat. Lowlands to 1500m or more; the usual mountain form of the species.
Distribution. C. and S. Europe, esp. in Alps, Pyrenees and mountainous districts of Spain, Portugal, and Sicily, but more stable on the whole than local races of *H. s. semele.* Absent from Sardinia, Corsica, Malta and Balearic Islands.
Variation. The unh markings are especially brilliant in some southern races, which have a conspicuous white pd band.
Similar species. *H. aristaeus* below. No reliable external characters have been found by which to distinguish between all races of these two species; where they overlap examination of the genitalia will be necessary for certain identification.

HIPPARCHIA ARISTAEUS   *Southern Grayling*
Range. Madeira, Azores, N. Africa and the larger Mediterranean Islands to Greece and Asia Minor.   Map 238

H. aristaeus aristaeus Bonelli 1826   TL: Sardinia   **Pl. 40**
    syn: *sardoa* Spuler 1902
Description. ♂fw 25–27mm, ♂ like *H. semele* but ups with extensive orange flush, upf pd ocellus in s2 small or vestigial, uph pd area broadly orange, crossed by dark veins. ♀ ups brightly marked orange-yellow, which extends widely across the disc of fw.
Flight and Habitat. Late June or July, flies over rough heathy ground often at 800m or more, at lower levels on Elba. Larval food plants not identified, but certainly grasses.
Distribution. Corsica, Sardinia, Elba, Giglio, Lipari Islands.

H. aristaeus algirica   Oberthur 1876   **Pl. 40**
Description. ♂fw 26–27mm, very like *H. semele* in both sexes, ups markings not
very bright, yellowish, lacking an orange flush. Uns as *H. semele*.
Flight. May, June and later, depending upon locality and altitude. A partial autumn
brood has been reported in Tunisia. At high levels often darker.
Habitat. Dry, stony places with grass, from about 1300m and upwards to 1800m.
Distribution. Mountains of Morocco, Algeria, Tunisia.

H. aristaeus blachieri   Fruhstorfer 1908   TL: Italy, Sicily
syn: *siciliana*   Oberthur 1915
Description. ♂fw 25–27mm, ups like *H. a. algirica* but all pale markings brighter
fulvous; upf ocellus in s2 well developed. ♀fw 26–28mm, large, ups markings
brilliant, dark pattern reduced.
Flight and **Habitat.** Late June and July, common on rough ground at 1000m.
Distribution. Sicily; Ficuzza, Madonie Mts., Mt. Etna etc. S. Italy; restricted to
Mt. Faito near Reggio, Calabria.

H. aristaeus senthes   Fruhstorfer 1908   TL: Greece (Taygetos)
Description. Like *H. s. semele*, ups markings often partly obscured by dark suffusion, but variable. ♂uph pd band usually grey but submarginal orange macules
constant. ♀ like *H. s. semele*.
Flight and **Habitat.** June/July, flying from about 500m upwards, often shelters
among fir-trees.
Distribution. Greece, mainland and Peloponnessos.

H. aristaeus maderensis   Bethune Baker 1891   TL: Madeira   **Pls. 59, 40**
Description. ♂fw 24–25mm, ups both wings heavily suffused with smoky-brown,
in most specimens only traces present of the usual ocelli and pd markings; unh white
pd band prominent. ♀ larger, fw 27–28mm, ups ocelli well developed, orange
markings reduced, but variable.
Flight and **Habitat.** July/August, flying on grassy and stony slopes from 1000m
upwards. A very local butterfly.

HIPPARCHIA AZORINA   *Azores Grayling*
Range. Confined to the Azores.   No map

H. azorina   Strecker 1899   TL: Azores   **Pl. 40**
Description. ♂fw 21/22mm, ups very dark, fuscous suffusion nearly obscures very
pale yellow gc and markings; upf small blind ocelli in s2, 5, sex-brand conspicuous,
in isolated patches in s1b, 2, 3 and cell; unh basal area very dark brown, *pd band
conspicuous, sinuous, white*, marginal area very dark and slightly mottled with fine
striae. ♀ slightly larger, ups wing-pattern less obscure.
Flight. July/August.
Habitat. Grassy slopes of crater lip at 700m.
Distribution. Azores, on Fayal Island, Isle de Pico, Sao Miguel.
Note. *H. azorina* is regarded as a subspecies of *H. aristaeus* by some authors.

NEOHIPPARCHIA STATILINUS *Tree Grayling*
Range. From N. Africa, Spain and Portugal through C. and S. Europe to Asia Minor. Map 239

N. statilinus statilinus Hufnagel 1766 TL: Berlin **Pl. 41**
Description. ♂fw 22/23mm, ups dark grey-brown obscurely marked; upf with blind ocelli in s2, 5, and *small white spots in s3, 4*; unh suffused grey-brown, discal area more or less defined by darker brown sinuous lines, often incomplete, but colour contrast minimal; scalloped submarginal line not sharp. ♀upf pd area with obscure yellowish markings, ocelli better defined, usually with white pupils; unh brown, with very variable rather indefinite markings.
Flight. July/August/September.
Habitat. Sandy heaths, bushy places or sparse woodland at low or moderate levels. Larval food plants various grasses, esp. *Bromus sterilis*.
Distribution. C. and S. Europe to 50°N in west. In C. and N. Germany local, becoming scarce and already absent from many earlier known localities. Poland, Madeira, very local. Absent from NW. Germany, Denmark, Fennoscandia, Britain, Bavaria, NW. Switzerland, N. Tirol and Carpathians.
Variation. *N. statilinus* is a most variable species. In general, northern races are small; in central Europe larger, f. *onosandrus* Fruhstorfer, unh grey, discal area defined by dark lines but without much colour contrast. In Portugal and S. Spain often very large, f. *allionia* Fabricus, unh variegated with pale grey and dark brown. In f. *maritima* Rostagno from C. Italy unh is almost uniform dark brown.

N. statilinus sylvicola Austaut 1879 TL: Algeria **Pl. 41**
Description. ♂fw 26/28mm, ups resembles *N. s. statilinus*, sex-brand very broad; unh grey-brown, usually with an irregular dark pd line, but other markings vestigial. ♀ similar, pd area vaguely paler, white spots in s3, 4 larger and apical ocellus with small white pupil.
Flight and **Habitat** as for *N. s. statilinus*, stony slopes at 1500–1800m in early July or later.
Distribution. Morocco, Algeria and Tunisia in Atlas Mts.
Similar species. *Neohipparchia fatua* below. Balkans only, unh scalloped submarginal line sharply defined.

NEOHIPPARCHIA FATUA *Freyer's Grayling*
Range. Greece, Bulgaria and SE. Yugoslavia, Lebanon, Syria. Map 240

N. fatua Freyer 1844 TL: not stated **Pl. 41**
syn: *allionii* Hübner 1824 (invalid homonym)
Description. ♂fw 30/34mm, resembles *N. statilinus* but larger; uph dark submarginal line of *externally concave lunules better defined*, usually continuous; unh discal band clearly defined by irregular dark transverse lines, the whole finely striated and irrorated with brown scales; outer margin of hw deeply scalloped, submarginal line sharp. ♀upf pd markings yellowish, prominent white pd spots in s3, 4; uph small ocellus in s2, white spots in s3–6.
Flight. July/August.
Habitat. Among trees in hilly country but at moderate levels.
Distribution. This fine eastern species reaches Europe only in Turkey, Bulgaria, Greece and SE. Yugoslavia.
Similar species. *N. statilinus* above.

NEOHIPPARCHIA HANSII *Austaut's Grayling*
Range. From Morocco to Tunis, extending far into Tripolitania. Map 241

N. hansii Austaut 1879 TL: Bône, Algeria **Pl. 42**
Description. ♂fw 24/28mm, very variable; ups gc medium brown; upf pd area usually paler with *yellowish suffusion around ocelli in s2, 5, and white spots in s3, 4*, a smallish sex-brand below'median vein; unh central band defined by dark transverse lines. ♀ups yellow suffusion in pd area more extensive, sometimes present also on uph, uph with small ocellus in s2 and white spots in s3–6.
Flight. September/October.
Habitat. Rough ground and stony slopes at 1500–2100m. Larval food plant grasses.
Distribution. Atlas Mts. in Morocco, Algeria and Tunisia, not recorded from the Rif.
Variation. On unh ground colour varies from light to dark brown, often with pale grey or nearly white pd area.

NEOHIPPARCHIA POWELLI *Powell's Grayling*
Range. Restricted to Algeria. Map 242

N. powelli Oberthur 1910 TL: Algeria (Geryville) **Pl. 41**
Description. ♂fw 22–24mm, like *N. hansii* but ups darker, upf lacks discal markings, ocelli black, yellow rings vestigial, sex-brand not well defined; uph without yellow submarginal markings; unh veins lined pale grey in characteristic pattern. ♀ often larger, ups wing markings slightly better defined.
Flight and **Habitat.** September, in desert areas south of Geryville and Aflou (Algeria), perhaps also in Tunisia, probably in localized colonies.
Distribution. Algeria, in southern and eastern districts; Tunisia.
Note. The taxonomic status of *powelli* is uncertain and the distribution is not well known. While the ♂ genitalia do not differ from those of *N. hansii*, external features are distinct and far more constant than those of *N. hansii*.

PSEUDOTERGUMIA FIDIA *Striped Grayling*
Range. Confined to N. Africa and SW. Europe. Map 243

P. fidia Linnaeus 1767 TL: Algeria **Pl. 42**
Description. ♂fw 28/31mm, outer margin of hw distinctly scalloped; fringe of fw chequered; ups gc dark brown with markings as in *H. statilinus*; upf with ocelli in s2, 5, white spots in s3, 4 and sometimes with vague yellow-grey pd markings; *unh* variegated pale grey and brown with *striking pattern of zig-zag dark lines*. ♀ larger, upf with white or yellowish pd markings on costa and in s(1)2, ocelli in s2 and 5, and rather large white spots in s3, 4.
Flight. July/August according to locality.
Habitat. Stony slopes, often among trees, from lowlands to 1800m on foothills or mountains. Larval food plants various grasses, esp. *Oryzopsis*.
Distribution. SE. France, local in Provence, Languedoc and E. Pyrenees, northwards to Ardèche. Italy, only in Maritime Alps. Spain and Portugal, Balearic Is. (Majorca), widely distributed in suitable localities among mountains. N. Africa, local but widely distributed in High and Middle Atlas in Morocco, Algeria and Tunisia.
Variation. In N. Africa ups wing-markings are slightly more developed and unh pale grey markings more prominent, sometimes with conspicuous pale lining along veins, f. *albovenosa* Austaut.

PSEUDOTERGUMIA WYSSII *Canary Grayling*
Range. Confined to Canary Isles. No map

P. wyssii wyssii Christ 1889 TL: Tenerife, Canary Isles **Pl. 41**
Description. ♂fw 28/32mm, fw narrow, pointed, fringes chequered, sex-brand conspicuous; hw outer margin slightly scalloped; ups gc dark brown with slight golden lustre; upf cell very dark and markings obscure, *blind ocelli in s2, 5 and white spots in s3* and 4 much better developed on uns; uph brown unmarked; unh paler brown finely irrorated with dark scales, discal band defined by irregular dark transverse lines narrowly edged white distally. ♀ups gc paler and markings more prominent, including upf yellowish discal markings in s2, 5 and larger white spots in s3, 4.
Flight. July.
Habitat. Among trees at 1800m, perhaps also at lower levels. Larval food plants not known.
Distribution. Tenerife, esp. Las Canadas, Parador de Tiede, etc.

P. wyssii bacchus Higgins 1967 TL: Hiero, Canary Isles **Pl. 41**
Description. ♂fw 30mm, ♀ 30/33mm, wings less pointed, outer margins of hw more deeply scalloped; uns gc darker more smoky brown, unh white pd markings more extensive and forming continuous irregular stripe. ♀ups dark brown with purple iridescence, slight golden lustre over basal area; upf conspicuous white costal spot and mark in s2 larger, yellowish; unh white markings enlarged, pd area richly marbled.
Flight. July/August.
Habitat. In vineyards and sparse woodland, at about 300m.
Distribution. Canaries on Hiero Island and Gomera Island.

CHAZARA BRISEIS *The Hermit*
Range. From N. Africa, Spain and S. France through Europe to W. Asia, Iran, Altai Mts. and Pamirs. Map 244

C. briseis Linnaeus 1764 TL: Germany **Pl. 42**
Description. ♂fw 21/30mm, size variable; ups gc dark brown, *pd bands cream-white, broken by gc along veins on fw*, but not on hw; upf costal margin almost white, more or less irrorated brown, a wide sex-brand below cell and often a pale area at cell-base; unh cream-white irrorated brown, large brown mark from costa to cell and another similar near inner margin, marginal border grey. ♀ larger, fw to 34mm, upf white pd band less regular; unh markings confused, irrorated and mottled grey-brown; dimorphic, white markings sometimes replaced by buff, f. *pirata* Esper, rare in S. Europe, not uncommon in Asia.
Flight. June or later.
Habitat. Dry stony places from lowlands to 1800m in N. Africa. Larval food plants grasses, esp. *Sesleria coerulea*.
Distribution. C. and S. Europe to about 50°N. Africa, common in Morocco, Algeria and Tunisia. Absent from N. and NW. France, Britain, Corsica, Sardinia, Elba, Balearic Islands and Crete.
Variation. In S. Europe and N. Africa often large, with ♂fw 29mm, f. *major* Oberthur.
Similar species. *C. prieuri* below, upf no white mark in s4.

CHAZARA PRIEURI *Southern Hermit*
Range. Confined to Spain and N. Africa.   Map 245

C. prieuri   Pierret 1837   TL: Oran, Algeria   **Pl. 42**
Description. ♂fw 27/33mm, resembles *C. briseis*; upf costa and diffuse area in cell
pale buff, white pd band more broken, with larger blind ocelli in s2, 5 but *no white
mark in s4*; uph irregular white pd band broad in s5, not reaching costa; unh long pale
v-shaped submarginal markings on v2–6, very long on v6. ♀ larger, upf blind ocellus
in s2 often very large and buff mark in cell absent; unh dark irroration more general.
Flight. June or later.
Habitat. Rocky slopes in mountainous country from 900m in Spain, to 2100m in
N. Africa. Larval food plants not recorded.
Distribution. Morocco, Algeria, local in Middle Atlas. Spain, very local in central
mountains, esp. Teruel (Albarracin, etc.) and Saragossa.
Variation. In Spain the ♀ is dimorphic, white markings sometimes replaced by
buff, f. *uhagonis* Oberthur Pl. 42.
Similar species. *C. briseis* p. 267.

PSEUDOCHAZARA ATLANTIS *Moroccan Grayling*
Range. Confined to Morocco.   Map 246

P. atlantis   Austaut 1905   TL: High summits of Moroccan Atlas   **Pl. 58**
syn: *maroccana* Meade-Waldo 1906
Description. ♂fw 26/28mm, ups gc light grey-brown with *wide, clear orange pd
bands* and narrow grey marginal borders; upf black white-pupilled ocelli in s2, 5, sex-
brand not conspicuous; unh gc pale yellow with grey and sandy brown irrorations.
♀ similar, unh striations better defined. Fringes not chequered.
Flight. June/early July.
Habitat. Mountains, flying on stony, barren slopes at 2100–2700m. Larval food
plants not recorded.
Distribution. Morocco, Er Rif, local in Middle Atlas, High Atlas.

PSEUDOCHAZARA HIPPOLYTE *Nevada Grayling*
Range. Isolated on the Sierra Nevada in Spain; S. Russia (TL of *P. hippolyte* Esper
1784), Asia Minor and east to Tian Shan.   Map 247

P. hippolyte williamsi   Romei 1927   TL: Sierra Nevada, Spain   **Pl. 58**
Description. ♂fw 25/26mm, ups pale grey-brown with *broad pale straw-coloured pd
bands*; upf ocelli in s2, 5; uph small ocellus in s2; unh gc yellow-grey with darker
striations, basal area darker, dark lunular sub-marginal marks in series. ♀ slightly
larger, upf darker basal area extended along v4.
Flight. End June/July.
Habitat. Stony slopes at altitudes of 2100–2700m.
Distribution. Spain, in Sierra Nevada and esp. on Mt. Mulhacen and Sierra de
Maria.
Note. The species was first known from Orenberg in southern Russia, distant about
3000 miles as the crow flies from the Spanish colony. It is not known from any
intermediate locality.

PSEUDOCHAZARA AMYMONE *Brown's Grayling*
Range. Confined to NW. Greece.   Map 248

P. amymone Brown 1976   TL: NW. Greece   **Pl. 59**
Description. ♂fw 26–27mm, ups dark grey with wide, pale buff pd bands; upf pale band from s1a–s5, 5–6mm wide, with or without dark crossing veins, v4 may be emphasized, and white pd spots present in s3 and s4; uph dark grey, pd band 6–7mm wide with dark marginal border 1mm. Uns pale buff, unf base and disc lightly striated and suffused fuscous; unh base and disc fuscous, distal border well defined, pd area paler.
Flight. Early August (specimens worn). Habitat, rough ground at 200–300m.
Distribution. Known only from NW. Greece.

PSEUDOCHAZARA GRAECA *Grecian Grayling*
Range. Known only from Greece.   Map 249

P. graeca Staudinger 1870   TL: Greece (*Sat. mamurra graeca*)   **Pl. 59**
Description. ♂fw 25–26mm, ups basal areas dark grey-brown, pd bands pale buff (variable); upf black ocelli present in s2 and s5, often small, rarely with white pupils and *without white spots in s3 and s4*; uph buff pd bands darker near dark marginal borders; uns pale grey with few markings. ♀ slightly larger, ups pd bands paler, often almost white. In N. Greece, in some colonies variable, both sexes darker, f. *coutsisi*, ups pale bands largely obscured by smoky-brown suffusion.
Flight and **Habitat.** Occurs in late July and August on mountains at 1700m and over.
Distribution. Mainland Greece and Peloponnesos; Mt. Taygetos; Mt. Chelmos; Mt. Timphristos; Mt. Olympos etc.
Similar species. The Asiatic *P. mamurra* H.–S., upf white spots present in s3 and s4.
Note. The specimen figured on Pl. 58 no. 6 was incorrectly identified as *P. graeca*. It is probably *P. beroe* Freyer, described from Asia Minor.

PSEUDOCHAZARA CINGOVSKII *Macedonian Grayling*
Range. Confined to S. Yugoslavia and NW. Greece.   Map 250

P. cingovskii Gross 1973   TL: S. Bosnia (Prilep)   **Pl. 59**
Description. ♂fw 25–27mm, ups dark smoky-brown, fulvous pd bands narrow; upf band broken by dark ground-colour along v4, ocelli in s2 and s5 clearly *white-pupilled, white pd spots prominent in s3 and s4*; uph fulvous band in s1b to s5 crossed by dark veins; small white-pupilled ocelli present in s2 and s3, dark marginal border 2–3mm wide; uns ground-colour grey, unf pd band pale buff, ocelli as on ups; unh heavily irrorated and powdered with fuscous. ♀fw 28mm, ups fulvous markings much brighter.
Flight. Late July. Habitat steep rocky slopes at 1100m or more.
Distribution. Identified in Yugoslavia, Macedonia and in NW. Greece. (Joannina).

PSEUDOCHAZARA ANTHELEA   *White-banded Grayling*
Range. Southern Balkans and Crete through Asia Minor (TL of *P. anthelea* Hübner 1824) to Kurdistan.   Map 251

H. anthelea amalthea   Frivaldsky 1845   TL: Crete   **Pl. 45**
Description. ♂fw 23/25mm, ups gc brown; upf conspicuous *black sex-brand* in cell, *narrow white pd band*, large ocelli in s2, 5 often blind; uph white pd band short, wide and suffused distally with fulvous; uns gc white; unh basal area and marginal border very dark, somewhat mottled darker. ♀ larger, unh less dark with confused irrorations and mottling, white pd area reduced or vestigial.
Flight. June/early July.
Habitat. Rough stony ground, usually among hills or mountains, lowlands to 1500m. Larval food plants not recorded.
Distribution. Greece, SE. Yugoslavia, Albania, Bulgaria, Crete (Psyloriti Mts.). The European white ♀ form does not occur in Asia, where all females have gc orange-yellow.

PSEUDOCHAZARA GEYERI   *Grey Asian Grayling*
Range. From S. Balkans through Asia Minor (*Satyrus geyeri* Herrich-Schäffer 1846, TL: Ararat) to Turkestan.   Map 252

P. geyeri occidentalis   Rebel and Zerny 1931   TL: Albania   **Pl. 58**
Description. ♂fw 24mm, ups gc yellowish-grey, basal and submarginal markings slightly darker; upf ocelli white-pupilled; unf yellowish, boldly marked; *unh submarginal area with sagittate brown chevrons.* ♀ups gc whiter, with bolder black markings; uns as in ♂.
Flight. July/August.
Habitat. Dry stony slopes at 1200–1800m. Larval food plants not known.
Distribution. In Europe known only from mountains in Albania and in SE. Yugoslavia north of Lake Ochrid.

OENEIS NORNA   *Norse Grayling*
Range. Lapland, Altai and Tarbagatai Mts, boreal W. Asia.   Map 253

O. norna   Thunberg 1791   TL: Lapland   **Pl. 45**
Description. ♂fw 26/28mm, fringes slightly chequered; ups gc grey-brown with wide yellowish pd bands; upf ocelli, often blind, in s2, 5, additional ocelli frequent; uph commonly with small ocelli in s2, sometimes also in 3; unh dark brown *discal band edged white,* pd area mottled and irrorated with brown, white and yellow, best seen in fresh specimens. ♀ similar, gc often paler yellow-buff, pd ocelli variable, often with white pupils.
Flight. July.
Habitat. Rough moorland, from 900m on Dovrefjeld to sea-level in far north. Larval food plants grasses, perhaps also sedge.
Distribution. Fennoscandia, from 62°N in Jotunheim to North Cape, locally common. Finland, less common, occurs principally in mountainous subarctic regions.
Similar species. *O. bore* below, slightly smaller, paler, markings unh similar but without ocelli. *O. glacialis* p. 271.

OENEIS BORE   *Arctic Grayling*
Range. Northern Fennoscandia, northern Russia, Siberia, and N. America. Map 254

O. bore Schneider 1792   TL: Lapland   **Pl. 45**
Description. ♂fw 22/25mm, fringes slightly chequered; ups gc pale fuscous, *ocelli absent* except rarely a very small, white-pupilled ocellus in s5 on upf; upf often with small yellow patches between veins in pd area, esp. in ♀; uph broad discal band usually present, lighter pd area often with small white or yellow spots between veins; unh dark discal band with white borders, pd area irrorated dark brown, yellow and white, with small pale spots between veins. ♀ similar, ups paler, sometimes with slight yellow flush on upf. *O. bore* is quickly worn, the wings losing scales and becoming nearly transparent.
Flight. June/July, depending upon weather.
Habitat. Stony slopes in hilly country, from sea-level to 600m esp. mountain summits. Larval food plant grasses, e.g. *Festuca ovina*.
Distribution. Norway and northern Finland, north of 67°N.
Similar species. *O. norna* p. 270.

OENEIS GLACIALIS   *Alpine Grayling*
Range. Confined to Alps.   Map 255

O. glacialis   Moll 1783   TL: Zillertal, Austria   **Pl. 45**
  syn: *aello* Hübner 1804
Description. ♂fw 25/28mm, fringes slightly chequered; ups gc light fuscous, yellowish in pd areas; upf ocelli in s2 and s5, often blind, inconspicuous, sex-brand along median vein conspicuous in fresh specimens; uph ocelli in s2 and s3; unh irrorated dark brown with *conspicuous white-lined veins.* ♀ larger, ups pale yellow-brown, wing-bases shaded grey, margins darker; unh pd area paler, ocelli usually white-pupilled on both wings.
Flight. End June/July.
Habitat. Rocky places, near tree-line, at 1800m or more, rarely at lower levels. Larval food plant *Festuca ovina*.
Distribution. Maritime Alps and eastwards to Carnic Alps, Bavarian Alps and North Tirol; commonest in Valais and Engadine. Absent from Jura and Vosges.
Similar species. *O. norna* p. 270, which does not show the distinctive white veins on unh.

OENEIS JUTTA   *Baltic Grayling*
Range. From Scandinavia across N. Russia and Siberia to Alaska, Labrador and Nova Scotia, thence extending to Maine and New Hampshire.   Map 256

O. jutta   Hübner 1806   TL: Lapland   **Pl. 45**
Description. ♂fw 27/28mm, fringes chequered; *ups gc dark smoky brown*, somewhat variable; upf sex-brand conspicuous, ocelli in s2(3) and 5 enclosed in yellow rings, usually blind; uph pd ocelli in s2, 3, sometimes absent, enclosed in yellow patches; *unh densely irrorated dark brown and mottled pale grey*, dark discal band often indicated by obscure grey shading. ♀ larger, pd ocelli ups larger and more constant, yellow pd patches often fused into a continuous band; unh resembles ♂.
Flight. End May to July.
Habitat. Among sparse pine trees growing around lowland bogs, etc.; the butterflies settle on the tree-trunks. Not a mountain species. Larval food plant not known.
Distribution. Fennoscandia, esp. around the lakes and bogs of Sweden and Finland, rare in Lithuania and East Prussia (Olsztyn).

SATYRUS ACTAEA *Black Satyr*

Range. SW. Europe and again in Asia Minor, Syria and Iran. Map 257

S. actaea Esper 1780 TL: S. France **Pl. 44**

Description. ♂fw 24/28mm, *sex-brand in s1–3 erect*; ups gc black; upf a single white-pupilled ocellus in s5 (rarely a small ocellus in s2); unh wing-pattern often obscure, a dark basal area generally present followed by a grey band. ♀ slightly larger, ups gc paler brown; upf basal area dark, paler pd band grey and often a small ocellus in s2; *unf gc light brown*, white spots in s3, 4; unh dark basal area or discal band often followed by white band, but very variable.

Flight. July/August in a single brood.

Habitat. Dry stony slopes at 900–1800m. Larval food plants various grasses (*Brachypodium, Bromus*, etc.).

Distribution. Spain and Portugal, widely distributed. France, from E. Pyrenees, Lot, Lozère and Aveyron to Maritimes and Basses Alpes. Italy, only in Maritime Alps and Cottian Alps northwards to Susa.

Variation. A variable species with many local races. Upf apical ocellus may be very large; in ♀ups yellow suffusion around ocelli is not uncommon and may extend to uph as a pd band, sometimes extensive.

Similar species. *S. ferula* below.

SATYRUS FERULA *Great Sooty Satyr*

Range. Morocco and southern Europe (excluding Spain and Portugal) to Asia Minor, Iran and the Himalayas. Map 258

S. ferula ferula Fabricus 1793 TL: Italy **Pl. 44**
syn: *bryce* Hübner 1800; *cordula* Fabricius 1793

Description. ♂fw 25/30mm, *sex-brand absent*; upf gc black with *white-pupilled ocelli in s2 and s5*; uph a small ocellus often present in s2; unh brown, usually strongly marked; unf white spots in s3, 4 and ocelli as on ups; unh dark basal area usually distinct, followed by paler grey band and a dark pd band beyond, but variable, sometimes with very bright markings. ♀ larger, ups gc paler brown with more or less extensive yellowish suffusion around ocelli; *unf gc orange-yellow* with prominent black ocelli; unh grey or yellow-grey with light brown basal, discal and submarginal bands and dusting, the discal band sometimes clearly defined.

Flight. July/August.

Habitat. Rocky hillsides at 450–1500m. Larval food plants various grasses.

Distribution. S. Europe, rarely north of 47°N. France, throughout southern regions of Central Massif, Provence and northwards through the Alps to Savoie and Isère, thence through the entire chain of southern Alps, including Switzerland northwards to Rhône valley, Bolzano, Etschtal, Trient, etc., but more local in Tirol. C. Italy in Apennines and south to Aspromonte. Serbia. SE. Yugoslavia, Greece and Bulgaria. Absent from Portugal, Spain. In Pyrenees rare and very local, reported near Luchon, and from Val d'Aran, probably also near Canfranc (Basses Pyrenees). Absent from Mediterranean islands.

S. ferula atlanteus Verity 1927 (Sept.) TL: Meknes, Morocco
syn: *meknesensis* Strand 1927 (Oct.)

Description. ♂fw 24/28mm, upf a single apical ocellus in s5, closely resembling *S. actaea, no sex-brand*; ♀upf a prominent white-pupilled ocellus in s5, a smaller ocellus in s2, occasional faint traces of orange suffusion around ocelli.

Flight. End June to August.
Habitat. Barren mountain slopes at 1500–2100m.
Distribution. Morocco, in High, Middle and El Rif.
Similar species. *S. actaea* p. 272, male upf with single apical ocellus and sex-brand in s1–3; ♀unf gc brown. *M. dryas* below.

MINOIS DRYAS *Dryad*
Range. From N. Spain through central Europe and C. Asia to Japan.   Map 259

M. dryas   Scopoli 1763   TL: Carniola   **Pl. 44**
  syn: *phaedra* Linnaeus 1764
Description. ♂fw 27/29mm, outer margin of hw scalloped; ups gc almost black; *upf blue-pupilled ocelli in s2 and s5*; uph a small ocellus in s2 in some specimens; unh dark brown, basal area sometimes followed by vestigial pale band and vague darker submarginal markings. ♀ larger, fw to 35mm, margin of hw deeply scalloped; ups gc paler brown, ocelli larger; unh paler brown, traces of dark discal band usually present and sometimes bordered with pale grey; unf white pd spots in s3, 4 very small; unh markings variable in both sexes.
Flight. July/August.
Habitat. Grass slopes or light woodland from lowlands to 900m. Larval food plants various grasses.
Distribution. Central Europe to 54°N, a local species absent from wide areas. From N. Spain through France, including Pyrenees and Massif Central to Fontainebleau and Vosges. Switzerland. N. Italy, Austria, Yugoslavia, Bulgaria and Romania. Germany, extending locally to Baltic coast. Absent from S. Spain, Rhone Valley, S. Provence, Italy south of Florence, Greece and Mediterranean islands.
Similar species. *S. ferula* p. 272, upf ocelli with white pupils; unh with pale bands.

BERBERIA ABDELKADER *Giant Grayling*
Range. Confined to Africa north of the Atlas Mts.   Map 260

B. abdelkader abdelkader   Pierret 1837   TL: Constantine Province,   **Pls. 43, 44**
Algeria
Description. ♂fw 35/39mm, first brood ups very dark brown; upf blue-pupilled ocelli in s2 and s5, bluish-white spots in s3, 4; uph small blue-pupilled ocelli in s2, 5, bluish-white spots in s3, 4 sometimes absent; unh discal band defined by thick dark lines, the distal line strongly angled at v4, proximal line broken, sometimes absent. ♀ups gc paler; upf some yellowish suffusion common around ocelli; unh veins strongly lined pale yellow-grey. ♂upf with an extensive sex-brand in s2–4. Second brood, *f. nelvai Seitz*, both sexes upf apex and outer margin broadly cream-white.
Flight. May/June and August/September in two annual broods.
Habitat. Rough ground and mountain slopes with esparto grass at 1800–2400m in Morocco, at lower altitudes in Algeria. Sometimes congregates on lucerne fields. Larval food plants grasses, esp. *Stipa tenacissima* (l'Alfa).
Distribution. Morocco and Algeria in Middle and High Atlas Mts.

B. abdelkader marteni   Chneour 1935   TL: Mines, Tunisia
Description. Smaller, ♂fw 28mm, upf pale apical suffusion reduced, to a wide ring around the sub-apical ocellus, with vestigial extension into s4 and s3. Late brood males only available for description.
Flight. In two broods like *B. a. abdelkader*.

Habitat. Recorded from relatively low altitudes.
Distribution. Tunisia and Tripoli, esp. coastal areas.

BRINTESIA CIRCE *Great Banded Grayling*
Range. From western Europe through Asia Minor to Iran and Himalayas.
Map 261

B. circe Fabricius 1775 TL: Europe (Germany, Verity 1953)
  syn: *proserpina* Denis and Schiffermüller 1775   **Pl. 43**
Description. ♂fw 33/36mm, ups black with single *milk-white broken pd band across both wings*; upf a single apical ocellus, generally blind; unh markings cryptic, white pd bands prominent. ♀ similar, larger, with fw to 40mm.
Flight. June/July.
Habitat. Light woodlands, lowlands to about 1400m. Larval food plants various grasses, *Bromus, Lolium*, etc.
Distribution. South and central Europe to 50°N in west, but extending farther to north in eastern Europe. Widely distributed and generally common from Spain, Portugal and France eastwards, with northern limits in central Germany. Czechoslovakia, Hungary and Romania. Absent from Britain, Belgium, Holland, Balearic Islands, Crete and N. Africa.

ARETHUSANA ARETHUSA *False Grayling*
Range. N. Africa and western Europe to Asia Minor, S. Russia and central Asia. Map 262

A. arethusa arethusa Denis and Schiffermüller 1775 TL: Vienna   **Pl. 43**
Description. ♂fw 22/24mm, upf sex-brand prominent; ups gc brown with broken *orange pd bands across both wings*, sometimes narrow or incomplete; upf a single blind dark ocellus in s5; uph small ocellus often present in s2; unh pale brown, irrorated with dark scales, basal area defined by a white band in many races. ♀ similar, ups orange bands better developed.
Flight. End July/August.
Habitat. On heaths and grassy places to 1200m. Larval food plants various grasses, esp. *Festuca*.
Distribution. Local in S. Europe, esp. on calcareous soils. Widely distributed in Spain, Portugal and France. Switzerland, in Jura and perhaps in a few localities in south-west. Italy, Ligurian Apennines and in a few scattered colonies at Oulz and NE. Italy. Absent generally from central Alps. In eastern Europe more generally distributed, esp. in Danube countries to 50°N and Balkans to Greece, but always local.

A. arethusa dentata Staudinger 1871 TL: Western France   **Pl. 43**
Description. ♂ups orange bands wide (4mm) and bright, each segment pointed externally; uns markings more brilliant; unf with lunulate inner border to grey wing-margin. ♀ similar, wing-markings better defined, with firm distal edge to brown basal areas on both wings; unf with elbowed brown pd line.
Flight and **Habitat** as for *A. a. arethusa*.
Distribution. France, in the south-west, Gironde, Basses Pyrénées, Landes, etc. Transitional to *arethusa* in Basses Alpes, Alpes Maritimes, etc., also in N. and E. Spain and Portugal. Morocco, very loccal in High Atlas, like *A. a. dentata* but unh veins very pale.

A. *arethusa boabdil*   Rambur 1842   TL: Andalusia   **Pl. 43**
Description. ♂ups gc dark brown, orange pd markings vestigial; uns all markings more brilliant; unh veins lined white and white pd band sometimes conspicuous. ♀ups orange markings slightly more developed.
Flight and **Habitat** as for *A. a. arethusa.*
Distribution. Spain, only recorded from Andalusia, esp. Sierra Nevada, Sierra de Alfacar, etc., flying at 1200–1500m in mountains.

EREBIA LIGEA   *Arran Brown*
Range. From Europe across Asia to Kamchatka and Japan.   Map 263

E. ligea ligea   Linnaeus 1758   TL: Sweden (Verity 1953)   **Pl. 46**
Description. ♂fw 24/27mm, ups gc black with wide red pd bands enclosing 3 or 4 ocelli on fw, generally white-pupilled, and 3 on hw; unh dark basal area limited by *white streak from costa to s5*, followed by white marks. ♀ups gc dark brown, pd bands orange=red; unh brightly marked, white streak longer and wider. In both sexes fringes chequered black and white. ♂ with *sex-brand* on *upf* from inner margin to s5.
Flight. End June to August.
Habitat. In hilly country from 300–1500m, often in light woodland, esp. among spruce; a lowland species in northern range. Larval food plants grasses, *Digitaria* and *Milium effusum.*
Distribution. From Auvergne and SW. Alps through Jura and Vosges eastwards through the Alps, Carpathians and Balkans to N. Greece; also in lowland Fennoscandia and very locally in Ligurian and Roman Apennines (Monte Penna). Absent from Pyrenees, Spain, Portugal, Mediterranean islands, C. and N. Germany (escept Harz Mts.), Poland. The reported occurrence of *E. ligea* on the Scottish island of Arran and mainland need confirmation.
Variation. Only minor local variation occurs; races flying at high altitudes are often small with ups red markings somewhat reduced.

E. ligea dovrensis   Strand 1902   TL: Dovre, Norway   **Pl. 46**
Description. ♂fw 21/24mm, small, ups ocelli often small and blind; unh brown, markings reduced, white streak often obsolescent. ♀unh markings better defined, white streak from costa often reaching s2 but narrow and broken, 3 submarginal ocelli.
Flight. July.
Habitat. In mountainous country in S. Norway, from sea-level to 900m in Dovrefjeld.
Distribution. Fennoscandia, chiefly Norway, from Hardanger and Dovrefjeld to North Cape. Sweden, Abisko. Finland, Ivalo.
Similar species. *E. euryale* below.

EREBIA EURYALE   *Large Ringlet*
Range. From Cantabrian Mts. through Pyrenees, Alps, Carpathians and Balkans to Urals and Altai Mts.   Map 264
E. euryale euryale   Esper 1805   TL: Riesengebirge   **Pls. 38, 46**
Description. ♂fw 21/23mm, resembles *E. ligea* but smaller and without sex-brand; ups gc black with wide red pd bands enclosing small ocelli (usually blind); unh gc reddish-brown, paler submarginal band often irrorated white or yellow, enclosing three or four small red-ringed ocelli, often blind. ♀ups gc dark brown, pd bands

paler, yellowish; unh dark discal band bordered externally by white or yellowish f. *ochracea* Wheeler; number and size of ocelli variable.

Flight. July/August.

Habitat. In mountains at 900–1800m, often among spruce. Larval food plants various grasses.

Distribution. Cantabrian Mts, Pyrenees, Central Massif of France, Jura, N. Switzerland, Alps of Germany, Austria, Sudeten Mts., Carpathians and Balkans to SE. Yugoslavia, N. Greece and Bulgaria.

Variation. The number of ocelli on upf varies locally, 4–6 spots in Riesengebirge, Erzgebirge and Böhmer Wald; farther south in much of Austria and Carpathians ocelli smaller, often absent in s3, f. *isarica* Rühl.

E. euryale adyte Hübner 1822 TL: Valais, S. Switzerland **Pls. 38, 46** (Verity 1955)

Description. ♂fw 21/23mm, ups ocelli generally with conspicuous white pupils, red pd band constricted at v4; unh markings generally obscure. ♀ups usually with white-pupilled ocelli on both wings, but distinction from *E. e. euryale* less marked.

Flight and **Habitat** as for *E. e. euryale*.

Distribution. Replaces *E. e. euryale* in SE. France and Italy, from Alpes Maritimes to Savoie, Cottian and Graian Alps. S. Switzerland to Ortler. Italy, local in Abruzzi, Gran Sasso, etc.

E. euryale ocellaris Staudinger 1861 TL: Styria and Carinthia **Pl. 46**

Description. ♂fw 20/22mm, differs from *E. e. euryale* on ups in reduction or absence of red pd bands, leaving only small blind red-ringed ocelli. ♀ups gc paler brownish, traces of normal markings more often present; unh as in *E. e. euryale*.

Flight and **Habitat** as for *E. e. euryale*.

Distribution. E. Alps, Dolomites and Alto Adige to Hohe Tauern.

Variation. Intermediate populations with ups red bands broken into separate spots often occur, with minor variation, between areas occupied by *E. e. euryale* and *E. e. adyte*, esp. at Bolzano, Glarus, Gemmi, Lenzerheide, Moléson, Gurnigel.

Similar species. *E. ligea* p. 275, which often flies with *euryale*, is larger with bolder markings, esp. unh, where conspicuous white mark on costa is distinctive. Males can be distinguished by the presence (*ligea*) or absence (*euryale*) of sex-brands on upf.

EREBIA ERIPHYLE *Eriphyle Ringlet*
Range. Confined to European Alps. Map 265

E. eriphyle eriphyle Freyer 1839 TL: Grimsel Pass, Switzerland **Pl. 48**

Description. ♂fw 16/18mm, upf pd red band obscure, sometimes with small black dots in s4, 5; uph small red spot in s4 very constant; *unf red flush extending towards base of wing*; unh red spot in s4 never with black central spot. ♀ slightly larger, markings usually paler and often slightly more extensive.

Flight. July.

Habitat. Among rocks in grassy places at 1500–1800m or more. Larval food plants unknown.

Distribution. Very local in SE. Switzerland, Grimsel Pass, Furka Pass, Flüela Pass, Davos, Val Tschitta, etc.

E. eriphyle tristis Herrich-Schäffer 1848 TL: not stated **Pls. 38, 48**

Description. Resembles *E. e. eriphyle* but markings better defined; upf red pd band narrow but bright, often enclosing three or four black points; uph red spot in s4 constant, smaller red spots often present in s2, 3, 5; unf marked reddish suffusion extending from pd band towards wing-base; unh generally three or four red pd spots, never with black central points.

Flight. July.

Habitat. On mountain slopes from 1200–2100m, seems to prefer damp places often on northern slopes.

Distribution. Alps of Bavaria (Nebelhorn), Austria (Arlberg, Innsbruck), Styria, Carinthia (Gr. Glockner, Gr. Sau Alp).

Variation. *E. e. tristis* is relatively constant in the eastern Alps and locally not uncommon. In specimens from the Gr. Glockner all ups red markings are greatly reduced but clearly defined.

Similar species. *E. melampus* p. 281, smaller with black dots in the red spots on unh; *E. manto pyrrhula* below, unh red spot in s4 elongate. *E. epiphron* p. 278.

EREBIA MANTO *Yellow-spotted Ringlet*
Range. Confined to Europe. Map 266

E. manto manto Denis and Schiffermüller 1775 TL: Vienna **Pl. 49**
Description. ♂fw 20/21mm, upf pd band variable but usually present, composed of *elongate red marks* long in s4, 5, shorter in s1a, 2, 3, each enclosing a small black spot; uph small red marks generally present in s4, 5, 6; unh gc distinctly reddish, markings more complete, often orange-yellow, longest in s4, 5, 6, basal red markings variable, often absent. ♀ups pd bands often paler and better defined; unh brown discal band bounded proximally by yellow basal marks and distally by yellow pd markings.
Flight. July/August.
Habitat. Subalpine meadows at 900–1800m.
Distribution. Alps and Tatra Mts., local in Balkans.

E. manto vogesiaca Christ 1882 TL: Vosges Mts. **Pl. 54**
Description. ♂fw 21–22mm, large, upf pd band narrow but complete, black subapical dots often absent. ♀unh pale discal and pd spots often white, ♀ f. *bubastis*.
Flight and **Habitat** as for *E. m. manto*.
Distribution. Confined to Vosges Mts.

E. manto constans Eiffinger 1908 TL: Hautes Pyrénées **Pl. 38**
Description. Resembles *E. m. manto* but black, ups unmarked, uns very rarely with traces of usual markings. ♀ often slightly larger and more often with traces of uns red markings.
Flight. End June/July.
Habitat. Flies in subalpine meadows at 1500–1800m, usually in damp places.
Distribution. Hautes Pyrénées, Gavarnie, Luchon and eastwards to Aulus. Slightly smaller and local in Cantal and Auvergne, Le Lioran, Plomb de Cantal, etc. Recently found in N. Spain (Santander).

E. manto pyrrhula Frey 1880 TL: Albula Pass, Engadine **Pl. 48**
Description. ♂fw 17/19mm, small and variable, markings always reduced or absent on both surfaces. ♀upf has twin subapical black spots in narrow red area.
Flight. July.
Habitat. High alpine meadows and slopes above tree-line at 1800–2100m.
Distribution. Engadine, Albula, Guarda, etc. Dolomites, rather local and not quite so small. Hte Savoie, Mt. Blanc, less extreme.
Similar species. *E. eriphyle* p. 276.

EREBIA CLAUDINA *White Speck Ringlet*
Range. Confined to eastern Alps. Map 267

E. claudina Borkhausen 1789 TL: Austria **Pl. 47**
syn: *arete* Fabricius 1787 (invalid homonym)
Description. ♂fw 17/18mm, upf pd red band narrow; uph two or three minute white submarginal points, sometimes traces of red submarginal band; *unh six white points forming a regular submarginal series.* ♀ups gc paler brown; upf pd band paler red, enclosing twin black spots in s5, 6; unh pale yellow-grey, white submarginal points larger.
Flight. July.
Habitat. Flies over short grass slopes at 1800m or more. Larval food plant grass, esp. *Deschampsia caespitosa.*
Distribution. Only in eastern Alps of Salzburg, Styria and Carinthia, including Zirbitzkogel, Gr. Sau Alp, Mallnitz.
Similar species. *E. epiphron* below; *E. melampus* p. 281.

EREBIA FLAVOFASCIATA *Yellow-Banded Ringlet*
Range. Confined to Alps of S. Switzerland. Map 268

E. flavofasciata Heyne 1895 TL: Campolungo Pass, Tessin **Pl. 47**
Description. ♂fw 17/18mm, ups gc black; upf small red-ringed black pd spots in s4, 5, often also in s2, 3, always in straight row; uph black red-ringed submarginal spots in s2–5; unf disc suffused reddish, pd spots better defined; *unh a wide yellow submarginal band* enclosing small black spots in s2–5. ♀ups gc paler, brownish; upf pd spots ringed yellow, series often complete.
Flight. July.
Habitat. On rocky slopes with grass at 2100m or more. Larval food plant grass, esp. *Festuca ovina.*
Distribution. Restricted to a few localities in S. Switzerland, Tessin (Campolungo Pass), Engadine (Pontresina), etc.
Variation. In the Engadine, f. *thiemei* Bartel, unh yellow band narrow, sometimes broken up.

EREBIA EPIPHRON *Mountain Ringlet*
Range. Mountains of Europe, excluding Fennoscandia. Map 269

E. epiphron epiphron Knoch 1783 TL: Harz Mts., W. Germany **Pl. 48**
The species is probably extinct in the Harz Mts., and the following description is based upon the closely related Silesian form, *silesiana* Meyer-Dur.
Description. ♂fw 17/19mm, fw pointed; *upf red pd bands brilliant, lustrous,* enclosing blind *round black spots in s2–5;* uph with similar pd band with three black spots; *unh brown,* generally with small dark submarginal spots narrowly red-ringed. ♀ similar, ups black spots usually larger and often with minute white pupils on upf.
Flight. July.
Habitat. Flies in clearings among fir trees at 600–1000m. Larval food plants grasses, esp. *Deschampsia caespitosa.*
Distribution. S. Bavaria, Czechoslovakia, Tatra Mts. and Carpathians.
Variation. In Tatra Mts. and Carpathians slightly smaller with ups red pd bands slightly reduced, upf black spot in s3 often absent.

E. epiphron fauveaui   de Lesse 1947   TL: E. Pyrenees   **Pl. 48**
Description. ♂fw 19/21mm, resembles *E. e. epiphron* but fw less pointed; upf red pd band reduced, rarely reaching s1b, enclosing four round black spots in most specimens. ♀ similar.
Flight. End June/July/August.
Habitat. Grass slopes at 1800m or more.
Distribution. E. Pyrenees, Mt. Canigou, Cambre d'Aze, etc., and westwards, with *aetheria*-forms becoming increasingly common, to Luchon.

E. epiphron mnemon   Haworth 1812   TL: Scotland   **Pl. 48**
   syn: *scotica* Cooke 1943
Description. ♂fw 17/19mm, size variable, general appearance dark; upf red pd band narrow and often incomplete, usually enclosing four small black spots. ♀ similar, ups markings sometimes better defined; unh gc grey-brown.
Flight. July.
Habitat. On rough moorland to 900m or over. Larval food plants various grasses, esp. *Nardus stricta*.
Distribution. Scotland, on higher mountains in the Grampians, Ben Nevis, above Loch Rannoch, etc. England, Westmorland and Cumberland.
Variation. English specimens are small, ♂fw 14/17mm, upf markings so reduced that basic features may be obscured. Similar forms occur in the Vosges and in Auvergne.

E. epiphron aetheria   Esper 1805   TL: not stated   **Pl. 48**
Description. ♂fw 17/19mm, upf red pd band reduced, *constricted in s3* with absence of black spot; sometimes only twin apical black spots present. ♀ups paler, markings better developed, upf often with four black spots, white pupils not rare in s4, 5; unh brown, pd area slightly paler.
Flight. July/August.
Habitat. Grass slopes on high mountains from 1700m upwards.
Distribution. S. Alps generally, including Tirol, S. Switzerland and Apennines. Central Pyrenees and Cantabrian Mts. West Balkans.
Variation. At very high altitudes smaller, ♂fw 16/17mm, markings very dark and obscure, f. *nelamus* Boisduval Pl. 48, a relatively constant form in many localities in Engadine, Oberland, Urschweiz, Dolomites, etc.

E. epiphron orientalis   Elwes 1900   TL: Rila Mts., Bulgaria   **Pl. 48**
Description. ♂fw 18/20mm, fw narrow, pointed; upf red pd band narrow, broken, twin black white-pupilled ocelli in s4, 5; uph with round black red-ringed pd spots and generally white-pupilled ocelli in s2, 3, 4(5); uns all ocelli small and white-pupilled. ♀ slightly larger, ups pd bands paler, unbroken, all ocelli larger, four ocelli on upf, four or five on uph.
Flight. July.
Habitat. Grass slopes at 1500–2100m.
Distribution. Bulgaria, in Rila and Pirin Mts. A little-known subspecies, habitats remote and difficult of access. In several respects it differs from other forms of *E. epiphron*, and perhaps would be better ranked as a distinct species. Also on Stara Planina.
Similar species. *E. pharte* below, upf without pupils in red pd spots; *E. claudina* p. 278, unh with series of minute white pd spots; *E. christi* p. 280, upf red pd band not constricted in s3, unh pd area distinctly paler; *E. eriphyle* p. 276, unh a round red

spot always present in s4; *E. sudetica* p. 281 and *E. melampus* p. 281, both with orange submarginal spots on unh.

EREBIA SEROTINA   *Descimon's Ringlet*
Range. Only known from the Central Pyrenees at Cauterets.   Map 270

E. serotina   Descimon and de Lesse 1953   TL: Cauterets   **Pl. 54**
Description. ♂fw 21/22mm, resembles *E. epiphron fauveaui*, with three or four ocelli on upf of which the *apical pair have small white pupils*; uph with three or four small submarginal ocelli, red-ringed and sometimes with *white pupils*; unf red pd band clearly defined; unh basal area dark brown with a paler pd band which recalls *E. aethiopella*. The ♀ is not known.
Flight. September.
Habitat. All known specimens have been taken at about 900m.
Distribution. Near Cauterets in the Hautes Pyrénées. About twenty specimens, all males, are known. The rarity and unusual flight period of this insect are most difficult to explain. Now accepted as hybrid, probably *E. epiphron* × *E. manto*. No specimens have been seen for about 20 years.

EREBIA CHRISTI   *Rätzer's Ringlet*
Range. Confined to S. Alps of Switzerland.   Map 271

E. christi   Rätzer 1890   TL: Laquintal, Simplon   **Pl. 48**
Description. ♂fw 18/20mm, resembles *E. epiphron*, upf *red pd band not constricted in s3*, crossed by dark veins, enclosing two to four black oval subapical dots in a straight row, the band of even width but slightly variable in extent; uph generally with three slightly oval red-ringed black dots; unh paler, with *vague grey-brown pd area without ocelli* or rarely with two or three small dark dots. ♀ all markings paler, upf pd band orange-yellow, wider; uph oval submarginal dots ringed fulvous; unh light brown, with paler pd area, sometimes a vague darker discal band.
Flight. End June/July.
Habitat. Grassy places among rocks at 1400–1800m. Larval food plant *Festuca ovina*.
Distribution. S. Switzerland, Simplon Pass, Laquintal, Alpien, Hossaz Alp, Zwischbergental, Eggen. Colonies very restricted.
Similar species. *E. epiphron aetheria* p. 279.

EREBIA PHARTE   *Blind Ringlet*
Range. Confined to European Alps and Tatra Mts.   Map 272

E. pharte pharte   Hübner 1804   TL: Alps of Switzerland   **Pl. 48**
Description. ♂fw 17/19mm, upf narrow red pd band of even rectangular spots continued on uph as a series of smaller rounded spots well separated; markings repeated on uns; *red spots are without black pupils or ocelli on either surface*. ♀ups gc paler, brownish-grey; uns suffused yellow.
Flight. July.
Habitat. Moist alpine meadows from 1700m upwards. Larval food plants unknown.
Distribution. Alps of Savoie, Valais, Vosges and N. Switzerland.
Note. The form illustrated in Hübner's original figure, of moderate size and with well-developed markings, occupies a central position on the cline of variation.

E. pharte eupompa Fruhstorfer 1918 TL: Schliersee and **Pls. 48, 54**
Tegernsee, Bavaria
  syn: *fasciata* Spuler 1901 (invalid homonym)
Description. ♂fw 19/20mm, large, brightly marked, upf pd band orange-red. ♀ups
paler yellow-brown, pd bands and spots yellow.
Flight and **Habitat** as for *E. p. pharte.*
Distribution. Eastern Alps, Bavaria, Styria, Julian Alps, Tatra Mts.

E. pharte phartina Staudinger 1894 TL: Central Alps **Pl. 54**
Description. ♂fw 16/17mm, small, ups red markings greatly reduced, sometimes
absent.
Flight and **Habitat** as for *E. p. pharte*, rarely seen below 1800m.
Distribution. High mountains from the Dauphiné to the Gross Glockner, very
typical at Pontresina, Guarda, Misurina and other localities in the Dolomites.
Variation. In all localities *E. pharte* is very variable in size and markings.
Similar species. *E. epiphron* p. 278.

EREBIA MELAMPUS *Lesser Mountain Ringlet*
Range. Confined to Alps of C. Europe. Map 273

E. melampus Fuessli 1775 TL: Switzerland **Pl. 47**
Description. ♂fw 15/18mm, upf red band narrow but extending from s1b–s6,
crossed by dark veins and enclosing small black spots in s4, 5; uph two to four round
red pd spots each enclosing a small black point, *spot in s3 displaced slightly outwards
and out of line with other spots in series*, spot in s4 largest; uns pattern as on ups.
♀ similar, ups gc paler, uns often suffused yellow.
Flight. End June/July/August.
Habitat. Alpine valleys from 1000m upwards to over 1800m, flying on grassy slopes
and meadows. Larval food plants grasses, esp. *Poa.*
Distribution. Graian and Cottian Alps to Savoie and through Switzerland and
N. Italian Alps to Dolomites, Styria and Carinthia. More local and scarce in Basses
Alpes, S. Bavaria, N. Tirol and Lower Austria. Absent from Pyrenees, Apennines,
Carpathians, Balkans, Jura and Vosges.
Variation. At higher altitudes often small, larger at lower altitudes. Additional
black spots are sometimes present on upf.
Similar species. *E. eriphyle* p. 276; *E. sudetica* below. *E. claudina* p. 278, unh with
series of minute white pd spots.

EREBIA SUDETICA *Sudeten Ringlet*
Range. Confined to Europe. Map 274

E. sudetica sudetica Staudinger 1861 TL: Silesian Mts. **Pl. 47**
Description. ♂fw 16/17mm, resembles *E. melampus* but uph with four to five red pd
spots in regular series and *unh six spots conspicuously regular* and well graded, spot in
s3 often largest, each spot usually enclosing a small black point. ♀ups gc slightly
paler, otherwise similar.
Flight. July.
Habitat. Grassy places among woodland at 600–1200m. Larval food plants not
known.
Distribution. Altvater Mt., Carpathians, Retezat Mts.

E. sudetica liorana de Lesse 1947   TL: Cantal, C. France   **Pl. 47**
Description. Resembles *E. s. sudetica* but markings less bright; uph series of red pd
spots often reduced to four spots; unh four or five spots only, but the regular graded
character of series fully maintained.
Flight and **Habitat** as for *E. s. sudetica*.
Distribution. France, in Massif Central, e.g. Lozère, Le Lioran, Puy-de-Dôme,
etc. Another colony with markings even more reduced exists near Grindelwald in the
Bernese Oberland of Switzerland.
Similar species. *E. melampus* p. 281, unh pd spots usually two to four in number,
not regularly graded, spot in s3 displaced slightly distad, spot in s4 noticeably the
largest. A black-centred small fulvous pd spot on upf in s6 is common in *E. sudetica*,
rare in *E. melampus*.

EREBIA AETHIOPS   *Scotch Argus*
Range. From W. Europe through Asia Minor, Urals and Caucasus to Sajan
Mts.   Map 275

E. aethiops Esper 1777   TL: S. Germany   **Pls. 49, 54**
Description. ♂fw 22/26mm, upf góc black, a conspicuous sex-brand from inner
margin to s5(6), pd band bright red, often constricted at s3 and enclosing white-
pupilled ocelli in s2, 4, 5; uph with small white-pupilled pd ocelli in s2, 3, 4(5), red-
ringed or enclosed in red pd band; *unh* dark red-brown, pd band pale greyish with
minute white points in s2–4. ♀ups gc paler brown, upf pd band orange or yellow; uph
three or four larger red-ringed ocelli; unh yellow-brown, often with darker discal
band defined by paler yellowish basal and pd areas; fringes slightly chequered light
and dark brown.
Flight. August/September.
Habitat. In hilly districts, generally among coniferous trees from 300–1800m or
more, exceptionally at sea-level on sand-dunes near Ostend. Larval food plants
various grasses, including *Molinia caerulea, Agropyron*, etc.
Distribution. France, in woodlands, etc., in NE., also Auvergne, Cevennes (?), Jura
and Vosges; Belgian Ardennes. From Hautes Alpes (Gap) northwards to Haute
Savoie and throughout central Alps. N. England, Scotland, mountainous districts
of Germany, Silesia, Baltic coast, Lithuania, Carpathians and Balkans. Italy, in
Ligurian Apennines and Apuane Alps but absent from peninsular Italy. Absent
from Pyrenees, Denmark, Fennoscandia, Greece.
Variation. Size is variable. A small race, f. *caledonia* Verity ♂fw 21/22mm. Pls. 49,
54, flies in S. Scotland and elsewhere at high altitudes. Large races are common on
southern alpine slopes, ♂fw 23/26mm. In ♀unh pale pd band varies in colour from
yellow-buff to violet-grey, ♀ f. *violacea* Wheeler.
Similar species. *E. neoridis* p. 298; *E. pronoe* p. 293; both these lack the white points
unh in pd band.

EREBIA TRIARIA   *de Prunner's Ringlet*
Range. Confined to Europe.   Map 276

E. triaria triaria de Prunner 1798   TL: Exilles, Piedmont   **Pl. 49**
   syn: *evias* Godart 1823
Description. ♂fw 23/25mm, upf red pd band wide near costa, tapering towards anal
angle, enclosing white-pupilled ocelli in s2–6, the small ocellus in s6 nearly constant;

uph three or four ocelli enclosed in red pd band or widely ringed red; *unh* gc very dark, *obscurely irrorated grey*, with darker discal band. ♀upf pd band orange-red; unh gc and markings lighter, discal band better defined.
Flight. End May/June/July.
Habitat. Flies on open grassy slopes at 900–2100m often near tree-line. Larval food plants unknown.
Distribution. Very localised in scattered colonies. Portugal, Serra da Gerez. Spain, Cantabrian Mts., Guadarrama and Pyrenees. France, in Pyrenees, Vaucluse, Basses and Hautes Alpes. Switzerland, widely distributed in southern Alps, Simplon, Albula, Ofen Pass, etc. Austria, Italy, Alto Adige, Trentino. Yugoslavia, in Julian Alps, Hercegovina, Montenegro. Albania.

E. triaria hispanica Gumppenberg 1888 TL: Teruel
Description. ♂fw 22/24mm, small, ups pd bands yellowish and ocelli small. ♀ups gc paler; unh dark discal band usually well defined.
Flight. End May/June.
Habitat. On grassy slopes at 1200–1500m.
Distribution. Spain, in provinces of Logrono, Teruel and Cuenca, e.g. Sierra Alta near Albarracin, Canales.
Similar species. *E. meolans* p. 299, ♂unh black, nearly unmarked.

EREBIA EMBLA *Lapland Ringlet*
Range. Arctic Europe, Siberia to Altai Mts., Sajan Mts. and Kamschatka without notable variation. Map 277

E. embla Thunberg 1791 TL: Västerbotten, Sweden **Pl. 48**
Description. ♂fw 25/26mm, upf with large twin apical ocelli, often blind, small ocelli in s2, 3, rarely also in 1b, all ringed tawny-yellow; *uph* smaller *yellow-ringed ocelli in s2–4(5)*; unh brown with paler grey pd area, small white mark on costa and in s4, fringes slightly chequered. ♀ups gc and markings paler.
Flight. End May/June.
Habitat. On moorlands or among sparse pine trees, from 150–400m. Larval food plants unknown.
Distribution. Fennoscandia, from 60°N to North Cape, rather local, most common in S. Finland. Also recorded in Latvia.
Similar species. *E. disa* below, in which uph ocelli are absent.

EREBIA DISA *Arctic Ringlet*
Range. Arctic Europe, Sajan Mts., Irkutsk, Yakutsk, Yablonoi Mts. and arctic N. America in Alaska, Yukon, British Columbia and Alberta, circumpolar. Map 278

E. disa Thunberg 1791 TL: Lapland **Pl. 48**
Description. ♂fw 23/25mm, upf resembles *E. embla* but all four ocelli are approximately equal in size, ringed tawny and sometimes fused into a pd band; *uph brown, without ocelli*; unh grey, with wide dark brown discal band; fringes chequered grey and brown. ♀ resembles ♂, ups gc sometimes paler brown; unh markings well defined with increased contrast.
Flight. June/early July, according to season.
Habitat. Wet moorland and bogs, in Europe usually a lowland insect, sometimes at sea-level. Larval food plants not known.

Distribution. Fennoscandia, not south of 64°N, most common near coast and in far north, e.g. Saltdalen, Inari, Petsamo.
Similar species. *E. embla* p. 283.

EREBIA MEDUSA *Woodland Ringlet*
Range. Europe and Asia Minor. Map 279

E. medusa medusa Denis and Schiffermüller 1775 TL: Vienna **Pl. 50**
Description. ♂fw 21/24mm, upf white-pupilled ocelli in s4, 5 widely ringed tawny yellow and a smaller ocellus in s2, together making an incomplete band interrupted at v3, additional small ocelli in s1b and 6 in some specimens; uph three or four small ocelli ringed yellowish; *unh gc paler uniform brown* with four or five white-pupilled ocelli, otherwise unmarked. ♀ups paler brown, markings orange-yellow, often larger, more or less confluent.
Flight. May/June.
Habitat. Moorlands, damp meadows and light woodland, in northern range often a lowland species, but flying to 1200m in hill country. Larval food plants grasses, esp. *Digitaria sanguinale* and *Milium effusum*.
Distribution. Belgian Ardennes. NE. France to Paris, Jura and Vosges, and southwards to Dijon and Lyon. Switzerland, in Geneva district. Italy, Susa in Piedmont, Etruscan Apennines. Poland, recorded from Baltic coast at Szczecin (Stettin) and Gdansk (Danzig) to 58°N. Germany, except in north-west. Austria. Hungary. Czechoslovakia. Yugoslavia. Greece. Absent from W. France, Spain, Pyrenees, SW. Alps, peninsular Italy and Mediterranean islands.
Variation. Typical *E. medusa*, which flies at moderate altitudes near Vienna, occupies an intermediate position on the cline of variation in size and wing-markings. The two extreme forms are described below.

E. medusa psodea Hübner 1804 TL: Hungary **Pl. 54**
Description. ♂fw 23/25mm, ups markings brighter, orange-yellow, often confluent; uns similar, gc smooth rather pale brown. Characters usually best marked in ♀, ocelli larger and orange-yellow areas more extensive, often six large ocelli and gc quite pale.
Flight and **Habitat** as for *E. m. medusa*, but flies to 1500m in Carpathians.
Distribution. Especially in E. Europe in favourable habitats. Hungary and Romania in Carpathians, with tendency to smaller brightly marked races at high altitudes. Yugoslavia (very variable). Bulgaria. Often transitional to *E. m. medusa*, with which it blends insensibly farther west.

E. medusa hippomedusa Ochsenheimer 1820 TL: Styria **Pl. 50**
Description. ♂fw 19/21mm, ups gc dark brown to black, markings greatly reduced, in extreme examples only two small subapical ocelli on upf, three on uph, all narrowly ringed orange-red; unh gc dark grey-brown. ♀ similar.
Flight. June/July.
Habitat. In mountains at high altitudes, usually near tree-line at 1500–1800m.
Distribution. In southern and eastern Alps and Balkans, Dolomites, Monte Baldo.
Variation. Still small but rather more brightly marked in Ticino (Fusio), Styria, Carinthia, Bosnia, S. Carpathians.
Similar species. *E. oeme* p. 299, usually smaller, ocelli ringed fulvous-red (yellowish in *medusa*), their pupils gleaming white; antennae in *oeme* tipped black (brown

in *medusa*). *E. alberganus* below, small specimens of f. *caradjae* may resemble *hippomedusa*, but ocellar rings are oval. *E. polaris* below.

EREBIA POLARIS *Arctic Woodland Ringlet*
Range. Lapland, probably across boreal Asia to Lena River.   Map 280

E. polaris Staudinger 1871   TL: Lapland   **Pl. 50**
Description. ♂fw 20/22mm, ups gc dark brown; upf with small white-pupilled ocelli in s4, 5, often with additional small pd ocelli or fulvous spots in s2, 3; uph one to three fulvous-ringed submarginal ocelli; unf as above; *unh pd area faintly paler.* ♀ups gc slightly paler; uph ocelli often more numerous; unf brown to red-brown with brown outer margin, ocelli ringed paler; unh pale grey-brown, pd band better defined, usually enclosing ocelli.
Flight. End June/July.
Habitat. Lightly wooded valleys and hillsides from sea-level to 300m. Larval food plant unknown.
Distribution. Scandinavia, Porsanger, Utsjoki, Kautokeino, etc., not south of 68°N.
Similar species. *E. medusa hippomedusa* above, unh lacks the pale pd band. There is no similar butterfly in the high north. The characters given above will distinguish *E. polaris* from specimens of *E. medusa* that lack data.

EREBIA ALBERGANUS *Almond-eyed Ringlet*
Range. Confined to Europe.   Map 281

E. alberganus alberganus   de Prunner 1798   TL: Piedmont   **Pl. 52**
   syn: *ceto* Hübner 1804
Description. ♂fw 20/22mm, ups dark brown, pd bands represented by series of *orange-red lanceolate spots*, which enclose ocelli with minute white pupils, in s2, 4, 5 upf and s1–5 uph, additional ocelli often present on fw; uns the same pattern is repeated. ♀ups resembles ♂, uns gc yellowish-brown, pd spots often pale yellow, with markings as in ♂.
Flight. Late June/July.
Habitat. Alpine meadows at 900–1800m. Larval food plants grasses, *Poa annua, Festuca*, etc.
Distribution. Alpes Maritimes to Savoie, Valais, Engadine, Dolomites, Oetztal, Hohe Tauern and locally in Apennines. In Switzerland rare and local north of the Rhône valley. Recently found in N. Spain (Santander Prov.).
Variation. At 1800–2100m in Engadine, Savoie, etc., very small, ♂fw 18/20mm, all orange markings greatly reduced, f. *caradjae* Caflisch; development of markings on ups very variable in many localities. On southern slopes of western Alps often large with very brilliant orange markings, f. *tyrsus* Fruhstorfer Pl. 52.

E. alberganus phorcys   Freyer 1836   TL: Turkey (Bulgaria)   **Pl. 52**
Description. ♂fw 23mm, ups orange markings extended; unh lanceolate spots long, pale yellow to white. ♀ similar.
Flight. Early July.
Habitat. Open woodland at 900m.
Distribution. Bulgaria, near Karlovo in Balkan Mts., not recorded elsewhere.
Similar species. *E. oeme* p. 299 and *E. medusa* p. 284.

EREBIA PLUTO *Sooty Ringlet*
Range. Confined to the Alps. Map 282

E. pluto pluto de Prunner 1798   TL: Val Varodisiana, Piedmont   **Pl. 51**
syn: *belzebub* Costa 1839
Description. ♂fw 22/25mm, ups *velvet-black, unmarked*; unf margin of discal area sometimes indicated by a darker shade, pd area with faint deep-chestnut flush; ♀ similar, ups paler, unf with broad chestnut-brown pd band which may extend to base; unh basal area grey-brown, pd area paler.
Flight. End June/July/August.
Habitat. On stony screes and moraines from 1800–2700m. Larval food plants grasses, esp. *Poa.*
Distribution. Alpes Maritimes and through Cottian and Graian Alps northwards to Savoie, where it occurs mixed with *E. p. oreas*; also in Bernese Oberland (Dent de Morcles), Todi Group, W. Dolomites, Triglav massif and in the Abruzzi on Gran Sasso, Monte Rotondo and perhaps elsewhere.

E. pluto alecto Hübner 1804   TL: Lermoos, Bavaria   **Pl. 51**
Description. ♂fw 24/25mm, ups resembles *E. p. pluto* but *upf with white-pupilled ocelli in s4, 5*; unf reddish pd area usually present. ♀upf often with traces of red suffusion in pd area.
Flight and **Habitat** as for *E. p. pluto.*
Distribution. Widely distributed in the central and north-central Alps, but often with transitional characters towards other forms of the species complex. Most characteristic in the Allgäuer Alps, Bavarian Alps, Karwendel Alps and Dolomites. In Ortler Alps ups red pd bands usually broad, f. *velocissima* Fruhstorfer Pl. 51.

E. pluto nicholli Oberthur 1896   TL: Campiglio, Brenta Alps
Description. ♂fw 20/23mm, ups sooty-black; upf dense black white-pupilled pd ocelli in s2–s5, usually small in s2, 3; uph similar ocelli in s2, 3, 4; uns black, markings as on ups. ♀ slightly larger; ups white-pupilled ocelli larger, often set in indistinct narrow brown pd bands; unf disc red-brown, outer margin and unh grey-brown to sooty-black, ocelli as on ups.
Flight and **Habitat** as for *E. p. pluto.*
Distribution. N. Italy (Trentino). Restricted to Alps of Brenta Group north of Lake Garda, also on Monte Baldo, with markings especially constant and well developed.
Variation. Farther north ocelli become less numerous with transitional forms blending with *E. p. alecto.*

E. pluto oreas Warren 1933   TL: Chamonix, Savoie   **Pl. 51**
syn: *glacialis* Esper 1804 (invalid homonym)
Description. ♂fw 21/24mm, ups gc very dark silky brown to black without ocelli; upf with *wide reddish pd band*; uph with or without broken red-brown pd band; unf pd band brighter with red flush to base; unh black, unmarked. ♀ups gc and markings paler and better defined; unf wholly reddish except margins; unh basal area brown with paler grey-brown pd band.
Flight and **Habitat** as for *E. p. pluto.*
Distribution. From Haute Savoie eastwards through Pennine Alps, Ticino and Grisons to the Albula Pass and Pontresina, also northwards in mountains of Upper Engadine. Farther east commonly transitional to *E. p. pluto* or *E. p. alecto.*

Similar species. *E. lefebvrei astur* and *pyrenaea* p. 295 and *E. melas* p. 294, none of which occurs in the Alps; unf not flushed chestnut-brown.

EREBIA GORGE Silky Ringlet
Range. Confined to Europe. Map 283

E. gorge gorge Hübner 1804 TL: Switzerland and Tirol **Pl. 47**
Description. ♂fw 17/20mm, upf with inconspicuous sex-brand in s1–3, *red pd band with gleaming texture*, wide, enclosing two subapical ocelli; uph pd band narrower, sometimes with small submarginal ocelli; unf red with dark grey marginal border; *unh* variable, usually *marbled light and dark* grey, often with dark discal band. ♀ups gc and pd bands lighter in tone, unh gc paler, discal band more sharply defined.
Flight. End June/July.
Habitat. Moraines and rocky slopes from 1500m upwards. Larval food plants grasses.
Distribution. E. Pyrenees, Savoie, Pennine and Bernese Alps, Tirol, Styria, Carinthia.
Variation. Large races with ♂fw 19/20mm, f. *gigantea* Oberthur, occur in the Cantabrian Mts., Allgauer Alps and Tatra Mts., apical ocelli usually small. Pl. 47.

E. gorge ramondi Oberthur 1909 TL: Gavarnie, Hautes Pyrénées **Pls. 47, 54**
Description. ♂fw 17/20mm, differs from *E. g. gorge* in having four to five well-formed white-pupilled ocelli on both surfaces of hw. Occasional specimens with triple apical ocelli on upf are not distinguishable from *E. g. triopes*.
Flight and **Habitat** as for *E. g. gorge*.
Distribution. Basses Pyrénées and eastwards to Andorra.

E. gorge triopes Speyer 1865 TL: Bernina Pass **Pl. 47**
Description. ♂fw 17/18mm, resembles *E. g. ramondi*, but upf ocelli in s4, 5, 6 conjoined, often nearly equal in size, forming a striking apical row, additional ocelli in s2, 3 may be present; uph three or four well-formed submarginal ocelli usually present near the outer border of the red pd band. ♀ similar.
Flight and **Habitat** as for *E. g. gorge*.
Distribution. Preponderates in Ortler group in Upper Engadine, Sulden, Pontresina, Monte Baldo. Occasional examples occur elsewhere in eastern Alps, Dolomites, etc. Rare in W. Alps.
Variation. Specimens with twin apical ocelli on upf, indistinguishable from *E. g. ramondi*, are not very uncommon.

E. gorge erynis Esper 1805 TL: Chamonix, Haute Savoie **Pl. 54**
Description. Differs from *E. g. gorge* in the absence of twin apical ocelli on upf, though occasional specimens occur with vestigial ocelli.
Flight and **Habitat** as for *E. g. gorge*.
Distribution. Alpes Maritimes, Basses Alpes. Abruzzi and Monte Sibillini.
Variation. Italian specimens are small, with unh very dark and obscurely marked, f. *carboncina* Verity Pl. 47.

In France the racial character of *E. g. erynis* is marked in the Maritimes and Basses Alpes with about 90% entirely without upf apical ocelli and the remaining 10% with one or two small ocelli, unlike *E. g. gorge*. North of the Basses Alpes the incidence of *gorge*-forms increases to about 50% in Savoy. In Switzerland *erynis*-forms are not rare in the Pennine and Bernese Alps, and occasional eastwards to Pontresina.

E. gorge albanica Rebel 1917 TL: Gropa Strelit, Albania
Description. ♂fw 18mm, upf red pd band short, indistinct, ocelli present in s4 and s5, absent in s2; unh very dark, lacking ocelli and markings.
♀fw 20mm, ups paler, unh with few markings, ocelli absent.
Flight. On mountains in July.
Distribution. Known only from Albania. Perhaps also in Montenegro.
Similar species. *E. aethiopella* below, resembles *E. gorge*, unh brown, markings in regular bands, ocelli always small, frequents alpine meadows; *E. gorgone* p. 289, larger, darker, unf deep chestnut, confined to Pyrenees; *E. mnestra* p. 288, unh medium brown, almost unmarked.

EREBIA AETHIOPELLA   *False Mnestra Ringlet*
Range. Confined to Europe.   Map 284

E. aethiopella aethiopella Hoffmannsegg 1806   TL: Piedmont   **Pl. 47**
syn: *gorgophone* Bellier 1863
Description. ♂fw 18/20mm, with conspicuous sex-brand in s1a to 4, red pd band wide, often extending to cell-end, with or (rarely) without small white-pupilled ocelli in s4, 5; uph pd band wide on costa, tapering to s2, ocelli absent; *unh rich brown with paler pd band*, the whole densely irrorated with white scales in northern range, less so in Alpes Maritimes. ♀ups gc paler brown, pd bands orange-red; upf ocelli constant, often larger; unh brightly marked, gc grey or yellow-brown, paler at base, pale pd band conspicuous.
Flight. July/August.
Habitat. Grass slopes at 1800m or more. Larval food plants not known.
Distribution. Alpes Maritimes and northwards to Cottian Alps and Mont Genèvre.

E. aethiopella rhodopensis Nicholl 1900   TL: Rila Mts., Bulgaria   **Pl. 47**
Description. ♂fw 19/20mm, resembles *E. a. aethiopella*; upf apical ocelli larger and small ocellus in s2; uph three submarginal ocelli; unh ocelli very small or absent. ♀ups dark basal areas well defined; upf pd bands orange-red; uph submarginal ocelli larger; unh markings much brighter, brown and yellow-grey with paler irroration and marbling, submarginal ocelli usually present but small.
Flight and **Habitat** as for *E. a. aethiopella*.
Distribution. Bulgaria. Stara Planina, Pirin Mts., Rila and Rhodope Mts.
Variation. A slightly smaller brighter form, f. *sharsta* Higgins, with unh grey and prominent white irroration, occurs in the Schar Planina, S. Yugoslavia. The distribution of this species and its forms corresponds closely with that of *Boloria graeca* Staudinger.
Similar species. *E. mnestra* below, often slightly larger, upf ♂ sex-brand inconspicuous, uph the red band shorter and more broken; unh markings generally obscure in both sexes; range overlaps that of *E. aethiopella* in the Hautes Alpes near Mont Genèvre; *E. gorge* p. 287.

EREBIA MNESTRA   *Mnestra's Ringlet*
Range. Confined to central Alps of Europe.   Map 285

E. mnestra Hübner 1804   TL: Swiss Alps   **Pl. 47**
Description. ♂fw 17/19mm, sex-brand very faint and inconspicuous; upf a broad red pd band extending in s4, 5 to cell-end, sometimes enclosing minute subapical

twin ocelli; uph pd band narrow, broken, usually restricted to s3, 4, 5, without enclosed ocelli, sometimes vestigial; unf red with brown marginal border; *unh chestnut-brown, unmarked or (rarely) with vague paler pd band.* ♀upf twin white-pupilled subapical ocelli rarely absent, sometimes very small; uph with or without pd ocelli; unh paler brown, sparsely irrorated with white scales, mostly concentrated along veins and in pd band which is well defined in this way.

Flight. July.

Habitat. Grass slopes at 1700–2200m.

Distribution. France, in Isère, Savoie, Hte Savoie, Htes Alpes and eastwards through Switzerland (excepting NW.) to the Ortler, Oetztal and Adamello groups, and northwards to Allgäuer Alps, Salzburg Alps and Karwendel Mts. Recorded from High Tatra Mts. Colonies are mostly very localised and not too common.

Variation. There is individual variation in the presence or absence of ocelli, etc., but local races have not been described.

Similar species. *E. aethiopella* p. 288; *E. gorge* p. 287.

EREBIA GORGONE *Gavarnie Ringlet*
Range. Confined to Pyrenees. Map 286

E. gorgone Boisduval 1833 TL: Pyrenees **Pl. 50**
Description. ♂fw 20/21mm, sex-brand in s1a to 5 prominent; *ups very dark*; upf pd band dark mahogany-red enclosing twin apical ocelli and small ocellus in s2; uph red pd band in s2–4, divided by dark veins, each red mark enclosing a small ocellus; *unf dark red-brown* with brown marginal border; unh dark brown with obscure paler pd band, ocelli vestigial if present. ♀ups gc paler brown, pd band also paler; unf paler with orange-brown discal area and grey marginal border; unh gc speckled dark grey-brown, veins lined pale buff, pd area pale buff, ocelli if present very small, brown marginal markings irregular.

Flight. July/August.

Habitat. Grass slopes at 1800–2400m.

Distribution. Pyrenees, Puy de Carlitte (Lac Lanoux) and westwards through Ariège and Hautes Pyrénées to Luchon, Gavarnie and Basses Pyrénées.

Similar species. *E. gorge ramondi* p. 287.

EREBIA EPISTYGNE *Spring Ringlet*
Range. Confined to SW. Europe. Map 287

E. epistygne epistygne Hübner 1824 TL: not stated (Provence) **Pl. 50**
Description. ♂fw 22/25mm, *upf a small area in cell and all pd band yellow-buff*, ocelli in s4–6 fused into a conspicuous row and small ocelli often present in s2–3; uph four or five submarginal ocelli each broadly ringed red; unf very dark brown, often reddish in cell and in pd area; unh with dark discal band, basal and pd areas mottled paler grey-brown. ♀ups markings slightly paler; unh basal and pd areas much marbled and irrorated brown on grey or yellow-grey, and veins conspicuously lined yellow-buff.

Flight. End March/April.

Habitat. Rough places and woodland clearings among low hills at 400–900m. Larval food plants esp. grasses *Festuca*, *Poa*.

Distribution. France, in Alpes Maritimes, Basses Alpes, Var, Bouches du Rhône, Hautes Alpes, Vaucluse, Gard, Hérault.

E. epistygne viriathus Sheldon 1913 TL: Losilla
Description. ♂fw 20/23mm, unf reddish suffusions more extensive, unh gc paler brown, brightly marked.
Flight. May/June.
Habitat. At 1200–1500m.
Distribution. Spain, Teruel, Albarracin, Losilla, etc.

The Erebia tyndarus group of species

The six small species that form this group provide special features of interest in their distribution and special difficulties in identification since their wing-markings are very similar in all. The chromosome numbers have been investigated by de Lesse and others and marked differences have been found, confirming the existence in Europe of six distinct species. Distribution patterns have been carefully checked, and it is found that, in effect, only a single species occurs in any given locality. Flight places rarely overlap, but the pattern is complicated especially in the Pyrenees and western Alps. In some areas where an overlap appears on a map, it is found that the species are separated by altitude. Individual variation can be confusing, and it is not possible to define key characters for specific identification by these alone, but with good data of place, date, altitude, etc., confident identification is nearly always possible, especially if a series of specimens is available. With the single exception of *E. ottomana*, the species of this group are endemic Europeans. Closely allied species fly in the Pontic Mts., in the Elburz, in C. Asia and in N. America.

EREBIA TYNDARUS *Swiss Brassy Ringlet*
Range. Confined to the Alps. Map 288

E. tyndarus Esper 1781 TL: Scheidegg, Switzerland **Pl. 52**
Description. ♂fw 17/18mm, apex blunt, gc dark brown with metallic greenish reflections, tawny pd band wide in s4, 5 and enclosing very small oblique twin subapical ocelli, but narrower below and extending to s2 or s1b, divided by brown cross veins, without additional ocelli; *uph without ocelli*, generally unmarked, small tawny spots occasional; uns apex of fw and all hw shining grey with bluish reflections in fresh specimens and brown striae, including a sinuous discal line across hw. ♀ similar, ups gc paler; upf subapical ocelli very small; uns apex of fw and all hw yellow-grey with brown markings.
Flight. July/August.
Habitat. High grassy slopes at 1800m or more. Larval food plant *Nardus strictus*.
Distribution. A restricted area in the central Alps from Val Ferret west of Mt. Blanc to the Oetztal, including Valais (Simplon), Oberland, Grisons, Engadine, Ortler, Brenner, Allgäuer Alps and Bergamasker Alps.
Variation. Specimens without upf ocelli are not rare in some districts, f. *caecodromus* Villiers and Guenée.
Similar species. *E. cassioides* below, a common species in the SW. Alps, can be distinguished by its more pointed fw with larger and less oblique subapical ocelli, pd tawny band usually short, rarely extending below s3 and white-pupilled ocelli present also on uph. The two species rarely fly together. *E. nivalis* p. 292.

EREBIA CASSIOIDES *Common Brassy Ringlet*
Range. Confined to Europe, from Cantabrian Mts. to Balkans. Map 289

E. cassioides cassioides Hohenwarth 1793 TL: Heilegenblut, Austria **Pl. 52**
Description. ♂fw 16/19mm, resembles *E. tyndarus* but apex more pointed; *upf tawny band short*, rarely extending beyond v3 and not invading cell, enclosing larger white-pupilled twin subapical ocelli; *uph three pd ocelli*, well formed and white-pupilled, generally present, enclosed in tawny spots; unh grey, a darker discal band more or less clearly indicated by darker brown transverse lines. ♀ups gc and markings paler; upf pd band tawny-yellow; unh grey or yellow-grey irrorated with darker scales, sometimes with distinct darker discal band.
Flight. End June/July/August.
Habitat. Grass slopes at 1700–1800m. Larval food plant *Nardus strictus*.
Distribution. Widely distributed. France. Switzerland. Austria, Hohe and Niederer Tauern. Italy, Dolomites, Apennines (Gran Sasso), Lucania (Pollino). Balkans, in S. Yugoslavia, Albania and Pirin Mts. Romania, Retezat Mts. Nearly every colony exhibits some minor racial peculiarity and many have been named.

E. cassioides arvernensis Oberthur 1908 TL: Mont Dore **Pl. 54**
Description. Resembles *E. c. cassioides* very closely, slightly larger, upf subapical twin ocelli larger. ♀unh usually distinctly yellowish.
Flight and **Habitat** as for *E. c. cassioides*.
Distribution. Auvergne, Mont Dore. Pyrenees, from Campcardos in the east to the Basses Pyrénées, but apparently absent between Salau and Gavarnie. Cantabrian Mts., Picos de Europa. Etruscan Apennines and Abruzzi.
Variation. External characters are not well marked, but the subspecies is of interest on account of its situation on mountains unconnected with the central Alps. The race of the central Pyrenees is referable to f. *pseudomurina* de Lesse Pl. 54.
Similar species. *E. tyndarus* p. 290; *E. nivalis* p. 292; *E. ottomana* p. 292.

EREBIA HISPANIA *Spanish Brassy Ringlet*
Range. Confined to Spain and the Pyrenees. Map 290

E. hispania hispania Butler 1868 TL: Spain **Pl. 52**
Description. ♂fw 20/21mm, ups gc dark brown; *upf pd band orange-yellow*, wide in s4–6, enclosing large twin ocelli, becoming rapidly narrower to s1b or s2; uph three smaller ocelli in fulvous spots; unh grey with rather indistinct discal line and other markings brownish. ♀upf gc and markings in paler tones; uph markings vestigial or absent; unh grey to pale brown with transverse markings in darker brown more distinct.
Flight. End June/July.
Habitat. Stony slopes from 2000m upwards. Larval food plant not known.
Distribution. S. Spain on Sierra Nevada. Not recorded from central Sierras.

E. hispania rondoui Oberthur 1908 TL: Cauterets, Hautes Pyrénées **Pl. 52**
Description. ♂fw 17/19mm, smaller with fw shorter; upf pd orange band often wider; uph pd ocelli better developed; unh grey with darker discal and marginal bands often defined. ♀uph orange submarginal markings and ocelli well developed.
Flight. July.
Habitat. Grassy slopes at 1500–1800m or more.
Distribution. From Mt. Canigou in E. Pyrenees westwards to Basses Pyrénées.
Variation. In E. Pyrenees on French and Spanish slopes, often rather small and markings very brilliant, f. *goya* Frühstorfer.
Note. *E. cassioides* and *E. h. rondoui* fly in contiguous areas but rarely occur together on the same ground.

EREBIA NIVALIS *De Lesse's Brassy Ringlet*
Range. Confined to the Alps. Map 291

E. nivalis Lorkovič and de Lesse 1954 TL: Gross Glockner **Pl. 52**
Description. ♂fw 15/17mm, resembles *E. tyndarus* with short square-cut fw; upf apical ocelli very small, scarcely oblique, with brilliant white pupils, pd band tawny, short, usually not beyond v3, but extending basad to cell-end in s4, 5; uph with or (generally) without small tawny blind pd spots; *unh with characteristic brilliant blue-grey* almost metallic lustre in fresh specimens. ♀unh also with bright silvery tone, veins paler.
Flight. July/August.
Habitat. Grass slopes at 2100m or over, flying about 300m above *E. cassioides* often on the same mountain. Larval food plant *Nardus stricta*.
Distribution. Austria, east of the Oetztal, including Hohe Tauern and Niederer Tauern. Switzerland, in a small area near Grindelwald (Faulhorn).
Similar species. *E. tyndarus* p. 290, which does not occur in the eastern Alps; upf basal extension of the tawny band in s4, 5 less well marked, unh browner, without bluish-grey lustre; *E. cassioides* p. 290, fw more pointed with larger ocelli; ocelli present also on uph.

EREBIA CALCARIA *Lorkovic's Brassy Ringlet*
Range. Confined to the eastern Alps. Map 292

E. calcaria Lorkovič 1953 TL: Julian Alps **Pl. 52**
Description. ♂fw 18/20mm, resembles *E. tyndarus* but slightly larger with fw square-cut and apex rounded; *ups dark*, tawny markings subdued; *upf apical ocelli very small*; uph two or three small obscure ocelli sometimes present; unh smooth silver-grey with dark sinuous line across disc and dark marginal markings. ♀ups paler; unh gc silver-grey with some yellowish scaling.
Flight. July.
Habitat. Grass slopes from 1200m upwards. Larval food plant *Festuca*.
Distribution. Yugoslavia, on Karawanken and Julian Alps. NE. Italy, recorded from Monte Cavallo and Monte Santo near Piave di Cadore.
Similar species. No other species of this group is known from the Julian Alps.

EREBIA OTTOMANA *Ottoman Brassy Ringlet*
Range. A few widely separated colonies in Europe, more generally distributed in Asia Minor (TL of *Erebia dromus* var. *ottomana* Herrich-Schaeffer 1851). Map 293

E. ottomana bulgarica Drenowski 1932 TL: Ali Botus **Pl. 52**
  syn: *bureschi* Warren 1936
Description. ♂fw 19/22mm, upf twin subapical ocelli enclosed in tawny patch which rarely extends beyond v3; uph with small ocelli ringed tawny in s2–4(5); unh gc silvery-grey with darker discal band outlined in brown, brown marginal marks, and sometimes small dark vestigial pd ocelli. ♀ups gc and tawny markings paler; unh gc yellow-grey, a brown discal band usually well defined and small brown pd ocellar spots and submarginal markings.
Flight. July.
Habitat. Grass slopes at 1500–1800m. Larval food plants not known.
Distribution. Greece on Mt. Veluchi. SE. Yugoslavia, Mt. Perister. No doubt also on other mountains in this region.

E. ottomana balcanica Rebel 1913 TL: Rila Mts., Bulgaria **Pl. 52**
Description. ♂fw 19/20mm, slightly smaller and fw appears less pointed; ups less brightly marked; upf ocelli small; unh with less colour-contrast, often appearing brown, dusted with pale grey especially at base and in pd area, and without vestigial ocelli.
Flight and **Habitat** as for *E. o. bulgarica.*
Distribution. Widely distributed in Balkans. Bulgaria, Rila, Rhodope and Pirin Mts. Yugoslavia, Serbia, Bosnia, Montenegro, Hercegovina and Macedonia on Schar Planina. Albania. NE. Italy.
Variation. Very small specimens with fw only 17mm occur on the Schar Planina at high altitudes on exposed mountain slopes. In Italy on Monte Baldo, ups rather dark with tawny markings slightly reduced. f. *benacensis* Dannehl.

E. ottomana tardenota Praviel 1941 TL: Mt. Mézenc, Haute Loire **Pl. 52**
Description. ♂fw 17/19mm, resembles *E. o. balcanica,* small in both sexes; upf ocelli small; unh often well marked with distinct brownish discal band. ♀unh yellow, usually with well-defined darker discal band and marginal markings.
Flight. July.
Habitat. On grass slopes at 1200m or more.
Distribution. C. France, widely distributed in Massif Central esp. in Ardèche and Haute Loire, e.g. Mont Mézenc, Gerbier de Jonc, Forêt de Bauzon, etc.
Similar species. *E. cassioides* p. 290, which may be confusing in the Balkans and in Italy, flies later, smaller, unf marginal band narrower.

EREBIA PRONOE *Water Ringlet*
Range. Confined to Europe. Map 294

E. pronoe pronoe Esper 1780 TL: Styria **Pl. 53**
Description. ♂fw 21/25mm, sex-brand not conspicuous; upf red pd band 3–5mm wide, generally clearly defined from s1b–s6, enclosing twin subapical ocelli and small ocellus in s2; uph two or three small red-ringed submarginal ocelli; *unh with scattered silver-grey irroration producing a violet-grey tone, dark brown discal band prominent.* ♀ups gc and markings paler; unh greyish to pale yellow-brown with discal band and marginal border darker.
Flight. End July/August/September. Larval food plant grasses, e.g. *Poa.*
Habitat. Woodland clearings and damp mountain slopes from 1000–1800m, flying in local colonies.
Distribution. Brightly marked typical specimens only on the Hohe Tauen, Styria and limestone mountains of Austria, Bavaria, High Tatra and Carpathians.

E. pronoe glottis Fruhstorfer 1920 TL: C. Pyrenees (Cauterets)
Description. Like *E. p. pronoe,* but upf red pd band reduced, ocellus in s2 often absent, uph ocelli vestigial or absent. ♀ups markings better developed.
Flight and **Habitat** as for *E. p. pronoe.*
Distribution. Basses and Hautes Pyrénées.

E. pronoe vergy Ochsenheimer 1807 TL: S. Switzerland **Pl. 53**
syn: *pitho* Hübner 1804 (invalid homonym)
Description. ♂fw 23/25mm, ups black, sometimes with inconspicuous sub-apical ocelli and traces of red pd band on fw; unf very dark, pd band vestigial, dull red-brown; unh as in *E. p. pronoe.* ♀ups gc brown, small subapical ocelli usually present; unh gc pale buff with brown discal band and marginal markings.

Flight and **Habitat** as for *E. p. pronoe*.
Distribution. Rather local. France, in Haute Savoie, Doubs (Jura), Grande Chartreuse. Switzerland, in Cantons Jura, St. Gall, Appenzell, Berne, Vaud, Valais, Grisons.
Variation. Races occur with intermediate characters of every grade.
Similar species. *E. styx* p. 296, unh pd area grey-brown or brown, discal band ill-defined; *E. aethiops* p. 282.

EREBIA MELAS   *Black Ringlet*
Range. Confined to SE. Europe.   Map 295

E. melas melas   Herbst 1796   TL: Perzenieska, Romanian Banat
Description. ♂fw 21/24mm, ups black; upf twin white-pupilled apical ocelli dead-black, a small ocellus often present in s2; uph two or three ocelli near outer margin; unh sometimes obscurely mottled, with traces of ocelli as on ups and obscure pale pd band. ♀ larger, usually strongly marked with large ocelli; upf fulvous pd band usually more or less present; unh brown, marbled with dark grey, paler pd band usually defined.
Flight. Late July/August.
Habitat. On moraines, rockfalls etc. from 200–1500m or more, usually on calcareous mountains. Larval food plants not known.
Distribution. Romania, at Herculiane in the Banat, Cernatal and surrounding mountains. S. Carpathians esp. Retezat Mts.
Variation. The species varies locally in development of ocelli and of the red pd band in ♀.

E. melas leonhardi   Fruhstorfer 1918   TL: Velebit, Yugoslavia   **Pl. 50**
Description. ♀fw 21/22mm, smaller, ups ocelli variable, often well developed; ♀ with larger ocelli, upf red pd band vestigial or absent.
Flight and **Habitat** as for *E. m. melas*, usually at 1200–1500m.
Distribution. NW. Yugoslavia, Mt. Nanos and Velabit Mts. (Karst).
Variation. In S. Balkans and Greece, f. *schawerdae*, slightly larger, ups markings more prominent in both sexes.
Similar species. *E. lefebvrei astur* and *pyrenaea* below, perhaps only distinguishable by examination of the male genitalia. No species occurs in E. Europe that could be confused with *E. melas*. *E. pluto* p. 286.

EREBIA LEFEBVREI   *Lefèbvre's Ringlet*
Range. Confined to Pyrenees and Cantabrian Mts.   Map 296

E. lefebvrei lefebvrei   Boisduval 1828   TL: Pyrenees   **Pl. 46**
Description. ♂fw 22/24mm, ups gc deep black with *ocelli placed close to outer margins of wings*; upf red pd band (sometimes absent) poorly defined enclosing twin white-pupilled apical ocelli and small ocellus in s2; uph with three to four sub-marginal ocelli; uns very dark, black on hw, with markings as on ups. ♀ups gc dark brown, ocelli larger, often more numerous and red pd band better defined; unh brown with paler pd band.
Flight. End June/July.
Habitat. Moraines and rocky slopes at 1800m and upwards. Larval food plants unknown.

Distribution. Pyrenees, from Ariège westwards including most high mountains in Hautes and Basses Pyrénées.
Similar species. *E. meolans* p. 299, in the Pyrenees, upf brightly coloured with a wide red pd band.

E. lefebvrei astur Oberthur 1884   TL: Picos de Europa, Cantabrian Mts.   **Pl. 46**
Description. ♂fw 20/23mm, upf without or (rarely) with traces of red pd band, ocelli small; uph ocelli often absent or represented by white pupils only. ♀ups ocelli very variable, on uph reduced to white pupils or absent; unh heavily irrorated with pale grey with paler pd band.
Flight and **Habitat** as in *E. l. lefebvrei.*
Distribution. Known only from the Picos de Europa, Cantabrian Mts.

E. lefebvrei pyrenaea Oberthur 1884   TL: Mt. Canigou, E. Pyrenees
Description. ♂fw 20/21mm, upf as in *E. l. astur;* uph ocelli usually present but small; uns black, unmarked except for ocelli as on ups. ♀ups with normal ocelli; upf red pd band usually indicated, sometimes vestigial; uph ocelli variable, often small or represented by white pupils; unh brown with paler pd area, ocelli variable, often absent.
Flight and **Habitat** as in *E. l. lefebvrei.*
Distribution. Eastern Pyrenees from Mt. Canigou to Fourmiguères, Pas de la Case and Pic Carlitte, on most high peaks and on French and Spanish slopes.
Similar species. *E. melas* p. 294, Balkans only; *E. pluto alecto* and *E. p. nicholli* p. 286, only in central Alps; *E. meolans* ♀ p. 299.

EREBIA SCIPIO *Larche Ringlet*
Range. Confined to SW. Alps.   Map 297

E. scipio Boisduval 1832   TL: Basses Alpes   **Pl. 49**
Description. ♂fw 23/25mm, fw pointed; upf red pd band pale, crossed by dark veins and enclosing twin subapical ocelli, sometimes with small ocelli also in s3, 4; uph pd band narrow, broken by dark veins, rarely with small ocelli; unf fulvous-red except the dark brown margins, apical ocelli conspicuous; *unh smooth dark brown,* usually with faint paler pd band, very rarely with minute ocelli. ♀ups red pd bands slightly paler and wider; unh pale grey, almost unmarked.
Flight. End June/August.
Habitat. Steep rocky places at 1500–2400m. Larval food plant not known.
Distribution. Maritime Alps, including the Italian slopes (rare), Basses Alpes and Vaucluse. Well-known localities include Digne, Beauvezer, Draix, Mont Ventoux, Mont de Lure, Col de Larche. It is said that the species has disappeared from some of its former localities.

EREBIA STYRIA *Styrian Ringlet*
Range. Restricted to SE. Alps.   Map 298

E. styria styria Godart 1824   TL: Klagenfurt, Carinthia   **Pl. 53**
syn: *nerine* Freyer 1831
Description. ♂fw 24/26mm, outer margin of hw often rather wavy, ups gc velvet-black; upf pd band dull red, not sharply defined, tapering below, rarely extending beyond v2, enclosing twin white-pupilled apical ocelli in s4, 5, rarely a small ocellus also in s2; uph broken red submarginal band with ocelli in s2, 3, 4; unf smooth chestnut brown with basal area limited by short darker mark from costa to about v4,

marginal dark border narrowing in s1b; *unh smooth, very dark*, sometimes with pale scaling along margin of darker basal area which may be scarcely indicated, pd area generally slightly paler with three white-pupilled black ocelli. ♀ups gc dark brown, ocelli sometimes larger but additional ocelli rare, pd band orange-red, not well defined, often broken at v3 and with small red-ringed ocellus in s2; *unh smooth pale grey* from base to wavy darker grey discal line, three dark ocelli conspicuous in the pale pd area; fringes slightly chequered.

Flight. Late July/August/September.

Habitat. Stony slopes from 700–1500m. Larval food plants grasses esp. *Poa* and *Sesleria coerulea*.

Distribution. Eastern Alps. Widely distributed in Karawanken Alps, Triglav and mountains near the Trenta Valley, Mt. Nanos in the Karst; but not seen from anywhere west of Seiser Alp near Bolzano; Mt. Baldo. Reports from Trafoi and Lower Engadine need confirmation.

E. styria morula   Speyer 1865   TL: Seiser Alp, Dolomites   **Pl. 53**
Description. ♂fw 23/24mm, upf red markings reduced to an obscure area round the twin ocelli; uph pd ocelli small; uns all markings rather small, obscure, but unh paler grey pd area is distinct. ♀ markings better developed on both surfaces.

Flight and Habitat. No information, probably at high levels in late summer.

Distribution. Dolomites, on the Seiser Alp (Grodnertal) and Brenta; recorded from the Gross Glockner, transitional to *E. s. styria*. The respective distribution ranges of *styria* and *morula* are imperfectly known.

Note. The distinction between *E. styria* and *E. styx* was defined first by Lorković in 1952. Before that the species were so often confused that old records are of little value. The distribution areas indicated here are based as far as possible on specimens actually examined, and on Lorković's records. In the Julian Alps (Trenta Valley) the specific distinction is very obvious, but west of the Gr. Glockner the characters are less definite, variation seems to be more common and identification may be difficult.

Similar species. *E. styx* below.

EREBIA STYX *Stygian Ringlet*
Range. Confined to central and eastern Alps.   Map 299

E. styx styx   Freyer 1834   TL: not stated   **Pl. 53**
   syn: *reichlini* Herrich-Schäffer 1860
Description. ♂fw 23/25mm, resembles *E. styria* very closely but differs as follows: upf red pd band well developed, extending generally to s1b, internally angled in s3 (inconstant in some races); unf darker basal area usually defined by distinct distal border which often extends from costa to inner margin, dark marginal border of even width to anal angle with short projection basad in s1b (in *styria* it tapers away and vanishes); *unh less smooth*, markings better defined, dark basal area often bordered with white. ♀unh often yellowish-grey, irrorated darker, basal area usually defined, sometimes with white along distal border.

Flight. July/August.

Habitat. Among rocks, precipices, mountain paths etc. to 1800m. Larval food plants grasses, probably *Poa* and *Sesleria*.

Distribution. Tirol and northern Alps. Among localities recorded are the following: Sulden, Cortina, Brenner Pass, Mendel Pass, Sorapiss, Allgäuer Alps, N. Switzerland, Karwendel Mts., Vosges (Ballon d'Alsace).

E. styx triglites Fruhstorfer 1918 TL: Monte Generoso
Description. ♂fw 23/24mm, upf red band wider, extending to inner margin and enclosing large apical ocelli; uph large ocelli in wide red submarginal band; unf and unh markings well developed. ♀fw apical ocelli larger, all red bands wide with brilliant ocelli; unf margin of basal area may be straight; unh with or without ocelli.
Flight and **Habitat** as for *E. s. styx.*
Distribution. Bergamasker Alps, Monte Generoso, Riva.

E. styx trentae Lorković 1952 TL: Trenta valley, Julian Alps **Pls. 53, 54**
Description. ♂fw 25/28mm, resembles *E. s. styx* but larger, ups ocelli prominent with brilliant white pupils, pd bands deep chestnut-red; unf gc dark mahogany-red with dark pd stripe from costa to inner margin; unh dark grey, discal band darker, the whole slightly marbled and irrorated with pale grey. ♀ups ocelli larger, conspicuous; upf usually with four or five ocelli; unh light grey, brightly marbled with darker, discal band prominent.
Flight. End July/August.
Habitat. Rocky slopes at 700–1200m.
Distribution. Julian Alps, recorded only from Trenta valley and Mojstrovka Pass.
Note. This subspecies is full of character and differs greatly from the form that occurs in the central Alps of Austria etc.
Similar species. *E. pronoe* p. 293; *E. styria* p. 295; *E. montana* below. Satisfactory definition of these three species is extremely difficult and the fact that the male genitalia are slightly variable does not help. The characters given above should permit identification of *styria* and *styx*, at any rate in their eastern ranges. In both sexes of *E. montana* the brilliant marbling on unh is usually distinctive, but resemblance to *E. styx* can be very close in the central Alps. The shape of the brown marginal border on unf in s1b, when clearly defined, is a small but important character.

EREBIA MONTANA *Marbled Ringlet*
Range. Confined to Alps and Apennines. Map 300

E. montana montana de Prunner 1798 TL: Piedmont **Pl. 50**
syn: *homole* Fruhstorfer 1918
Description. ♂fw 22/24mm, upf pd band dull chestnut-red, narrow, tapering to v2 or s1b, enclosing small twin white-pupilled apical ocelli; uph pd band variable with ocelli in s2, 3, 4; unf slightly darker basal area clearly defined by dark discal line, brown marginal border tapering slightly to v1; unh gc dark brown, with darker discal band, the whole *mottled and irrorated white*, esp. in paler pd area. ♀ *fringes chequered*; outer margin of hw slightly wavy; ups pd bands orange-red and ocelli larger; unh gc paler yellow-brown, *brightly mottled with pale grey and white*, veins lined white.
Flight. July/August.
Habitat. Rocky mountain slopes, generally at 1500–2100m, sometimes at lower levels. Larval food plant grasses (not identified).
Distribution. SW. Alps from Alpes Maritimes northwards to Savoie and Graian Alps. Italy, in Ligurian Apennines and Abruzzi, but more local, Gran Sasso, Mt. Portella and Corno Grande.

E. montana goante Esper 1805 TL: Switzerland **Pl. 50**
Description. ♂fw 23/25mm, upf pd band brighter red and wider with larger ocelli, often with small ocellus in s2; unh very dark, white irroration less extensive but

border of basal area usually defined. ♀ups resembles *E. m. montana* but unh white lining of veins much less prominent. The features of *E. goante* are most definite in the Alps of E. Switzerland and Austria.

Flight and **Habitat** as for *E. m. montana*.

Distribution. From southern Switzerland eastwards through the Alps to the Engadine, Brenta Group, Brenner Pass and Oetztal Alps. Less common in N. Switzerland and occasional only in Allgäuer Alps.

Similar species. *E. styx* p. 296.

EREBIA ZAPATERI *Zapater's Ringlet*

Range. Confined to mountains of Central Spain, Teruel and Cuenca.   Map 301

E. zapateri   Oberthur 1875   TL: Sierra de Albarracin   **Pl. 51**

Description. ♂fw 19/20mm, upf *pd band orange-yellow, wide* on costa and tapering to anal angle, enclosing twin apical ocelli; uph dark brown with occasional traces of red submarginal markings; unh brown with paler pd band. ♀ups gc paler brown, pd band yellow; unh light brown with grey pd band.

Flight. End July/August.

Habitat. Open woodland and rough ground at 1000–1500m. Larval food plant not known.

Distribution. Central Spain. Recorded from Bronchales, Griegos, Albarracin, Tragacete, Noguera etc.

EREBIA NEORIDAS *Autumn Ringlet*

Range. Confined to southern Europe.   Map 302

E. neoridas neoridas   Boisduval 1828   TL: Grenoble   **Pl. 51**

Description. ♂fw 20/23mm, upf fulvous-red *pd band wide near costa and tapering to anal angle*, enclosing twin apical and other ocelli; uph with ocelli in s2–4 enclosed in red rings or a narrow interrupted fulvous-red band; unh dark brown with paler pd area. ♀ similar with markings on both surfaces in paler tones.

Flight. August/September.

Habitat. Hill country and mountain foothills at 600–1500m.

Distribution. E. Pyrenees, Maritime Alps and northwards to Isère and Hautes Alpes, Gard, Vaucluse and Var, Lozère and Cantal (Puy de Dôme). Italy in Cottian Alps and north to Susa valley. Spain, recorded from Val d'Aran, Pyrenees.

Variation. Specimens from the Central Massif of France (Lozère) are small with ♂fw 18/19mm, unh paler brown with little contrast.

E. neoridas sibyllina   Verity 1913   TL: Monte Sibillini, C. Italy

Description. ♂fw 19/20mm, ups ocelli small; unh more brightly marked with dark discal band bordered grey.

Flight and **Habitat** as for *E. n. neoridas*.

Distribution. C. Italy, recorded from Monte Sibillini, Monte Rotondo, Gran Sasso, and Apuane Alps.

Similar species. *E. aethiops* p. 282.

EREBIA OEME *Bright-eyed Ringlet*

Range. Confined to Europe.   Map 303

E. oeme oeme   Hübner 1804   TL: Tirol   **Pl. 50**

Description. ♂fw 20/22mm, ups gc black or very dark brown; upf with small white-pupilled twin subapical ocelli enclosed in a small red patch, and a small ocellus in s2; uph three red-ringed submarginal ocelli, the *white pupils conspicuously brilliant*; uns markings of ups repeated, often with larger ocelli; unf gc paler grey-brown, often with reddish flush; unh with five ocelli in a very even row. ♀ups paler with larger ocelli; unf flushed cinnamon-brown; unh yellow-grey, generally with six ocelli set in yellow band or yellow spots. *Antennae black-tipped.*

Flight. June/July.

Habitat. Wet meadows or damp woodland at 900–1800m. Larval food plant woodrush (*Luzula*).

Distribution. France, widely distributed throughout the Pyrenees, Mont Dore, Monts du Forez, Aveyron, Isère, Savoie, S. Jura. Bavaria. Upper Austria. N. Greece. Reported occurrence in Czechoslovakia needs confirmation.

E. oeme lugens Staudinger 1901 TL: Gadmen, Switzerland **Pl. 47**
Description. ♂fw 19/21mm, ups ocelli very small or partly obsolete; all red markings reduced on both surfaces. ♀ups ocelli small, better developed on uns and ringed yellow.

Flight and **Habitat** as for *E. o. oeme*.

Distribution. Switzerland, widely distributed esp. north of R. Rhône. Bavaria esp. in Allgäuer Alps, with some colonies transitional to *E. o. oeme*.

E. oeme spodia Staudinger 1871 TL: Austria **Pl. 50**
Description. ♂fw 19/23mm, ups ocelli and red pd band usually better developed; unf gc reddish-brown; unh with six ocelli widely red-ringed. ♀ups pd bands generally complete and enclosing ocelli with large white pupils; upf often with additional ocellus in s6; unh markings exceptionally brilliant, submarginal ocelli large and enclosed in a yellow band.

Flight and **Habitat** as for *E. o. oeme*.

Distribution. Eastern Alps, esp. Styria, and locally in Balkans (Velebit). Bulgaria. N. Greece (Drama).

Similar species. *E. medusa* p. 284; *E. meolans valesiaca* p. 299, ♂unf red pd band usually well defined; *E. alberganus* p. 285, ocellar rings almond-shaped.

Note. *E. oeme* shows very marked variation on a cline, of which the main forms are described above, from rather small dark forms sometimes almost without markings to larger specimens with large bright ocelli.

EREBIA MEOLANS Piedmont Ringlet
Range. Confined to Europe. Map 304

E. meolans meolans de Prunner 1798 TL: Piedmont
syn: *calaritas* Fruhstorfer 1918 **Pls. 49, 54**
Description. ♂fw 19/21mm, upf red band entire, enclosing white-pupilled subapical ocelli in s4, 5, a smaller ocellus in s2 and sometimes others; uph red band narrower, broken by dark veins and with three or four ocelli; unf gc very dark, the *pd band wider and well defined* in s1b–6, enclosing ocelli as on ups; unh black when fresh, pd area usually slightly paler, ocelli without red rings. ♀ups gc brown, pd bands orange-red with larger more prominent ocelli, usually five on fw, four on hw; unh paler brown, the basal area separated by a white band (sometimes absent) from the paler pd area, three inconspicuous ocelli.

Flight. End June/July.

Habitat. Stony slopes with grass, precipices etc., at 1500–1800m. Larval food plants various grasses.

Distribution. Alpes Maritimes and Basses Alpes and northwards through Savoie to Jura with minor local variation. Massif Central of France, present on most mountains and often small and variable, esp. Mont Dore, Le Lioran, etc. More brightly marked and often with more numerous ocelli in Black Forest. Ligurian Apennines, central Apennines (rare).

E. meolans bejarensis Chapman 1902   TL: Sierra de Gredos, Spain   **Pl. 49**
Description. ♂fw 22/27mm, upf tawny bands wide and bright, extending often below v1, with four or five ocelli; unh slightly marbled dark grey in some specimens, pd area distinctly paler. ♀ often very large, all colour tones paler with conspicuous ups ocelli; unh white border to darker basal area reduced or vestigial.
Flight and **Habitat** as for *E. m. meolans*.
Distribution. C. Spain, Sierra de Gredos, Sierra de Guadarrama, Sierra de la Demanda.
   This subspecies represents the maximum development in size, brilliance of markings and in number of ocelli. These characters diminish further north in the Cantabrian Mts. to blend insensibly into the smaller races flying in the Hautes Pyrénées.

E. meolans stygne Ochsenheimer 1808   TL: Alps of Tirol and Switzerland
Description. ♂fw 21/23mm, upf red pd band narrow, often incomplete and interrupted by dark veins; upf usually with three ocelli; uph ocelli small and inconstant; unf pd band reduced in size but remaining well defined and entire; unh pd area sometimes faintly paler with vestigial ocelli. ♀gc brown, unh basal area slightly darker, rarely bordered white.
Flight and **Habitat** as for *E. m. meolans*, sometimes at lower levels.
Distribution. Local and uncommon in the E. Alps, Thuringia, Allgäuer Alps, Hochschwab, Brenner district, etc. Switzerland, widely distributed north of Rhône valley. Carpathians?

E. meolans valesiaca Elwes 1898   TL: Valais, Switzerland   **Pl. 49**
Description. Smaller ♂fw 20/21mm, markings reduced to very small red-ringed apical twin ocelli on fw, on hw ocelli vestigial or absent; unf red pd band narrow, short. ♀ups markings only slightly increased.
Flight and **Habitat** as for *E. m. meolans*.
Distribution. Switzerland, in Graubünden (Grisons) and westwards to Rhône Valley.
Similar species. *E. oeme* p. 299; *E. triaria* p. 282; *E. palarica* below: *E. lefebvrei* ♀ p. 294, unh paler pd area not clearly defined.

EREBIA PALARICA   *Chapman's Ringlet*
Range. Confined to NW. Spain.   Map 305

E. palarica Chapman 1905   TL: Pajares, Cantabrian Mts.   **Pl. 51**
Description. ♂fw 28/30mm, closely resembles *E. meolans* but larger; unh dark brown, *slightly mottled with 'roughened' appearance*, discal dark band often present, sometimes defined by scanty pale grey markings before the faintly paler pd area which contains small inconspicuous ocelli. ♀ sometimes smaller, with gc and markings in paler tones; unh much paler grey-brown, discal band edged darker and bordered pale grey, ocelli small and variable.
Flight. End June/July.
Habitat. Rough places among rocks and long grass, especially associated with tall broom (*Cytisus*). Larval food plant not known.

Distribution. Cantabrian Mts., in Provinces of Oviedo and Leon.
Similar species. *E. meolans* (p. 299) smaller, unh surface smooth, unf pd band with proximal border straight (slightly concave in *E. palarica*).

EREBIA PANDROSE   *Dewy Ringlet*
Range. Arctic and Alpine zones on high mountains from E. Pyrenees to central Asia and in Fennoscandia.   Map 306

E. pandrose   Borkhausen 1788   TL: Styria   **Pls. 49, 54**
  syn: *lappona*   Thunberg 1791
Description. ♂fw 20/25mm, ups gc dusky-brown; upf with dark striae in cell, dark transverse pd line, and *broad tawny pd area enclosing blind black spots* in s2–5; uph sometimes with similar spots ringed reddish-brown; unh gc silver-grey, discal band more or less distinctly outlined by irregular dark transverse lines. ♀ similar with paler gc; upf pd spots sometimes absent; unh more variable, gc yellowish-grey with discal band sometimes filled darker.
Flight. End June/July.
Habitat. Stony slopes and pastures at 1800m or more in Pyrenees and Alps, at lower levels in Fennoscandia. Larval food plants grasses, esp. *Festuca* and *Poa*.
Distribution. From eastern Pyrenees through the whole Alpine chain to Julian Alps and higher Carpathians. More local in Balkans, but recorded from Prenj and Durmitor in S. Yugoslavia and Rila Mts. in Bulgaria. Fennoscandia, in the south as a mountain insect at 900m; in the High North from sea-level. Italy, Apennines (Monti della Laga), *E. p. sevoensis* Willien and Racheli. Absent from Jura, Vosges and Spanish Sierras.
Variation. This is slight through most of the range. In the Carpathians the ♀unh has a stronger pattern with discal band filled dark brown and edged pale grey ♀-f. *roberti* Peschke Pl. 54.
Similar species. *E. sthennyo* below.

EREBIA STHENNYO   *False Dewy Ringlet*
Range. Confined to Hautes and Basses Pyrénées.   Map 307

E. sthennyo   Graslin 1850   TL: Bagnères de Bigorre, Pyrenees   **Pl. 49**
Description. ♂fw 20/22mm, resembles *E. pandrose* but differs as follows; smaller; upf dark pd spots nearer to outer margin, dark striae in cell and dark pd line absent or vestigial; unh pale grey nearly unmarked. ♀ resembles ♂; ups slightly paler brown; unh pale grey.
Flight. End June/July.
Habitat. Grass slopes at 1800m or more. Larval food plants not known.
Distribution. Basses and Hautes Pyrénées eastwards to Andorra at Pic de Coullac near Salau.
  The distributions of *E. sthennyo* and *E. pandrose* above do not overlap although in Andorra and in Aulus the species fly in close proximity. The small differences in markings and in male genitalia appear to be constant.

EREBIA PHEGEA   *Dalmatian Ringlet*
Range. Dalmatia and S. Russia (*Papilio phegea* Borkhausen 1788 TL: Volga) to C. Asia.   Map 308

E. phegea dalmata   Godart 1824   TL: Sibenik, Dalmatia   **Pl. 54**
syn: *afer* Esper 1783 (invalid homonym)
Description. ♂fw 22/24mm, ups gc brown; upf apex and most of outer margin
yellowish-grey; fused twin white-pupilled ocelli in s4 and 5, additional ocelli placed
more distally in s1b (twin) 2, 3, and 6; uph ocelli in s1b–6 in regular series, small; uns
brown; unf apex paler with veins lined pale yellow-grey and disc slightly reddish;
unh veins conspicuously yellow-grey, 8 small pale-ringed ocelli. ♀ similar with
markings in paler tones.
Flight. May.
Habitat. Rocks and boulder-strewn slopes at comparatively low levels.
Distribution. Dalmatia, Zara, Sibenik, appears to be very local and rare.
Note. This species has several unusual features including a precostal vein in the
hind-wing. It is not well placed in the genus *Erebia*.

MANIOLA JURTINA   *Meadow Brown*
Range. Canary Islands and N. Africa through Europe to Urals, Asia Minor and
Iran.   Map 309

M. jurtina jurtina   Linnaeus 1758   TL: Europe and Africa (Sweden, Verity
1953)   **Pl. 55**
Description. ♂fw 22/25mm, a large black sex-brand from near wing-base extending along and below median vein; *ups* gc dark brown, nearly or quite *without orange
markings; upf a single white-pupilled apical ocellus* unh grey to yellow-brown, basal
area darker, small black dots in s2 and s5 in paler pd band. ♀fw 24/26mm, upf with
yellow or orange discal and pd areas; unh often yellowish and brightly marked,
without small black spots in paler pd band.
Flight. June to August with long flight period, females appearing late.
Habitat. Meadows and grassy places from sea-level to 1800m. Larval food plants
various grasses, esp. *Poa*.
Distribution. Europe, S. of 62°N; northern specimens slightly smaller than those
from southern areas; replaced in SW. by *M. j. hispulla*.

M. jurtina hispulla   Esper (*ante* 1805)   TL: Lisbon   **Pl. 55**
Description. ♂fw 24/27mm, large, sex-brand appears very large; resembles *M. j.
jurtina*; unh additional small dark spots are common in paler pd band. ♀fw 26/29mm,
ups orange markings much extended and upf apical ocellus large; uph orange pd
band wide; unh darker brown basal area often bordered with yellowish suffusion.
Variation. In Africa and Canary Islands mostly very large, females brightly coloured, f. *fortunata* Alpheraky. Local races of large size with brightly coloured
females, transitional to *M. j. jurtina*, occur in many districts in S. Europe.
Flight and **Habitat** as for *M. j. jurtina*.
Distribution. Canary Islands, Morocco, Algeria, Tunisia, Portugal, Spain, E.
Pyrenees and Provence, Mediterranean islands to Malta, S. Italy.

M. jurtina splendida   White 1872   TL: Lunga Island, W. Scotland
Description. ♂fw 21/22mm, upf brightly marked, with fulvous pd area in s2–4
usually well developed, often enclosing the ocellus in s5; uph very dark, basal area
vaguely indicated; unf apical ocellus a little larger; unh sometimes with very small
black pd ocelli in s2, 5. ♀ larger, upf fulvous pd area extends into cell; uph often with
slightly fulvous pd flush.
Flight and **Habitat** as for *M. j. jurtina*.

Distribution. N. Scotland in Western Isles – Canna, Lunga, S. Uist, etc., on mainland to W. Sutherland – Lochinver, etc. Orkneys. Ireland. Isle of Man. Scilly Isles. South of the Firth of Forth, *M. j. splendida* does not occur, and is replaced by *M. j. jurtina*, sometimes with traces of fulvous pd flush.
Similar species. *M. nurag* below. *H. lycaon* and *H. lupina* p. 304, in which upf apical ocellus is blind. *P. janiroides* p. 307, upf apical ocellus twin-pupilled. *Maniola telmessia* Zeller, sometimes considered a subspecies of *Maniola jurtina*, is quite distinct. It flies in Asia Minor; there are no reliable records from Europe.
Note. Typical *jurtina* and typical *hispulla* are so different in appearance that they have often been regarded as distinct species. However, between the north-eastern *jurtina* and the south-western *hispulla* a wide belt occurs which is populated by races with intermediate characters that link them together.

MANIOLA NURAG *Sardinian Meadow Brown*
Range. Confined to Sardinia. Map 310

M. nurag Ghiliani 1852   TL: Mt. Gennargentu, Sardinia   **Pl. 56**
Description. ♂fw 20mm, *resembles M. jurtina hispulla but smaller*; upf sex-brand conspicuous; ups brown with broad yellow pd suffusions on both wings; unh gc paler, grey-brown, almost unmarked, a trace of yellow in pd area where very small dark spots may be present. ♀ larger, upf broadly orange with brown marginal border and darker transverse striae from costa; uph with broad yellow pd band; unh without dark spots in pd area.
Flight. End June/July, flight of females prolonged.
Habitat. Open bushy places at moderate altitudes. Larval food plant grasses.
Distribution. Local in Sardinia, probably most frequent in northern areas.
Similar species. *M. jurtina* p. 302, ♂ distinguished by larger size and absence of yellow suffusion on uph. The rather similar species of *Pyronia* can be distinguished by having twin white pupils in the fw apical ocellus.

HYPONEPHELE MAROCCANA *Moroccan Meadow Brown*
Range. Confined to Morocco.   Map 311

H. maroccana marocanna Blachier 1908   TL: High Atlas   **Pl. 55**
Description. ♂fw 21/22mm, ups gc medium brown; upf narrow sex-brand bordering median vein, *orange-yellow pd suffusion sometimes extending towards base of wing*, small ocellus often present in s2, larger ocellus constant in s5; uph unmarked; unf single white pupil in apical ocellus; unh pale grey-brown, discal band generally indicated by slightly darker broken transverse lines. ♀hw outer margin wavy; upf orange-yellow pd area brighter, extending to wing-base, dusky basal area clearly defined by brown elbowed discal line, ocelli larger, sometimes very large, apical ocellus occasionally with white pupil; uph vague darker discal and submarginal lines sometimes present; unh pale grey-brown, discal band indicated by brown striae.
Flight. June/July.
Habitat. Rough ground at 1800–2100m. Larval food plants not recorded, probably grasses.
Distribution. Local in the High Atlas.

H. maroccana nivellei Oberthur 1920   TL: Taghzeft and   **Pl. 55**
Djebel Hebbri, Middle Atlas
Description. ♂fw 18/20mm, resembles *H. m. maroccana* but smaller; upf apical

ocellus small, often double; unh paler grey with brown discal striae less regular. ♀unh gc pale grey.
Flight and **Habitat** as for *H. m. maroccana.*
Distribution. Middle Atlas on Taghzeft Pass, etc. Appears to be confined to Middle Atlas in Morocco; not recorded from Algeria. In series distinction from *H. m. maroccana* is quite marked.
Similar species. *H. lupina mauritanica* below, common in Morocco, is a larger species, and lacks orange-yellow suffusion on upf.

HYPONEPHELE LYCAON *Dusky Meadow Brown*
Range. From W. Europe through S. Russia, Asia Minor, Lebanon and Caucasus, to Central Asia. Map 312

H. lycaon Kühn 1774 TL: Berlin **Pl. 55**
Description. ♂fw 20/24mm, ups gc grey-brown; upf a *narrow brown sex-brand* below median vein *cut by paler* gc on *v2 and v3*, and often with slightly fulvous flush in pd area; uph unmarked; unf apical ocellus with single white pupil; unh grey-brown, irrorated darker to pale grey, darker discal band often vaguely indicated by vestigial brown elbowed pd transverse line. ♀hw slightly scalloped; *upf disc orange-yellow* with dusky basal area defined by dark distal edge; uph gc grey-brown, basal area defined by darker transverse line followed by paler, often yellowish, pd band.
Flight. July/August; female emerges late.
Habitat. Dry, rocky places, often at low altitudes, exceptionally to 1800m. Larval food plants grasses, esp. *Poa.*
Distribution. C. and S. Europe from Mediterranean to Finland. Absent from Britain, France, Belgium, Holland, Denmark, Scandinavia, Mediterranean islands (except Sicily) and N. Africa.
Variation. Variation is slight. Males with an ocellus on upf in s2 are not rare in some colonies; ♀ups varies in extent of yellow-suffusion.
Similar species. *H. lupina* below; *M. jurtina* p. 302.

HYPONEPHELE LUPINA *Oriental Meadow Brown*
Range. From N. Africa and south-western Europe, S. Russia and Asia Minor to Iran, perhaps to the Himalayas and Mongolia. Map 313

H. lupina lupina Costa 1836 TL: Otranto, Naples **Pl. 55**
Description. ♂fw 21/24mm, resembles *H. lycaon*; ups gc yellow-brown with brassy reflection; upf a conspicuous *dark sex-brand, not cut by veins*, small blind apical ocellus, otherwise unmarked; hw outer margin scalloped, uph unmarked; unf light orange-brown with grey marginal border, black apical ocellus conspicuous, white pupilled; unh light grey-brown with fine darker irrorations, position of discal band often indicated by darker striae. ♀hw outer margin scalloped; *ups gc grey-brown* with blind ocelli in s2 and s5 on upf each surrounded by pale yellow, but always separated by *brown gc along v4*; uph generally with darker basal area followed by paler band.
Flight. July/August.
Habitat. Hot rocky places from lowlands to 900m. The butterflies shelter in bushes and fly out when disturbed, but vanish immediately into a different shelter. Larval food plants not recorded.
Distribution. Italy, very local in Apennines, etc. France, in Vaucluse, Gard, Alpes Maritimes, very local. Hungary, Flamenda, Deliblat. Dalmatia, Krk.

H. lupina rhamnusia Freyer 1845 TL: Etna, Sicily
Description. ♂fw 26/28mm, resembles *H. l. lupina* but larger; ups gc yellow-brown with brassy-golden pile at wing-bases; upf dark sex-brand conspicuous; hw outer margin deeply scalloped. ♀ups as in *H. l. lupina*.
Flight and **Habitat** as in *H. l. lupina*.
Distribution. Sicily. SE. Yugoslavia, Mt. Perister, slightly smaller. Greece, Mt. Parnassus, Mt. Olympus. Crete.

H. lupina mauritanica Oberthur 1881 TL: Algeria **Pl. 55**
Description. ♂fw 21/24mm, ups gc nearly uniform dark grey-brown with little brassy reflection; upf dark sex-brand less conspicuous on darker gc. ♀upf yellow markings slightly paler in tone and often reduced in extent, but distinction from *H. l. lupina* less marked in this sex.
Flight and **Habitat** as for *H. l. lupina*, but flies in Spain at 900–1200m and up to 1800m in Morocco.
Distribution. Morocco. Algeria. Spain, common in mountainous districts. Portugal, in the Serra da Estrela.
Similar species. *H. lycaon* p. 304, ♂ sex-brand uph inconspicuous, narrow, and cut by veins 2 and 3; ♀upf orange-yellow markings more extensive, generally without dark shade along v4 in pd area; *M. jurtina* p. 302.

APHANTOPUS HYPERANTUS *Ringlet*
Range. Europe, except Mediterranean and arctic regions, and across N. Asia to Ussuri. Map 314

A. hyperantus Linnaeus 1758 TL: Europe (Sweden Verity 1953) **Pl. 43**
Description. ♂fw 20/24mm, ups gc almost black; upf with inconspicuous sex-brand along median vein, and with or without obscure ocelli in s3 and s5; uph obscure ocelli in s2, 3; fringes very pale; uns gc pale brown with golden reflection, *conspicuous yellow-ringed ocelli* with white pupils in s3, 5 on fw, and s(1), 2, 3, 5, 6 in uneven series on hw. ♀ups gc paler brown with ocelli, constantly present, usually white pupilled on hw.
Flight. June/July.
Habitat. Damp grassy places, often in light woodland, from lowlands to 1500m. Larval food plants grasses, e.g. *Milium, Poa*, also *Carex* and more rarely sedges.
Distribution. Western Europe to 64°N except Mediterranean region, C. and S. Greece. Cantabrian Mts. France including Pyrenees and generally through C. Europe, Britain, Ireland and S. Scotland. Absent from Portugal, C. and S. Spain, peninsular Italy, Mediterranean islands; local and scarce in central Balkans and Greece.
Variation. Individual variation occurs in the development of the ocelli on uns.
Similar species. *Coenonympha oedippus* p. 316, smaller with an ocellus on unh in s4.

PYRONIA TITHONUS *Gatekeeper*
Range. From Spain and western Europe to Asia Minor and Caucasus. Map 315

P. tithonus Linnaeus 1771 TL: Germany **Pl. 56**
Description. ♂fw 17/19mm, upf sex-brand in and below cell in s1–4, base of wing not suffused fuscous; uph base dusky, orange pd area variable, sometimes small, occasional ocellus in s2; unh gc reddish to pale yellow-brown, margin of dark basal area bounded by paler yellowish area with very *small white-pupilled ocelli in s2 and s5*

both enclosed in yellow-brown shades. ♀ larger, ups gc brighter orange-yellow, unh gc yellow.

Flight. July/August in a single brood, females appear late.

Habitat. Around bramble-bushes, etc., in lowlands, rarely to 900m. Larval food plants various grasses, e.g. *Poa, Milium*.

Distribution. Local but widely distributed in western, central and southern Europe, including southern Ireland and Britain, to about 52°N; Morocco (Er Rif), Sardinia, Corsica and Elba; eastwards to the Balkans. Broadly absent from the Alps except along their southern slopes; absent from S. Italy, Sicily and other Mediterranean islands.

Variation. On upf in ♂ additional ocelli are not uncommon.

Similar species. *P. cecilia* below, unh without ocelli.

PYRONIA CECILIA *Southern Gatekeeper*

Range. From Morocco and Spain through S. Europe to Asia Minor (Bursa). Map 316

P. cecilia Vallantin 1894 TL: Morocco **Pl. 56**
  syn: *ida* Esper 1785 (invalid homonym)

Description. ♂fw 15/16mm, ups resembles *P. tithonus*; upf with striking *quadrilateral sex-brand*, usually divided by fulvous veins, extending into outer angle of cell; uph without ocelli; *unh no ocelli*, gc pale grey marbled olive-brown, irregular darker basal area bounded by pale gc in pd area but sometimes indistinct in ♂. ♀ larger with fw 20mm, uns as in ♂.

Flight. May/August perhaps in a succession of broods.

Habitat. Rough, bushy places in hot localities, usually in lowlands but rising in Spain to 1200m, and to 1800m in Morocco. Larval food plants grasses, esp. *Deschampsia caespitosa*.

Distribution. Morocco, Algeria, Tunisia, Portugal. Absent from NW. Spain and southern slopes of Pyrenees, present in Catalonia and in Balearic Islands. France in Pyrenees, Basses Alpes, Alpes Maritimes, Var, Bouches du Rhône, Hte. Garonne, Hérault, Lozère, Corsica, Sardinia, Elba, Giglio. Italy, local and scattered in north, more common in peninsular Italy and Sicily. Recorded from Dalmatia, Albania, Greece and Turkey in Europe. Records from Romania need confirmation.

Similar species. *P. tithonus* p. 305.

PYRONIA BATHSEBA *Spanish Gatekeeper*

Range. Confined to W. Europe and N. Africa. Map 317

P. bathseba bathseba Fabricius 1793 TL: Morocco ('Barbaria') **Pl. 56**
  syn: *pasiphae* Esper 1781 (invalid homonym)

Description. ♂fw 18/19mm, upf orange gc partly obscured by dark basal suffusion which encloses sex-brand; uph small submarginal ocelli in s2, 3, 5; unf basal area not usually defined; *unh* gc brown, a very *narrow pale yellow discal stripe* with sharply defined inner border followed by obscure, yellow-ringed white-pupilled ocelli, sometimes very small, in s1c, 2, 3, 5, 6. ♀ larger, fw to 23mm, upf dark basal suffusion less extensive; unh gc paler, pale discal stripe wider, ocelli more conspicuous.

Flight. May/June or later.

Habitat. Rough places, hedges, etc., to 1700m in Middle Atlas. Larval food plants grasses, esp. *Brachypodium*.

Distribution. Morocco, Algeria, widely distributed. Not recorded from Tunisia.

P. bathseba pardilloi Sagarra 1924   TL: Barcelona   **Pl. 56**
Description. Slighter larger, unf distal margin of basal area more clearly defined; unh yellow discal line wider, generally extending along v4 into pd area; ocelli on both surfaces more conspicuous esp. in the larger female.
Flight and **Habitat** as for *P. b. bathseba* but at lower altitudes.
Distribution. Portugal, Algarve, Torres Vedras, etc. Spain, widely distributed except in NW. France, in Basses Alpes, Lozère, Bouches du Rhône, Var, E. Pyrenees. In S. Spain often transitional to *P. b. bathseba*.

PYRONIA JANIROIDES   *False Meadow Brown*
Range. Confined to eastern Algeria and Tunisia.   Map 318

P. janiroides Herrich-Schäffer 1851   TL: 'Spain' (error)   **Pl. 56**
Description. ♂fw 23mm, upf brown, with narrow orange pd band restricted by wide dark basal area covering sex-brand; uph orange pd band much wider; unh gc grey-brown, discal band slightly darker with paler pd area enclosing *three or four very small blind yellow ocelli*. ♀ slightly larger, upf dark basal suffusion greatly reduced.
Flight. July/September.
Habitat. Rough ground, esp. near coast and at low altitudes. Larval food plants not known.
Distribution. Algeria, Blida, Bône, Collo, etc. Tunisia, common in July/September.
Similar species. *Maniola jurtina* p. 302.

COENONYMPHA TULLIA   *Large Heath*
Range. From NW. Europe across temperate Asia to Pacific; N. America, local in eastern States, but extending through western mountains to California.   Map 319

C. tullia tullia Müller 1764   TL: Fridrichsdal (Seeland), Denmark   **Pl. 57**
syn: *philoxenus* Esper 1780.
Description. ♂fw 19/20mm, ups gc dingy grey-brown, variable; upf with small yellow-ringed apical ocellus and paler orange-brown suffusion over base and disc, *but without dark margin*; uph yellow-ringed submarginal ocelli (variable) in s1, 2, 3; unf gc pale golden-brown with yellow or white pd stripe and white-pupilled ocelli in s(2), 5; unh grey, sometimes flushed fulvous, an irregular white pd band generally broken in s2/3 and black white-pupilled yellow-ringed submarginal ocelli in s1–6, often very small in s4, 5. ♀upf gc paler orange-brown, yellow pd stripe of uns indicated on costa; uph often darker with pale pd mark in s3, 4, 5; two or three submarginal ocelli present in some specimens.
Flight. June/early July.
Habitat. Bogs, peat mosses and rough meadows, esp. among cotton grass, from lowlands to lower mountain slopes. Larval food plants cotton grass (*Eriophorum*) and beaked rush (*Rhynchospora alba*).
Distribution. Denmark, becoming extinct. Germany, esp. in NW, Hanover, Hamburg, etc. England in NE counties from Northumberland to Yorkshire and in Cumberland. Scotland in southern counties to about 56°N. Wales, in northern districts, now rare. Ireland, widely distributed and very variable. Scandinavia, lowland districts in S. and W.
Variation. It is difficult to give precise characters as nearly every colony shows

minor local features and individual variation is also marked. Some specimens from north-eastern England and southern Scotland closely resemble *C. t. tiphon*.

C. tullia rothliebii   Herrich-Schäffer 1851   TL: not stated   **Pl. 57**
syn: *philoxenus* auct.
Description. Compared with *C. t. tullia* ♂ups darker grey-brown, upf orange-brown suffusion reduced; uph variable, usually with 3 to 5 ocelli; unf gc darker orange-brown, 2–4 submarginal ocelli; unh grey-brown, six large pd ocelli. ♀ similar, ups gc slightly paler, pale pd markings well-defined, uph generally with 4–5 ocelli.
Flight and **Habitat** as for *C. t. tullia*.
Distribution. England, in a restricted area in N. Shropshire, Lancashire and Westmorland. Extinct in Cheshire and Staffordshire. Extent of remaining habitat rapidly shrinking.

C. tullia lorkovici   Sirajić and Cornalutti 1976
Description. ♂fw 18–22mm, resembles *C. t. rothliebii* in rather dark colour, submarginal ocelli usually well-developed; ♀fw 19–25mm, paler buff. The large size of the race is remarkable. Flies very locally in lowland meadows in Bosnia near Jaice etc.

C. tullia tiphon   Rottemburg 1775   TL: Halle, W. Germany   **Pl. 57**
Description. ♂fw 17/20mm, ups gc light orange-brown, pd area of fw and much of hw slightly grey; upf apical ocellus usually present; uph with or without submarginal ocelli; unf ocelli present in (2), 5; unh grey but often with brown flush over disc, pd ocelli usually well developed. ♀ups gc paler ochre-yellow; uph slightly grey with pale discal mark and ocelli more clearly marked.
Flight. End June/July.
Habitat. Wet meadows, moorland, etc., in lowlands.
Distribution. Belgium, Ardennes. France, Aisne, Jura. Switzerland, north of Rhône valley. Bavaria. Austria. Czechoslovakia. Rare or absent in south Tirol.

C. tullia scotica   Staudinger 1901   TL: Scotland   **Pl. 57**
Description. ♂fw 18/19mm, ups gc pale yellow-brown or yellow-grey; upf single apical ocellus sometimes present; uph pale discal mark nearly constant; unf pale pd band enlarged, ocelli small or absent, grey apical area more extensive; *unh grey, ocelli small or absent*. ♀ups gc golden-buff, pale whitish areas often enlarged on both surfaces.
Flight. End June/July.
Habitat. Bogs and rough grassy places from lowlands to about 700m.
Distribution. Scotland north of 56°N but including Argyll, also Hebrides and Orkney Islands; characters are best marked in northern areas.
Variation. Less typical south of 56°N and transitional to *C. t. tullia*.

C. tullia demophile   Freyer 1844   TL: Lapland   **Pl. 57**
syn: *suecica* Hemming 1936
Description. ♂fw 15/18mm, upf gc light yellow-brown, outer border and uph tending more to grey, rarely a small apical ocellus; unf paler, a single apical ocellus, pale pd stripe well-marked, outer border and all hw grey; unh ocelli reduced or absent. ♀ups yellow with rather grey hw; pale markings show through from uns.
Flight. End June/July.
Habitat. Rough grassy places, moorland, etc.

Distribution. Fennoscandia at lowland levels on fjelds and in arctic regions to 70°N, with transitions to *C. t. tiphon* in Baltic countries.
Similar species. *C. pamphilus* below, nearly always smaller and ups gc clear yellow-buff with narrow grey wing borders, unh small submarginal ocelli indistinct if present; ocelli always well formed in s2 and s6 in all European forms of *C. tullia*. *C. glycerion* p. 315.

COENONYMPHA RHODOPENSIS *Eastern Large Heath*
Range. Balkan Mts. and C. Italy.   Map 320

C. rhodopensis rhodopensis Elwes 1900   TL: Bulgaria.   **Pl. 57**
syn: *occupata* Rebel 1903; *italica* Verity 1913.
Description. ♂fw 16/17mm, ups gc *clear orange-buff*, slightly variable, often with small black basal suffusion; upf apical ocellus usually shows through faintly from uns, fuscous shading along outer margin slight or absent; uph sometimes slightly darker, rarely with ocelli in s2, 3 (Balkan Mts.); unf broadly orange-yellow, pale pd stripe absent or (rarely) vestigial; unh grey with fulvous discal flush, *small white mark in s3, 4, 5* constant, pd ocelli well developed. ♀ups paler, upf clear orange-yellow without black basal suffusion; uph pale discal mark plainly visible.
Flight. July.
Habitat. Mountain meadows at 1400–2100m.
Distribution. Confined to SE. Europe and C. Italy. Probably flies on all higher mountains from Sarajevo (Trebević) southwards to Mt. Perister; N. Greece.
Variation. Markings vary slightly in different colonies. Italy, local on a few high mountains in Abruzzi, Monte Sibillini and Monte Baldo, closely resembling Balkan specimens, f. *italica* Verity Pl. 57. Romania, only at high altitudes in Retezat Mts.

COENONYMPHA PAMPHILUS *Small Heath*
Range. All Europe and N. Africa, Asia Minor, Lebanon, Iraq, Iran and Turkestan, perhaps further east into Siberia.   Map 321

C. pamphilus pamphilus Linnaeus 1758   TL: not stated   **Pl. 58**
(Sweden, Verity 1953)
Description. ♂fw 14/16mm, ups gc bright yellow-buff with *grey marginal borders* 1–2mm wide; upf, apical ocellus small, grey; uph a pale discal mark may show through from uns; unf apical ocellus black, white-pupilled and yellow-ringed, indications of pale pd line sometimes present; unh grey nearly unmarked in many northern specimens, basal area often darker and followed by pale pd mark and obscure submarginal ocelli in s1–6. ♀ similar, larger.
Flight. Throughout summer with succession of broods from April in N. Africa and Spain and from end May in N. Europe. Some larvae from each brood hibernate until following spring.
Habitat. Open grassy places from sea level to 1800m. Larval food plants various grasses, e.g., *Poa, Nardus stricta*, etc.
Distribution. Throughout W. and N. Europe and N. Africa.
Variation. In some districts of S. Europe summer broods have conspicuous dark grey ups marginal borders f. *marginata*. In such specimens unh gc is often brown instead of grey, f. *latecana* Verity.

C. p. pamphilus f. *lyllus* Esper 1805   TL: Portugal   **Pl. 58**
Description. ♂Differs on ups in wider grey marginal borders; unf with black shade

along outer margin near anal angle and pd transverse line reddish; unh gc pale buff
with dark basal area, markings brown, often indistinct. ♀ similar, unh basal area
slightly darker, pd area usually unmarked.
Flight. May or later.
Distribution. The common summer form in the W. Mediterranean region, including the islands, but not fully developed in all localities. It occurs constantly in
N. Africa, Spain and Portugal, and often with commoner intermediate forms in
S. France and peninsular Italy and Greece, uph sometimes with small ocellar pd
points.

C. pamphilus thyrsis   Freyer 1845   TL: Crete   **Pl. 56**
Description. ♂fw 13/14mm, resembles f. *latecana* Verity; ups dark marginal bor-
ders conspicuous; uph frequently with small pd ocellar points; unf dark pd line well
defined; unh gc pale buff, dark brown basal area sharply defined, 5 or 6 small black
white-pupilled pd ocelli, fuscous shade in s2, 3, 4 followed by metallic antemarginal
line. ♀ similar, slightly larger, uph black pd dots constantly present.
Flight. Early April to July in two broods.
Habitat. Waste ground and rough places among grass, from sea-level.
Distribution. Isle of Crete.
Note. *C. p. thyrsis* is regarded as a distinct species by some authors. On Sicily
C. p. sicula Zeller, very similar, unh brightly marked.
Similar species. *C. tullia* p. 307.

COENONYMPHA CORINNA   *Corsican Heath*
Range. Corsica, Sardinia.   Map 322

C. corinna   Hübner 1804   TL: Sardinia   **Pl. 58**
Description. ♂fw 14/15mm, ups bright fulvous with dark fuscous apical and
marginal borders, including costal margin of hw; upf with small blind yellow-ringed
apical ocellus and narrow yellow antemarginal line; uph unmarked fulvous, apart
from black costal border; unh gc fulvous with margin of darker grey, basal area
defined by *very irregular yellowish pd line often incomplete*, small yellow-ringed
ocellus in s6, other pd ocelli absent or if present very small in a *straight row in s2, 3, 4*.
♀ similar, ups dark wing-borders often reduced; unh markings better defined and
basal area usually more grey.
Flight. May/June and later with succession of broods through summer.
Habitat. Open grassy places, commonest at about 900m. Larval food plants not
recorded.
Distribution. Corsica and Sardinia.
Variation. In Corsican specimens unh gc is more fulvous, and there is a small pale
mark in cell opposite origin of v2.

COENONYMPHA ELBANA   *Elban Heath*
Range. Elba, Giglio and neighbouring Italian mainland.   Map 323

C. elbana   Staudinger 1901   TL: Elba   **Pl. 58**
Description. ♂fw 12.5/14mm, like *C. corinna*, uph pd ocelli in a straight row from
s2 to s4, small or absent in slc; uns black ante-marginal and submarginal lines equally
well developed on both wings; unh pd band narrow, irregular, yellowish, followed by
a complete series of six ocelli, small in s1c and in s5. ♀ similar.
Flight and **Habitat.** Occurs in May and later on open grassland.

Distribution. Confined to Elba, Giglio, mainland on Monte Argentario and locally in this area.

COENONYMPHA DORUS   *Dusky Heath*
Range. N. Africa and SW. Europe to C. Italy. Map 324

C. dorus dorus   Esper 1782   TL: Toulouse, France   **Pl. 58**
Description. ♂fw 16/17mm, upf grey-brown with yellow undertones, yellow-ringed apical ocellus blind, pd spaces sometimes partly filled yellow; uph gc orange-yellow with wide fuscous costal border, blind *ocelli in s1–4 in internally convex curve*, a very small ocellus in s6; uns metallic antemarginal and orange marginal lines; unf a single black white-pupilled apical ocellus; unh basal area yellow-grey, bordered by slightly irregular pale yellow or white pd band with distal bulge in s4, 5, pd area paler with black white-pupilled yellow-ringed ocelli as on ups. ♂ with a wide sex-brand on upf partly obscured by fuscous gc. ♀upf orange-fulvous, marginal borders grey with double lines in some races, uph often with fuscous shading along costa.
Flight. End June/July, in a single brood.
Habitat. Dry stony places from lowlands to 1500m or more. Larval food plants not recorded.
Distribution. France, Provence to Aveyron, Lozère and E. Pyrenees. Spain, widely distributed south of Pyrenees, replaced in NW. by *C. d. bieli* (see below). Portugal, common except in north. Local in C. Italy.
Variation. A very variable species with many named local races.

C. dorus bieli   Staudinger 1901   TL: N. Spain   **Pl. 58**
Description. ♂fw 15/16mm, ups dark smokey brown, ocelli small or absent; unf apical ocellus small; unh markings grey or yellow-grey, pale pd band variable and often extending into pd area, ocelli small, grey and inconspicuous. ♀upf orange-brown with dark brown marginal border, with or without apical ocellus; uph fuscous flushed orange-brown, one or two yellow-ringed ocelli present in s2, 3; unh as in ♂ with small ocelli.
Flight and **Habitat** as for *C. d. dorus*.
Distribution. NW. Spain in Galicia and Leon. N. Portugal, widespread in Minho and Tras os Montes.
Variation. In ♂ups orange-brown discal flush not rare, esp. uph; small yellow-ringed ocellus uph in s2 common, more rarely also apical ocellus upf.

C. dorus aquilonia   Higgins 1969   TL: l'Aquila, C. Italy
Description. ♂fw 14/16mm, upf grey with fulvous-yellow pd band 2–3mm wide; uph yellow area includes most of cell, ocelli small, sometimes incomplete; unf apical ocellus small, usual dark markings reduced; unh gc yellow-grey with darker basal area, ocelli small but in complete series. ♀ups light orange-fulvous, lightly marked with small ocelli; uns resembles ♂ but gc paler.
Flight and **Habitat.** July, on rough ground at 900m.
Distribution. C. Italy, local in Marche and Abruzzi, Bolognola, l'Aquila, Lucania.

C. dorus fettigii   Oberthur 1874   TL: Tuelagh, Algeria   **Pl. 58**
Description. ♂fw 15/16mm, ups resembles *C. d. aquilonia*; upf fulvous-yellow pd patch sometimes extending basad; uph pd ocelli small; unf apex pale grey, dark antemarginal line obsolete; unh gc pale grey, dark basal area defined only near costa, ocelli small or minute but rarely absent. ♀upf fulvous patch extended to cover base and discal area.

Flight and **Habitat.** End June/July, on rough ground at 1500–1800m.
Distribution. Algeria, in Oran. Morocco, more widely distributed in Middle and High Atlas. Not recorded from Tunisia.
Variation. In High Atlas unh almost uniform pale grey with very pale pd area and minute ocelli.
Note. *C. d. fettigii* is regarded as a distinct species by some authors.
Similar species. *C. austauti* below, unh white discal band narrow, almost straight.

COENONYMPHA AUSTAUTI   *Austaut's Algerian Heath*
Range. Confined to Algeria.   Map 325

C. austauti   Oberthur 1881   TL: Nemours, Algeria   **Pl. 56**
Description. ♂fw 14/15mm, resembles *C. dorus*, upf with sex-brand, but apex of fw more rounded, apical ocellus large, clearly yellow-ringed; unh gc yellow-grey, *distal border of darker basal area not uneven*, followed by a narrow nearly straight white or pale yellow stripe, ocelli enclosed in yellow-grey band, a yellow antemarginal patch in s1c, 2, 3. Metallic antemarginal lines very bright on uns of both wings. ♀ups fuscous suffusion greatly reduced, resembling *C. dorus*.
Flight. June/July, and perhaps later with continuous emergence.
Habitat. Probably at low or moderate altitudes but little information.
Distribution. Only recorded from Province of Oran in Algeria, in neighbourhood of Nemours, e.g., Masser Mines, Lalla Marnia, Zough-el-Beghal, etc.
Remarks. The relationship between *C. d. fettigii* and *C. austauti* is confusing. Both forms have been recorded from Lalla Marnia, but whether flying together or not is not known. Existing records suggest that *austauti* is more generally distributed near the coast, perhaps at low altitudes, and *fettigii* is known to fly more commonly in mountains at levels of 1200m or more.
Similar species. *C. dorus* p. 311.

COENONYMPHA VAUCHERI   *Vaucher's Heath*
Range. Confined to Morocco.   Map 326

C. vaucheri vaucheri   Blachier 1905   TL: High Atlas, Morocco   **Pl. 56**
Description. ♂fw 17/18mm, ups gc sandy-orange with slight fuscous shading; upf a large blind apical ocellus across s4, 5; uph small blind ocelli in s1c–s4 (5); unf gc much paler beyond darker basal area, apical ocellus with twin silver pupils; unh *striking dark basal area with pale mark in cell*, bordered by pale discal band and regular series of six ocelli enclosed in fuscous pd area. ♀ similar.
Flight. June/July in a single brood.
Habitat. Rough stony ground at altitudes of 2400–2700m. Larval food plant unknown.
Distribution. Only in High Atlas esp. on Toubkal Massif, e.g., Amizmiz, etc.

C. vaucheri annoceuri   Wyatt 1952   TL: Annoceur, Middle Atlas
Description. ♂fw 15mm, small, ups without fuscous suffusion; upf blind apical ocellus smaller; uph two or three very small submarginal ocelli; unf gc paler with little contrast between basal and pd areas; unh pd area mostly pale sandy yellow, ocelli small. ♀ similar.
Flight and **Habitat.** Flies June on barren mountain-sides at 1500–2100m.
Distribution. Middle Atlas, local, esp. Taghzeft Pass, Annoceur. In Er Rif paler on both surfaces and dark shading reduced *C. a. rifensis* Weiss. 1975.

COENONYMPHA ARCANIA   *Pearly Heath*

Range. From W. Europe through Asia Minor and S. Russia to southern Urals. Map 327

C. arcania   Linnaeus 1761   TL: Sweden   **Pl. 57**
syn: *amyntas* Poda 1761

Description. ♂fw 17/20mm, ups gc yellow-orange; upf fuscous marginal borders wide; uph dark fuscous with traces of orange marginal line at anal angle and sometimes a small pd ocellus; unf dark border reduced, sometimes replaced by orange marginal and metallic antemarginal lines; unh gc orange-brown to grey, *conspicuous white irregular pd band wide in s4, 5*, black white-pupilled yellow-ringed ocelli in s2–3 in pd area, often with additional small ocelli in s1c, 4, 5, *prominent ocellus proximal to pd band in s6*, orange marginal and metallic antemarginal lines as on fw. ♀ similar.

Flight. June/July usually in a single brood, partial second broods may occur in southern localities.

Habitat. Grassy banks and light woodland from lowlands to 1200m in Alps to Jura, to over 1800m in Pyrenees, commonest in hilly country. Larval food plants grasses, esp. *Melica*.

Distribution. W. Europe, widely distributed to 60°N. Spain, local in northern and central districts, San Ildefonso, Cuenca, etc. Portugal. Absent from S. Spain, Britain, Sicily, Corsica, Sardinia, Elba and Crete.

Variation. In C. Spain uph often with a slight fulvous flush.

COENONYMPHA DARWINIANA   *Darwin's Heath*

Range. Restricted to southern Alps from France to the Dolomites.   Map 328

C. darwiniana   Staudinger 1871   TL: Switzerland (Valais)   **Pl. 57**

Description. ♂fw 16/17mm, like *C. arcania* but usually smaller, unh fulvous-grey, pd band *narrow*, white or yellowish, often slightly irregular, ocelli usually well developed, encircled with wide, yellow rings, small in s5, in ♂ ocellus in s6 usually proximal to pale band, but in ♀ more often enclosed within it. ♀ similar.

Flight. July/August in a single brood.

Habitat. Subalpine meadows at 1500m or more, rarely at lower altitudes.

Distribution. France, Maritimes and Basses Alpes. Switzerland on southern alpine slopes in Valais, Tessin, Graubünden and eastwards locally to Mendel, Schlern and Dolomites.

Similar species. *C. gardetta* below, unh ocelli without external yellow rings.

COENONYMPHA GARDETTA   *Alpine Heath*

Range. Confined to Alps.   Map 329

C. gardetta   de Prunner 1798   TL: Val Varaita, Alpes Maritimes   **Pl. 57**
syn: *satyrion* Esper 1804; *philea* Hübner 1800 (invalid homonym); *neoclides* Hübner 1805

Description. ♂fw 15/16mm, upf grey-brown with slight fulvous discal flush in some specimens; uph grey, orange marginal line at anal angle vestigial; unf gc tawny, apex and outer border grey, often with small apical ocellus; unh grey with *regular white postdiscal band* enclosing ocelli in s1–6, and metallic antemarginal and orange marginal lines. ♀upf orange-brown with fuscous border from apex down outer margin; uph grey-brown, orange marginal line usually present.

Flight. July/August.
Habitat. High alpine meadows at 1500–2100m, often very abundant; exceptionally at lower levels, e.g., Gimel, Switzerland at 800m. Larval food plants not known.
Distribution. Hautes Alpes, Savoie and Haute Savoie and eastwards through the higher Alps including Bavarian Alps, Dolomites and Hohe Tauern to Karawanken Mts.
Variation. At high altitudes in northern Alps ♂ ups may be plain grey without fulvous and ♀ paler with upf fulvous area reduced. At lower altitudes upf fulvous area is often increased, sometimes with enlarged submarginal ocelli on unh, f. *macrophthalmica* Stauder, esp. in eastern Alps from Berchtesgaden, Dolomites, etc.
Similar species. *C. darwiniana* p. 313.

COENONYMPHA ARCANIOIDES　*Moroccan Pearly Heath*
Range. Confined to Morocco, Algeria and Tunisia, north of Atlas Mts.　Map 330

C. arcanioides　Pierret 1837　TL: Oran, Algeria　　　　　　　　　Pl. 57
Description. ♂fw 14/15mm, upf gc fulvous, dark fuscous border along outer margin wide, extending over apex and enclosing blind apical ocellus; uph fuscous with orange marginal line at anal angle; unf a large white-pupilled apical ocellus preceded by transverse yellow pd line; unh gc dark brown with *narrow irregular white pd stripe* followed by small ocelli; metallic antemarginal lines along outer margins of both wings. ♀ similar.
Flight. April to September in continuous broods without obvious seasonal variation.
Habitat. Uncultivated grassy places; especially common near coast and up to 1500m. Larval food plants not recorded.
Distribution. Morocco, Algeria and Tunisia, in coastal regions and on northern slopes of Middle Atlas.

COENONYMPHA LEANDER　*Russian Heath*
Range. From S. Carpathians and Balkans through S. Russia, Asia Minor and Armenia to Iran.　Map 331.

C. leander leander　Esper 1784　TL: Russia, Volga　　　　　　　　Pl. 57
Description. ♂fw 16/17mm, ups gc dark brown; upf fulvous flush often present from base to cell-end; uph sometimes with two or three submarginal blind ocelli and an orange mark at anal angle which may spread into s2, 3; unf gc light fulvous with small white-pupilled apical ocellus; apex not grey, distinction from forms of *C. gardetta*, unh light fulvous with pale grey basal shade, six white-pupilled yellow-ringed black submarginal ocelli in regular series, and *prominent orange band between ocelli and metallic antemarginal line*. ♀upf yellow-buff, more or less shaded fuscous towards outer margin, often with small apical ocellus; uph *yellow anal submarginal marks* often expanded into a band sometimes enclosing small ocelli; uns as in ♂.
Flight. May/June, in a single brood.
Habitat. Rough grassy places from lowlands to moderate altitudes. Larval food plants unknown.
Distribution. Carpathians, Romania, Bulgaria, NE. Greece (Florina).
Similar species. *C. iphioides* p. 315.

C. leander orientalis　Rebel 1913　TL: E. Bosnia　　　　　　　　　Pl. 23
　syn: *skypetarum* Rebel & Zerny 1931; *katarae* Coutsis 1975

Description. Ups as in *C. leander leander*, upf fulvous discal suffusion extensive; unh pale ocellar rings widely extended into pd area, forming a prominent, white band when fully developed but somewhat variable; usually prominent in females.
Flight and **Habitat.** June early July, flying with *C. arcania* at 1500m.
Distribution. SE. Bosnia, Montenegro, Albania and N. Greece (Pindus Mts.).
Similar species. *C. arcania* p. 313; *C. gardetta* p. 313.

COENONYMPHA GLYCERION   Chestnut Heath
Range. From W. Europe across Russia to Siberia.   Map 332

C. glycerion glycerion Borkhausen 1788   TL: not stated (Bavaria)   **Pl. 57**
   syn: *iphis* Denis and Schiffermüller 1775 (invalid homonym)
Description. ♂fw 16/18mm, ups gc chestnut brown; upf without apical ocellus; uph usually unmarked, occasionally with one or two blind submarginal ocelli; unf tawny brown with wide grey border at apex and down outer margin; unh grey, *with white discal marks in s(1c) and s4*, six pale-ringed pd ocelli of uneven size *with brilliant white pupils* (rarely very small or absent in s4, 5), and usually an orange antemarginal line near anal angle. ♀ both wings ups and uns with faint orange antemarginal lines, usually preceded on unh by a narrow metallic line; *upf orange-buff; uph dark grey*, sometimes with two or three small ocelli; unf gc as upf; unh pale grey, ocelli larger, with brilliant pupils, but often absent at high altitudes in W. Europe f. *bertolis* Prunner.
Flight. June/July in a single brood.
Habitat. Grassy places from foothills to 1500m, not uncommon, but local. Larval food plants various grasses, e.g., *Melica, Brachypodium, Cynosurus, etc.*
Distribution. N. Spain (Aragon). E. Pyrenees and central France, through Switzerland and central Europe to S. Finland, Baltic countries, Romania, Bulgaria and N. Yugoslavia. Italy in northern Alps and Apennines, but very local. Absent from Britain, W. and N. France, Basses and Hautes Pyrénées, Spain (except Aragon), Portugal, Belgium, Holland, NW. Germany, Scandinavia, S. Italy and Greece.
Similar species. *C. pamphilus* p. 309 and *C. tullia* p. 307, both of which have an apical ocellus on upf.

COENONYMPHA IPHIOIDES   Spanish Heath
Range. Confined to N. and C. Spain.

C. iphioides Staudinger 1870   TL: Castile, Spain.   **Pl. 57**
Description. ♂fw 17/20mm, resembling *C. iphis* but larger; ups gc dark brown; upf a tawny flush from base across disc, *apical ocellus absent*; uph with or without two or three blind submarginal ocelli, a narrow orange marginal line near anal angle; unf fulvous, apex grey with small ocellus; unh gc grey with white pd mark in s4, often small sometimes absent, *six white-pupilled yellow-ringed ocelli of nearly uniform size in s1c–s6*, and metallic antemarginal and *orange marginal line* from anal angle to s5.
♀upf gc orange-buff with grey outer margin and *yellow marginal line*, often with small apical ocellus; uph dark grey with yellow marginal line, with or without ocelli; unh ocelli conspicuous.
Flight. June/July.
Habitat. Rough moist grassy uplands to 1700m. Larval food plants not known.
Distribution. Spain, northern and central districts south of Pyrenees, including southern slopes of Cantabrian Mts. to Leon (Brañuelas) and south to Teruel and Sierra de Guadarrama. Not recorded from Portugal.

Variation. At high altitudes on southern slopes of Pyrenees often small, unh ocelli small, f. *pearsoni* transitional to *C. g. glycerion*. Borkh.
Similar species. No confusion should occur. The combination of absence of upf apical ocellus with a complete series of pd ocelli unh, is not found in any other species of *Coenonympha*.

COENONYMPHA HERO   *Scarce Heath*

Range. From N. France and Scandinavia across C. Europe to Urals Mts., Amur, Korea and Japan.   Map 333

C. hero Linnaeus 1761   TL: S. Sweden   **Pl. 56**
Description. ♂fw 15/17mm, *ups uniformly dark grey-brown*; upf unmarked; uph usually with *yellow-ringed generally blind submarginal ocelli* in s1c, 2, 3, (4) (variable) and orange marginal line at anal angle; unf grey-brown with pale pd transverse shade and small apical ocellus; unh an irregular white pd line before a series of six black white-pupilled yellow-ringed ocelli, metallic antemarginal and orange marginal lines. ♀ slightly larger and paler; upf a small apical ocellus; uph ocelli more prominent.
Flight. End May/June in a single brood.
Habitat. Damp meadows, moorlands, etc., at moderate altitudes. Larval food plants various grasses, esp. *Elymus arenarius*.
Distribution. Southern Scandinavia. France, only in NE. Belgium. Holland. Germany (rare). Czechoslovakia. Baltic countries, Lithuania, etc. An extremely local species with colonies widely scattered.
Similar species. *C. oedippus* below.

COENONYMPHA OEDIPPUS   *False Ringlet*

Range. From W. Europe through Russia and C. Asia to China and Japan.
Map 334

C. oedippus oedippus Fabricius 1787   TL: S. Russia   **Pl. 57**
Description. ♂fw 17/21mm, resembles *A. hyperantus* but smaller; ups gc dark brown (black), fw unmarked; uph small ocelli often dimly visible in s2, 3; uns gc yellow-brown; unf small pd ocelli usually present in s2, 3 and (4); unh silver-pupilled pd ocelli present in s1–4 and *s6 (large, displaced basad)*, ocellus in s5 small or absent, *metallic antemarginal line* constant on hw, vestigial on fw. ♀ similar, larger, with ocelli better developed on both surfaces, often bordered proximally by pale band.
Flight. June/July in a single brood.
Habitat. Wet meadows and boggy places in lowlands, but sometimes also in dry woodland or scrub with open grassy places. Larval food plants include *Lolium, Carex, Iris pseudacorus*.
Distribution. France, very local in widely distributed colonies in Isère, Hte Garonne, Basses Pyrénées, E. Pyrenees, Landes, Deux Sèvres, Charente, etc. Belgium (rare). Italy, near Turin, etc., Venezia Giulia. Germany, no recent records.

C. oedippus hungarica Rebel 1900   TL: not stated
Description. ♂fw 17/19mm, ups ocelli absent; uns ocelli rudimentary on fw, small on hw, but ocellus in s6 remains conspicuous, with pale proximal bar present in both sexes.
Flight and **Habitat** as above.
Distribution. Austria ('Vienna'), Hungary.

Variation. Minor local variation in size and development of markings occurs in most colonies.

Similar species. *C. hero* above, smaller, ocelli usually well developed on uph, and on unh preceded by conspicuous white band. *A. hyperantus* p. 305, larger, unh large ocellus in s4 absent.

PARARGE AEGERIA *Speckled Wood*
Range. From W. Europe through Asia Minor, Syria and Russia to C. Asia. Map 335

P. aegeria aegeria Linnaeus 1758 TL: S. Europe and N. Africa **Pl. 60**
syn: *vulgaris* Zeller 1847
Description. ♂fw 19/22mm, fw outer margin concave below v5; hw outer margin rather deeply scalloped; ups gc orange-yellow with dark criss-cross markings; upf a small apical ocellus and a broad sex-brand from inner margin below median vein to v4 and extending along v2 and v3; uph ocelli in s2, 3, 4 (5); *unh* yellow-brown with *greenish tint*, markings confused, darker area along outer margin enclosing small white spots between veins. ♀ similar.
Flight. March or later with successive broods until October.
Habitat. Shady places and woodland from sea-level to 1200m in Europe, to 1700m in Africa. Larval food plants various grasses, esp. couch grass (*Agropyron*), also *Triticum repens*, etc.
Distribution. S. and C. France; S. Switzerland. Italy, esp. peninsular Italy. Spain and Portugal. Recently taken in Madeira. Mediterranean islands. Morocco. Algeria. Tunisia and Scilly Isles.

P. aegeria tircis Butler 1867 TL: France **Pl. 60**
syn: *egerides* Staudinger 1871
Description. Resembles *P. a. aegeria* but gc on ups pale yellow to white, on uns cream-white, paler in late broods. ♀ similar.
Flight and **Habitat** as for *P. a. aegeria* but appears first about April.
Distribution. Northern, central and eastern Europe to 63°N, including British Isles and Balkan countries.
Variation. The distribution areas of the two colour forms are not clearly defined; late broods of the northern *P. a. tircis* incline in their southern range to *P. a. aegeria*. The *aegeria*-form is constant in the western Mediterranean as far east as Sicily, reappearing in Lebanon.

PARARGE XIPHIOIDES *Canary Speckled Wood*
Range. Confined to Canary Islands. No map.

P. xiphioides Staudinger 1871 TL: Canary Islands **Pl. 56**
Description. ♂fw 21/24mm, size variable, smaller in late broods; resembles *P. aegeria* in colour but outer margin of fw not concave at v5; upf apical ocellus small; unh light brown with darker chestnut markings, prominent white costal mark generally extending to cell; pd ocelli often strongly marked. ♀ similar, larger, ups gc paler; unh gc yellow-grey with brown markings as in ♂.
Flight. May to September or later.
Habitat. Widespread and common. Larval food plants grasses.
Distribution. Canary Islands, but not known from Hierro, Fuerteventura or Lanzarote.

PARARGE XIPHIA   *Madeiran Speckled Wood*
Range. Restricted to Madeira.   No map.

P. xiphia   Fabricius 1775   Madeira   **Pl. 56**
Description. ♂fw 26/27mm, fw bluntly pointed with outer margin gently convex;
hw outer margin rather deeply scalloped; ups resembles *P. aegeria* but dark criss-
cross markings more extensive, orange gc darker and reduced to small spots; upf
apical ocellus vestigial, narrow sex-brand below cell extends from v1 to v4, covered
with long hair that fills cell; unf gc orange-fulvous; unh bright chestnut-brown with
small white mark on costa and grey marginal border. ♀unh gc paler grey-brown,
basal area darker with larger white costal mark.
Flight. May and later to August.
Habitat. From sea-level to 800m or more, often common in Funchal.

LASIOMMATA MEGERA   *Wall Brown*
Range. From W. Europe and N. Africa through Russia and Asia Minor to Syria,
Lebanon and Iran.   Map 336

L. megera megera   Linnaeus 1767   TL: Austria and Denmark   **Pl. 60**
Description. ♂fw 19/25mm; *ups gc orange-yellow* with black lattice wing-pattern;
upf apical ocellus and sex-brand conspicuous; uph smaller pd ocelli in s1c, 2, 3, 4;
unh grey with confused basal and discal markings including brown-ringed pd ocelli
in s1c–s6. ♀ similar, ups often slightly paler.
Flight. March or later, two broods in C. Europe, three in S. Europe.
Habitat. Rough ground, gardens, woodland glades, etc., from sea-level to 1500m.
Larval food plant grasses esp. *Poa* and *Dactylis*.
Distribution. Widely distributed in N. Africa and Europe to 60°N, including
Ireland and Mediterranean islands. Absent from Madeira and Canary Islands;
replaced in Corsica and Sardinia by following subspecies.

L. megera paramegaera   Hübner 1824   TL: Sardinia (Verity 1953)   **Pl. 60**
syn: *tigelius* Bonelli 1826
Description. ♂fw 18/19mm, resembles *L. m. megera*, but upf black pd line in s1b
and s2 thin, sometimes incomplete; uph fuscous pd line internal to ocelli lacking.
Flight. April to September, probably three broods.
Habitat. Rough places esp. open moorland at about 900m.
Distribution. Sardinia and Corsica. Balearic Islands (Majorca), most specimens
indistinguishable from Sardinian race.
Variation. Corsican specimens are more lightly marked, and on upf the pd line in
s1c and s2 is usually absent; the thin, partly obsolete appearance of the black
markings on ups is especially noticeable in females. Similar forms have been re-
ported from Sicily and Majorca.
Similar species. *L. maera* below, ♀ larger, upf with single dark bar in cell.

LASIOMMATA MAERA   *Large Wall Brown*
Range. From N. Africa and W. Europe across Russia, Asia Minor and Syria to Iran,
central Asia and Himalayas.   Map 337

L. maera maera   Linnaeus 1758   TL: Sweden (Verity 1953)   **Pl. 60**
syn: *monotonia* Schilde, 1885; *hiera* Fabricius 1777
Description. ♂fw *first brood* 25/28mm, *second brood* 22/23mm, ups brown; upf a
large white-pupilled apical ocellus in s4 and 5, sometimes with two pupils, and

sometimes a small ocellus in s6, fulvous pd area broken by dark veins, sex-brand somewhat obscured by brown discal area; *uph* yellow-ringed white-pupilled ocelli in s2, 3, 4, *discal area unmarked*; unh grey with confused markings and small brown-ringed pd ocelli in s2–s6. ♀upf fulvous pd band brighter and wider, enclosing apical ocellus.

Flight. June/July in a single brood in northern range; May/June and August/September in two broods in southern range.

Habitat. Rough places and rocky paths in hills and mountains from lowlands to 1800m. Larval food plants various grasses, e.g., *Poa, Glyceria fluitans*.

Distribution. Common and widely distributed in W. Europe from Mediterranean coasts to 68°N. Absent from Britain, Corsica, Sardinia, Crete and Atlantic islands.

Variation. In S. France, Spain and Portugal fulvous markings are more extensive in both sexes, in ♀upf orange-yellow, lightly marked, f. *adrasta* Illiger. In all localities late broods emerging August/September are generally small with ups fulvous markings more extensive. In northern Scandinavia males are small, often dark but in ♀upf pale yellowish apical patch is well defined, f. *borealis* Fuchs.

L. maera meadewaldoi   Rothschild 1917   TL: Algeria
   syn: *alluaudi* Oberthur 1922

Description. ♂fw 28mm, large with exaggerated *adrasta*-features; ups fiery orange-fulvous and uns more brown than grey, suggesting a well-defined subspecies. Smaller specimens, probably of late broods, have been taken occasionally in the Middle Atlas and in the Rif. Very similar forms occur in S. Spain.

Distribution. Algeria and Morocco on High Atlas June and July.

Similar species. *L. petropolitana* below; *L. megera* p. 318.

LASIOMMATA PETROPOLITANA   *Northern Wall Brown*

Range. From Pyrenees through Alps, Carpathians and Fennoscandia, Russia and N. Siberia to the Amur.   Map 338

L. petropolitana   Fabricius 1787   TL: Petrograd   **Pl. 60**
   syn: *hiera* auct.

Description. ♂fw 19/21mm, like *L. maera* but smaller; upf with two, often obscure, dark cross-bars in cell; unf dark line between apical ocellus and cell-end close to ocellus; *uph with dark curving wavy transverse discal line*. ♀ similar.

Flight. May/July, according to locality, usually in a single brood, but perhaps in some warm localities a partial second brood in August/September.

Habitat. Frequent in open spaces in woodland of pine or spruce, from sea-level in the high north to 1800m in southern Alps. Larval food plants grasses, esp. *Festuca*.

Distribution. Fennoscandia to 68°N; as a mountain butterfly in Pyrenees, Alps and probably on all higher mountains to Bulgaria, SE. Yugoslavia and Greece (Pindus Mts.). Not recorded from Spain, Jura, Vosges, Apennines.

Similar species. *L. maera* above, uph without wavy transverse discal line.

LOPINGA ACHINE *Woodland Brown*
Range. From N. France and S. Scandinavia through C. Europe, Russia and north-central Asia to Amur, Ussuri and Japan. Map 339

L. achine Scopoli 1763 TL: Carniola **Pl. 43**
syn: *deianira* Linnaeus 1764
Description. ♂fw 25/27mm, outer margins of wings slightly wavy; ups gc uniform light grey-brown, each wing with an evenly curved *row of large yellow-ringed blind ocelli* in pd area; uns paler, ocelli as on ups with or without white pupils and prominently yellow-ringed, preceded on fw by pale buff and on hw by a white stripe; both wings with double pale buff antemarginal lines. ♀ similar, slightly larger and paler. Males are without a sex-brand but androconia are abundant on uph.
Flight. Early June/July in a single brood; females emerge later than males.
Habitat. Shady woodland from lowlands to 900m. Larval food plants various grasses, *Lolium, Agropyron*.
Distribution. Very local in widely scattered colonies. S. Fennoscandia, Baltic countries, Germany. France, widely distributed esp. in N. and E.; Spain, only in Catalonia; Italy, north of the Po and eastwards to Yugoslavia and Bulgaria. Not recorded from Poland or Czechoslovakia.

KIRINIA ROXELANA *Lattice Brown*
Range. From SE. Europe through Asia Minor to Cyprus, Syria and Iraq. Map 340

K. roxelana Cramer 1777 TL: Istanbul **Pl. 24**
Description. ♂fw 29/31mm, fw narrow, pointed; hw cell long; ups gc brown; upf with fulvous flush and small apical ocellus in s5, a complicated pattern of sex-brands occupies basal and much of discal areas causing distortion of v1 and shape of wing; uph ocelli show through faintly from uns; unh series of white-pupilled yellow-ringed pd ocelli smallest in s4 and s5. ♀fw of normal shape; upf with white costal and apical spots; unh wing-markings much better defined.
Flight. End May/June/July from lowlands to 1100m.
Habitat. Rough ground, hill paths, etc., prefers to sit in low bushes and rarely flies unless disturbed. Larval food plant not known.
Distribution. Eastern Hungary, Romania, southern Balkans including Yugoslavia, Bulgaria, Greece, Albania and Turkey.

KIRINIA CLIMENE *Lesser Lattice Brown*
Range. S. Russia, Caucasus, N. Iran. Map 341

K. climene Esper 1783 TL: S. Russia (Ukraine) **Pl. 59**
Description. ♂fw 23–24mm, ups dark brown; upf discal area orange-fulvous spreading across s4, s3 and into s2; uph medium brown, with or without small pd ocelli in yellow rings, hw margin scalloped; unh yellow grey, a pale mark often present at cell-end, pd ocelli black, yellow-ringed, variable. ♀ slightly larger, upf with small, yellowish sub-apical markings.
Flight. June/July in rough grassy places.
Distribution. Single specimens have been reported from Bulgaria, Romania and Yugoslav Macedonia; an established colony reported near Drama, N. Greece.

DANAIDAE

Bates 1861

Large butterflies, characteristic especially of the tropics of Africa and the Far East, of which two species occur in the Canary Islands. They are distasteful to birds, have an unpleasant smell, tough leathery integuments and are extraordinarily tenacious of life. In both sexes the forelegs are small, useless for walking; antennal club slender and slightly flexed.

DANAUS PLEXIPPUS   *Milkweed or Monarch*

Range. America from Peru to Canada; Australia, New Zealand, Papua and larger East Indian islands; Canary Islands. Absent from Africa and continental Asia.   No map

D. plexippus   Linnaeus 1758   TL: Pennsylvania   **Pl. 24**
Description. ♂fw 47mm, variable; ups chestnut-brown, veins and wing-borders lined black or dark brown, the latter including two marginal rows of small white spots; upf with scattered pale pd spots near apex; uph with small black sex-brand on v2; uns gc paler with similar markings. ♀gc paler, veins darker, esp. on hw, no sex-brand.
Flight. April or later in a succession of broods, perhaps throughout the year.
Habitat. Open places with flowers, etc, at low or moderate altitudes, very wide ranging. Foodplants *Asclepias curassavica, Gymnocarpus?*
Distribution. Canary Islands, recorded from Tenerife, Gran Canary, La Palma, Hiero, sometimes common. Azores. Occurs as a rare vagrant in Portugal, Spain, France, Ireland and England.
This remarkable American migratory butterfly made spectacular extensions of its range during the nineteenth century. It reached New Zealand in 1840, Australia in 1870 and the Canary Islands in 1880.

DANAUS CHRYSIPPUS   *Plain Tiger*

Range. Africa, south of the Atlas Mts., Arabia and thence throughout tropical Asia to Australia. Canary Islands.   No map

D. chrysippus   Linnaeus 1758   TL: Egypt   **Pl. 24**
Description. ♂fw 35/42mm, variable; ups light tawny-brown; upf darker chestnut-brown near base, apex broadly black with white transverse band and small white marginal spots; uph with three small black discal spots, black sex-brand on v2, black marginal border enclosing small white spots; uns gc paler, markings similar. ♀ similar, without sex-brand.
Flight. Throughout warm months.
Habitat. Open places at low or moderate altitudes. Foodplant *Asclepias.*
Distribution. Appears to be resident in the Canary Islands on Tenerife, La Palma, Gomera. Occasionally reported from the Mediterranean area, esp. Greece and S. Italy; a rare migrant in Morocco. Not reported from Algeria or Tunisia.

HESPERIIDAE

Latreille 1809

Skippers

These are small butterflies which differ widely from all others in the following characters. In the imago the head is wide, antennae widely separated, thorax robust. All wing-veins arise directly from the wing-base or from the discoidal cell, and all run without branching to the costa or outer margin. The antennal club often ends in a pointed tip – the apiculus. Larvae are cylindrical or fusiform, and the larval head appears large in relation to the slender neck and narrow first body segment. So far as known, all European species live in shelters made of grass or leaves, in which they pupate. The family is cosmopolitan. Males of the genera *Pyrgus*, *Syrichtus* and *Carcharodus* have the costa of the forewing folded over enclosing androconia.

PYRGUS MALVAE *Grizzled Skipper*
Range. Widely distributed throughout Europe and eastwards to Mongolia and Amurland.   Map 342

P. malvae malvae Linnaeus 1758   TL: Aland Is, Finland   **Pl. 61**
Description. ♂fw 11/13mm; ups white markings and spots sharply defined on both wings; *uph with clear-cut row of small white pd spots*; unh gc brown, often with green or yellowish tint, discal row of pale marks often broken in s2 and 3. ♀ usually slightly larger otherwise similar.
Flight. April/June and July/August in two broods in southern districts; in N. Europe and at high altitudes more often a single brood in May/June or later.
Habitat. Flowery banks, bogs and meadows from sea-level to 1800m. Food plants *Potentilla, Fragaria, Malva, Agrimonia*, etc.
Distribution. Central, northern and eastern Europe to 65°N. Absent from N. Scotland and Ireland.

P. malvae malvoides Elwes and Edwards 1897   TL: Biarritz
Description. Indistinguishable from *P. m. malvae* on external characters, but genitalia distinct.
Flight. April/June and July/August in two broods at low altitudes, a single brood in June/July at high altitudes.
Habitat. As for *P. m. malvae*.
Distribution. Throughout Spain and Portugal. France only in S. and SE. Switzerland in southern Alps to about 47°N. Istria and throughout Italy to Sicily. Absent from Corsica, Sardinia, Malta and Balearic Islands.

The next seven species form a difficult group. They are all closely related, lack well-marked specific characters, and show considerable local variation. It may be impossible to make a confident specific determination by external features, but most species are easily identified by the male genitalia.

The widely distributed and variable species *Pyrgus alveus* provides a convenient standard for comparison of specific characters with those of other species.

322

PYRGUS ALVEUS *Large Grizzled Skipper*
Range. From N. Africa and Spain through most of Europe to Caucasus, Altai Mts.
and Siberia. Map 343

P. alveus alveus Hübner 1803 TL: Germany (Verity 1940) **Pl. 61**
Description. ♂fw 14/16mm; ups gc dark grey-brown (nearly black when fresh)
often with yellowish flush; upf white spots of small to moderate size; uph rectangular
discal mark in s4 and 5, *small pd spots usually very obscure*; unh gc *olive-brown* to
greenish, pale discal band usually complete, but *spots in s2, 3 small*. ♀upf white spots
smaller, gc sometimes with golden reflection when fresh.
Flight. End June to August in a single brood.
Habitat. Flowery meadows, most often in hilly districts or in mountains at
900–1800m, rarely below 900m. Larval food plants *Potentilla, Helianthemum, Rubus,*
etc.
Distribution. France in Central Massif, Pyrenees, Jura, Vosges, thence through
Alps, Balkans and SE. Yugoslavia to N. Greece (Pindus); northwards through
Belgium, Germany and Poland to the Baltic countries but local and usually rare in its
northern range. Absent from Britain and Mediterranean islands except Sicily.

P. alveus centralhispaniae Verity 1925 TL: C. Spain **Pl. 61**
Description. ♂fw 14/16mm, often large, ups markings well developed, on uph often
extensive; ♀ ups pale markings usually reduced.
Flight and **Habitat** as for *P. a. alveus.*
Distribution. Common on the Montes Universales of C. Spain (Teruel), and from
there northwards, with a small anatomical modification (*P. a. accretus* Verity) in the
Cantabrian Mts and Pyrenees, thence across S. France to Dijon. A closely related
race occurs locally in the high Sierras of S. Spain, also C. Italy (Monte Sibillini etc.).
Similar species. *P. carthami* p. 327 is easily confused, but on upf has pale spot in
cell oblique, inclined very close to pale discoidal mark; in *alveus* these two spots are
well separated. *P. foulquieri picenus* p. 325, distinction very difficult, perhaps impossible without dissection.

P. alveus scandinavicus Strand 1903 TL: Dovre, Norway **Pl. 61**
syn: *ballotae* Oberthur 1910
Description. ♂fw 11/12mm, small, upf markings well defined, usually also on hw;
uns markings complete, often large, ♀ similar.
Flight. End June/July.
Habitat as for *P. a. alveus.*
Distribution. Fennoscandia, local but appears to be widely distributed to about
63°N.
Note. The small size and relatively large pale markings of *P. a. scandinavicus* are
distinctive, recalling *P. armoricanus.* The genitalia characters are unusual, but
variable; possibly two species are present in Scandinavia. The taxonomic status of
scandinavicus is uncertain; it is sometimes considered specifically distinct.

P. alveus numidus Oberthur 1910 TL: Lambessa, Algeria **Pl. 61**
Description. ♂fw 14/15mm; slightly larger than *P. a. alveus;* ups white markings
well developed; uph discal and pd spots prominent; unh pale markings rather
inconspicuous against pale yellowish gc. ♀ similar.
Flight. End May and August in two broods.
Habitat. Flowery slopes and meadows at 1500–1800m.

Distribution. Algeria (Lambessa). Morocco, Ifrane, Azrou, Anosseur, etc.; recorded from High Atlas.
Similar species. *P. armoricanus* below, smaller, broods emerge before and after *P. alveus*, flies commonly at lowland levels (*P. alveus* more in mountains); uph pale rectangular mark in s4 and 5 usually distinct; unh discal markings complete. *P. foulquieri* below, compared with *P. alveus*, ups more hairy, pale spots and markings much better defined; distribution restricted. *P. serratulae* p. 325, smaller, unh smooth olive-brown, pale markings well defined.

PYRGUS ARMORICANUS *Oberthur's Grizzled Skipper*
Range. From N. Africa and Europe to Iran.   Map 344

P. armoricanus armoricanus Oberthur 1910   TL: Rennes   **Pl. 61**
Description. ♂fw 12/14mm; upf white markings complete; *uph pale markings usually present* and discal spot sometimes prominent; unh resembles *P. alveus* with pale discal band well defined esp. in s4, 5, 6 and with large round spot in s1c. ♀ similar or ups white spots may be reduced. Specimens of *second brood* are often small.
Flight. May/June and August/September in two broods in S. Europe, a single brood in June/July in parts of northern range.
Habitat. Flowery banks from lowlands to 1200m or more.
Distribution. Widely distributed across Europe to 60°N, rare and local in northern range. Spain and Portugal; Corsica, Sardinia and Sicily; Hungary, the Balkans and Greece. Recorded from Denmark in N. and S. Seeland and Bornholm.
Similar species. *P. alveus* p. 323.

P. armoricanus maroccanus Picard 1950   TL: Morocco   **Pl. 61**
Description. ♂fw 14mm, slightly larger than *P. a. armoricanus*; ups white markings more prominent; uph pale submarginal spots well defined. ♀ similar.
Flight. June; probably a second brood in late summer.
Habitat. Flowery banks and rough ground at 1500–1800m.
Distribution. Flies in Middle Atlas in Morocco and Algeria, not recorded from High Atlas.
Similar species. *P. onopordi* p. 326, easily separable by yellowish gc and distinctive unh marking in anal area. *P. alveus numidus* p. 323 is larger.

PYRGUS FOULQUIERI *Foulquier's Grizzled Skipper*
Range. Confined to SW. Europe and Italy.   Map 345

P. foulquieri foulquieri Oberthur 1910   TL: Larche, Basses Alpes   **Pl. 61**
syn: *bellieri* Oberthur 1910
Description. ♂fw 14/15mm, ups noticeably hairy at wing-bases; resembles *P. alveus centralhispaniae, uph pale markings complete* and only lightly suffused, *pd spots large*, esp. *in s2 and 3*; unh gc yellow-brown, white markings usually slightly more extensive than in *P. alveus*. ♀ups with marked yellowish reflections and with smaller white markings.
Flight. Late July/August in a single brood.
Habitat. In mountains from valleys to 1800m.
Distribution. France, widely distributed in south-east and in Central Massif, Alpes Maritimes, Var, Bouches du Rhône, Isère, Aveyron, Hautes and Basses Alpes. Spain, only in Catalonia.

P. foulquieri picenus Verity 1920   TL: Bolognola, C. Italy
Description. ♂fw 13/14mm, small, ups general colour tone paler, yellowish, ups pale markings complete; unh yellowish, usually slightly mottled darker, white markings large and complete. ♀ similar.
Flight. July/August.
Habitat. Mountainous districts at 600–1300m.
Distribution. Central Italy in Monti Sibillini, Abruzzi, Monte Aurunci, etc., but very local.
Similar species. *P. alveus centralhispaniae* Verity p. 323.

PYRGUS WARRENENSIS   *Warren's Skipper*
Range. Local in the Eastern Alps.   Map 346

P. warrenensis Verity 1928   TL: Switzerland, Grisons   **Pl. 61**
syn: *alticola* Evans nec Rebel
Description. ♂fw 12mm or less; like *P. alveus* but very small, ups dark, white markings minute and scanty; unh markings small but complete. ♀ups basal hair yellowish.
Flight and **Habitat.** July/August in a single brood, flying over short grassy slopes from 1800m upwards, often with *P. alveus*.
Distribution. Very local in E. Alps, Brenner, Stelvio, Hohe Tauern. Switzerland in Grisons. Reported from Basses Alpes, Piedmont, Ortler Alps and Savoie.

PYRGUS SERRATULAE   *Olive Skipper*
Range. From Spain across C. Europe to Transbaical.   Map 347

P. serratulae Rambur 1839   TL: Spain   **Pl. 61**
Description. ♂fw 12/14mm, upf markings variable, white spots sometimes very small; *uph pale markings generally obscure* or vestigial; *unh gc olive to yellow-green without secondary mottling.* ♀ups white markings usually very small, sometimes absent in s1b and s2 on upf, often with brassy suffusion over the whole wing.
Flight. End June/August in a single brood, one of the first species to appear in early summer.
Habitat. Usually in hilly or mountainous districts, from low levels (rare) to 2400m in late summer. Larval food plants *Potentilla, Alchemilla.*
Distribution. S. and C. Europe to 52°N, occasional farther north, absent from NW. France, Holland and NW. Germany; a mountain species in peninsular Italy.
Variation. Size varies, large specimens, f. *major* Staudinger Pl. 61 with fw 15/16mm occur in lowlands in SW. France and elsewhere (Vendée, Gironde, Charente, etc.) and in Balkans, racial in Greece.
Similar species. Other small *Pyrgus* esp. *P. alveus.* The pattern of well-defined pale markings on a smooth olive-brown or yellowish unh gc is distinctive of *P. serratulae. P. carthami* p. 327, which often flies with *P. serratulae* in mid-June is larger and has well-defined small pale pd spots on uph.

PYRGUS CARLINAE   *Carline Skipper*
Range. Confined to south-western Alps.   Map 348

P. carlinae carlinae Rambur 1839   TL: Dalecarlia (error)   **Pl. 61**
Description. ♂fw 13/14mm, *upf white cell mark narrow, divided, shaped like letter C* outwardly concave; uph pale markings obscure; *unh gc usually pale reddish-brown,* discal markings in s2 and s3 minute or absent, *white marginal mark on vein 5*

prominent. ♀ups usually with yellowish flush, white markings very small or partly obsolete. See text figure p. 328.
Flight. July/August.
Habitat. Mountain pastures, often assembling in scores at damp places on paths, most common at 1500–2400m, occasional at lower altitudes. Larval food plant *Potentilla verna*.
Distribution. France, from Maritime Alps northwards to Savoie and on Italian slopes in Piedmont. Switzerland, on Alps of Valais and east to Ticino and Campiglio, northwards to Interlaken but uncommon north of Rhône valley.

P. carlinae cirsii   Rambur 1839   TL: Fontainebleau, France Map 349   **Pl. 61**
Description. ♂fw 13/14mm, upf all white markings prominent, *cell spot usually wide, rectangular; uph pale markings, esp. spot at base of s4 and 5*, and submarginal spots *distinct*, often yellowish; unh gc yellowish olive to reddish-brown, spots of discal band small, mark on margin on v5 brownish, inconspicuous; veins paler. ♀ similar.
Flight. Late July/August in a single brood.
Habitat. Flowery slopes, often at low altitudes, rarely above 1300m. Larval food plant *Potentilla verna*, etc.
Distribution. Spain in Catalonia, Aragon, Andalusia, etc. France, E. Pyrenees, Central Massif and northwards to Paris, more common in SE., e.g., Var, Alpes Maritimes, Bouches du Rhône and northwards to Haute Savoie. Switzerland in Canton Vaud. Germany, Nurnberg (Pottenstein) and occasional in S. Bavaria and probably further east to Vienna and beyond. Not recorded with certainty from N. Italy.
Similar species. *P. serratulae* p. 325, which may fly at the same time and in the same localities; unh olive-grey, without reddish tints, uph white marginal mark on v5 not especially prominent.
Note. It is known that these two taxa breed together freely where their distributional frontiers meet. On this account they are graded in this book as subspecies of a single taxon. Treated as semi-species by some authors.

PYRGUS ONOPORDI   *Rosy Grizzled Skipper*
Range. Confined to SW. Europe and N. Africa.   Map 350

P. onopordi   Rambur 1839   TL: Granada, S. Spain   **Pl. 61**
Description. ♂fw 11/14mm, ups gc dark brown with slightly yellow tint; upf markings clearly defined; uph pale markings generally distinct, yellowish, esp. a pale mark near costa in s7; unh gc light yellow-brown, marbled darker, with yellow veins, a *prominent anvil-shaped discoidal spot in s4 and 5* and another large spot in 1c (signe de Blachier). See text figure p. 328. ♀ usually slightly larger and ups darker, with fewer yellow scales.
Flight. April/June and July/September in two broods.
Habitat. Flowery meadows from lowlands to 1300m in Europe and to 1700m in N. Africa.
Distribution. SW. Europe to 46°N, including the Rhône valley and the southern slopes of the Alps, but commonest in Spain, Portugal, peninsular Italy and SE. France. N. Africa, widely distributed in Middle Atlas and High Atlas in Morocco and Algeria, up to 2200m. Absent from Mediterranean islands.
Similar species. *P. c. cirsii* above, which flies in late summer, ups darker, less yellow, upf white spots prominent, quadrate. *P. armoricanus* p. 324.

PYRGUS CINARAE *Sandy Grizzled Skipper*
Range. C. Spain, S. Balkans and eastwards locally through S. Russia to Turkestan. Map 351

P. cinarae cinarae Rambur 1839 TL: Sarepta **Pl. 62**
Description. ♂fw 15/16mm, ups gc very dark; *upf white spots large* esp. dumb-bell shaped spot near cell-end; uph two small basal spots, discal markings clear and well defined; unf white markings large; unh gc olive-brown, white spots conspicuous but not large. ♀ups *gc medium brown; ups pale markings less distinct and very small*; unh gc pale yellow-brown, white markings small, pearly, discrete.
Flight. End June.
Habitat. Dry stony slopes with scanty grass at 900m. Larval food plant not known.
Distribution. SE. Yugoslavia (Skopje). N. Greece. Albania. Bulgaria (Sliven).

P. cinarae clorinda Warren 1927 TL: Spain, Prov. Cuenca
Description. Differs from the eastern form in the slightly yellowish ups gc; unh gc definitely yellow. ♀ups with noticeable yellow flush.
Flight. July.
Habitat. In mountainous districts.
Distribution. C. Spain, local in Province Cuenca, e.g., Villacabras, Jardin Encatada, etc.

PYRGUS SIDAE *Yellow-banded Skipper*
Range. From Provence, C. Italy and Balkans to Asia Minor and Iran. Map 352

P. sidae sidae Esper 1782 TL: Volga, S. Russia **Pl. 61**
Description. ♂fw 16/18mm, ups dark brown with greyish hair at wing-bases; upf cell-spot large, small submarginal spots usually all present; uph markings variable, pale spots sometimes prominent; *unh gc white, discal and pale pd bands bright yellow*; upf costal fold inconspicuous. ♀ similar, ups pale basal hair less conspicuous.
Flight. June/July in a single brood.
Habitat. Open places and flowery meadows, lowlands to 1500m. Larval food plants Malvaceae, esp. *Abutilon avicennae.*
Distribution. Balkans; Bulgaria, Greece, Yugoslavia south of Mostar and Sarajevo. Romania, Dobrogea, Banat.

P. sidae occiduus Verity 1925 TL: Tuscany **Pl. 61**
Description. ♂fw 13/16mm, ups spots smaller; unh discal and pd bands pale yellow.
Flight. June/early July in a single brood.
Habitat. Flowery banks and meadows, from lowlands to 1300m.
Distribution. Italy, local in Apennines from Modena to Monte Aurunci; Florence; Liguria, Alassio, Genoa District, Belluna and Istria etc. France, only in Provence, i.e., Alpes Maritimes, Var, Basses Alpes, Bouches du Rhône and Hérault.

PYRGUS CARTHAMI *Safflower Skipper*
Range. S. and C. Europe, including N. Greece. S. Russia to C. Asia. Map 353

P. carthami Hübner 1819 **Pl. 61**
syn: *fritillarius* auct. nec Poda
Description. ♂fw 15/17mm, ups gc dark charcoal-grey with pale hair at wing-bases; upf usual white markings well developed; uph submarginal pale spots gen-

erally well defined; unh gc yellow-grey, *white markings narrowly bordered darker grey with distinctive mottled appearance.* ♀ similar, often larger, ups pale downy hair absent.
Flight. End June to early September in a single prolonged brood.
Habitat. Flowery banks and meadows from lowlands to 1500m or more. Larval food plants mallow, *Potentilla, Althaea,* etc.
Distribution. Generally distributed and often abundant in S. and C. Europe northwards to Baltic. Absent from Britain, Denmark, Holland, NW. Germany, NW. France, and Mediterranean islands. Reported from Sicily.
Variation. In S. Spain ups often brightly marked with larger white spots, f. *nevadensis* Oberthur.
Similar species. *P. alveus* p. 323.

PYRGUS ANDROMEDAE   *Alpine Grizzled Skipper*
Range. Confined to Europe.   Map 354

P. andromedae Wallengren 1853   TL: Dovre, Norway   **Pl. 61**
Description. ♂fw 13/15mm, ups resembles *P. alveus*; upf white spots well defined in standard pattern, *small spot present at base of s2* with twin longitudinal spots just below in s1b; uph pale markings generally heavily obscured; unh gc olive-brown to yellowish, discoidal spot large and extended basad along median vein, gc dark grey in s1a–1b with prominent round white spot in s1c and a short white streak above it (see text figure p. 329). ♀ generally similar.
Flight. June/July in a single brood.
Habitat. Rough hillsides, moorland, etc., often near water; flies from 1500m upwards in Pyrenees and Alps, at low altitudes in N. Norway. Larval food plants not known.
Distribution. Scandinavia, on main mountain system from Dovre to North Cape, most common within the Arctic Circle. C. and S. Europe, occurs at high levels on all principal mountain ranges from C. Pyrenees through Alps to Grossglockner and Julian Alps (Triglav) and northwards to Bavaria; Bosnia and SE. Yugoslavia (Schar Planina), probably widely distributed. Absent from Portugal, Spain, including Cantabrian Mts. (but reported from the Val d'Aran), E. Pyrenees (?), peninsular Italy and Greece, Tatra Mts. and Carpathians.
Similar species. *P. centaureae* p. 329, upf lacks small white spot at base of s2; unh dark grey, veins lined white, *P. cacaliae* below, ups white spots generally very small; upf lacks white spot at base of s2 and twin white marks below it; unh markings often rather indistinct.

PYRGUS CACALIAE   *Dusky Grizzled Skipper*
Range. Confined to Europe.   Map 355

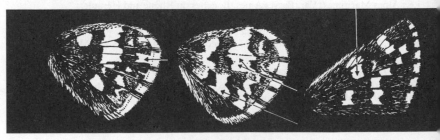

Pyrgus carlinae unh   *P. onopordi* unh   *P. cirsii* upf

P. cacaliae   Rambur 1839   TL: 'Alps'   **Pl. 61**

Description. ♂fw 13/15mm; ups gc grey-brown; upf white spots often very small, sometimes partly absent or minute, *no white spot at base of s2*; unh gc grey to grey-brown, markings white, not sharply defined, inner margin scarcely darker, a white spot in s1c and a short white streak above it. ♀ similar.

Flight. End June/July/August in a single brood, flight lasts about four weeks.

Habitat. Only on high mountains at alpine levels from 1800m upwards. Larval food plants *Potentilla, Sibbaldia*.

Distribution. Alpes Maritimes and eastwards to Grosser Sau Alp and Gross Glockner, northwards to Allgäuer Alps; recorded from Rilo Dagh in Bulgaria and local in Romania in S. Carpathians (Bucegi Mts.). Also reported in Pyrenees.

Variation. Upf white spots larger in Carpathians.

Similar species. *P. andromedae* p. 328.

PYRGUS CENTAUREAE   *Northern Grizzled Skipper*

Range. N. Scandinavia and Arctic Russia, Altai Mts., Sajan Mts. N. America widely distributed in arctic regions and extending to Appalachians and through Rocky Mts. to S. Colorado (Pike's Peak).   Map 356

P. centaureae   Rambur 1839   TL: Lapland   **Pl. 61**

Description. ♂fw 13/15mm, ups dark grey, usually clouded with pale hair; upf white spots well developed in usual pattern but *no spot at base of s2*; uph white markings prominent, including pd spots, a conspicuous pale mark in s7 near costa; unh gc rather dark grey, pale markings bold, *veins lined white*, the large discal spot produced basad along median vein. ♀ similar.

Flight. June/July depending upon climate; flies in a single brood.

Habitat. Heathy bogs and tundra, from sea-level to 900m, in mountainous districts. Larval food plant *Rubus chamaemorus*.

Distribution. Fennoscandia, widely distributed except in cultivated southern districts.

Similar species. *P. andromedae* p. 328.

Note. The American subspecies *Pyrgus freija* Warren, has been reported from Lapland, perhaps based upon mis-identified specimens.

SPIALIA SERTORIUS   *Red Underwing Skipper*

Range. N. Africa, S. Europe, W. Asia to Chitral, Altai Mts., Tibet and Amur. Map 357

S. sertorius sertorius   Hoffmannsegg 1804   TL: Germany   **Pl. 62**
(Hemming 1936)
   syn: *sao* Hübner (invalid homonym); *hibiscae* Hemming 1936

Description. ♂fw 11/13mm, ups dark brown to black, white spots small; upf pd

P. andromedae unh   *P. alveus centralitaliae* upf   *P. carthami* upf

spots often absent in s4 or s5 or both, submarginal series generally complete; uph discoidal spot small; unf dark grey; unh *brick red*, less commonly yellowish, discal band of white spots sharply curved with large round spots on costa in s7, 8, *discoidal spot curved*. ♀ similar, usually larger.

Flight. April/May/June and July/August in two broods; in late broods often very small.

Habitat. Rough ground and mountainsides from lowlands to 1500m in its southern range. Larval food plants *Sanguisorba, Rubus, Potentilla*.

Distribution. Widely distributed from Spain and Portugal through S. and C. Europe to 52°N, eastwards to Bavaria, Trieste, peninsular Italy. Reported from Czechoslovakia, N. Hungary and on two recent occasions from Corsica. Absent from Britain, N. France, Belgium north of Ardennes.

S. sertorius therapne   Rambur 1832   TL: Corsica   **Pl. 62**
Description. ♂fw 9/10mm, the smallest European Skipper; ups dark brown shaded yellow, pale markings all yellowish and rather large, esp. upf cell-spot which is more or less square; submarginal spots rarely present; uns red-brown with pale markings arranged as in *S. s. sertorius*. ♀ slightly larger.

Flight. April and September in two broods.

Habitat. Mountainous country to 1500m. Larval food plant not known.

Distribution. Confined to Corsica and Sardinia. Typical *S. s. sertorius* has been reported from Corsica more than once, and specimens taken at Corte and Evisa have been described as being intermediate between it and *S. s. therapne*.

S. sertorius ali   Oberthur 1881   TL: Morocco   **Pl. 62**
Description. ♂fw 9/11mm, ups markings slightly larger and faintly shaded yellow; *unh pale brown marbled with dark striae*, white markings sometimes nacreous, the discoidal spot prominent with pointed proximal and distal projections, veins conspicuously pale brown. ♀ similar.

Flight. April/June and September in two broods.

Habitat. Rough mountain sides and flowery slopes. Larval food plant not known.

Distribution. Morocco, in Middle Atlas, High Atlas and El Rif. Algeria. Tunisia. Widespread but rarely common.

Similar species. *S. phlomidis* p. 331, larger, uph discoidal spot large and rectangular, unh large pale costal spot not round.

SPIALIA ORBIFER   *Orbed Red-underwing Skipper*
Range. E. Europe with Sicily and Balkan countries, S. Russia and W. Asia to Afghanistan, Tibet and the Amur.   Map 358

S. orbifer   Hübner 1823   TL: not stated   **Pl. 62**
Description. ♂fw 12/14mm, like *S. sertorius*, ups white markings better defined (except in Sicily); unh *gc olive grey* (not red) pale basal mark on costa *round, usually prominent*. ♀ similar, often slightly larger.

Flight. April/June and July/August in two broods. Late brood specimens often small, ♂fw 11mm.

Habitat. As for *S. sertorius*, on rough, open ground. Larval food-plant *Sanguisorba minor*. (Rosaceae).

Distribution. In Europe, Hungary, Romania, Istria, Sicily and throughout the Balkans and Greece. In Hungary the range overlaps that of *S. sertorius*.

SPIALIA PHLOMIDIS *Persian Skipper*
Range. From S. Balkans through S. Russia and Asia Minor to Iran. Map 359

S. phlomidis Herrich-Schäffer 1845   TL: Sea of Marmora, Turkey   **Pl. 62**
Description. ♂fw 14/15mm, ups gc black, markings as in *S. sertorius* but white spots larger, base of costa white, a white mark at base of s1b; uph discoidal spot large, rectangular, submarginal spot in s4 large; *unh gc pale olive-grey*, white markings well defined, *costal spot not round* but *linked to white discoidal spot.* ♀ similar.
Flight. June/early July. No record of a second brood.
Habitat. Flies at low or moderate altitudes in rough flowery places.
Distribution. Greece, SE. Yugoslavia and Albania. A very local species.
Similar species. *S. sertorius* p. 329. *S. doris* below, smaller, unh white mark in s7 well separated from large discoidal spot.

SPIALIA DORIS *Aden Skipper*
Range. High Atlas of Morocco, Egypt, Somaliland (Tajora, TL of *S. doris* Walker 1870) and Arabia to India.   Map 360

S. doris Evans 1949   TL: High Atlas, Ziz Valley   **Pl. 62**
Description. ♂fw 12mm, very similar to *S. phlomidis* but smaller and fw more pointed; ups gc black, white markings large; upf white crescentic discoidal spot and subapical spots well marked, base of costa grey; uph discoidal spot large, square; uns gc dull greenish-grey, markings as on ups; unf costal area pale grey; *unh spot in s7 well separated from large white discoidal spot.* ♀ similar.
Flight. April/May and September.
Habitat. Dry valleys with sparse vegetation. Food plant in Egypt *Convolvulus lanatus.*
Distribution. Morocco, southern slopes of High Atlas, Ziz Valley at 900–1200m, El Aioun du Drââ, 400m.

SYRICHTUS TESSELLUM *Tessellated Skipper*
Range. S. Balkans, S. Russia and eastwards to Iran and Amurland.   Map 361

S. tessellum Hübner 1803   TL: S. Russia   **Pl. 62**
Description. ♂fw 16/18mm, ups gc dark grey, *white markings large, fully developed on both wings*; upf a *single pair of discal spots in s1b*; uns gc pale olive-brown, darker at base of fw, white markings as above. ♀ similar.
Flight. End May/June in a single brood.
Habitat. Flowery meadows from lowlands to 900m or more. Larval food plant not known. Larval food plant *Phlomis tuberosa.*
Distribution. S. Balkans, N. Greece and SE. Yugoslavia.
Note. The form *nomas* Lederer, with uns of both wings nearly white and inconspicuous markings, has not yet been found in Europe although common in Asia Minor.
Similar species. *S. cribrellum* below, smaller, markings larger, upf normally with two pairs of discal spots in s1b.

SYRICHTUS CRIBRELLUM *Spinose Skipper*
Range. From Romania across S. Russia to Altai Mts. and Amurland.   Map 362

S. cribrellum Eversmann 1841   TL: S. Russia   **Pl. 62**
Description. ♂fw 13/16mm, resembles *S. tessellum*, slightly smaller but markings

larger, clear white and sharply defined; upf *two pairs of discal spots in s1b*; unh gc olive-yellow, *white markings large and tending to coalesce*, esp. those in submarginal area.
Flight. End May/June.
Habitat. Dry steppe country. Larval food plant *Potentilla* sp.
Distribution. In Europe known only from W. Romania on Pannonian plain at Cluj and Hunedoara.
Similar species. *S. tessellum* p. 331.

SYRICHTUS PROTO   *Sage Skipper*
Range. From N. Africa, Portugal and Spain through S. Europe to Asia Minor.
Map 363

S. proto   Ochsenheimer 1808   TL: Portugal   **Pl. 62**
Description. ♂fw 14/15mm; ups gc dark grey, often somewhat obscured by yel-lowish hair, discal spots white or yellowish, well developed, *submarginal markings lunular, indistinct*; unh gc variable, yellow-grey to sandy-red, pale markings as above in white or sandy, often indistinct. ♀ similar, but ups without yellow hair.
Flight. April/May or later, in a single brood, but emergence sometimes occurs at intervals throughout summer.
Habitat. Waste ground in lowlands or lower mountain slopes; to 1700m in Morocco. Larval food plant *Phlomis*.
Distribution. Portugal. Spain (common). France, many localities in Provence, esp. near coast, rare north of Hautes Alpes. Italy and Sicily. Greece, on Mt. Taygetos, Mt. Parnassus, etc. Morocco. Algeria, Constantine, not rare.
Variation. In spring and early summer often large, with unh gc olive-grey; in late summer often smaller with unh gc brown or red-brown. Large forms with ♂fw 15/17mm, f. *fulvosatura* Verity Pl. 62, are common in Morocco.
Similar species. *S. mohammed* below, in N. Africa, ups markings more yellow-brown; unh with some spaces filled dark brown, veins lined pale brown. *S. leuzeae* p. 332.

SYRICHTUS MOHAMMED   *Barbary Skipper*
Range. Confined to Morocco and Algeria.   Map 364

S. mohammed   Oberthur 1887   TL: Lambessa, Algeria   **Pl. 62**
Description. ♂fw 15/16mm, resembles *S. proto*; outer margin of hw distinctly wavy; ups all markings better defined, yellowish; small submarginal spots generally distinct; unh gc brown or red-brown, *veins paler*, in pd area *some spaces filled dark brown* esp. s1c, 2, 3, white markings small, sometimes partially ringed black, prominent pale discal spot usually shining (nacreous).
Flight. March/June and August/September in two broods.
Habitat. Rough places and flowery banks at 1500–1800m. Food plant *Phlomis*.
Distribution. Morocco, Azrou. Algeria, Aflou, Teniet-el-Haad, etc.
Variation. *First brood* small, ♂fw about 14mm, f. *caid* Le Cerf, unh gc dark brown. The *second brood* described above is larger with unh red-brown.
Similar species. *S. proto* above.

SYRICHTUS LEUZEAE   *Algerian Grizzled Skipper*
Range. Confined to Algeria.   Map 365

S. leuzeae Oberthur 1881 TL: Algeria **Pl. 62**
Description. ♂fw 15mm, ups resembles *S. proto*; ups gc dark grey; upf discal spot in cell very large; uph white markings reduced; uns both wings suffused pale grey with rather obscure markings; *unh*, white discal band narrow but regular and complete, submarginal pale spots present, pattern faintly reticulate.
Flight. May and July.
Habitat. Flowery meadows.
Distribution. Algeria.
Similar species. *S. proto* p. 332, uph discal markings less complete; upf discal cell-spot smaller; unh markings not reticulate.

CARCHARODUS ALCEAE *Mallow Skipper*
Range. From N. Africa and Spain through S. and C. Europe to C. Asia. Map 366

C. alceae Esper 1780 TL: Germany **Pl. 62**
Description. ♂fw 13/16mm, ups gc brown marbled darker brown and grey; upf hyaline cell-spot very narrow, sometimes absent; *uph with vague paler discal and pd markings*; uns gc paler brown; *unf without hair-tuft*; unh a small white or yellow spot near base of cell, spots in s1c, 2, 4, 5 and 7 forming a discal row, traces of submarginal series. ♀ often larger, otherwise similar.
Flight. April/May and later in two or three broods throughout summer.
Habitat. Flowery banks, etc., to 1500m usually in hilly country. Larval food plants *Malva, Althaea, Hibiscus*, etc.
Distribution. N. Africa, widely distributed in Morocco, Algeria and Tunisia. S. and C. Europe to 52°N. Absent from Denmark, Fennoscandia, Baltic countries and Britain.
Variation. Seasonal changes may be marked. Specimens of the *first brood* are usually dark; in warm districts *second and third broods* are often paler brown. In S. Italy, Sicily, etc., the last brood (September) is very dark and small, ♂fw 13/14mm.
Similar species. *C. flocciferus* p. 334, hw markings better defined, esp. uph discoidal spot; ♂ with hair pencil on unf from v1 near base.

CARCHARODUS LAVATHERAE *Marbled Skipper*
Range. From N. Africa through S. Europe to Asia Minor. Map 367

C. lavatherae Esper 1780 TL: S. France **Pl. 62**
Description. ♂fw 14/17mm, upf light olive-brown often suffused greenish and marbled darker, with white streaks at outer margin esp. in s4 and s5, vitreous spots prominent esp. cell-spot and spot in s2; uph darker with *conspicuous white discal spots*, pd spots sagittate, pointed basad; uns very pale greenish-white, slightly darker in discal areas, markings vestigial. ♂unf without hair-tuft. ♀ similar.
Flight. May/June or later, usually a single brood, but second broods have been reported.
Habitat. Dry flowery slopes esp. on calcareous soils, usually in hilly districts, from lowlands to 1500m or more. Larval food plant *Stachys*.
Distribution. S. and C. districts of Europe to 50°N, local and scarce N. of the Alps. Widely distributed through the Middle Atlas in Morocco, Algeria and Tunisia. Absent from Corsica, Sardinia, Sicily.
Variation. In Spain and S. Balkans gc may be darker, more grey-brown.

CARCHARODUS BOETICUS *Southern Marbled Skipper*
Range. N. Africa, SW. Europe and C. Italy; Asia Minor to Iran. Map 368

C. boeticus boeticus Rambur 1839 TL: Andalusia **Pl. 62**
syn: *marrubii* Rambur 1840

Description. ♂fw 13/14mm, upf grey, slightly marbled darker grey-brown, a narrow pale grey discal band limiting a darker basal area, hyaline spots not large; uph darker brown, usually with small pale basal spot and discal and pd series of pale spots and lunules, the discoidal spot generally prominent; unf gc grey-brown with paler veins; unh pale yellow-grey, *veins, basal spots, discal spots and pd lunules* all almost white and *together producing a reticulate pattern*; fringes chequered. ♀ similar. ♂unf *with hair-tuft.*

Flight. May to September/October in two or three broods.

Habitat. Rough places and flowery slopes to 1500m, usually in hot localities, most frequent among mountains. Larval food plants *Marrubium vulgare, Ballota foetida,* etc.

Distribution. Portugal. Spain, south of Pyrenees and Cantabrian Mts. France in E. Pyrenees and Provence. Switzerland in a single brood in Valais. N. Italy, Susa, and very local in Apennines and Sicily. Records from Yugoslavia and Greece need confirmation.

Variation. Colour varies through the seasons; in *first brood* (May) dark on ups; *second brood* (end June) paler grey-brown, often inclining to sandy; *late broods* (August/September) light sandy brown. The hair-tuft on unf also varies, being large and dark in early summer but pale sandy-brown and sometimes small in late broods.

C. boeticus stauderi Reverdin 1913 TL: El Kantara, Algeria **Pl. 62**
Description. ♂fw 13/14mm, like *C. b. boeticus* in size and appearance; unh pale veins and lattice pattern usually rather less well developed. The distinctive character is a slight difference in the structure of the male genitalia.

Flight and **Habitat** as for *C. b. boeticus.*

Distribution. N. Africa, from Morocco to Cyrenaica, flying in the Middle Atlas. Not known from Europe.

Similar species. *C. flocciferus* below and *C. orientalis* p. 335, unh markings are not reticulate.

CARCHARODUS FLOCCIFERUS *Tufted Marbled Skipper*
Range. From Spain across S. Europe to Bulgaria and Greece. Map 369

C. flocciferus Zeller 1847 TL: Sicily **Pl. 62**
syn: *alchymillae* Hemming 1936; *altheae* Hübner 1803 (invalid homonym).

Description. ♂fw 14/16mm; ups gc dark grey-brown marbled with darker striae which form a wide band across fw before the vitreous cell-spot; uph basal and discal spots pale, pd markings vague; unf grey-brown, paler, with white marginal striae and *prominent dark hair-tuft; unh grey-brown,* white markings better defined than on ups, including small submarginal spots. ♀ similar.

Flight. End May/June and end July/August in two broods.

Habitat. Flowery banks and rough ground esp. among mountains to 1800m, less common at low levels. Larval food plants *Marrubium, Stachys.*

Distribution. S. and C. Europe to 48°N, somewhat farther N. along Rhine into Baden and eastwards to SE. Yugoslavia, Bulgaria and Greece. Absent or scarce in N. and W. France, S. Spain, Portugal, Corsica and Sardinia.

Similar species. *C. alceae* p. 333; *C. boeticus* above; *C. orientalis* p. 335.

CARCHARODUS ORIENTALIS *Oriental Marbled Skipper*
Range. From Montenegro and Greece widespread in W. Asia to Iran.
Map 370

C. orientalis Reverdin 1913 TL: S. Greece **Pl. 62**
Description. ♂fw 14/15mm, ups gc variable, usually grey rather than brown, often slightly yellowish; upf markings as in *C. flocciferus*; uph white discal and submarginal markings well developed, often complete; unf gc grey; *unh gc pale grey with obscure white markings.* ♀ similar. ♂unf dark hair-tuft generally conspicuous.
Flight. April onwards, probably in two broods.
Habitat. Flowery meadows usually in mountainous country, to 1200m. Larval food plant not recorded.
Distribution. Montenegro, Albania, Greece, Bulgaria.
Note. Though both *C. flocciferus* and *C. orientalis* occur in Greece and in Macedonia, they do not fly together. The former flies at 1100–2000m, the latter in hot, low-lying localities. Their ♂ genitalia are distinct.
Similar species. *C. flocciferus* p. 334, unh gc dark grey-brown. *C. boeticus* p. 334.

ERYNNIS TAGES *Dingy Skipper*
Range. Europe to 62°N, thence across Russia and Siberia to China. Map 371

E. tages Linnaeus 1758 TL: Europe **Pl. 62**
Description. ♂fw 13/14mm, ups gc brown; upf three white dots on costa near apex, *complete series of white marginal dots,* oblique sub-basal and pd sinuous dark brown bands enclosing powdered pale grey area; uph white marginal dots as on fw and white or yellowish pd spots in some specimens; uns paler brown with white marginal dots on both wings, otherwise unmarked. ♀ similar. ♂ with costal fold.
Flight. May/June or later with a partial or complete second brood in some southern localities.
Habitat. Flowery banks to 1800m, often associated with calcareous soils. Larval food plants *Lotus corniculatus, Eryngium, Coronilla,* etc.
Distribution. S. and C. Europe to Britain and S. Scandinavia. Absent from Mediterranean islands. Local in N. Germany and rare in Lithuania.
Variation. Colour forms range from typical dark brown through medium brown, f. *brunnea* Tutt, to grey, f. *clarus* Caradja. Of these, f. *brunnea*, with vestigial ups markings, is very common in S. Europe. Ireland, in Co. Clare, Galway and Co. Mayo, brightly variegated, ups dark brown and pale grey, f. *baynesi* Huggins.
Similar species. *E. marloyi* below (Greece only), upf dark transverse bands distinct, ♂ without costal fold.

ERYNNIS MARLOYI *Inky Skipper*
Range. S. Balkans through Asia Minor and Syria to Iran and Chitral. Map 372

E. marloyi Boisduval 1834 TL: S. Greece **Pl. 62**
Description. ♂fw 14/15mm, ups dark brown, *marginal white dots inconspicuous or absent*; upf narrow black sub-basal and oblique pd transverse black bands mixed with grey, with two or three white dots before apex; uph unmarked; unf white dots before apex as on ups. ♀ often larger, ups gc paler. ♂ without costal fold.
Flight. May/June, perhaps a second brood in some places.
Habitat. Mountainous districts to 1800m or more. Larval food plant not recorded.
Distribution. In Europe only in Greece, Albania and SE. Yugoslavia. The Catalonian record on p. 28 of the 2nd and 3rd editions is mistaken.
Similar species. *E. tages* above.

HETEROPTERUS MORPHEUS   *Large Chequered Skipper*
Range. From N. Spain through much of S. and C. Europe and C. Asia to Amurland and Korea.   Map 373

H. morpheus   Pallas 1771   TL: Samara, S. Russia   **Pl. 63**
    syn: *steropes* Denis and Schiffermüller 1775
Description. ♂fw 16/18mm, ups dark brown; upf with three or four small yellow pre-apical spots near costa; uph unmarked; unf with yellow markings at apex and along outer margin; unh gc yellow with twelve large whitish black-ringed spots, wide black band down inner margin and black marginal line. ♀upf yellow apical markings larger; fringes chequered black and white; uns as in ♂.
Flight. End June/July in a single brood.
Habitat. Shady and woodland roads to 1000m. Larval food plant *Brachypodium*, *Molinia caerulea*, *Phragmitis* and *Calamgrostis*.
Distribution. Local in widely dispersed colonies. Spain in coastal area near Santander. France, only N. and W. of Central Massif and S. to Basses Pyrénées. Switzerland in warm valleys of Ticino. Italy, in Piedmont and E. to Alto Adige and Gorizia, also in Lazio, not rare in damp places. More widely distributed in N. Germany and Lithuania. Bosnia, Serbia and Romania. Recorded also from Jersey, NW. Germany, Holland and Denmark. Throughout its extensive range geographical variation is negligible.

CARTEROCEPHALUS PALAEMON   *Chequered Skipper*
Range. From W. Europe across C. and N. Asia to Japan; N. America.   Map 374

C. palaemon   Pallas 1771   TL: Russia   **Pl. 63**
Description. ♂fw 14mm, *upf dark brown with large basal and pd dark yellow spots*, small submarginal spots in series; uph one basal and two discal spots all large and a row of small pd spots, all yellow; unh dark brownish powdered yellow, yellow markings as on ups but paler on hw. ♀ups gc more grey, markings in paler yellow.
Flight. June/July in a single brood.
Habitat. Usually in light woodland, to 1500m in S. Alps. Larval food plants grasses esp. *Bromus*.
Distribution. Widely distributed in NE. and C. Europe, extending across N. and C. France with colonies in Pyrenees, England and Scotland. A very local species absent from large areas including Denmark, peninsular Italy, SE. France and Spain but recorded from the Val d'Aran. In Balkans recorded from Bosnia, Hercegovina and Bulgaria.
Similar species. *C. silvicolus* below, upf gc yellow with dark markings; uph with an additional yellow spot near costa.

CARTEROCEPHALUS SILVICOLUS   *Northern Chequered Skipper*
Range. Fennoscandia and through Siberia to Amurland and Kamschatka. Japan. Map 375

C. silvicolus   Meigen 1829   TL: Brunswick, Germany   **Pl. 63**
    syn: *sylvius* Knoch 1781 (invalid homonym)
Description. ♂fw 12/13mm, *upf gc light yellow with discal and very small submarginal spots* all black; uph gc black with yellow discal and submarginal spots arranged as in *C. palaemon* but with prominent *additional spot near costa*; uns markings as on ups. ♀upf dark markings greatly extended, basal area and outer margin dark.

Flight. End June/July in a single brood.

Habitat. Woodland and warm valleys with abundant vegetation at low altitudes. Food plants *Cynosurus* and other woodland grasses.

Distribution. Fennoscandia, not in mountainous districts, extending through Baltic countries including N. Poland, to Neubrandenburg and Holstein.

Similar species. *C. palaemon* p. 336.

THYMELICUS ACTEON *Lulworth Skipper*

Range. From Canary Islands and N. Africa across S. and C. Europe to Cyprus, Lebanon and Asia Minor. Map 376

T. acteon acteon Rottemburg 1775 TL: Lansberg-an-der-Warthe, **Pl. 63**
Germany

Description. ♂fw 11/13mm, ups gc dusky fulvous; upf a yellow streak in cell and a *bowed series of small yellow pd spots* in s3–9, often very obscure; uph unmarked; uns gc uniformly orange-yellow, except the black base of s1 on unf. ♀ similar. In both sexes palpi are white below with orange hair in front; hw with distinct anal lobe. ♂ with prominent sex-brand on upf from wing-base across v1 to v3.

Flight. May or later in a single brood.

Habitat. Grass banks and meadows to 1500m, usually in damp places. Food plant Brome grass.

Distribution. Local in S. and C. Europe. Baltic Coast. England only near coast in Dorset, Devon; rare or occasional in Alps of N. Italy; absent from Corsica and Sardinia.

Variation. In some districts gc is paler, more yellow, esp. in SW. Alps; gc much darker in NW. Spain and Portugal f. *virescens* Agenjo.

T. acteon oranus Evans 1949 TL: Algeria

Description. ♂fw 10/11mm, ups gc darker, slightly greenish with yellow marking distinct, esp. in ♀ in which a yellow discal band on upf is usual; uns both wings sometimes slightly shaded grey.

Flight. May or later in a single brood.

Habitat. Grassy banks, etc., in damp places in Atlas Mts. at 1200–1800m.

Distribution. Morocco. Algeria. Tunisia. Widely distributed.

T. acteon christi Rebel 1894 TL: Canary Islands **Pl. 63**

Description. ♂fw 10/11mm, ups gc darker, all markings better defined in orange-yellow, including uph discal band; uns disc of fw orange with indistinct markings as on upf, dark grey in s1; unh s1b and s1c orange.

Flight. April and throughout summer.

Habitat. Grass banks, etc., to 1800m or more.

Distribution. Canary Islands, recorded from Tenerife, Gran Canary, La Palma, Gomera.

Similar species. *T. hamza* below, ♂ups gc brighter foxy-red; upf lacks pale pd spots; unh grey except fulvous inner marginal area.

THYMELICUS HAMZA *Moroccan Small Skipper*

Range. N. Africa, Asia Minor. Map 377

T. hamza Oberthur 1876 TL: Oran, Algeria **Pl. 63**

Description. ♂fw 11/13mm, resembles *T. acteon*; ups bright fulvous; upf with slightly paler fulvous shade through cell and beyond, no trace of pd band; sex-brand continuous from v1–v3; uns bright fulvous; unh *greyish between v2* and *v7*. ♀ similar, ups paler.

Flight. May/June in a single brood.

Habitat. Flowery places and rough slopes at 1500–1800m. Larval food plants not known.

Distribution. Local in Morocco, Algeria and Tunisia. Not reported from Europe.

Similar species. *T. acteon* p. 337.

THYMELICUS LINEOLA　*Essex Skipper*

Range. From N. Africa across Europe and C. Asia to Amurland; also in N. America, probably introduced.　Map 378

T. lineola lineola　Ochsenheimer 1808　TL: Germany　　　　　　　**Pl. 63**

Description. ♂fw 12/14mm, ups gc fulvous; upf unmarked except for *narrow dark inconspicuous sex-brand, broken at v2*, and not reaching v3; unf fulvous, apex usually yellow-grey, a conspicuous black basal mark below cell; unh pale yellow-grey with fulvous streak in s2. *Tip of antenna black* beneath. ♀ similar.

Flight. End May to August in a single brood.

Habitat. Grassy banks and meadows to 1800m. Larval food plants various grasses.

Distribution. Widespread in S. and C. Europe to 62°N, including S. England. Absent from Balearic Islands and Crete. Doubtfully recorded from Corsica and Sardinia.

T. lineola semicolon　Staudinger 1892　TL: Lambessa, Algeria

Description. ♂fw 13mm, ups resembles *T. l. lineola* but veins conspicuously lined black beyond cell and dark marginal borders wider; upf sex-brand larger; uns as in *T. l. lineola*. ♀ups gc paler with slight general fuscous suffusion.

Flight and **Habitat** as for *T. l. lineola*.

Distribution. Widely distributed in Morocco and Algeria; not recorded from Tunisia.

Variation. In some southern European localities extremely small with ♀fw 10mm. Large races, ♂fw 14mm, are common in E. Europe.

Similar species. *T. flavus* below, ups gc clear orange with little dark suffusion along veins; in ♂upf black sex-brand conspicuous, slightly curved; tip of antenna fulvous beneath.

THYMELICUS FLAVUS　*Small Skipper*

Range. From Morocco and Spain across Europe and Asia Minor to Iran.　Map 379

T. flavus　Brünnich 1763　TL: Denmark　　　　　　　　　　**Pl. 63**
　　syn: *thaumas* Hufnagel 1766; *sylvestris* auct.

Description. ♂fw 13/15mm, ups clear fulvous yellow, outer margins and veins lightly lined black; upf *conspicuous black sex-brand* below cell *from v1 to v3*; uph costa dark grey, otherwise unmarked; uns fulvous, tip of fw and most of hw greyish. *Tip of antenna fulvous* beneath. ♀ similar.

Flight. June or later in a single brood.

Habitat. Grass banks and meadows to 1800m or more. Larval food plants various grasses, *Deschampia, Oryzopsis, Holcus*, etc.

Distribution. Generally common throughout Europe to 56°N. N. Africa, common in Atlas Mts. in Morocco and Algeria, not recorded from Tunisia. Absent from N. England, Ireland and Mediterranean Islands except Sicily.

Variation. Very large, brilliant races occur in S. Europe, ♂fw 15/16mm, f. *syriacus* Tutt Pl. 63.
Similar species. *T. lineola* p. 338.

HESPERIA COMMA   *Silver-spotted Skipper*
Range. From N. Africa and Spain through C. and N. Europe and temperate Asia to Western N. America.   Map 380

H. comma comma   Linnaeus 1758   TL: Sweden (Verity 1940)   **Pl. 63**
syn: *sylvestris* auct. nec Poda.
Description. ♂fw 14/15mm, ups gc fulvous with wide dark brown borders on both wings; upf veins black, a conspicuous ridged black sex-brand, and small yellow subapical spots; hw anal lobe pronounced; uph discal area fulvous, with small paler pd spots; unf apex olive-green, pale spots as on ups; *unh olive-green with silvery discal spots.* ♀ups usually darker with markings more prominent; uns resembles ♂.
Flight. July/August in a single brood.
Habitat. Grass banks and meadows, on calcareous soils, from sea-level to 2100m or more. Larval food plants various grasses, esp. tussock grass.
Distribution. Widely distributed in suitable localities but local in Europe; rare in S. Spain; absent from S. Italy, Corsica, Sardinia, Ireland. In England, confined to chalk hills in S.

H. comma benuncas   Oberthur 1912   TL: Algeria
Description. Unh white spots slightly larger and fused into an irregular pd band, veins often lined white. ♀ups fulvous markings sometimes extensive.
Flight and **Habitat.** Flies July in mountainous districts of Morocco, Taghzeft Pass; Algeria, Djebel Aures, etc.
Similar species. *O. venatus* below, unh yellowish, pale markings indistinct.

OCHLODES VENATUS   *Large Skipper*
Range. From W. Europe through temperate Asia to China (TL of *Hesperia venata* Bremer and Grey 1857) and Japan.   Map 381

O. venatus faunus   Turati 1905   TL: Italy and S. France   **Pl. 63**
syn: *sylvanus* Esper 1779 (invalid homonym)
Description. ♂fw 14/17mm; upf bright fulvous with wide dark outer margin, veins dark, a prominent black sex-brand without central ridge; uph fulvous with dark margins and a few faintly paler discal spots; unf paler fulvous with markings as on ups; *unh yellow*, variable discal spots faint, markings as on uph. ♀upf fulvous, base dusky and disc with series of dusky markings; uph dusky brown with series of paler discal spots; uns as in ♂.
Flight. June/July/August, in northern range a single brood, two or three broods reported from S. Italy.
Habitat. Grass banks and meadows to 1800m. Larval food plants grasses, e.g., *Festuca, Poa, Triticum*, etc., also *Juncus*.
Distribution. Generally common throughout Europe to 64°N. Absent from Ireland and all Mediterranean islands except Sicily.
Variation. In some northern localities and at high altitudes often smaller and ups gc darker, f. *alpinus* Hoffmann Pl. 63.
Similar species. *H. comma* above.

GEGENES NOSTRODAMUS   *Mediterranean Skipper*

Range. From coastal districts of Mediterranean through Egypt and Asia Minor to Turkestan and India.   Map 382

G. nostrodamus   Fabricius 1793   TL: Morocco (Barbaria)   **Pl. 63**

Description. ♂fw 15/16mm, ups *pale brown, unmarked*; unf paler with two or three indistinct pale discal spots; unh pale sandy-brown unmarked fading to white along inner margin. ♀upf with angled series of pale discal spots, very small on costa, larger in s1b, s2 and s3, repeated on uns; unh as in ♂, faint paler discal spots sometimes present.

Flight. May/October, most common in late summer.

Habitat. Hot dry paths and rocky gorges, usually at low altitudes, most often near sea. Larval food plant grasses.

Distribution. Recorded from many localities around Mediterranean coast including NE. coast of Morocco at Rabat, etc. Occurs in Spain N. to Saragossa. Portugal.

Similar species. *G. pumilio* below, ups very dark brown. *B. borbonica* below, ups very dark with vitreous spots.

GEGENES PUMILIO   *Pigmy Skipper*

Range. From coastal districts of Mediterranean eastwards to Iran and Himalaya; also very generally throughout Africa.   Map 383

G. pumilio   Hoffmannsegg 1804   TL: Naples   **Pl. 63**
  syn: *pygmaeus* Cyrilli 1787 (invalid homonym); *aetna* Boisduval 1840; *lefebvrei* Rambur 1842

Description. ♂fw 14mm, outer margin of fw straight or slightly convex; *ups very dark brown, unmarked*; uns pale grey-brown with indistinct pale pd spots on both wings. ♀ups gc slightly paler with small indistinct pale pd spots on fw; uns pale grey-brown, both wings with small pale pd spots.

Flight. April/October, flies throughout summer.

Habitat. At low altitudes, often resting on hot paths or rocks in full sun. Larval food plant grasses.

Distribution. Recorded from many localities around the Mediterranean coasts.

Similar species. *G. nostrodamus* above; *B. borbonica* below.

BORBO BORBONICA   *Zeller's Skipper*

Range. Occasional along S. Mediterranean coast and widely distributed in Egypt, Syria, Africa, Mauritius and Reunion (TL of *Hesperia borbonica* Boisduval 1833).   Map 384

B. borbonica zelleri   Lederer 1855   TL: Syria   **Pl. 63**

Description. ♂fw 14/15mm, palpi pale yellow-brown below; ups dark brown; upf *with pd series of hyaline spots*, largest spot in s2, spot in s1b yellow; uph unmarked; unf base and disc brown, apex and all hind-wing rather bright yellow-brown, markings as on ups. ♀ generally larger and similar, unh often with a few small pale spots.

Flight. September/October.

Habitat. At low altitudes near sea-coast.

Distribution. Algeria, Hussein Day. Morocco at Rabat. Gibraltar. There are few Mediterranean records with satisfactory data.

Similar species. ♀ *G. pumilio* above, ♀ *G. nostrodamus* above, spots on fw not hyaline.

Distribution Maps

Distribution maps are necessary in order to show accurately the ranges of the species without regard to national frontiers. On these maps the black areas show breeding ranges of each species so far as these are known. It has not been possible to make a distinction between resident breeding species and summer visitors, of which several occur regularly in central and northern Europe, i.e. immigrant species which arrive and breed every summer, but which are not able to survive through winter in northern regions. Many migrants disperse far beyond their breeding ranges and such additional areas of dispersal are shown by parallel black lines. In N. Africa, in Tripolitania, Cyrenaica and Fezzan, where some Palearctic butterflies are known to occur although actual distribution is not understood, the presence of such species is indicated by dots.

The maps are intended to show where each butterfly may be expected to occur in suitable habitats. They do not always show the extreme limits of occasional dispersal ("strays"), nor do they show areas of earlier occurrence in which today the species is extinct.

The Atlantic Islands are not included on the maps, but a butterfly's presence on any of them is indicated by initial letters as follows: **C** = Canary Islands; **M** = Madeira; **A** = Azores.

The preparation of distribution maps is extremely laborious, often difficult, and without doubt some maps now presented will be imperfect in details. Accurate corrections can be made only by entomologists with personal knowledge of the countries concerned and suggestions for improvements will be welcomed by Dr L. G. Higgins, Focklesbrook Farm, Chobham, Woking, Surrey, England.

1 Papilio machaon
5 Zerynthia polyxena
9 Parnassius apollo
13 Pieris brassicae

2 Papilio hospiton
6 Zerynthia rumina
10 Parnassius phoebus
14 Artogeia rapae

3 Papilio alexanor
7 Zerynthia cerisyi
11 Parnassius mnemosyne
15 Artogeia mannii

4 Iphiclides podalirius
8 Archon apollinus
12 Aporia crataegi
16 Artogeia ergane

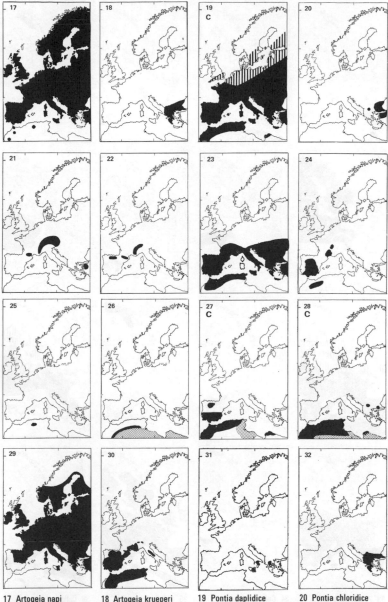

17 Artogeia napi
18 Artogeia krueperi
19 Pontia daplidice
20 Pontia chloridice
21 Pontia callidice
22 Euchloe ausonia
23 Euchloe simplonia
24 Euchloe tagis
25 Euchloe pechi
26 Euchloe falloui
27 Euchloe belemia
28 Elphinstonia charlonia
29 Anthocharis cardamines
30 Anthocharis belia
31 Anthocharis damone
32 Anthocharis gruneri

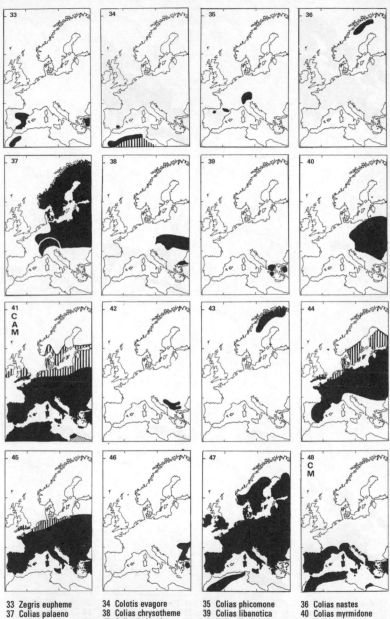

33 Zegris eupheme
37 Colias palaeno
41 Colias crocea
45 Colias australis
34 Colotis evagore
38 Colias chrysotheme
42 Colias balcanica
46 Colias erate
35 Colias phicomone
39 Colias libanotica
43 Colias hecla
47 Gonepteryx rhamni
36 Colias nastes
40 Colias myrmidone
44 Colias hyale
48 Gonepteryx cleopatra

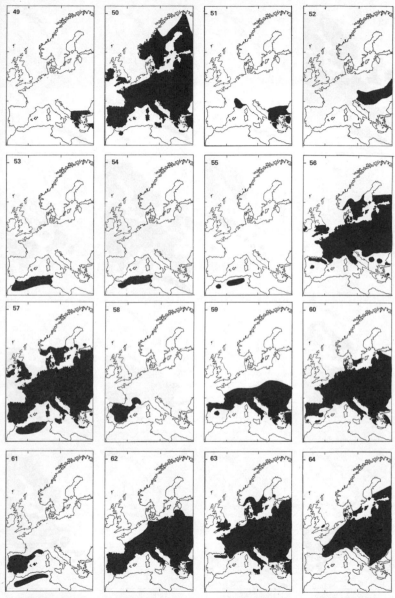

49 Gonepteryx farinosa
53 Cigaritis zohra
57 Quercusia quercus
61 Nordmannia esculi

50 Leptidea sinapis
54 Cigaritis siphax
58 Laeosopis roboris
62 Strymonidia spini

51 Leptidea duponcheli
55 Cigaritis allardi
59 Nordmannia acaciae
63 Strymonidia w-album

52 Leptidea morsei
56 Thecla betulae
60 Nordmannia ilicis
64 Strymonidia pruni

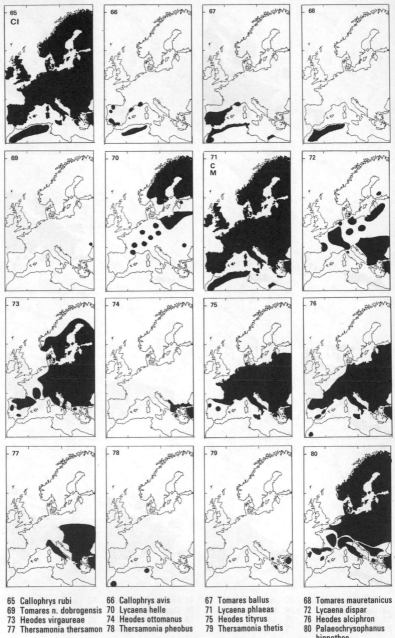

65 Callophrys rubi
66 Callophrys avis
67 Tomares ballus
68 Tomares mauretanicus
69 Tomares n. dobrogensis
70 Lycaena helle
71 Lycaena phlaeas
72 Lycaena dispar
73 Heodes virgaureae
74 Heodes ottomanus
75 Heodes tityrus
76 Heodes alciphron
77 Thersamonia thersamon
78 Thersamonia pheobus
79 Thersamonia thetis
80 Palaeochrysophanus hippothoe

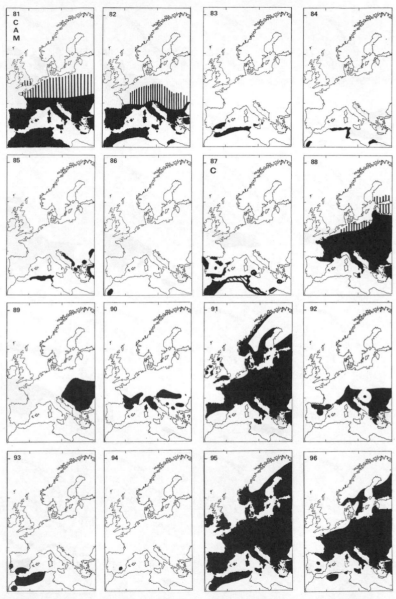

81 Lampides boeticus
82 Syntarucus pirithous
83 Taracus theophrastus
84 Tarucus rosaceus
85 Tarucus balkanicus
86 Azanus jesous
87 Zizeeria knysna
88 Everes argiades
89 Everes decoloratus
90 Everes alcetas
91 Cupido minimus
92 Cupido osiris
93 Cupido lorquinii
94 Cupido carswelli
95 Celastrina argiolus
96 Glaucopsyche alexis

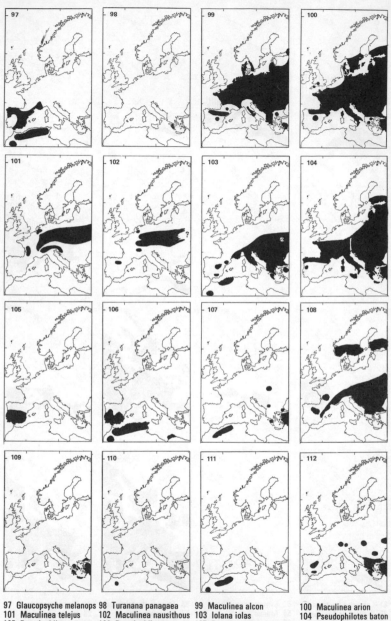

97 Glaucopsyche melanops 98 Turanana panagaea
101 Maculinea telejus 102 Maculinea nausithous 103 Iolana iolas
105 Pseudophilotes 106 Pseudophilotes 107 Pseudophilotes bavius
panoptes abencerragus 111 Plebejus martini
109 Freyeria trochylus 110 Plebejus vogelii

99 Maculinea alcon 100 Maculinea arion
104 Pseudophilotes baton
107 Pseudophilotes bavius 108 Scolitantides orion
112 Plebejus pylaon

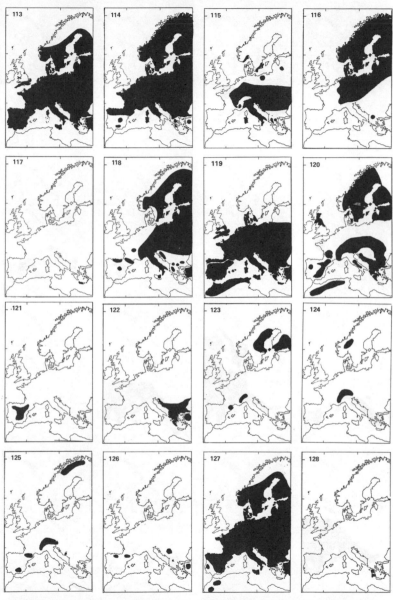

113 Plebejus argus
117 Kretania psylorita
121 Aricia morronensis
125 Agriades glandon

114 Lycaeides idas
118 Eumedonia eumedon
122 Aricia anteros
126 Agriades pyrenaicus

115 Lycaeides
    argyrognomon
119 Aricia agestis
123 Pseudaricia nicias
127 Cyaniris semiargus

116 Vacciniina optilete
120 Aricia artaxerxes
124 Albulina orbitulus
128 Cyaniris helena

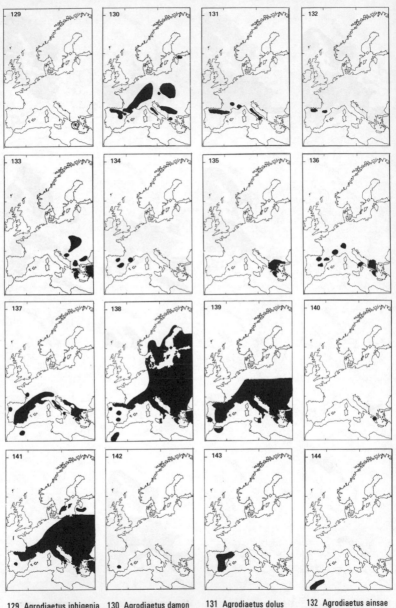

129 Agrodiaetus iphigenia 130 Agrodiaetus damon 131 Agrodiaetus dolus 132 Agrodiaetus ainsae
133 Agrodiaetus admetus 134 Agrodiaetus fabressei 135 Agrodiaetus 136 Agrodiaetus ripartii
137 Agrodiaetus escheri 138 Agrodiaetus amanda aroaniensis 140 Agrodiaetus
141 Plebicula dorylas 142 Plebicula golgus 139 Agrodiaetus thersites coelestinus
143 Plebicula nivecens 144 Plebicula atlantica

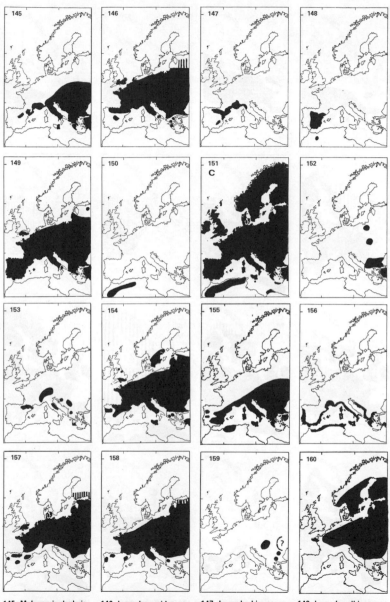

145 Meleageria daphnis
149 Lysandra bellargus
153 Polyommatus eros
157 Apatura iris

146 Lysandra coridon
150 Lysandra punctifera
154 Hamearis lucina
158 Apatura ilia

147 Lysandra hispana
151 Polyommatus icarus
155 Lybythea celtis
159 Apatura metis

148 Lysandra albicans
152 Polyommatus eroides
156 Charaxes jasius
160 Limenitis populi

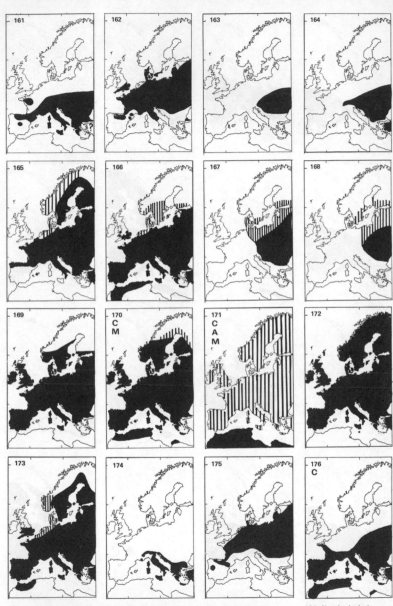

161 Limenitis reducta
165 Nymphalis antiopa
169 Inachis io
173 Polygonia c-album

162 Limenitis camilla
166 Nymphalis polychloros
170 Vanessa atalanta
174 Polygona egea

163 Neptis sappho
167 Nymphalis
   xanthomelas
171 Cynthia cardui
175 Araschnia levana

164 Neptis rivularis
168 Nymphalis vau-album
172 Aglais urticae
176 Pandoriana pandora

177 Argynnis paphia
181 Fabriciana niobe
185 Brenthis daphne
189 Boloria aquilonaris

178 Argyronome laodice
182 Fabriciana elisa
186 Brenthis ino
190 Boloria graeca

179 Mesoacidalia aglaja
183 Issoria lathonia
187 Boloria pales
191 Proclossiana eunomia

180 Fabriciana adippe
184 Brenthis hecate
188 Boloria napaea
192 Clossiana euphrosyne

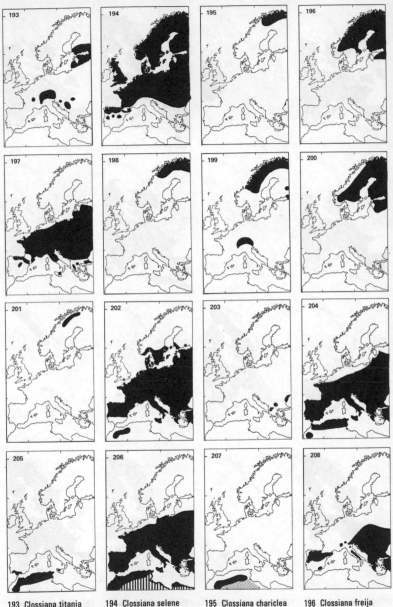

193 Clossiana titania
194 Clossiana selene
195 Clossiana chariclea
196 Clossiana freija
197 Clossiana dia
198 Clossiana polaris
199 Clossiana thore
200 Clossiana frigga
201 Clossiana improba
202 Melitaea cinxia
203 Melitaea arduinna
204 Melitaea phoebe
205 Melitaea aetherie
206 Melitaea didyma
207 Melitaea deserticola
208 Melitaea trivia

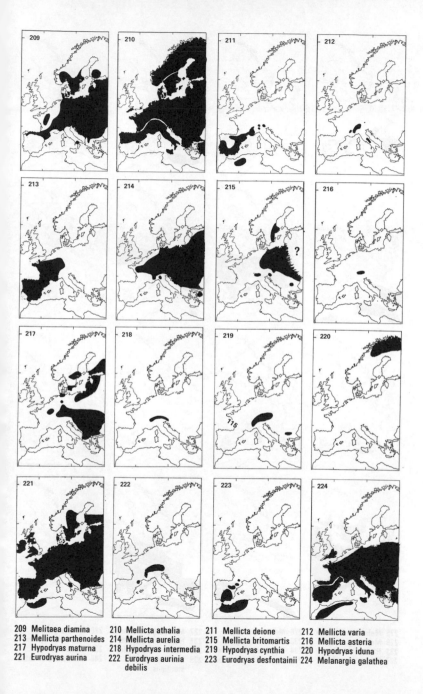

209 Melitaea diamina
210 Mellicta athalia
211 Mellicta deione
212 Mellicta varia
213 Mellicta parthenoides
214 Mellicta aurelia
215 Mellicta britomartis
216 Mellicta asteria
217 Hypodryas maturna
218 Hypodryas intermedia
219 Hypodryas cynthia
220 Hypodryas iduna
221 Eurodryas aurina
222 Eurodryas aurinia debilis
223 Eurodryas desfontainii
224 Melanargia galathea

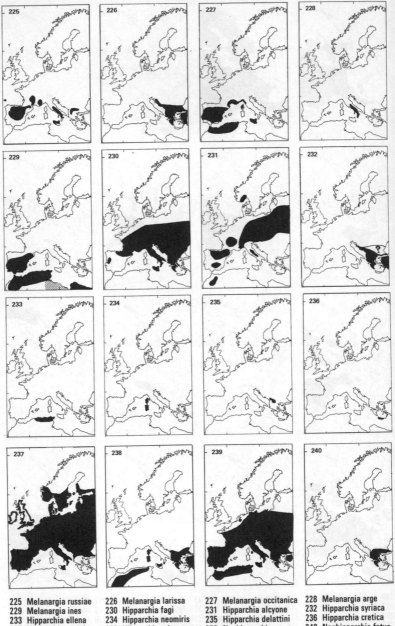

225 Melanargia russiae   226 Melanargia larissa   227 Melanargia occitanica   228 Melanargia arge
229 Melanargia ines   230 Hipparchia fagi   231 Hipparchia alcyone   232 Hipparchia syriaca
233 Hipparchia ellena   234 Hipparchia neomiris   235 Hipparchia delattini   236 Hipparchia cretica
237 Hipparchia semele   238 Hipparchia aristaeus   239 Neohipparchia statilinus   240 Neohipparchia fatua

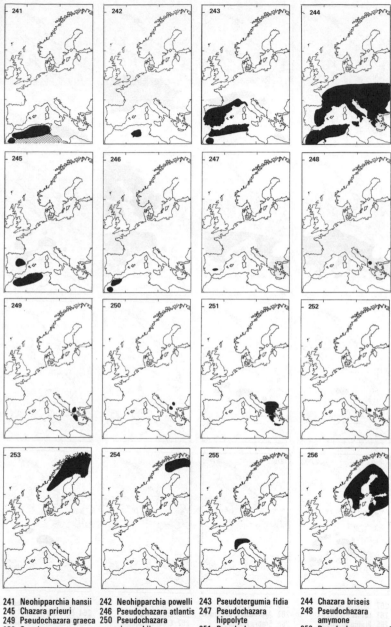

241 Neohipparchia hansii   242 Neohipparchia powelli   243 Pseudotergumia fidia   244 Chazara briseis
245 Chazara prieuri   246 Pseudochazara atlantis   247 Pseudochazara   248 Pseudochazara
249 Pseudochazara graeca   250 Pseudochazara   hippolyte   amymone
253 Oeneis norna   cingovskii   251 Pseudochazara   252 Pseudochazara geyeri
                       254 Oeneis bore   anthelea   256 Oeneis jutta
                                              255 Oeneis glacialis

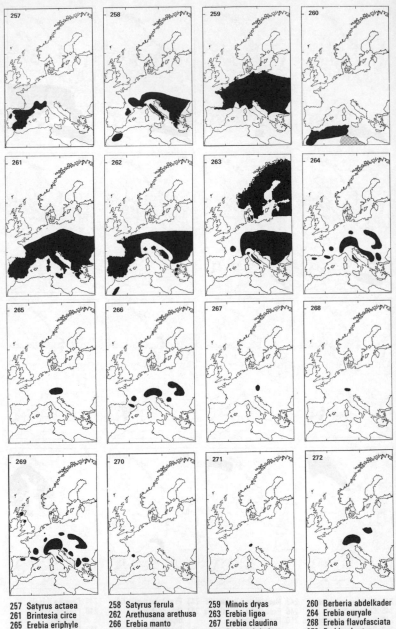

257 Satyrus actaea
261 Brintesia circe
265 Erebia eriphyle
269 Erebia epiphron

258 Satyrus ferula
262 Arethusana arethusa
266 Erebia manto
270 Erebia serotina

259 Minois dryas
263 Erebia ligea
267 Erebia claudina
271 Erebia christi

260 Berberia abdelkader
264 Erebia euryale
268 Erebia flavofasciata
272 Erebia pharte

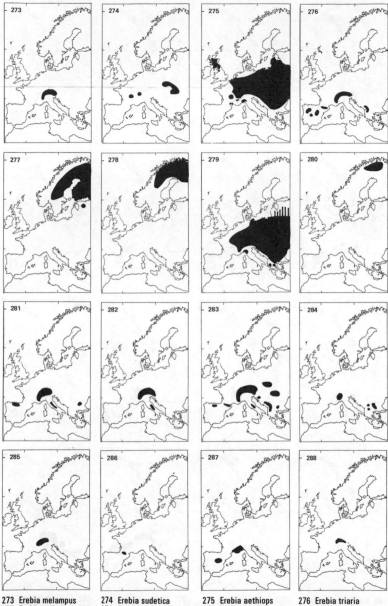

273 Erebia melampus
277 Erebia embla
281 Erebia alberganus
285 Erebia mnestra

274 Erebia sudetica
278 Erebia disa
282 Erebia pluto
286 Erebia gorgone

275 Erebia aethiops
279 Erebia medusa
283 Erebia gorge
287 Erebia epistygne

276 Erebia triaria
280 Erebia polaris
284 Erebia aethiopella
288 Erebia tyndarus

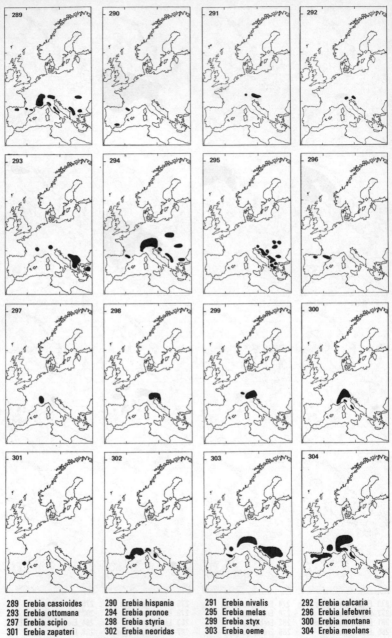

289 Erebia cassioides
293 Erebia ottomana
297 Erebia scipio
301 Erebia zapateri

290 Erebia hispania
294 Erebia pronoe
298 Erebia styria
302 Erebia neoridas

291 Erebia nivalis
295 Erebia melas
299 Erebia styx
303 Erebia oeme

292 Erebia calcaria
296 Erebia lefebvrei
300 Erebia montana
304 Erebia meolans

305 Erebia palarica
309 Maniola jurtina
313 Hyponephele lupina
317 Pyronia bathseba

306 Erebia pandrose
310 Maniola nurag
314 Aphantopus
    hyperantus
318 Pyronia janiroides

307 Erebia sthennyo
311 Hyponephele
    maroccana
315 Pyronia tithonus
319 Coenonympha tullia

308 Erebia phegea
312 Hyponephele lycaon
316 Pyronia cecilia
320 Coenonympha
    rhodopensis

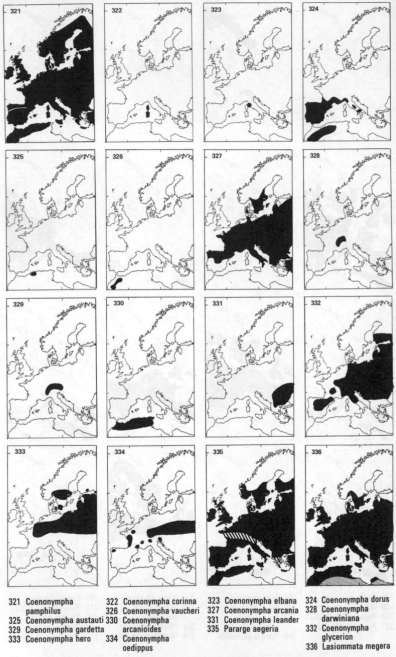

321 Coenonympha pamphilus
322 Coenonympha corinna
323 Coenonympha elbana
324 Coenonympha dorus
325 Coenonympha austauti
326 Coenonympha vaucheri
327 Coenonympha arcania
328 Coenonympha darwiniana
329 Coenonympha gardetta
330 Coenonympha arcanioides
331 Coenonympha leander
332 Coenonympha glycerion
333 Coenonympha hero
334 Coenonympha oedippus
335 Pararge aegeria
336 Lasiommata megera

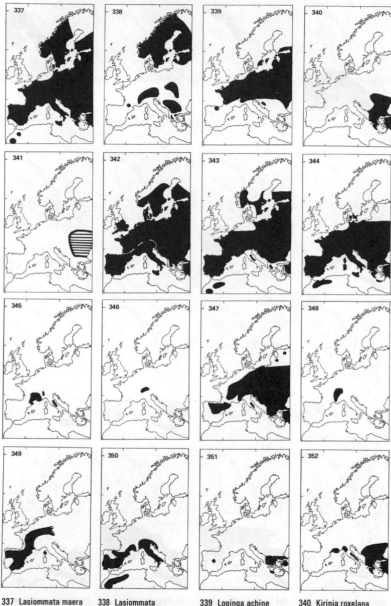

337 Lasiommata maera
338 Lasiommata
    petropolitana
339 Lopinga achine
340 Kirinia roxelana
341 Kirinia climene
342 Pyrgus malvae
343 Pyrgus alveus
344 Pyrgus armoricanus
345 Pyrgus foulquieri
346 Pyrgus warrenensis
347 Pyrgus serratulae
348 Pyrgus c. carlinae
349 Pyrgus c. cirsii
350 Pyrgus onopordi
351 Pyrgus cinarae
352 Pyrgus sidae

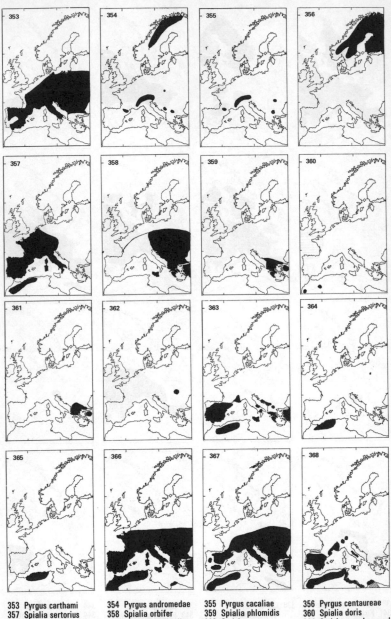

353 Pyrgus carthami
357 Spialia sertorius
361 Syrichtus tessellum
365 Syrichtus leuzeae

354 Pyrgus andromedae
358 Spialia orbifer
362 Syrichtus cribrellum
366 Carcharodus alceae

355 Pyrgus cacaliae
359 Spialia phlomidis
363 Syrichtus proto
367 Carcharodus
   lavatherae

356 Pyrgus centaureae
360 Spialia doris
364 Syrichtus mohammed
368 Carcharodus boeticus

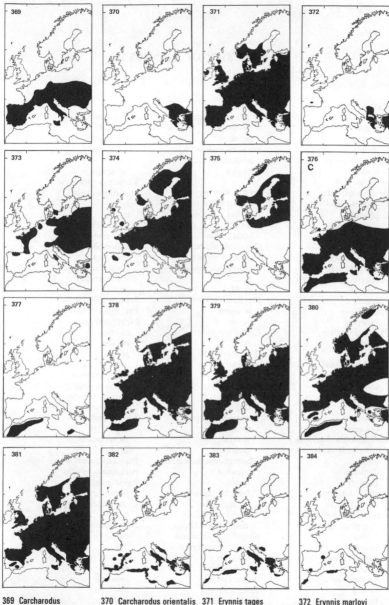

369 Carcharodus
    flocciferus
373 Heteropterus
    morpheus
377 Thymelicus hamza
381 Ochlodes venatus

370 Carcharodus orientalis
374 Carterocephalus
    palaemon
378 Thymelicus lineola
382 Gegenes nostrodamus

371 Erynnis tages
375 Carterocephalus
    silvicolus
379 Thymelicus flavus
383 Gegenes pumilio

372 Erynnis marloyi
376 Thymelicus acteon
380 Hesperia comma
384 Borbo borbonica

Checklist of Species

PAPILIONIDAE
Papilio machaon
  hospiton
  alexanor
Iphiclides podalirius
Zerynthia polyxena
  rumina
  cerisyi
Archon apollinus
Parnassius apollo
  phoebus
  mnemosyne

PIERIDAE
Aporia crataegi
Pieris brassicae
Artogeia rapae
  mannii
  ergane
  napi
  krueperi
Pontia daplidice
  chloridice
  callidice
Euchloe ausonia
  simplonia
  insularis
  tagis
  pechi
  falloui
  belemia
Elphinstonia charlonia
Anthocharis cardamines
  belia
  damone
  gruneri
Zegris eupheme
Colotis evagore
Catopsilia florella
Colias phicomone
  nastes
  palaeno
  chrysotheme
  libanotica
  myrmidone
  crocea
  balcanica
  hecla
  hyale
  australis

erate
Gonepteryx rhamni
  cleopatra
  farinosa
Leptidea sinapis
  duponcheli
  morsei

LYCAENIDAE
Cigaritis zohra
  siphax
  allardi
Thecla betulae
Quercusia quercus
Laeosopis roboris
Nordmannia acaciae
  ilicis
  esculi
Strymonidia spini
  w-album
  pruni
Callophrys rubi
  avis
Tomares ballus
  mauretanicus
  nogellii
Lycaena helle
  phlaeas
  dispar
Heodes virgaureae
  ottomanus
  tityrus
  alciphron
Thersamonia thersamon
  phoebus
  thetis
Palaeochrysophanus
  hippothoe
Lampides boeticus
Syntarucus pirithous
Cyclyrius webbianus
Tarucus theophrastus
  rosaceus
  balkanicus
Azanus jesous
Zizeria knysna
Everes argiades
  decoloratus
  alcetas
Cupido minimus

osiris
  lorquinii
  carswelli
Celastrina argiolus
Glaucopsyche
  alexis
  melanops
Turanana panagaea
Maculinea alcon
  arion
  telejus
  nausithous
Iolana iolas
Pseudophilotes baton
  panoptes
  barbagiae
  abencerragus
  bavius
Scolitantides orion
Freyeria trochylus
Plebejus vogelii
  martini
  pylaon
  argus
Lycaeides idas
  argyrognomon
Vacciniina optilete
Kretania psylorita
Eumedonia eumedon
Aricia agestis
  artaxerces
  morronensis
  anteros
Pseudaricia nicias
Albulina orbitulus
Agriades glandon
  pyrenaicus
Cyaniris semiargus
  helena
Agrodiaetus iphigenia
  damon
  dolus
  ainsae
  escheri
  amanda
  thersites
  admetus
  fabressei
  agenjoi
  humedasae

aroaniesis
pelopi
ripartii
violetae
nephohiptamenos
Neolysandra coelestina
Plebicula dorylas
  golgus
  nivescens
  atlantica
Meleageria daphnis
Lysandra coridon
  philippi
  hispana
  albicans
  bellargus
  punctifera
Polyommatus icarus
  eroides
  eros

RIODINIDAE
Hamearis lucina

LIBYTHEIDAE
Libythea celtis

NYMPHALIDAE
Charaxes jasius
Apatura iris
  ilia
  metis
Limenitis populi
  reducta
  camilla
Neptis sappho
  rivularis
Nymphalis antiopa
  polychloros
  xanthomelas
  vau-album
Inachis io
Vanessa atalanta
  indica
Cynthia cardui
  virginiensis
Aglais urticae
Polygonia c-album
  egea
Araschnia levana
Pandoriana pandora
Argynnis paphia
Argyronome laodice
Mesoacidalia aglaja
Fabriciana adippe
  niobe

elisa
Issoria lathonia
Brenthis hecate
  daphne
  ino
Boloria pales
  napaea
Boloria aquilonaris
  graeca
Proclossiana eunomia
Clossiana euphrosyne
  titania
  selene
  chariclea
  freija
  dia
  polaris
  thore
  frigga
  improba
Melitaea cinxia
  arduinna
  phoebe
  aetherie
  didyma
  deserticola
  trivia
  diamina
Mellicta athalia
  deione
  varia
  parthenoides
  aurelia
  britomartis
  asteria
Hypodryas maturna
  intermedia
  cynthia
  iduna
Eurodryas aurinia
  desfontainii

SATYRIDAE
Melanargia galathea
  russiae
  larissa
  occitanica
  arge
  ines
Hipparchia fagi
  alcyone
  syriaca
  ellena
  neomiris
  delattini
  lieghebi

cretica
semele
aristaeus
azorina
Neohipparchia statilinus
  fatua
  hansii
  powelli
Pseudotergumia fidia
  wyssii
Chazara briseis
  prieuri
Pseudochazara atlantis
  hippolyte
  amymone
  graeca
  cingovskii
  orestes
  tisiphone
  anthelea
  geyeri
Oeneis norna
  bore
  glacialis
  jutta
Satyrus actaea
  ferula
Minois dryas
Berberia abdelkader
Brintesia circe
Arethusana arethusa
Erebia ligea
  euryale
  eriphyle
  manto .
  claudina
  flavofasciata
  epiphron
  christi
  pharte
  melampus
  sudetica
  aethiops
  triaria
  embla
  disa
  medusa
  polaris
  alberganus
  pluto
  gorge
  aethiopella
  mnestra
  gorgone
  epistygne
  tyndarus

cassioides
hispania
nivalis
calcaria
ottomana
pronoe
melas
lefebvrei
scipio
styria
styx
montana
zapateri
neoridas
oeme
meolans
palarica
pandrose
sthennyo
phegea
Maniola jurtina
  nurag
Hyponephele maroccana
  lycaon
  lupina
Aphantopus hyperantus
Pyronia tithonus
  cecilia
  bathseba
  janiroides
Coenonympha tullia
  rhodopensis
  pamphilus
  corinna
  elbana

dorus
austauti
vaucheri
arcania
darwiniana
gardetta
arcanioides
leander
glycerion
hero
oedippus
Pararge aegeria
  xiphioides
  xiphia
Lasiommata megera
  maera
  petropolitana
Lopinga achine
Kirinia roxelana
  climene

DANAIDAE
Danaus plexippus
  chrysippus

HESPERIIDAE
Pyrgus malvae
  alveus
  armoricanus
  foulquieri
  warrenensis
  serratulae
  carlinae
  onopordi
  cinarae

sidae
carthami
andromedae
cacaliae
centaureae
Spialia sertorius
  orbifer
  phlomidis
  doris
Syrichtus tessellum
  cribrellum
  proto
  mohammed
  leuzeae
Carcharodus alceae
  tripolinus
  lavatherae
  boeticus
  flocciferus
  orientalis
Erynnis tages
  marloyi
Heteropterus morpheus
Carterocephalus
  palaemon
  silvicolus
Thymelicus acteon
  hamza
  lineola
  flavus
Hesperia comma
Ochlodes venatus
Gegenes nostrodamus
  pumilio
Borbo borbonica

Glossary

Abdomen. The free part of the body behind the thorax.

Aberration. An individual variety of rare occurrence; a freak.

Allopatric. Occupying different, mutually exclusive geographical areas.

Anal Angle. The point of the hind-wing opposite the butterfly's anus; i.e. at the junction of inner and outer margins.

Anal fold. A fold in the hind-wing parallel to and close to the inner margin.

Androconia. Wing scales of special form, often tufted, occurring only in males and often grouped in patches to form 'sex-brands'.

Antennae. Paired sensory organs arising from the insect's head; feelers.

Apex, of wing. The point where costa and outer margin meet, usually angular on fore-wing, rounded on hind-wing.

Auct. (*auctorum*) used following a specific name indicates its use by authors otherwise than as intended by the original author.

Available. Of names, one that satisfies all the requirements of the Code of Nomenclature.

Basad. Towards the base.

Base. Of a wing, the part nearest the body.

Caudal. Associated with the tail.

Cell. (i.e. in butterflies, the discoidal cell). The area in the basal half of each wing generally enclosed by veins. When the closure is incomplete the cell is said to be 'open'. See Fig. on p. 14.

Cephalic. Associated with the head.

Chevron. An arrow-headed mark.

Chitin. A horny material of which an insect's cuticle is composed.

Chrysalis. See *Pupa*.

Cline. A character gradient; a gradual and almost continuous change of size, colour or wing markings in a recognisable direction throughout a population or series of populations; often apparently related to climatic factors; especially common in such variable species as those of the genera *Erebia* and *Melitaea*.

Club. Of antenna. The thickened terminal part of the antenna.

Code. See *International Commission*.

Conspecific. Belonging to the same species.

Costa. The front edge of a wing.

Costal fold. A fold of the fw costa enclosing androconia; confined to certain Skippers (Hesperiidae).

Cryptic. Camouflage intended to hide an animal from predators or prey.

Dimorphism. Occurrence within a species of two distinct forms, e.g. the 'white' and 'yellow' females of *Colias*. See also *Polymorphism*.

Discal. Used of the disc or central area of the wing.

Discocellular. See *Discoidal*.

Discoidal. Used of the central area around the transverse discoidal veins at the end of the cell; discoidal spot, a conspicuous mark often present on these veins; discoidal cell, the central area enclosed by veins. See page 14.

369

Distad. Away from the base (of the wing).

Distal. Distant from the centre of the body.

Endemic. Native to and always present in a particular area or country; in zoology, confined to that area and not found elsewhere.

Falcate. Hooked.

Family. In zoology a group of genera all with certain similar characters and considered closely related on this account. Family names always end in -idae.

Fauna. Collective name for all the living creatures in a given region.

Fennoscandia. Geographical term embracing Norway, Sweden and Finland.

Filamentous. Like a fine thread.

Flora. Collective name for all the plants in a given region.

Form. Any recognisably distinct variant of a species, e.g. a female form, a seasonal or local form, a variety or aberration; an indefinite term unless qualified.

Frons. The front of the head between the eyes, often bearing a tuft of hair.

Fuscous. Dusky, grey-brown.

Fusiform. Spindle-shaped.

Genitalia. Sex organs. In butterflies the chitinous organs (partly external) at the end of the abdomen.

Genus. A unit including one species, or a group of species presumably of common origin, separated from related similar units by a different combination of characters.

Hibernation. Survival through winter in a dormant state.

Homonym. The same names used for different species are homonyms. The first published name only is valid.

Hyaline. Translucent; resembling glass.

I.C.Z.N. See *International Commission.*

Imago (pl. *imagines*). The fourth phase of a butterfly's life, the adult insect.

International Commission on Zoological Nomenclature. The body responsible for the International Code of rules that governs the application of the scientific names of animals.

Invalid name. A scientific name which does not conform with the international rules of nomenclature (the Code).

Irrorated. Minutely speckled: dotted with pale coloured scales.

Jullien Organ. A group of stiff rods (batons), formed from modified scales, on the dorsal surface of the last visible segment of the abdomen in certain Satyrid butterflies.

Larva. Caterpillar; an insect at the second (growth) stage of its life.

Linear. In the form of a line.

Lunule. A crescent-shaped mark.

Macular. Spotted.

Nacreous. Like mother-of-pearl.

Nom. nud. Nomen nudum. A name not accompanied by a description and therefore not available.

Ocellus. Of markings, a round spot usually black with a central pale spot or pupil; if the pupil is absent the ocellus is termed 'blind'.

Palearctic Region. The zoogeographical region that includes Europe, Asia north of the Himalayas, northern Arabia and Africa north of the Sahara, i.e. most of the Old World north of the tropics.

Palpi. Paired sensory organs arising on each side of the proboscis.

Pilose. Covered with fine short hair.

Polymorphism. Occurrence of different individual forms in a single species; the forms may appear constantly or as rare exceptions ('aberrations').

Postdiscal. The area of the wing between the discal and submarginal areas. See Fig., p. 14.

Proboscis. The spirally coiled organ, composed of two minute tubes united side by side to form a third tube, through which a butterfly imbibes liquids; when not in use it lies coiled between the palpi.

Proximal. Near the centre of the body; opposite of 'distal'.

Pupa. An insect in the third (resting) stage of its life-cycle; the chrysalis.

Pyriform. Pear shaped.

Race. A local form with distinctive characters, present in all or most individuals.

Reticulate. Marked with a network pattern.

Sagittate. Shaped like an arrow-head.

Sex-brand. See *Androconia.*

Space. An area of the wing lying between two veins and bounded outwardly by the wing margin; usually abbreviated to 's', e.g. s2, s3 etc. See diagram p. 14.

Species. The scientific term – which in practice cannot be precisely defined – for different kinds of butterflies. The specific name is written thus: *Pieris napi* or *P. napi* – *napi* being the name of the species, *Pieris* that of the genus.

Sphragis. A horny, pouch-like structure formed underneath the female abdomen during copulation.

Stria (pl. *striae*). A very slender streak.

Subspecies. Differing populations of a species that occupy separate, though often contiguous areas; geographical races. The subspecific name is written thus: *Pieris napi napi* (which can be abbreviated to *Pieris n. napi* or *P. n. napi*).

Symbiosis. Literally 'living together', e.g. the association of the larvae of some Lycaenid butterflies with ants. The association may or may not be of mutual advantage.

Sympatric. Living in the same area; opposite of allopatric (q.v.).

Synonyms. Different names given to the same species. Only the first published name is valid.

Taxon (pl. *taxa*). A unit of classification, e.g. Family genus or species, whether named or not.

Taxonomy. The classification of plants and animals.

Thorax. The part of the insect's body that bears the wings and legs; the chest.

Type locality. The locality in which the type specimen was collected.

Type specimen. The specimen actually described by the author of the name of a species (or subspecies or form).

Valid name. The name recognised as correct under the Code.

Vein. In insect wings, the minute rigid tubes that support the membrane of the wing. See Fig., p. 15.

Venation. The pattern of the veins in an insect's wing. See Fig., p. 14.

Bibliography

Albania. REBEL, & ZERNY H. 1931. *Die Lepidopterenfauna Albaniens.* Denkschriften der mathem. naturw. Klasse *103*: 37–161 (Acad. d. Wissensch. in Wien).

Algeria. OBERTHUR, C. 1914. *Faune des Lépidoptères de la Barbarie.* Études de Lépidopterologie Comparée *10*: 1–459. Rennes.

Austria, see Germany.

Balearic Islands. REBEL, H. 1926. *Lepidopteren von den Balearen.* Iris. Dresden. *40*: 135–141; id. 1934. *48*: 122–126.

Balkans. REBEL, H. 1903. *Studien über die Lepidopterenfauna der Balkanländer*
1. Bulgarien und Ostrumelien. Ann. naturh. Hofmuseum Wien *18*: 123–346.
2. Bosnien und Herzegovina. id. 1904. *19*: 97–377.
3. Montenegro. Albanien etc. id. 1913. *27*: 281–334.

Belgium. HACKRAY, J. & SARLET, L. G. 1969 et seq. *Catalogue des Macrolépidoptères de Belgique.* Lambillionea, Suppl. to vol. *67* etc.

Canary Islands. LEESTMANS, SCHWARZ, R. Motyli 1948. Prague.

Corsica. LEESTMANS, R. 1965. *Étude biogéographique sur les Lépidoptères diurnes de la Corse.* Alexanor *4*: 17 et seq.

Crete. TRONICEK, E. 1949. *Contribution to the Knowledge of the Lepidopterological fauna of Crete.* Acta Ent. Mus. Nat. Prague *26* (358): pp. 15.

Czechoslovakia. HRUBY, K. 1964. *Prodromus Lepidopter Slovenska.* pp. 1–962. Bratislava.

Denmark. LANGER, T. W. 1957. *Systematisk oversigt over de danske storsommerfügles . . .* Saertryk af Flora og Fauna 63:1–26. (English Summary).

Estonia. THOMSON, E. 1967. Die Grosschmetterlinge Estlands. Stollhamm.

VIIDALEPP, J. & MOLS, T. 1963. *Eesti Suurliblikate Määraja.* Eesti NSV Teaduste Akadeemia. Tartu.

Finland. NORDSTRÖM, F. 1955. *De Fennoskandiska Dagfjärilarnas Utbredning.* Acta Univ. Lund (2), *51.* Butterflies only, with excellent distribution maps.

France. LHOMME, L. 1923–1935. *Catalogue des Lépidoptères de France et de Belgique. 1*: 1–114. Le Carriol. Lot. Out of date but still the standard work for the Lepidoptera of France.

Germany. FORSTER, W. & WOHLFAHRT, T. A. *Die Schmetterlinge Mitteleuropas. 2*: 1–126. 1955. Tagfalter. Stuttgart.

Great Britain. HOWARTH, T. G. 1973. *South's British Butterflies.* pp. 1–320. London.

Greece. COUTSIS, J. G. 1969. *List of Grecian Butterflies.* Entomologist *102*: 264–268 id. 1972. Additional Records. Ent. Rec. 84: 145–151. A Collector's list with localities, etc.

Holland. LEMPKE, B. J. 1936, 1937. Tijdschr. Ent. *79*: 238–15, with supplements.

Hungary. GOZMANY, L. 1968. *Nappali Lepkek – Diurna.* Fauna Hungariae 91. pp. 1–204. Budapest.

Italy. VERITY, R. 1940–1953. *Le Farfalle Diurne d'Italia.* 5 vol. Florence.

Malta.

Morocco. OBERTHUR, C. 1922. *Les Lépidoptères du Maroc.* Études de Lépidopterologie Comparée *19*: 1–403. Rennes. Many coloured figures.

Norway. See under Finland.

Poland. ROMANISZYN, J. 1929. *Fauna Motyli Polski* (Fauna Lepidopterorum Poloniae). pp. 1–555. Krakow.

Portugal. ZERKOWITZ, A. 1946. *The Lepidoptera of Portugal.* J. New York Ent. Soc. 54: 51–87.

Pyrenees. RONDOU, P. 1932–1935. *Catalogue des Lépidoptères des Pyrénées.* Ann. Soc. Ent. Fr. *101*: 165–222. *105*: 253–255.

OBERTHUR, C. 1923. *Catalogue des Lépidoptères des Pyrénées-Orientales.* Études de Lépidopterologie Comparée 20: 1–54. Rennes.

OCHMIA, S. 1977. *Die Tagfalter Madieras.* E. Z. Stuttgart *87*: pp. 169. Borg P.

Romania. NICULESCU, E. 1961–1970. *Fauna Repub. Pop. Romine.* Lepidoptera. 11: fasc. 5–7, 10. Bucharest (Romanian Language).

Sardinia. HARTIG, F. & AMSEL, H. G. 1951. *Lepidoptera Sardinica.* Fragmenta Est. *1*: 1–152. Rome.

Scandinavia. See under Finland.

Sicily. MARIASI, M. 1939. *Fauna Lepidopterorum Siciliae.* Mem. Soc. ent. Ital. *17*: 129–187.

Spain. MANLEY, W. B. L. & ALLCARD, H. G. 1970. *A Field Guide to the Butterflies and Burnets of Spain.* Hampton, Middlesex.

Sweden. NORDSTRÖM, F. & WAHLGREN, E. 1935–1941. *Svenska Fjärilar.* pp. 1–353. Stockholm.

Switzerland. VORBRODT, K. & MÜLLER-RUTZ, J. 1911–1914 and later supplements. *Die Schmetterlinge der Schweiz.* Bern.

Tunisia. CNEOUR, A. 1954. Macrolepidoptéres de Tunisie. 1–2: Bull. Soc. Sci. Nat. Tunis. 7: 207–239.

Yugoslavia. See under Balkans.

The following foreign editions of the present Field Guide have appeared. Their translators have been at liberty to modify the text, and have in many cases introduced taxa which we did not think necessary to include:

Denmark	*Europas dagsommerfugle*	Gads Forlag	Niels Peder Kristensen Svend Kaaber Niels L. Wolff
Finland	*Euroopan päiräperhoset*	Tammi	Olavi Sotavalta
Holland	*Elseviers vlindergids*	Elsevier	B. J. Lempke J. Huisenga
Germany	*Schmetterlinge Europas*	Paul Parey	Dr Forster
France	*Guide des Papillons d'Europe*	Delachaux & Niestle	P. C. Rougeot
Norway	*En Felthandbok Sommerfugler*	Tiden Norsk Forlag	Magne Opheim
Spain	*Guia de Camp de las Mariposas de Espana y de Europa*	Omega	Olegario Escola
Sweden	*Europas fjärilar Dagfjärilar*	Almqvist & Wiksell	Per Douwes

Index of English Names

References in **bold** type are to plate numbers.

Index of Scientific Names

abdelaziz (Agrodiaetus) 84
abdelkader (Berberia) 273
abencerragus
PSEUDOPHILOTES 67
acaciae (Nordmannia) 45
aceris (Neptis) 99
achine (Lopinga) 320
acis (Cyaniris) 80
actaea (Satyrus) 272
acteon (Thymelicus) 337
adalwinda (Artogeia) 25
adippe (Fabriciana) 106
admetus (Agrodiaetus) 85
adonis (Lysandra) 92
adyte (Erebia) 276
aegeria (Pararge) 317
aegidion (Plebejus) 71
aegon (Plebejus) 71
aegus (Lycaeides) 73
aelia (Hipparchia) 261
aello (Oeneis) 271
aestivus (Papilio) 17
aetheria (Erebia) 279
aetherie (Melitaea) 118
aethiopella (Erebia) 288
aethiops (Erebia) 282
africana (Zerynthia) 19
agenjo (Agrodiaetus) 86
agestis (Aricia) 75
agestor (Agrodiaetus) 85
AGLAIS 102
aglaja (Mesoacidalia) 105
AGRIADES 78
AGRODIAETUS 81
ahmar (Agrodiaetus) 84
ainsae (Agrodiaetus) 83
albanica (Erebia) 288
alberganus (Erebia) 285
albicans (Lysandra) 91
alboocellatus (Agriades) 79
albovenosa (Pseudotergumia) 266
ALBULINA 78
alceae (Carcharodus) 333
alcetas (Everes) 60
alciphron (Heodes) 53
alcon (Maculinea) 64
alcyone (Hipparchia) 261
alecto (Erebia) 286
alexanor (Papilio) 18

alexis (Glaucopsyche) 63
alfacarensis (Colias) 38
algerica (Melitaea) 118
algirica (Hipparchia) 264
algirica (Glaucopsyche) 63
ali (Spialia) 330
allardi (Cigaritis) 44
allionia (Neohipparchia) 265
allionii (Neohipparchia) 265
allous (Aricia) 76
alpicola (Hypodryas) 127
alpinus (Lycaeides) 72
alternans (Melitaea) 117
alticolus (Pyrgus) 325
altivolans (Agrodiaetus) 85
alveus (Pyrgus) 323
amalthea (Pseudochazara) 270
amanda (Agrodiaetus) 84
amathusia (Clossiana) 113
amphidamas (Lycaena) 49
amymone (Pseudochazara) 269
amyntas (Coenonympha) 313
andromedae (Pyrgus) 328
annoceuri (Coenonympha) 312
anonyma (Limenitis) 98
anteros (Aricia) 77
anthelea (Pseudochazara) 270
ANTHOCHARIS 31–2
antiopa (Nymphalis) 99
APATURA 96
APHANTOPUS 305
aphirape (Proclossiana) 112
apollinus (Archon) 20
apollo (Parnassius) 20
APORIA 23
aquilo (Agriades) 79
aquilonaris (Boloria) 111
aquilonia (Coenonympha) 311
ARASCHNIA 104
arcania (Coenonympha) 313
arcanioides (Coenonympha) 314
arcas (Maculinea) 66
ARCHON 20
arctica (Artogeia) 25
arduinna (Melitaea) 117

arete (Erebia) 278
arethusa (Arethusana) 274
ARETHUSANA 274
arge (Melanargia) 259
argester (Plebicula) 87
argiades (Everes) 59
argiolus (Celastrina) 62
argus (Plebejus) 71
ARGYNNIS 104
argyrognomon (Lycaeides) 73
ARGYRONOME 105
ARICIA 75–7
arion (Maculinea) 65
aristaeus (Hipparchia) 263
armoricanus (Pyrgus) 324
aroaniensis (Agrodiaetus) 86
artaxerxes (Aricia) 76
ARTOGEIA 24–7
arsilache (Boloria) 111
arvernensis (Erebia) 291
asteria (Mellicta) 126
astrarche (Aricia) 75
astrifera (Fabriciana) 108
astur (Erebia) 295
asturiensis (Agriades) 80
asturiensis (Lysandra) 90
atalanta (Vanessa) 101
athalia (Mellicta) 122
athene (Parnassius) 22
atlanteus (Satyrus) 272
atlantica (Plebicula) 88
atlantica (Artogeia) 26
atlantis (Artogeia) 26
atlantis (Pseudochazara) 268
atlantis (Melitaea) 117
aurantiaca (Papilio) 17
aurelia (Mellicta) 125
auresiana (Fabriciana) 107
aurinia (Eurodryas) 128
ausonia (Euchloe) 28
austauti (Coenonympha) 312
australis (Colias) 38
avis (Callophrys) 48
AZANUS 58
azorina (Hipparchia) 264

bacchus (Pseudotergumia) 267
baetica (Eurodryas) 129
boeticus (Lampides) 56

378

NYMPHALIDAE [i]

Apatura ilia [25]

Limenitis reducta [26]

Polygonia c-album [26]

Vanessa atalanta [27]

Inachis io [27]

Aglais urticae [27]

Cynthia cardui [27]